The world's largest collection of visual travel guides

The French Riviera

Original edition by Lisa Gerard-Sharp
Photography by Lyle Lawson
Editorial Director: Brian Bell

Part of the Langenscheidt Publishing Group

INSIGHT GUIDES

THE FRENCH RIVIERA

CONTACTING THE EDITORS: Although every effort
is made to provide accurate information in this
publication, we live in a fast-changing world and would
appreciate it if readers would call our attention to any
errors or outdated information that may occur by
writing to us at Apa Publications,
P.O. Box 7910, London SE1 8ZB, England.
Fax: (44) 171-403 0290.
e-mail: insight@apaguide.demon.co.uk.

First Edition 1992
Second Edition (Revised) 1999

Distributed in the United States by
Langenscheidt Publishers Inc.
46–35 54th Road
Maspeth, NY 11378
Fax: (718) 784 0640

Distributed in the UK & Ireland by
GeoCenter International Ltd
The Viables Centre, Harrow Way
Basingstoke, Hampshire RG22 4BJ
Fax: (44) 1256-817988

Distributed in Australia & New Zealand by
Hema Maps Pty. Ltd
24 Allgas Street, Slacks Creek 4127
Brisbane, Australia
Tel: (61) 7 3290 0322
Fax: (61) 7 3290 0478

Worldwide distribution enquiries:
APA Publications GmbH & Co. Verlag KG
(Singapore branch)
38 Joo Koon Road, Singapore 628990
Tel: 65-8651600
Fax: 65-8616438

Printed in Singapore by
Insight Print Services (Pte) Ltd
38 Joo Koon Road
Singapore 628990
Fax: 65-8616438

Discovery CHANNEL

This guidebook combines the interests
and enthusiasms of two of the
world's best known information pro-
viders: Insight Guides, whose range of titles
has set the standard for visual travel guides
since 1970, and Discovery Channel, the
world's premier source of nonfiction television programming.

The editors of Insight Guides provide both
practical advice and general understanding
about a destination's history, culture, institutions and people. Discovery Channel
and its Web site, www.discovery.com, help
millions of viewers explore their world from
the comfort of their own home and also
encourage them to explore it firsthand.

A travel guide to the French Riviera
inevitably presents problems: how do
you say something fresh about a region which has been for centuries a holiday
destination favoured by royalty and some of
the worlds most famous writers, and how do
you give an honest appraisal of a place which
is frequently cited by critics as a chastening
example of how untramelled tourism can turn
beauty into beastliness?

This new edition of *Insight Guide: The
French Riviera* has been painstakingly updated by its original editor, **Rosemary Bailey**,
whose love of the South of France has led her
to live there most of the year. She fell in love
with the Côte d'Azur at the end of the 1970s,
when she stayed on a rose farm near Vence.

Bailey

An author and journalist, Bailey contributes
articles to the London *Sunday Times* and
many other publications. Here she has written
about the regions she knows best: Cagnes
and St-Paul, Grasse and Cap Ferrat. She has
also explored the famous perched villages of
the Alpes Maritimes, and has contributed features on history and contemporary life.

A distinguishing characteristic of the Insight
series is its superb photography, and this
guide combines the work of two of its most
talented photographers: **Catherine Karnow**,
an American whose sensual appreciation of
France combines with a particular skill for
revealing portraiture, and **Douglas Corrance**,

Karnow

Miles

Gerard-Sharp

Rocca

Stratte-McClure

a Scot whose photojournalist's eye produces an exciting immediacy.

Bailey was assisted by **Barry Miles**, whose books include acclaimed biographies of Allen Ginsberg, Sir Paul McCartney and William Burroughs. He has been a frequent visitor to the Riviera since 1968 and a devoted fan of Brigitte Bardot for even longer. Here he writes about the BB phenomenon, and about Picasso and the many other writers and artists inspired by the region.

A formidable team of contributors explored the myriad aspects which make the region such a rich subject. **Lisa Gerard-Sharp**, a London-based writer and broadcaster, and a regular contributor to Insight Guides, here applies her fearsome research skills and trenchant perceptions to the impact of the British and other expatriates, as well as contributing chapters on Monaco, Menton and the Border Country of the mountains. She has been a regular visitor to the French Riviera since childhood family holidays, when, she says, "our caravan holiday in St-Tropez was enlivened by the proximity of a nudist colony."

Tony Rocca, who has spent many years living on the Côte d'Azur is a British writer based in Le Cannet, he offers an enticing insider's guide to Nice and Cannes. After spending 20 years working for Britain's national newspapers, mainly the *Sunday Times* and the *Daily Mail*, Rocca escaped in the early 1980s to Cannes, from where he contributes to a variety of UK and US publications.

Peter Graham, another frequent contributor to Insight Guides, here writes about the region's distinct cuisine, his favourite subject, and the contretemps between Graham Greene and Nice's headline-making mayor, Jacques Médecin. Graham lives in a small village in the Auvergne, writing regularly for London's *Guardian*, *Times* and *Sunday Times*. His book *Classic Cheese Cookery*, was the winner of the André Simon Memorial prize. Appropriately, he was responsible for translating Jacques Médecin's very own Niçois cookbook into English.

Philip Sweeney, another Insight regular, writes frequently about travel and music and has published a guide to world music. For someone addicted to people-watching, St-Tropez proved a honey-pot.

Chris Peachment, a film writer and former arts editor of London's *Times*, has contributed a wry and amusing behind-the-scenes look at the Cannes Film Festival.

Joel Stratte-McClure, an American-born Côte d'Azur resident, is based in Valbonne. He has written a number of guidebooks and is a regular contributor to *Time, People,* the *International Herald Tribune* and a host of other publications. In this book, he explains the wheeling and dealing involved in the business life of the area.

Sophie Radice, who has explored Hyères and the surrounding region, was *Vogue*'s Young Writer of the Year in 1988 and now contributes articles on France to a variety of publications from the rambling mill-house in the forests of Compiègne.

Rowlinson Carter, whose many Insight contributions have proved that historical narratives need never contain a dull moment, provides a dramatic description of the wartime Riviera. **Mike Meade**, the Canadian editor of the *Riviera Reporter* and a devoted yachtee, explains the niceties of yachting culture to the uninitiated.

Jill Adam, who has put together fact-packed Travel Tips sections for several of Insight's France titles and has also edited the *French Farm and Village Holiday Guide* for some years, has compiled the comprehensive information listings at the end of this guide. She welcomes any opportunity to spend more time in her house in southwest France.

Nicky Burton made an invaluable contribution to picture research and information on hotels and restaurants. She is based in Tourrettes-sur-Loup, from where she writes for *New Riviera Côte d'Azur* magazine, and travels throughout the region as sales representative for Penguin Books.

The original book was proofread and indexed by **Carole Mansur**.

CONTENTS

Preceding pages: *trompe l'oeil* in Nice; on the beach at Menton.

THE BUSINESS OF GAIETY

The Côte d'Azur, the French Riviera: the names alone retain an enduring allure. Strung along the Mediterranean coast of France is a glittering necklace of exotic towns redolent of glamour and luxury: Cannes, Nice, Monte-Carlo, Antibes, St-Tropez.

The coast's plentiful pleasures include not only sun and sea but magnificent art and architecture, glorious perfumes and flowers, world-class yachts, casinos, film and jazz festivals, food, wine and spectacular scenery. As one of the world's most glamorous holiday destinations, the French Riviera has attracted visitors for over two centuries, from Queen Victoria to Madonna, Picasso to Brigitte Bardot.

The actual geographical limits of the region are a matter of debate. Traditionally the Côte extends from Menton to Cannes. The French Riviera usually designates the coast, despite its infinite variety, all the way to Marseille. Certainly property developers like to think so.

This guide takes a middle path, starting from Hyères and its islands in the west, one of the destinations first favoured by early visitors such as Queen Victoria. It extends as far as Menton and also includes the Haut-Pays in the east, where the villages close to the border are more Italian than French – appropriate since the Italian influence is a significant aspect of the region.

The Côte d'Azur for most people is the classic image of a summer holiday. Its clichés persist: glorious blue sea, virtually guaranteed sunshine, waving palm trees and serious sun-tans. For most of its visitors the Côte d'Azur continues to supply all in liberal quantity; satisfaction guaranteed. Today, however, tourism is no longer the sole *raison d'être* of the region, which is now also aspiring to become a "technological Eden", the high-tech capital of the Southern European sun-belt.

We have tried in this guidebook to present an accurate picture of the contemporary Côte d'Azur, from its yacht culture to Grimaldi gossip; from the best restaurants to the crime figures; from where the financial investment is coming from to the best museums and the most perfect gardens, views and beaches. We have also delved into its history to put it all in context: its early beginnings; the influence of the British; the hedonistic jazz age of the Americans; the sun cult of Bardot and St-Tropez. We describe the many writers and artists who have been inspired by the region, and those, like Graham Greene, who have sometimes been enraged by it.

We have tried to be honest, to acknowledge the problems as well as exploring the pleasures, because it is these issues as much as its traditional diversions that make the Côte d'Azur today such a fascinating place to explore.

Preceding pages: St-Tropez sun-lover; the Carlton Hotel, Cannes; Harley-Davidsons, the quintessential accessory in St-Tropez; a game of *boules*; artist in the Café des Arts, St-Tropez. Left, a fête at Biot.

"It is to be tranquilly overwhelmed to see the Mediterranean just before dawn, stretching out beneath your windows. There will be the grey satin of the sea, the mountains behind, the absolutely convincing outline of Reinach's Greek villa at the end of Beaulieu Point. And the memory of Greek gods…

"It is one of the greatest pleasures of my life that a legend avers that Ulysses once sheltered in the sea cave below my garden. If I close my eyes I can see Pallas Athene with shield and spear stand in the sky and brood above her sea. Or if you quote to me, *Saepe te in somnis vidi…* or merely mention to me the name of Catullus you will have me in such a state that I must leave my writing and walk from end to end of the terrace for some minutes."

– Ford Madox Ford: *It Was The Nightingale* (1933)

A first glance at the stretch of Mediterranean coast which we now call the Côte d'Azur suggests that little evidence of the past can possibly remain amongst the super-high-ways and shopping centres. While it is true that this region of France is not as rich in antiquity as some, it does have a past and the clues are there for those who wish to imagine the lives of earlier inhabitants. The region has numerous museums of archaeology and early human habitation as well as many delightful local museums devoted to Provençal daily life and traditional crafts.

The history of travel to the region is a story in itself; antiquarian travel books abound from the days when 18th-century visitors like Tobias Smollett were more concerned with discovering antiquities or restoring their health than with suntans and casinos.

The writers of these books, rattling about in their horse-drawn carriages along dusty roads lit only by fireflies or moonlight, or clambering over headlands still rich with fragrant *maquis* in search of Roman inscriptions and rare butterflies and plants, supply us with a wealth of classical learning and

Preceding pages: tuna-fishing in the Mediterranean. Left, Roman legionnaires in stone basrelief. Right, 19th-century travel guide.

acute observation about the region, both as it used to be in ancient times and as it appeared to them in their own time.

Some of the most fascinating include the Rev. Hugh Macmillan's scriptural reflections in his 1885 *The Riviera*, Edward Strasburger's *Rambles on the Riviera*, with its loving detail of the long-lost flora of the region, Sir Frederick Treves's highly-coloured historical anecdotes in *The Riviera of the Corniche Roads* (1923), or the altogether racier picture painted by Charles Graves in

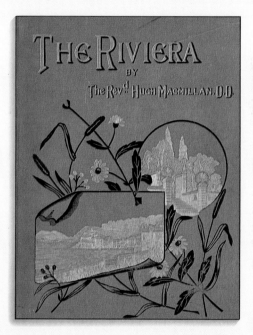

The Riviera Revisited, written just after World War II, and rather more concerned with the price of a good *coq-au-vin* than with anything else. Their tales of hoary peasants, newly discovered ruins or 1946 menus provide us with an excellent reference point for linking the rich history of the region with its all too present reality.

Some of the very first signs of human habitation have been discovered here; in the Vallée des Merveilles are Bronze Age rock carvings, and evidence of Cro-Magnon man has been found in caves around Grasse.

The earliest known settlers along the coast were the Bronze Age Ligurians but little survives of their passing except the faint remains of their forts, built of unworked stone, and some fragments of pottery and beads. Anyway, according to Norman Douglas: "Their reputation was none of the best; they were more prompt, says Crinagoras, in devising evil than good."

Roman occupation: It is not until the Greeks and Romans that we have much knowledge of everyday life. The Greeks traded throughout the Mediterranean and were responsible for founding both the city of Nice, which they called Nikea after Nike, the goddess of Victory, and subsequently, Antibes, called Antipolis, meaning "the city opposite" (to Nice). Traditionally all trading was done

outside the city walls and today the Antibes covered market is still located in almost the same place on the Cours Masséna.

The Roman occupation began in 125 BC and there is considerable evidence to be seen today; although their primary intentions were military, the Romans can in a sense be regarded as the first visitors to appreciate the pleasures of the coast, building themselves luxurious villas on the shore of St-Raphaël, near to their headquarters at Fréjus.

One of the most magnificent sights in the entire region is the gargantuan monument at La Turbie, which still towers over the landscape today, dwarfing the little village of the same name, and providing an enduring emblem of the power and self-confidence of the Romans. On the base of the monument, a long inscription lists all the subjugated tribes of the region.

The Via Aurelia, the main Roman road from Rome to Arles, passed through Menton, La Turbie and Cimiez, part of the route following what is now the Grande Corniche. La Turbie was the highest point of the road and a landmark which was visible for miles; and what is today a charming backwater of a village was then an important staging-post, bustling with merchants, centurions, slaves and gossip from Rome.

The Romans set up their capital in Narbonne and founded substantial towns throughout Provence including Arles, Nîmes and Fréjus. Everywhere they built arenas, baths and temples of which substantial ruins still remain today; in some cases entire towns like Cimiez have been excavated, and everywhere there are stones with Latin inscriptions which have been re-used in much later buildings.

In Fréjus the amphitheatre and arena is one of the largest built in Gaul by the Romans. The cathedral in Vence was built on the site of a Roman temple and throughout the town are scattered fragments of blocks with Roman inscriptions. Vallauris was founded by the Romans and was famous for its pottery even then, thanks to the quality of the red clay of the surrounding mountains.

Roman rule brought peace to the region for a time and the hill tribesmen ventured down from their fortified hill settlements to establish themselves in towns along the coast. However, with the fall of the Roman Empire chaos reigned once again, and Goths, Vandals and Lombards ravaged the area, leaving little in their savage wake.

Saracen invaders: Marauders also came from the sea; the Saracens were to devastate great swathes of the Mediterranean coastline from Rhodes to Spain and foray inland as far as the Loire river. They were Arabs originating from North Africa and the Eastern Mediterranean coast, and appear to have been exceptionally violent and terrifying. By about the year 800 they had taken power in Èze, La Turbie and Ste-Agnès and by the 10th century occupied nearly all the coast.

Finally in 980 a concerted effort was made to drive them out by the Count of Provence, who numbered amongst his soldiers a Genoese named Gibellino Grimaldi, the first mention in the region of a Grimaldi, the name of Monaco's name ruling house today.

It was a period of internal strife in which everybody fought with everybody else for dominance. As Sir Frederick Treves succinctly puts it: "They fought in a vague, confused, spasmodic way, with infinite vicissitudes and in every available place, for over 500 years." The history of almost every small village records the constant turmoil suffered by the people as they were attacked by invader after invader.

The history of Èze in particular is an astonishing summary of violent attack and subju-

Genoa at war with Nice, even tiny Gorbio at war with neighbouring Roquebrune.

Siege of Nice: The famous long-running conflict between the Guelphs and Ghibellines, defenders and enemies of the Pope, also engulfed the towns and villages of the region. Nice itself has been a constantly shifting pawn on the Mediterranean chessboard, and was frequently besieged, often by the French. On one memorable occasion, usually referred to as *the* siege of Nice in 1543, the town was saved by the heroic action of a stout laundrywoman who beat back the Turkish invaders scaling the walls, with her washing stick. From the 14th century, Nice and the surrounding region was under the protec-

gation, with generations of inhabitants being murdered and pillaged, the village itself continually burnt and razed to the ground. What is remarkable is the tenacity with which the village has always risen from its ashes – and today continues to flourish on the lucrative proceeds of tourism.

Neither France nor Italy was a united nation in the way that we know them today. Instead, both were divided into warring little fiefdoms, with towns constantly at war with each other, Pisa at war with Genoa, and

tion of Savoy and did not elect to become part of France until 1860. The Italian influence is everywhere apparent, both in architecture, place names and the Niçois dialect.

Monks and pirates: Religion, of course, played a great part in the area's early history and a wealth of religious art survives. It sometimes seems as if almost every village has a religious festival or procession to celebrate, often revived for the benefit of tourists, but authentic nonetheless. One curious example is "*La procession aux escargots*" which takes place in Gorbio. It is not in fact a promenade of snails, but a festival celebrated by the White Penitents when all the

<u>Left</u>, 19th-century Cagnes. <u>Above</u>, Nice in its nautical heyday, as seen in the Naval Museum.

streets and houses are illuminated by oil flames lit in a multitude of snail shells.

There are Penitents' chapels in Nice, Cannes and Sospel near the Italian border; these were lay brotherhoods that appeared in the 14th century and proliferated throughout the Midi. They were denoted by the colours of their hoods, the most important being Penitents Gris, Blancs and Noirs, and were devoted to charitable and sacred duties.

All over the Côte d'Azur are sanctuaries and pilgrimage centres, often in high mountain reaches, and heavily festooned with votive offerings. The Knights Templar also had a presence here and there are vestiges of their castles near Vence and La Gaude.

Among the most interesting ecclesiastical locations are the Îles de Lérins; the monastery on the Île de St-Honorat was for hundreds of years after it was founded in the 5th century the centre of Christianity in Southern Europe, described by the Rev. Hugh Macmillan as "the Iona of the South".

St Honorat was, like St Columba, a man of noble birth, born in Belgic Gaul in the 4th century. He renounced his worldly life and and went off on a pilgrimage to the East with his brother. Here he was inspired to return to one of the Lérins islands to found a monastery. The island was inhospitably swarming with serpents, crawling in and out of the

Roman ruins that remained. Undeterred, Honorat established himself, and his holy life attracted many followers. A well was rediscovered, a church built and a garden planted. Honorat's sister, Marguerite, also started a convent on the next island, now named after her.

St-Honorat rapidly became a centre of religious learning and was in the thick of the great religious controversies of the Middle Ages. It was a centre for missionaries and supplied bishops to Arles, Avignon, Lyon, Vienne, Fréjus, Nice. Many ecclesiastical names are associated with Lérins, including that of St Patrick, who according to tradition was educated at the monastery.

Lérins became very wealthy, and owned land right along the coast from Grasse as far as Barcelona, including the village of Cannes itself. At one time nearly 4,000 monks lived on the island. But such riches were a great temptation and attacks by pirates and quarrels between the monks and Pope-appointed abbots undermined the monastery. By the 17th century it had finally collapsed, and eventually the island was bought by the Cistercians, who built a new monastery, and today supply visitors with their home-made liqueurs and cultivate the land using traditional medieval methods.

Damsels and pirates: Romantic stories also abound; the history of the region is awash with pirates, troubadours, distressed damsels, grand feats of bravery, dramatic betrayals, and princesses both pure and poisonous. Even today, among the high-rises and pink villas, the remains of a staircase, a curiously carved door lintel or a Renaissance window can evoke a past both humble and heroic.

As Sir Frederick Treves observed in 1923, it was a time of "general and brilliant disorder... a time to read about rather than to live in; a period that owes its chief charm to a safe distance and to the distortion of an artificial mirage. In any case one cannot fail to realise that these scenes took place in spots where tramcars are now running, where the char-à-banc rumbles along, and where the anaemic youth and the brazen damosel dance to the jazz music of an American band." And little did he know what was yet to come.

Left, Brea's painting, *La Brigue*, is a reminder of the region's ecclesiastical traditions. **Right**, a fountain at Mougins.

SERPOLLET

THE BRITISH INVASION

"Cannes is for living, Monte-Carlo for gambling and Menton for dying." Such was the Victorian popular wisdom on the Riviera. During the days of the Grand Tour, France was considered a mere antechamber to classical Rome. But in the 1850s the South of France replaced Italy as the British home from home. Previously, the British invasion had been entirely bellicose: the Duke of Berwick, serving Louis XIV, razed Nice fortress to the ground in 1706.

The peaceful colonisation was led by Tobias Smollett, the Scots doctor and writer who pioneered sea-bathing as a cure for consumption. During his stay in Nice from 1763 to 1765, Smollett enjoyed the climate but deplored the uncultured locals, especially the "pot-bellied" women. He also found fault with the garlicky Niçoise cuisine but his ill-humour melted on contact with fruit sorbets. These "sorbettes, which are sold in coffee houses and places of public resort... are very agreeable to the palate."

In Smollett's day, medical fashion favoured spas such as Bath and Cheltenham but the prescription in the following century was for Riviera resorts. The avowed travel motive was health but, as William Chambers noted in 1870, "Fashion, *ennui* and love of gaiety seem to send quite as many abroad as absolutely bad health." At any rate, visitors in search of health were followed by social-climbers and pleasure-seekers. According to David Cecil, the British merely wanted to escape from "the chatter and clatter and hustle and guzzle of literary and fashionable London." One hidden impulse was the Victorian restlessness Alfred de Musset called "*la maladie du siècle*", the desire to flee.

The British followed the flock, migrating south in autumn and north in spring. As the American novelist W. D. Howells commented: "October was the month of the sunsets and the English." From May to September the Riviera villas were shuttered and the resorts deserted

by all but unfashionable merchants, gamblers, prostitutes and, horror of horrors, the locals. But the British stranded on the Riviera out of season were vocal. Christopher Home Douglas, in Nice in May, was distressed by "a toilet table festooned with spiders' webs; decayed boots and chicken bones are also objectionable in a bedroom, even though under the bed and supposed to be out of sight."

By the 1830s, the days of corsairs and Barbary pirates were over and the civilised world could travel freely once more. For the

British upper classes this meant travelling by private carriage to the Riviera, stopping at inns along the way. In 1832, the wealthy Boyle family travelled south in a drawing-room on wheels and, at a maximum speed of 35 miles (56 km) a day, there was time to admire the view. Money bought only comfort and convenience, not speed. The journey to the Riviera took up to three weeks, as long as in the time of the Roman Empire.

Alternatively, visitors could hire a *voiturin*, a French contractor, who provided coaches and horses all the way to the Côte. As late as 1875, Dr Bennet described this as "the most comfortable, pleasant and hygienic of any for

Preceding pages: early steam-powered car from series of tile pictures, Michelin Building, London. **Left**, Lord Brougham who first "discovered" Cannes in 1834. **Right**, a stroll in the Nice public gardens, 19th century.

tourists not much pressed for time or very particular about expense." Passengers who could not afford private transport were not so fortunate. Their fate was the diligence, a contraption built like an overgrown haywagon. Weighing up to five tons, the diligence carried 15 to 30 passengers and travelled at little more than walking pace.

In 1829 one disgruntled passenger, Dr James Johnson, likened French diligences to "locomotive prisons… in which one is pressed, pounded, and, what is worse than all, poisoned with mephitic gasses and noxious exhalations evolved from above, below and around." Passengers faced the unpleasant choice between the outside *banquette*, the

in light seas the ships swayed dangerously. British voyagers cried discrimination at every turn. In the 1880s the Rev. John Aiton complained that "the passengers are actually starved; English passengers are insulted by Frenchmen… and as to a Frenchman lending an English voyager a spyglass or telling him the name of an island, he would rather spit in his face."

The arrival of the railway in the 1850s dramatically reduced the hardships of travel to the Riviera. Yet horse-power was not rendered obsolete overnight since key stretches of railway were not complete before 1870. Until then, carriages bridged the gaps. Diligences would be placed on a rolling platform

cold, hard seat beside the driver, or the cowshed odours of the seats in the *intérieur* and the *coupé*. For the middle stretch of the journey south, travellers usually switched to a river steamer from Chalon to Avignon. The Austrian-built river steamers found favour with the British but nothing but scorn was poured on the French steamships.

From the 1830s, steamships linked the Riviera ports and, to avoid the stultifying diligence, the British often opted for this sea voyage. Despite the *fin-de-siècle* opulence of the later steamers, there were justified complaints about vibration and noise. In calm conditions the French steamers were fine, but

and hitched to a train: a forerunner of the modern Motorail service south. Dr Bennet enthused about the new service: "Railways have all but annihilated space… A traveller may leave the London Bridge station at 7.40 on a Monday morning, by mail train for Paris, and be at Nice or Menton for supper the following day." The most luxurious trains included private saloon carriages, each containing a bedroom, sitting-room, smoking-room and study.

Queen Victoria, travelling incognito as the Comtesse de Balmoral, arrived in such style that her identity was no secret. The royal train was hung with silk and was partly decorated with Louis XVI furnishings. Naturally, the Queen travelled with supplies of familiar foods, including Irish stew, kept lukewarm in red flannel cushions. In the mornings, the train was halted to allow the Queen an hour to dress and her male staff to shave. From 1882 onwards she was a regular winter visitor and her presence did much to soothe troubled Anglo-French relations.

Health was the Queen's motive for visiting the Riviera since her son, Prince Leopold, suffered from consumption. Until the 1870s, consumption was the killer disease in Victorian Britain. The only remedy was believed to be a warm climate. Climates were labelled as "tonic and exciting" or "sedative and relax-

British clientèle from the 18th century onwards. Robert Louis Stevenson came in search of a southern cure and settled in the romantic retreat of La Solitude. Luxuries were cheap but essentials were dear. By this token, the British freely purchased carriages, villas, wine and entertainment but stinted on fuel, food, servants and travel. By the 1890s, Hyères' date palms incongruously sheltered an Anglican church, English estate agencies and public tennis courts.

Compared with the privacy of Hyères, Nice was a more ostentatious resort, with British residents living in grand hotels in the public eye. By the 1820s Nice had a flourishing British community who sketched and botan-

ing". As tonic climates, Hyères, Menton and Cannes were considered ideal for invalids suffering from such esoteric illnesses as consumption, delicacy, gout and clergyman's sore throat. In no time, the Paris-Riviera Express became known as an ambulance train to death's waiting-room.

Queen Victoria wintered in Hyères before finding a more desirable address in Nice. Hyères was the first Riviera resort to be patronised by the British. Although later upstaged by Nice and Cannes, Hyères had a solid

ised their way through the mild Mediterranean winters. Visitors indulged in literary readings, *soirées musicales*, "quantities of gossip and a great deal of dressiness."

The Victorian obsession with standards and public works soon had an impact on Nice. Winter residents insisted on better roads, English plumbing, new bandstands and public parks. The British imported nurses and ladies' maids, gardeners and grocers, lawyers and estate agents, but the local labour force had to conform to quirky British requirements. Hotels advertised "drainage executed by English engineers." French hoteliers grumbled about the demands of English hygiene, the frostiness of English manners and the sibilance of English speech.

Yet British philanthropy was also grudgingly acknowledged. After the failure of the olive and citrus crops in 1821, the impoverished locals were offered employment by the Rev. Lewis Way and Charles Whitby. Funded by British families, the scheme subsidised the building of Camin des Angès, the coastal road now known as the Promenade des Anglais. Only the uncharitable questioned British motives: the Promenade provided better access to the shore and effectively shielded Victorian strollers from the hordes of beggars. In 1931, British interests were again served by an enlarged Promenade des Anglais.

of Wales and his yacht *Britannia* were regular fixtures from 1878. He used to say: "I go to the Riviera as I would a club. It's a place with good company where everyone mingles, just like a garden party."

However, it was an earlier and more endearing Englishman who put Cannes on the map. In 1834, Lord Brougham "discovered" this charming fishing village while looking for a suitable home for his invalid daughter. Brougham built several villas in Cannes and wintered there for almost 35 years. Under his patronage, the village became one of the Riviera's most British resorts and was home to over 1,000 English residents shortly after the arrival of the railway in 1862. The atmos-

The development of a British quarter known as Newborough attracted a new wave of Victorian visitors, as did the arrival of the railway link in 1864. Queen Victoria set the tone, wintering in the palatial Hotel Regina in the Cimiez district of Nice from 1895 onwards. There she entertained the Emperor Franz Josef, other European royals and heads of state.

Regal Nice was eventually eclipsed by stylish Cannes – in British eyes, at least. Queen Victoria's son, the future Edward VII, was not alone in thinking Cannes Cercle Nautique the most exciting club on the Côte. Still, in his inimitable way, Edward did as much to keep the *Entente Cordiale* as his mother. The Prince

phere, heavy with Victorian divinity and charitable works, changed with the Prince of Wales. By the Naughty Nineties, Cannes was a cosmopolitan resort with a reputation for vice second only to Monaco's.

Baptist ministers, such as Charles Spurgeon, condemned Monaco as "the serpent in paradise". Queen Victoria was not alone in refusing to stay in this "moral cesspool". Dr Bennet also feared "the proximity of a gaming table" in this warm and wicked resort. Before the turn of the century, Monaco was labelled "a sunny place for shady people," the haunt of arms dealers, courtesans and gold-diggers. But the glamour drew British gamblers such as Charles Wells, the fortune-hunter who became famous as "The Man Who Broke the Bank at Monte-Carlo". Cora Pearl, the Duke of Hamilton's extravagant mistress, was an *habituée* at the casino in the 1860s.

The archetypal British resort was Menton. In its heyday, in the 1890s, it boasted the largest British colony on the Continent. As the main Riviera sanatorium, the resort had at least 50 British doctors and several rest homes. It was quieter and cheaper than Cannes and combined a dowager-like atmosphere with a seductive setting. Yet the heady, Italianate exoticism could not be openly acknowledged in a resort favoured by Anglican clergymen and consumptive ladies. Instead, "Everyone

but to have as much fresh air and exercise as possible. Invalids followed the strict regime prescribed by local British doctors. Flannel underwear and woollen clothes were obligatory, as were shoes with india-rubber soles, designed to insulate one against cold stone floors. For the invalids there was little light relief: "Bath chairs monopolised the Promenade du Midi by day, and by night their premature retirement imparted a hospital hush to the atmosphere." Despite John Pemble's sombre comments, Menton, like Brighton, had British appeal.

Anglo-Saxon names flattered the insular vanity of the British and stores stocked British delicacies such as Guinness and port, York

indulged in *à la mode* church-going excess, with all its formality and display."

Menton's dullness could be attributed to Dr James Henry Bennet, an eminent Victorian doctor who came "to die in a quiet corner". Instead, his consumption was cured by "the bracing, stimulating climate." From 1859 to 1891, he promoted Menton as the ideal health resort and his book, *Winter and Spring on the Shores of the Mediterranean*, became a European best-seller.

Consumptives were told to wrap up warmly

Left, Queen Victoria on one of her visits. **Above**, high society in a Monte Carlo restaurant, 1907.

ham and smoked goose breast, as well as "strange red, green or blue sauces in boxes marked 'by royal appointment'."

In between shopping and prayer-meetings, there were sketching trips and rides in donkey-drawn buggies. The British introduced donkey rides to Menton. Even in cold weather, the *"Miss Anglaises"* took part in donkey races on the beach or went on picnic trips to perched villages. Much to the astonishment of the locals, the young ladies still had enough energy to ride all the way down to the Italian frontier before returning to Menton. From her Chalet des Rosiers overlooking the Bay of Menton, Queen Victoria also found time for donkey rides. In the event of a chill in the *Entente Cordiale*, the Queen had a carriage ready to whisk her to safety in Bordighera, just over the Italian border.

In Victorian times, Britannia literally ruled the waves. Such was British chauvinism that the Franco-German War of 1870 was interpreted in Britain as a capitulation of the south to the north. On the Riviera, belief in British supremacy was widespread, and British values reigned: deference was expected and granted. In 1879 Dr Edward Sparkes wrote: "English tastes are well understood and carefully consulted in all the hotels." English was often used as a generic term for all foreigners. As such, the *"Miss Anglaises"* were some-

times Russian or German.

The British rarely ventured into "foreign" shops and relied on safe English staples. English eating habits and appetites were notorious. Queen Victoria's typical Riviera lunch included risotto and mutton chops, chicken with noodles, followed by tapioca, meringue and strawberries. Dr Bennet wrote that "the dinners we positively require every day" were considered "festive dinners" by the natives. To supply the daily British intake "the country had to be ransacked for a hundred and fifty miles around." The Prince of Wales also had an enormous appetite and, as the unwitting inventor of *crêpes suzettes*, probably lost no

time in polishing off both the *crêpes* and Suzette herself.

Victorian life on the Riviera was deeply institutionalised. The British day followed a pattern: breakfast, early stroll, correspondence in the hotel, lunch, afternoon stroll and 5 o'clock tea. In Nice, there were English signs for "5 o'clock tea – any time". Afternoon variants included gentle shopping or a concert at the bandstand. The British community organised regattas and whist drives while the big hotels held weekly tea dances and balls.

Depending on taste and morals, residents spent their evenings in the casino, cabaret or at home, reading. Victorian music hall was popular as were theatrical performances by Sarah Bernhardt. By Edwardian times, Folies Bergères and Moulin Rouge troupes were often in residence in casinos along the Côte. Yet after Menton opened a casino, it incurred the wrath of the moral minority. The Rev. Eustace Reynolds Ball found Menton guilty of *fin-de-siècle* decadence, "infected by the Monte-Carlo contingent".

But Victorian puritanism was often outdone by patriotism. Well before the turn of the century, British competitive sports played a major role in life on the Riviera. The British upper classes were serious about sport but defensive about games in a sunny climate. Author Charles Kingsley scorned "the English hedge-gnats who only take their sport when the sun shines." Still, there were enough hedge-gnats to indulge in horse-racing at Cannes, skating in Menton and Nice as well as golf in Monte-Carlo and Sospel.

Sea-bathing was not in vogue on the Riviera until the 1930s. Although the Italians had been swimming just down the coast in San Remo since the 1850s, the British regarded this as Italian perversity. The British swam at home, of course, but believed that the Riviera's hot climate was suitable only for seaweed and anemone hunting.

The Menton Lawn Tennis and Croquet Club was founded in 1901 and held international tournaments. The dominance of British cultural values ensured a copycat reaction: King Gustav V of Sweden and the Queen of Siam were dedicated yet hopeless players.

The British drawn to the Riviera included sportsmen and statesmen, royals and writers, artists and intellectuals: in short, the missing apex of the British social pyramid. British politicians were part of Riviera life from Victorian times onwards. When Lord Salisbury was in his villa at Beaulieu and Victoria in residence at Cimiez, state business moved from London to Nice. The Queen bombarded the Prime Minister with her views on heads of state, foreign affairs, church and army appointments. A monument on Avenue George V in Nice pays tribute to the warmth of royal Franco-British relations on the Riviera: "*À la mémoire des membres augustes de la maison royale de Windsor qui depuis deux siècles furent nos hôtes.*"

British eccentrics were not thin on the ground. Trahorne Moggridge, the Victorian entomologist, published a book on indigenous spiders. James Bruyn Andrews translated lo-

However, if one had to select the quintessential Briton abroad, it would be Dr Bennet. As well as pioneering the Riviera as a sanatorium, James Bennet was a linguist, writer, botanist, environmentalist and man of action. He represented the best face of the eminent Victorian abroad: duty led him to set up a medical association which monitored public health and instigated street-cleaning services, sewers and abattoirs. It was largely thanks to his efforts that in 1892 the Association for the Advancement of Science declared Menton to be the cleanest, most efficient town in France.

Bennet also personified the British love of gardens. He pressured Menton council into creating public parks and funding nature cam-

cal legends and wrote works on the Mentonnais language. Edward VII's presence assured the Riviera of style. In more recent times, Amy Paget, an elderly Riviera resident, flew the Union Jack from her villa throughout World War II. Nora, Lady Docker, flew in the face of postwar austerity by flaunting zebra-skin upholstery on her Daimler (she found mink was just too hot to sit on). The latest candidate for eccentricity is the British academic John Cairncross, widely alleged to be the "Fifth Man" in the Cambridge spy-ring of the 1930s.

Left, the new fashion for sea-bathing. **Above**, a more cautious approach.

paigns to protect plants and wildlife. Queen Victoria and Princess Beatrice often sketched and strolled in Bennet's exotic garden, created with the help of "an intelligent peasant… raised to the dignity of head-gardener." Wherever the British settled in the area, they cultivated magnificent gardens.

In Menton's Jardin Botanique, Lord Redcliffe, the Governor of Malta, favoured a didactic approach, with thematic gardens illustrating the range of Mediterranean flora. Miss Campbell, a later owner, introduced exotic plants from Asia and Central America. Just around the corner, Major Lawrence Johnston changed the Riviera landscape by introducing rare trees from China, Japan, Asia and Africa. Sir Thomas Hanbury, a Victoran spice trader, made his fortune in China and retired to the hills on the French-Italian border. There he introduced Norfolk pines and exotic plants from all corners of the British Empire. In Cannes, an early Victorian, Thomas Woolfield, introduced the gooseberry and the sweet potato, eucalyptus and acacia.

The British landscaped large sections of Nice, Cannes, Menton and Cap Ferrat. To some locals, Somerset Maugham is merely the person who introduced the avocado to the Riviera. When it comes to garden snobbery on the Riviera, it is hard to know whether it is a British import or a French anomaly.

killjoys and the women as philistines or prudes. Henry James commented on the British "insular faculty to gush".

Katherine Mansfield confined herself to mocking English insularity, with liking for Dundee cake and familiar nursery foods. Mansfield, living in Menton in the 1920s, avoided the most anglicised spots, such as Monaco. Even so, she couldn't fail to notice the pervasive British influence. The Riviera was home to British charities, lending libraries, boarding schools and Scottish tea houses. Local British animal protection societies made sure bull-fighting did not spread to the Riviera. By 1928, Menton competed with Monaco in welcoming Girl Guides and Brownies.

But the British visitors offered more than blue blood and green fingers. For British writers and artists, the Riviera became a place to express smothered sensibilities. Enchanted by the soft light and dramatic scenery, these hot-house plants hoped to stretch out in the sun. Yet, once transplanted, they remained rooted to a British social code. Even for D. H. Lawrence and Somerset Maugham, the lotus-eating south was a miasma. Outsiders viewed the British on the Riviera more critically. Locals on the Côte d'Azur disliked patronising references to "our Gallic friends". Berlioz rued the day he married an Englishwoman on the Riviera. Stendhal saw the men as morose

Despite the virtuous Girl Guides, pleasure not duty was the keynote of the 1920s. A poster in Menton contrasts an ailing Victorian gentleman with an elegant 1920s flapper: "In the old days visitors apparently came here for their health. Today, it is a town of luxury and gaiety." If the Edwardian visitors were dutiful, the Americans embodied the pleasure principle. Riviera residents were now judged on the size of their pools and yachts, not their consciences. The British played only supporting roles in a glittering American show.

Although the Americans wrote the script, the British occasionally upstaged them. Glamorous stars such as the Duke of Westminster regularly sailed the Côte d'Azur. "Whose yacht is that?" Amanda asks in *Private Lives*. Elyot replies: "The Duke of Westminster's, I expect. It always is." Noël Coward and Gertrude Lawrence rehearsed the play in Edward Molyneux's villa on Cap d'Ail in 1930.

In 1934 the Prince of Wales stayed in Cannes with Wallis Simpson's party and presented her with a diamond charm as a sign of his infatuation. It was to Cannes that Mrs Simpson retreated when it became clear that the King would abdicate rather than give her up. The couple even contemplated marriage on the Riviera but bowed to George VI's wishes for a more discreet ceremony, far from the Riviera playground. The couple later spent

ish star of the period. Towards the end of his life he was an honoured guest on the Onassis yacht. Patrick Howarth in *When the Riviera was Ours* describes how Aristotle Onassis could be seen feeding the enfeebled Churchill caviare, a symbolic tribute from "the new power on the Riviera to the most famous representative of the grandeurs of the past".

From the 1950s, a new wave of expatriates settled in Haut-de-Cagnes, Vence and Grasse, attracted to the arts and crafts traditions in the foothills. In the 1970s, the British built Isola 2000, the skiing resort, and invested heavily in Cannes and St-Tropez. The current boom town is Sophia-Antipolis, the Riviera's Silicon Valley. Here, there is little sign of the

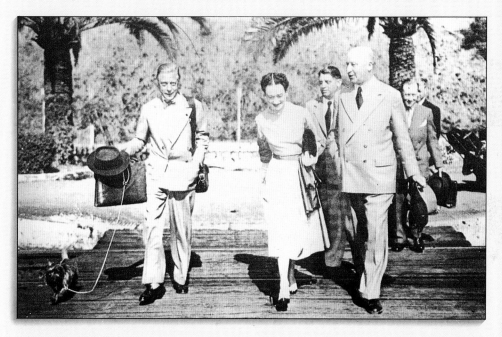

their early years of exile in a luxurious villa on the Cap d'Antibes.

In 1945 the Windsors' villa proved a major embarrassment to Winston Churchill. After her fraternisation with German officers, Coco Chanel was arrested as a collaborator but was quickly released after threatening to expose Churchill. He had made secret payments to the Germans to secure the protection of the Duke of Windsor's villa during the war.

Even so, Churchill was the best-loved Brit-

Left, Aristotle Onassis (left) and Sir Winston Churchill boarding the millionaire's yacht, 1959. **Above**, the Duke and Duchess of Windsor.

tweed-suited matron, the elderly naval captain, the Anglican clergyman or other British Riviera stereotypes. Mike Meade, editor of *Riviera Reporter*, claims never to have met "the retired colonel who doesn't speak a word of French, scowls continually at the natives, and thinks that the Queen's Birthday should be a national holiday here."

If this Riviera stereotype is extinct, *tant mieux*. In today's Riviera, the emphasis is on integration, aided by bilingual psychiatrists and dual-language colleges. There are Anglo-American schools in Mougins, Nice and Sophia-Antipolis. Monte-Carlo's Riviera Radio can be heard from St-Tropez to the

Italian border and the station claims that four out of five English speakers regularly tune in.

Socially, expatriates can choose from the Riviera Singles Group, the Conservatives Abroad, the Oxbridge Set or the Dog Exchange Club. The Anglo-American Group of Provence indulges in Scottish dancing and Marseille cuisine. The Franco-Irish Friendship Group competes fiercely with the Association Franco-Irlande. The British Association has branches in Cannes, Nice, Menton and Monaco.

The Riviera Establishment survives, nonetheless. One English agency supplies British nannies, housekeepers and butlers. British antique dealers regularly advertise for "1920s

cocktail watches, Fabergé enamels and Edwardian gem set jewellery'".

English lending libraries exist in Menton and Vence, as do English bookshops in Cannes, Antibes, Monaco and Sophia-Antipolis. Anglican churches are active in most large resorts, including Nice, Menton and Monaco. Elsewhere, there are British banks, pubs and the long-established John Taylor & Son estate agency. The British distrust of French plumbing remains as a relic of a bygone age. Still, one sign of the times is the existence of an Anglo-American hospital for alcoholism and drug dependency.

For some Britons, the Côte d'Azur was the place to die – D. H. Lawrence in Vence, Aubrey Beardsley in Menton. But today it is a place for the living, a second home to countless British celebrities, though Joan Collins, Ringo Starr, Michael Caine, George Michael or Elton John are hardly typical of British expatriates. Nor is the image of the retired English colonel, playing golf and downing snifters at sundown, very accurate either.

Mike Meade describes the difference between the Old Riviera Establishment and today's expatriates. A well-meaning English gentleman suggested that a Tuesday afternoon whist drive would attract young members to his club. But, as Meade points out, "The typical 25 to 55 Riviera anglophone is an executive at Sophia-Antipolis or a business whizz-kid. He could be an independent professional or part of a yacht crew. On weekends he's probably playing squash or tennis, sailing or skiing, or on a Hash House run... There's a 51 percent chance that 'he' is a 'she'. Whoever he is, it's quite likely that, at 4pm on a Tuesday afternoon, he's working. And whist isn't his thing."

The Riviera is arguably a British creation. Here they recreated decorous anglophile enclaves in balmy, lemon-scented surroundings. The British simplified the south yet were deeply affected by it. Nor was this aesthetic sensibilty a fey whim of the consumptive artist or the cultural élite. It was a creative urge to leave a lasting mark, whether a gallery or garden, a civic statue or a treatise on spiders. Even retired Empire-builders, spice traders and clergymen succumbed, becoming art collectors, landscape gardeners or benefactors.

The Noël Coward song *I went to a Marvellous Party* was inspired by his visit to a high society gathering on the Riviera. Yet the British legacy encompasses more than glamour. Frederic Harrison, a Victorian visitor, defined the British contribution more prosaically: "tea, tubs, sanitary appliances, lawn tennis and churches." Rather like a grand jumble sale, the British gift was a magnificent white elephant. Glorious gardens vied with eccentric institutions, alien churches and curious new games. British names and niceties, philanthropy and prejudice are part of the job lot. In the words of Edward VII, that notorious Riviera adventurer, *"Vive l'Entente Cordiale"*.

Left, a languid moment under the pines, Juan-les-Pins. **Right**, the winter season, Nice.

43

"The resplendent names – Cannes, Nice, Monte-Carlo – began to glow through their torpid camouflage, whispering of old Kings come here to dine or die, of rajahs tossing Buddha's eyes to English ballerinas, of Russian princes turning the weeks into Baltic twilights in the lost Caviare days."

Tender is the Night is a champagne toast to an end of an era. Published in 1934, Scott Fitzgerald's novel is infused with the American glamour that flooded the Riviera from the 1920s. This seductive vision of the "hot sweet south" is not a true mirror but a montage of magical moments. Strictly speaking, the kings, princes and rajahs ruled an earlier age and a moral climate conditioned by Victorian values. Even then, the balmy Mediterranean climate wrought its own magic: these were Victorian values on vacation.

The post-war Americans may have invented the summer season but the Victorians and Edwardians were pale winter migrants. Renoir called this winter sanatorium "a hothouse into which fragile people take refuge". During the *belle époque*, from 1862 until World War I, the Riviera became the royals' winter retreat. The arrival of the railway link to Cannes in 1863 stamped the Riviera with the public's seal of approval. Invalids were the pioneers of the Côte d'Azur, a trend started by the British in the 1850s. Within 10 years, Hyères, Cannes and Nice had large foreign colonies in the winter. A few years later, Beaulieu, Menton and San Remo competed for the aristocratic clientèle while Monte-Carlo catered exclusively to the rich and pleasure-loving.

It was a short step from royal retreat to winter playground. "Princes, princes, nothing but princes. If you like them, you're in the right place," complained Guy de Maupassant of Cannes in 1884. The royals were headed by Queen Victoria, the Empress of Russia and Emperor Frederick of Germany. At the turn of the century, Menton alone received the Kings of Italy, Sweden, Saxe, Belgium and Bulgaria, as well as visits by Count Pushkin and Russian Grand Dukes. The Shah of Persia and President Kruger of South Africa stayed in Menton at the same time. They narrowly missed Emperor Franz Josef of Austria and his wife. Sometimes the royals literally crossed paths: while on a carriage drive near Villefranche, Queen Victoria passed King Leopold, out on his regular daily stroll.

In the same year, the young Aga Khan III arrived on a steamer from India and found Queen Victoria in Nice and the Emperor

Franz Josef at Cap Martin. In addition, there were "a score or so Russian Grand Dukes and Austrian Archdukes in their villas and palaces, half the English peerage with a generous sprinkling of millionaires from industry and finance; and most of the Almanac de Gotha from Germany, the Austro-Hungarian Empire, the Balkan countries lately emancipated from Ottoman rule, and Tsarist Russia." As the Aga Khan modestly put it: "The young man from Bombay was dazzled and awed."

The royals visited not as Grand Tourists of the 18th century, explorers on a unique adventure, but as *habitués*, comfortable in their second homes. Second palaces would be a more accurate description. Queen Victoria had a huge residence in the Cimiez quarter of Nice. Menton's magnificent 18th-century Palais de Carnolès was owned by the Queen of Prussia in the 1860s and by Prince Metternich shortly afterwards. But given the difficulties of finding suitable French servants, royal visitors often preferred to spend the whole winter season in hotels.

Unsurprisingly, such hotels were known as *les palaces de la Côte d'Azur*. Amongst the grandest were L'Hermitage in Monte-Carlo and the Victoria Hotel on the Promenade des Anglais in Nice. Charles of Prussia stayed in the Victoria in the 1860s while

attended Anglican services at Christ Church in Cannes where he made it known that he hoped the hymns would include "The Son of God goes forth to war." Tea and tennis were immovable fixtures; Russian Grand Dukes wore starched white linen; Belgian and Swedish aristocrats challenged one another to jolly polo matches.

Chauvinism aside, the royal way of life on the Riviera was not so much English as regal. Crested dice were thrown in the Monte-Carlo Casino; coroneted carriages paraded the Promenade des Anglais in Nice; the aristocratic *jeunesse dorée* dined on caviare, blinis and pink champagne in the Hôtel de l'Hermitage. Leopold I of Belgium was

Tsarevitch Alexander made it his home until his accession to the Russian throne in 1881. Menton boasted two *belle-époque* hotels on the Avenue Riviera: the Winter Palace was favoured by Oriental royals while Grand Duchess Anastasia, Tsar Nicholas II's aunt, occupied the Riviera Palace in the 1880s. In the lovely *salon de musique*, a Parisian orchestra played Gregorian chants or gypsy music before Anastasia's afternoon nap.

When the Riviera was Ours, Patrick Howarth's wonderful but unashamedly chauvinistic account, argues that even foreign royals followed an English lifestyle on the Riviera. Prince Albert of Prussia regularly

Queen Victoria's domineering uncle but it was his son who made an indelible mark on the Riviera. As an ageing playboy, Leopold II wintered in the Riviera from the 1890s to his death in 1909. Leopold resided in Les Cèdres villa on Cap Martin and filled the grounds with lush vegetation he had transplanted from the Belgian Congo.

Princess Daisy of Pless described Leopold peeling grapes with "a look of cruelty on his face as if he were skinning alive all the members of the Aborigines Protection Society." Apart from rare orchids and palms, Leopold's only hobby was young girls. Princess Daisy describes how his lecherous pursuits were hampered by a dangling white beard and grotesquely long fingernails.

Empress Eugénie of France, often described as the *doyenne* of the Riviera royalty, also held court on Cap Martin in the 1890s. Although Spanish-born and married to a French Emperor, Eugénie was an anglophile who had been educated in England. After the Empire collapsed in 1870, she left Deauville for Kent. By the 1890s her husband and son had died and Eugénie relished her role of *grande dame* in exile, even managing to charm Queen Victoria. Eugénie had long been a diplomat behind the scenes and, after a dull period of suburban exile in Chislehurst in England, found the Riviera a more satisfy-

taneity offended Viennese society so she was delighted to find that the Riviera was not etiquette-bound. Considered the most beautiful Princess in Europe, she nonetheless had an unhappy marriage and was labelled neurotic. Her secluded villa, the Grand Hôtel du Cap Martin, represented comfort and privacy, and she found solace walking the long coastal path around the Cape. Having no wish to meet her husband in Monaco, she usually walked the other way, towards Menton.

Teutonic aristocrats regularly wintered in the Riviera, particularly after a German edition of Dr Bennet's *Winter and Spring on the Shores of the Mediterranean* appeared in

ing stage. From her rococo-style Villa Cyrnos, Eugénie quietly advised a variety of foreign sovereigns and ministers on world politics.

Eugénie's neighbour and contemporary was Elizabeth, Empress of Austria, married to Franz Josef I. Known as Sissi, Elizabeth was a daughter of a Bavarian duke and married her cousin at the age of 15. Sissi led a troubled life and, as Queen of Hungary, had a high political profile which was her downfall: she was assassinated by an Italian anarchist in Geneva. Sissi's restlessness and spon-

Left, Juan-les-Pins Casino by Edmond Lahaye, 1927. Above, the Grand Hotel, Juan-les-Pins.

1863. In the same year, Maximilian II of Bavaria bought a huge Niçois villa that had previously belonged to the Russian Empress Alexandra Feodrovna.

Cap Martin became a Germanic haunt by the turn of the century. The Grand Duke of Saxe-Weimar bought a villa there in 1894 and was soon joined by an exceedingly minor royal, Jean II, Prince of Lichtenstein. Frederick William, the last Crown Prince of Germany, wintered on the Cap and was known as "Little Willie" long before he retired to England in 1918. However, the German aristocrats were generally more discreet than their British and Russian counterparts. When a German claimed to be on the Riviera for health, not high jinks, he was generally believed.

The same could not be said for the Russians. Before World War I, the Russian community was second only to the British in size and influence. In 1856 Alexandra Feodorovna, the widow of Tsar Nicholas I, bought Villa Acquaviva in the Promenade des Anglais and forged the early Russian links with Nice. Not that the Russians needed much encouragement. French was the language of the Russian court and the Riviera made a restful second home, a welcome change from Russian winters and rebellious serfs. Alexandra's son, the Grand Duke Con-

stantine, followed in his mother's footsteps and bought Villa Lavit in the Promenade des Anglais. The seafront and the Boulevard Tzarewitch soon became distinct Russian colonies, set at a safe distance from the English camp at Cimiez. The Russians congregated in the Ferme Russe, Russian tea rooms run by the formidable Madame Chirikov. The pastries provided stiff competition to the cream cakes in Perrimond-Rumpelmayer, the German haunt. Below the domed winter garden of La Ferme Russe, imported Russian servants worked the samovars while their mistresses discussed charity balls or rheumatic gout.

The opening of the railway to Nice in 1864 had an immediate impact: Tsar Alexander II arrived a week later and was soon enthralled enough to consider building a Russian Orthodox church in Nice. The flamboyant green-and-gold domes remain a testament to the importance of the Russian community in the 19th century. In 1880 Grand Duchess Anastasia, Tsar Nicholas II's aunt, founded the Association Orthodoxe Russe which looked after consumptive soldiers and students. After the Revolution, the home became known as the Maison Russe and, linked to the Russian Red Cross, still welcomes Russian émigrés.

The Russian women had a particularly high social profile on the Riviera. One *grande dame* was the Princess Kotschouby whose ochre *belle-époque* villa is now the Chéret Museum in Nice. The Princess Caramachimay abandoned her troublesome Russian estates and emigrated to Cap Martin at the turn of the century. Princess Anna Chervachidzé settled in a grand estate nearby; it later sheltered a skulking Greta Garbo and is now owned by a Lebanese millionaire.

Unlike the Germans, the Russians were enthusiastic gamblers. Armed with boxes of gold and silver pieces, they whiled away the afternoons in the Monte-Carlo Casino. Princess Souvorov arrived in Monaco in 1869 with an "infallible" method. After visiting all the casinos in Europe, she had made copious notes of every winning number in all the games she had witnessed. But despite thousands of files, she lost 300,000 francs in a couple of hours. Suddenly her luck changed and she won eight nights in succession, breaking the bank twice.

To celebrate the win, she scandalised high society by holding a party for complete strangers. The only entry requirement was that guests should be amusing. The Monégasques closed ranks and refused to let her rent a room so she bought a villa and gave it away the next day. To encourage guests to perform party tricks, the Princess broke open thousands of cases of champagne and celebrated with a gypsy band and a Romanian dance troupe, the latest craze at the time on the Riviera.

Non-European royals were also drawn to the Riviera, including the Princess of Siam and the Bey of Algeria. One of the most eccentric visitors was the Maharajah of

Kaputhala. In 1897 he arrived at Monte Carlo's Hotel de Paris with a vast retinue. One servant, dressed in national costume and bedecked with gold and jewels, would stand behind the Maharajah's chair at dinner. When signalled, he sprinkled flakes of real silver on the royal curries. A later maharajah was instrumental in opening the Martinez Hotel in Cannes in 1926: he insisted on Louis XVI bedrooms for all the guests.

Sir Mohammed Shah, the Aga Khan III, was one of the few hereditary rulers whose affection for the Riviera has been echoed by his descendants. In 1908, the Aga Khan married an Italian dancer and installed her in a Middle Eastern-style villa above Monaco.

could be circumvented by importing staff or by choosing to live in hotels. Expatriates further down the social scale often ignored all other foreign residents.

"You may see English, German and French families pass many weeks together in the same house, eat twice a day at the same table, and sit for hours in the same salon without even exchanging a word." Such was Frederic Harrison's view of sour-faced Victorian visitors in 1887.

The Riviera was only relatively free from social restraints; even in Menton cemetery, each nationality and religion was accorded a separate burial tier. Nor were the pleasures of the South egalitarian; the Riviera was the

Their son, Major Aly Khan, was a member of the Free French forces that helped liberate the Riviera. Aly then went on to marry Rita Hayworth while his father competed by marrying Yvette, a "Miss France" bathing belle. The current Aga Khan lives in an art deco mansion in Antibes where "the only unguarded exit is the chute from the swimming pool to the sea".

Foreigners maintained a frontier mentality. The only local people they met were shopkeepers and servants; even this problem

Left, Tsarina Maria Alexandrovna, a frequent visitor, in 1865. **Above**, Nice Casino.

preserve of the rich until the Edwardian era. In the 1840s, a house in Nice could be rented for £300 a year while in the 1880s it cost £1,200 for the winter season. In 1896, the writer Augustus Hare commented approvingly: "Nice is a home for the millionaire and the working man. The intermediate class is not wanted. Visitors are expected to have money, and if they have to look at pounds, shillings and pence, had much better remain at home."

Victorian and Edwardian visitors were not exclusively aristocratic. "Money increases quickly," wrote Trollope in 1866, "and distances decrease." Bourgeois visitors were, however, in the minority until the 1920s.

While the flow of royal visitors continued during the inter-war years, a new élite emerged: the American dollar kings. Dr Bennet's *Winter and Spring in the Mediterranean* was published in New York in 1870 and provoked a new wave of wealthy visitors. The simple yet sophisticated pleasures of the Mediterranean appealed to jaded American tycoons. In 1898 Dr Allis, the art collector, was attracted to the unspoilt site of the Palais de Carnolès in Menton. After adding two new wings and replanting the gardens, Allis installed his priceless paintings. The watchword may have been simplicity but it was expensive simplicity.

James Gordon Bennett, the proprietor of the *New York Herald*, started a European edition of the paper as a pretext for living on the Riviera. As well as running the *International Herald Tribune*, Bennett found time to indulge fellow-Americans at his Beaulieu villa. As for his yacht, *Lysistrata*, even Vanderbilt was impressed. Manned by a 100-strong crew, the yacht had three decks, Turkish baths and a resident Alderney cow. The millionaire once invited Drexel, Biddle and Vanderbilt to dine at the Café Riche, his favourite restaurant in Monte-Carlo. The Americans were turned away from the restaurant terrace when the management decided that only cocktails should be served there. An outraged Bennett immediately bought the restaurant for $40,000 and sacked the manager. In appreciation for well-cooked lamb chops, Bennett promptly handed over the restaurant to Ciro, his favourite waiter, by way of a tip. The fortunate Ciro then went on to open successful restaurants all over Europe.

Bennett was only one of the profligate Americans who stayed on the Riviera. J. Pierpont Morgan, the steel magnate, was a notorious gambler at the Monte-Carlo Casino. Morgan asked if the individual limit for bets could be virtually doubled to 20,000 francs. When Blanc, the director, refused, Morgan left on the spot, complaining that he wouldn't waste his time gambling for such paltry amounts. Morgan, of course, went on to form the United States Steel Corporation with Andrew Carnegie. Charles M. Schwab, the President of the Corporation, was also an inveterate gambler. After tales of Schwab's profligacy reached the American press, Morgan somewhat hypocritically took him to task. Schwab's defence – "But I sin openly, not behind closed doors" – was countered with, "But that's exactly what doors are for."

Closed doors were needed with such colourful courtesans as Mata Hari and "La Belle Otéro" working their way through the foreign ranks. Although Mata Hari's spying was beyond the pale, until 1914 courtesans had an accepted status in Riviera society. As Mata Hari, the Dutch show-girl Gertrud Zelle came to Monte-Carlo to perform "exotic dances". Her stage name, meaning "sunrise" in Malay, was matched by exotic looks that captivated the French and German Ministers of Information. One night in the Casino, an agent accused her of secreting stolen documents in her bodice. Mata Hari promptly shot him and was excused on the grounds of self-defence.

By contrast, La Belle Otéro was apolitical. At the age of 14, Caroline Otéro, a Spanish gypsy, married an Italian baron and spent her honeymoon in Monaco. After her husband had lost in the Casino, she removed all the gold buttons from her dress and, as well as causing a stir, amassed a fortune on the tables. Caroline quickly abandoned her husband and began a new career as a *grande*

Left, The Riviera Express.

THE BLUE TRAIN

Along with the Santa Fe Superchief, the Orient Express and the Trans-Siberian Express, the Blue Train was never just a train; to travel on it from London to the Côte d'Azur in the 1920s and '30s represented the epitome of style and fashion. It was said that, for a woman to have made it in the world, she should have dined at the Ritz and Colony Restaurants in New York, the Everglades Club in Palm Beach, the Ritz in Paris, Claridge's in London and the Hôtel du Cap in Antibes, sailed on the *Berengaria* and the *Aquitania*, and, of course, travelled on the Blue Train. It was the *only* way to travel to the Côte d'Azur.

From the 1850s onwards the South of France was opened up to foreign visitors as trains reduced travelling times from about three weeks by carriage to just a couple of days by train. All that was then needed was sleeping accommodation, of the type pioneered by Pullman in the United States.

The first manufacturers of sleeping cars in Europe was the Compagnie Internationale des Wagons-Lits, founded by an enterprising Belgian, Georges Nagelmackers, in 1872. Its sleeping cars became famous, and the Calais-Nice-Rome Express, the first train to the south to be equipped with sleeping accommodation, began operating in 1883, about six months after the Orient Express. The Italian section was little used and the train eventually became known as the Calais-Mediterranean Express. It was popularly known as the Blue Train after 1922 when blue and gold painted sleeping cars first appeared. The words "*Train bleu*" were painted on the carriages only after 1949.

This luxurious palace on wheels, whose carriages catered to only 10 passengers, would leave Calais at 1pm, arriving in Monte-Carlo at 9.30 the next morning. For early British visitors travelling south for the winter, nothing could beat the pleasurable contrast of boarding under the grey skies and smog of London and waking the next morning to the blue skies, terracotta roofs and orange-trees of the Mediterranean.

It became known as the "millionaires' train" with some justification. The American James Gordon Bennett, owner of the *New York Herald* and famous for his profligacy, once, to the horror of his valet, tipped the conductor 20,000 francs. The conductor used the money to open a restaurant in Boulogne. When Charlie Chaplin came to stay with Frank Jay Gould, he arrived on the Blue Train. The Duke of Windsor had a carriage with a specially designed bathroom. When the casinos brought girls down from Maxim's in Paris they were guaranteed return tickets on the Blue Train (to be used if they failed to snare a rich husband). The fame of the Blue Train has been enshrined by the arts; Agatha Christie set a Hercule Poirot story on it, *The Mystery of the Blue Train*. Diaghilev directed a musical called *Le Train Bleu*, which was written by Jean Cocteau, with bathing costumes by Chanel and curtain by Picasso.

For Charles Graves in *The Riviera Revisited*, his account of the Côte d'Azur just after World War II, being able to board the Blue Train again meant the war was truly over. He even records the menu: "Off to the Gare de Lyons, where the Blue Train itself is waiting with a six-course dinner of clear soup, red mullet, pâté with truffles, chouxfleur au gratin, cheese, fruit and

coffee. Then bed in the same speckless sleeping compartment which has miraculously survived all bombing by the British and American aircraft."

Today the Blue Train is no more, though its name endures. Monte-Carlo Casino has a restaurant called Le Train Bleu, using its traditional decor. However, it is possible to travel in considerable comfort overnight through France, still a romantic journey; half-waking at dim-lit stations in the dead of night and rising to the golden sunlight glinting off the southern roofs and the blue waters of the Mediterranean. Plans for the new TGV line have been shelved and, for the time being at least, the train track still hugs the shore, providing tantalising glimpses of villas, pools and rocky coves – all the pleasures to come. ■

<u>Right</u>, a poster by Cassandre.

horizontale. Her voluptuous figure was appreciated by Edward VII and Kaiser Wilhelm II. One of her lovers was a hideous German millionaire but, as La Belle Otéro pointed out, "Such a rich man can never be ugly." Caroline retired to Monaco in 1922 but her legendary figure lives on in Cannes' Carlton Hotel: the twin domes are said to have been inspired by La Belle Otéro's perfect breasts.

There was a distinct change of climate after World War I. The courtesans were no more; the Russians were dead or in exile; the Kings of Italy, Spain, Albania and Yugoslavia clung to their thrones; most royals were in financial straits.

Only the Americans had the means to live

out their fantasies. With the glamorous new arrivals, winter was banished and the summer season launched. Writer E. Phillips Oppenheim slept aboard a yacht which was known as the floating double bed; the women were expected to stay awake at night to deal with the mosquitoes.

There was no shortage of eccentrics on the new summer stage. Mr Neal, an American millionaire guest at the Hôtel de l'Hermitage, installed an artificial moon in his window to remind him that it was night and therefore time to go to the Casino. One of his milder whims was to invite 80 guests to a free dinner, provided that they laughed at his jokes. His peremptory method of summoning staff consisted of firing one pistol shot for room service and two shots if he required a chambermaid for personal services.

Henry Clews, the wealthy American sculptor, was also a noted eccentric. In La Napoule, his Saracen castle, Clews recreated a medieval setting, complete with minstrel gallery and staff dressed in Provençal costume. His wife's pet peacocks were notorious, frequently straying onto the railway line where they often brought the Blue Train to a halt. As Patrick Howarth remarks, "It happened so frequently that the SNCF felt obliged to make a formal demand that the peacocks shouldn't be allowed on the line."

Not for nothing were the 1920s known as *les années folles*. Even if the bodies of bankrupt gamblers were no longer immured in the Casino walls, fortunes could still be won or lost on a dropped gold button. But, amidst the wanton partying, creativity seemed to flourish. Colette, Scott Fitzgerald, Somerset Maugham, Katherine Mansfield and Blasco Ibañez were writing themselves into different patches of the Riviera.

In Monte-Carlo, the impresario Raoul Gunsbourg was the first to stage Wagner outside Bayreuth and, as Director of the Monte Carlo Opera, also introduced the public to works by Berlioz, Massenet and Tchaikovsky. Ravel was invited to compose for the orchestra and created the *Ballet Pour Ma Fille*, based on Colette's work. But Gunsbourg's greatest coup was to convince Sergei Diaghilev and his Ballets Russes to settle in Monaco. In turn, Diaghilev persuaded the greatest composers of the age, including Debussy and Stravinsky, to write for the Ballets Russes. The company, starring Pavlova and Nijinsky, danced to such modern classics as *L'Après-midi d'un Faune* and *The Firebird*.

As if this were not enough, the costumes and sets were designed by Picasso and Matisse, Utrillo and De Chirico, Georges Braque and André Derain. Unsurprisingly, the ballets ran at a financial loss but Diaghilev was not deterred: "I don't spend a sou on myself. I have very simple tastes: only the best is good enough." Diaghilev praised Isadora Duncan for breaking with classical tradition but she spurned an invitation to see the Ballets Russes: "I don't care much for acrobats." Instead, she ran up huge hotel bills at the Negresco in Nice and, before her tragic entanglement with a silk scarf, indulged her penchant for chasing young men, including Zelda Fitzgerald's husband.

In the 1920s and '30s, the Riviera was in glamorous American hands. Scott Fitzgerald enthused about "the soft-pawed night and the ghostly wash of the Mediterranean far below." Gerald and Sara Murphy, the originals for Dick and Nicole Diver in *Tender is the Night*, had discovered it some years before. After being introduced to the Riviera by Cole Porter, the couple bought Villa America on the Cap d'Antibes and there entertained the Lost Generation. Dorothy Parker, Hemingway and the Fitzgeralds needed little

ence over the Riviera for 50 years. The tasteless splendour of Juan-les-Pins is their lasting imprint.

World War II drew the curtains on old American glamour but the Riviera has proved irresistible to Hollywood stars. The Hôtel du Cap-Eden Roc provides the sumptuous link. Situated on the tip of the Cap d'Antibes, this gilded white palace has long been the mecca for the American set, from the Murphys onwards.

A new wave brought such stars as Clark Gable, Humphrey Bogart and Rita Hayworth. At different times, John Wayne and Charlie Chaplin were entertained by the hotel's private funicular to the beach. While indulging

encouragement to sample swimming and sunbathing.

The Goulds, along with the Murphys, entertained *le beau monde*, welcoming André Gide and Giraudoux as well as American high society. Frank Jay Gould, heir to a railway empire, virtually created Juan-les-Pins. For Florence, his Californian wife, the Riviera was also a *coup de foudre*: she quickly opened a casino and hotel and created a neo-Gothic villa for herself. Although long treated as arrivistes, the couple exerted great influ-

Left, Frank Jay Gould and his wife, Florence. **Above**, Grand Hôtel du Cap-Eden Roc, 1929.

in cocktails and caviare, John F. Kennedy admired the exotic gardens from the gigantic stone terrace.

The star-spangled tradition continues. The Cote d'Azur has not lost its glamour, and continues to attract the rich and famous who rent or own villas hidden away on Cap Ferrat or Cap d'Antibes. Rock stars and supermodels still flock to St-Tropez, to dine at the beach clubs or sip cocktails on quayside yachts. The grand hotels retain their legendary status and helicopters, private planes and limousines still provide luxury transport for the privileged percentage to keep the dream of Caviare days alive for everyone else.

The 1939 summer season on the Riviera attracted the customary cosmopolitan crowd and, enlivened by the novelties of water-skiing and skin-diving, was said to have been the best yet. Colonel Josef Beck, the Polish Foreign Minister, rubbed shoulders with Sir Robert Vansittart of the British Foreign Office and Crown Prince Umberto of Italy. The Duke of Windsor, licking the wounds of the abdication which had ended his brief reign as Edward VIII of England, took a 10-year lease on a villa near Cannes, then preparing for its first film festival in September.

There were, however, intimations of the sinister clouds gathering over Europe. The shadowy face within a large car which cruised around San Remo – and was once seen parked advantageously above the annual military parade in Nice – belonged to Hermann Goering. In the Hôtel Beaulieu in Cannes, Dr E. Wightman Ginner gave a series of lectures on what to do in an air raid. Rumour spoke of secret landings at Cap Ferrat and Cap Martin – spies! Hitler occupied Austria, the Czech Sudeten, and then invaded Poland. World War II was on.

In the uneasy calm of the "Phoney War" while Hitler gathered strength for his attack on Western Europe, the Riviera prepared for the inevitable. Two British colliers arrived in Cannes to evacuate British subjects but some, such as the septuagenarian Miss Amy Paget, chose to stay put and ran up the British flag over her Cannes villa.

The Windsors, who also remained, invited Maurice Chevalier to their villa "in the perhaps forlorn hope," the controversial duchess wrote later, "that he might be inspired to supply a last flash of lightheartedness in that dismal atmosphere." The local labour force on which the expatriate colony depended was swallowed up by France's mobilisation. Waiters and tradesmen were transplanted to the concrete bunkers of the Maginot Line, facing Nazi Germany across the Rhine, the Moselle, the Saar and the Meuse. Yet still no shots were fired.

On 10 May 1940, Hitler's army simply side-stepped the Maginot Line by marching through the Low Countries and attacking France from the north. The Nazis marched into Paris, which had been declared an open city, on 14 June. From there they pushed south to Nantes, Vichy, Dijon and Lyon and west to Bordeaux and the Spanish frontier. More than 250,000 British and French troops cut off by the speed of the advance were evacuated from Dunkirk by the famous flotilla of small boats, but there were many who could not reach the coast.

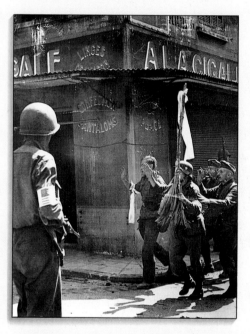

Most of the stranded troops joined the exodus south. For a while, however, the supposed sanctuary of the south looked threatened by Mussolini who, feeling that he had been rather left out of things, declared war on Britain and France and occupied Menton and a few villages just across the Italian border.

The Axis advance was suspended when the French government resigned and Marshal Pétain asked for, and was granted, an armistice. France was divided into two zones. Germany occupied the Atlantic coastline from Spain to the Low Countries and the industrial north above a line drawn roughly between Tours and Dijon. The unoccupied

Left, Resistance fighters in Hyéres. **Right**, American troops rounding up Germans.

zone consisted of the relatively barren mountain areas, the Rhône valley, the Mediterranean coast and a puppet government named after its "capital", Vichy.

There was, of course, no certainty that Germany would not renege on the armistice and take over "Free France" as well, but in the circumstances it was very much more congenial than the north for stranded soldiers, downed Allied air crews and persecuted minorities like Jews, gypsies and Communists. For the following four years, the war in the South of France was mostly about providing a safe passage for these fugitives. Many of the civilians were helped across the Mediterranean to French North Africa. The

lied officers reported on Monday mornings for a roll call, collected their rations, sold them on the black market, and applied the proceeds to renting lodgings in the city. Their ambition was somehow to slip away to Spain, and British Intelligence created a branch known as MI9 to help them realise that objective.

With a long history of underhand survival, the Marseille Mafia was fitter than most. To make contact with these dubious characters, British Intelligence turned to Nubar Gulbenkian, the son of the legendary Iranian oil dealer. Young Gulbenkian tackled the undertaking with the help of Bailey, his English valet, and it nearly came to grief at

escape route for Allied military personnel, including those arriving from Central Europe via Switzerland, was along the Riviera to neutral Spain.

Once the evaders had crossed the demarcation line into Vichy France they were still liable to arrest by the police but were not normally in danger of being handed back to the Germans. There were plenty of Vichy officials ready to give them a nod and a wink, but if caught they were assembled in Fort St-Jean in Marseille or, later on, at St-Hippolyte du Fort at Nîmes or La Turbie, outside Monte-Carlo. They were then neither quite prisoners nor free. In Marseille, for example, Al-

the outset in the Hôtel des Ambassadeurs in Vichy. Bailey, having borrowed an iron to press his employer's clothes, bumped into a delegation of German officers and dropped the iron on the foot of Field Marshal von Brauchitsch, Commander-in-Chief of the German Army. Brauchitsch stared at Bailey, assumed he must be American, and chose not to pursue the matter.

The pair were instructed by London to go to Perpignan and look out for a garage proprietor named "Parker". In time-honoured fashion, he would be reading the newspaper L'Indépendant upside-down. In case he was not alone in this curious habit, a test question was provided: "Have you got a Parker pen? A Parker Duo-fold?" The reader in question passed with flying colours. Within 20 minutes Gulbenkian had negotiated a price for guides to smuggle men across the frontier: £40 for an officer, £20 for other ranks. Payment was by results and the money would be deposited in England for collection after the war. "Parker" was clearly willing to bank on the ultimate outcome.

Several British officers who had recently escaped from France were sent back under the auspices of the Special Operations Executive, a unit established by Churchill to keep the enemy on its toes by organising and supplying national resistance movements.

and the whole affair was treated like a game. Churchill (no relation to Sir Winston) affected Damon Runyon prose in his official reports, the dubious theory being that any Germans intercepting his messages would be completely baffled.

"It is a lucky thing that the Chief Constable of the Department where this comic opera takes place is a great friend of England. He knows all about this particular performance and last night in a friend's house he is seen beating his hands against the wall and crying, 'I close my peepers to what the Albions do right under my nose, but in the name of the Holy Virgin why do they not help me and themselves by picking any one or all of the

They arrived by parachute, by submarine and from Gibraltar either in an armed British trawler flying false colours or in feluccas manned by Polish crews so exuberant that even the Polish Navy preferred to manage without them.

The Poles did not deign to conceal their activities. "The reception mob is there every night and... carry on like a Bank Holiday crowd on Derby Day," reported Peter Churchill, one of the British agents. Like many of the SOE operatives, he was in his early 20s

Left, the American landings. Above, beach at Juan-les-Pins in 1944.

17 to 20 nights in the month when there is no moon whatever'."

When not pretending to be Damon Runyon, Churchill was "Pierre Chauvet", estate agent. Flush with British War Office money, he moved into a comfortable flat in Cannes and had a regular table at Chez Robert. The British government seems unknowingly to have treated every secret agent passing through town – all the more so if they were female, young and pretty – to M. Robert's excellent fare. Churchill's memoirs are a litany of *pièces de résistance* and the search for a complementary wine. A bottle of 1911 Château Chambord was just the ticket to wash down a herb omelette and M. Robert's miraculous chicken on the occasion of Churchill's lunch with a charming "Madame Rondet". At their next meeting – at Chez Robert again, of course – they are joined by "an aristocratic Frenchman with a monocle". Churchill divides his attention between "an excellent *loup de mer*... with a dry white wine", Madame Rondet's beautiful face, and "the vast expanse of the blue Mediterranean, calm and untroubled below a cloudless sky". He has to tear himself away from the cheese, coffee and brandy – "all as delicious as the rest of the meal" – to mount his bicycle and race off to the station to attend to some urgent undercover business.

Churchill soon made the acquaintance of Lise, an agent who arrived by felucca and was, if possible, even lovelier than Madame Rondet. "This girl's dynamite," he noted in his journal and, as things turned out, he later married her. But it was about then, November 1942, that the Allies invaded North Africa. Hitler immediately terminated the French "free" zone, the occupation of which was entrusted to the Italians.

SOE and its guerrilla bands had worked out plans to blow up roads, tunnels and bridges in such an eventuality, but these were countermanded by superiors in London who were pleased at the prospect of troops being absorbed by garrison duties away from the active battleground. The disappointed saboteurs took up positions on the Rue du Canada to witness the arrival of the Italians. "Below the feathers of the Bersaglieri hats," Churchill observed, "their faces seemed ready enough to break into an answering smile." He subsequently conceded that under the Italian occupation forces, "if anything a greater atmosphere of peace prevailed in the district and all persecution of the Jews came to an end."

When Italy surrendered in September 1943, the Germans themselves took over the occupation. By then the fate of the Dunkirk stragglers had long been settled, and the combined efforts of SOE and the French Resistance were devoted to the repatriation of downed air crews and escaped prisoners-of-war and to longer-term planning of an uprising in support of an Allied invasion, whenever that happened. The most famous of the escape routes was the so-called "Pat Line" run by a "Lieutenant-Commander Patrick

O'Leary" who was in reality the Belgian Count Albert-Marie Guerisse. Hacksaws and other useful implements were smuggled to interned air crews at La Turbie to facilitate, in one instance, a mass escape down a coal-chute and through the sewers. About 90 percent of the 3,000 Allied airmen shot down in northwest Europe before the Normandy landings (the majority Americans) managed to avoid capture and were smuggled back to base via the Riviera.

Joint operations with the Resistance were complicated by the exiled General de Gaulle's notorious prickliness about foreigners, even friendly ones, giving orders to Frenchmen on French soil. The artist André Girard, who as "Carte" ran a section of the Riviera Resistance, shared these feelings and claimed to have no fewer than 300,000 Frenchmen under his independent command and ready to take up arms when the word was given. In the event, the word was cloaked in confusion as it rested on the misconception, which in the end may have been deliberately left uncorrected, that the Allies would crush the German forces in France between simultaneous and equal operations from north and south, "Hammer" against "Anvil".

The change in plans, Winston Churchill declared later, was "the first important divergence on high strategy between ourselves and our American friends." A simultaneous invasion of the Côte d'Azur would have drawn Allied troops from Italy, and he was keen to push through Italy and into the Balkans before the Russians got there. Nor were there sufficient invasion craft to mount two assaults.

Invasion plans: The Normandy operation was renamed "Overlord". "Anvil" was put back a few months and became "Dragoon". Even so, says Patrick Howarth in *When The Riviera was Ours*, the plans for the invasion of the south "were among the less well kept secrets of the Second World War, not least because of the frequency with which officers who were to take part in the operations themselves, or in their planning, asked for guidebooks to southern France in the bookshops of Rome."

The German defence strategy in the south was to concentrate forces around Marseille and Toulon while at the same time making an Allied landing anywhere along the coast as difficult as possible. Villas, hotels and restaurants overlooking the shore were bricked up and turned into strong-points.

Any spot that looked suitable for a landing was sown with "Rommel's asparagus", underwater posts tipped with explosive charges set to detonate on contact. The beaches were lined with trenches, tank traps and emplacements for flame-throwers; secondary defences ran 20 miles (32 km) inland and included sharp stakes to impale paratroopers and wires to impede glider landings.

Of the German 19th Army in the south, three divisions were withdrawn to fight in Normandy, leaving about 250,000 men made up largely of battle-weary veterans of the eastern front and non-Germans pressed into

too, and the Carlton Hotel in Cannes was only spared, so the story goes, by Herbert Matthews of the *New York Times* telling American naval gunners that in his opinion it was the best hotel in the world and they ought to take special care not to hit it.

Taking the bombardment as a signal for insurrection, the Resistance swung into action by blowing up bridges which isolated St-Laurent, Cagnes-sur-Mer, Antibes and Cannes, cutting power lines, and attacking factories and German installations. German reprisals were swift and unselective; 99 hostages were hanged at Tulle, for example, after the shooting of an SS officer. Even schoolboys were rounded up in Vence and

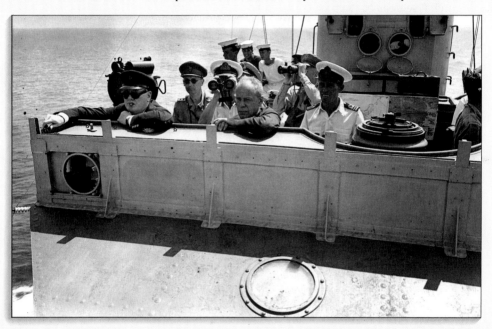

Hitler's service. German Intelligence estimates put the number of Allied troops available for Dragoon at 500,000. The Allies enjoyed enormous superiority in aircraft: 5,000 based in Corsica and Italy against 186 German aircraft.

Dragoon was preceded by naval and air bombardment which began towards the end of May. On the 26th, bombers hit marshalling yards and the St-Roch freight depot in Nice in a raid which killed 283 civilians and destroyed 500 houses. St-Tropez suffered

Above, Churchill watches St-Tropez landings from the destroyer *Kimberley*.

deported to concentration camps, many of them never to return. For their part, the Resistance fighters, who were soon uncomfortably aware that they had rather jumped the gun, were not slow to execute suspected collaborators.

German commanders were inclined to think that one of the most likely places for the seaborne invasion which had to follow was below La Croisette and they accordingly reinforced their positions with heavy gun emplacements disguised as bathing huts and beach cafés. Some officers were convinced they were facing a double-pronged assault on Marseille and Genoa, a deception encouraged by the pattern of pre-invasion bombing and, as time went by, thousands of rubber mannequins dropped by parachute over the mouth of the Rhône.

For weeks on end, however, the action remained stubbornly in the air, although the targets changed. "In the blue August sky," wrote an eye-witness subsequently, "formation after formation of silver planes no longer contented themselves flying overhead with that majestic indifference which until now had only drawn the glances of the curious: now the whole coast was itself attacked, point by point.

"Little by little, the fires caused by the explosions coalesced and huge eruptions of black smoke rose menacingly behind the rocky scarps… Thunderbolts and Liberators staged a veritable rodeo over Cap St-Pierre, near St-Tropez, and above the tiered vine terraces of Ste-Maxime. Allied aircraft making the most fantastic manoeuvres seemed to be playing cat-and-mouse with the coastal batteries, shooting up minefields and blockhouses, showering the corniches with explosions of water and flame, brewing up colours that even our skies had never known until that day." Between 28 April and 10 August, the Allies flew more than 10,000 sorties over the Côte d'Azur and dropped 12,500 tons of bombs on it.

On 14 August the cryptic "personal messages" which followed the BBC news bulletin provided what the Resistance had been waiting for. "Gaby is sleeping on the grass" and "Nancy has a stiff neck" were among those which signalled an Allied invasion the next day. The American 7th Army under General Patch and the French 1st Army led by General de Lattre de Tassigny landed along a 35-mile (55-km) stretch of coast east of Toulon while an airborne division dropped inland near Le Muy. The invasion force was carried in 500 troop transport ships and 1,200 smaller craft backed up by six battleships, four carriers, 21 cruisers and more than 100 destroyers.

Sir Winston Churchill, a regular pre-war visitor to the Riviera, watched the landings on Pampelonne Beach near St-Tropez from the destroyer *Kimberley*. He was frustrated to learn that his ship would remain 10,000 yards off St-Tropez for fear of mines. Had he been told in time, he said, he would have arranged a launch to take him ashore. "As far as I could see or hear," he wrote, "not a shot was fired either at the approaching flotillas or on the beaches."

He consoled himself in the captain's cabin with the novel *Grand Hotel*. It kept him, he said, "in good temper", his mood improving even more when he heard that in their cabin the Supreme Commander and the Naval Commander-in-Chief had spent "an equally dull day".

It was not so quiet nearer Cannes, where Germans and Americans fought for possession of the beaches at Agay and Dramont. The unluckiest unit in the invasion force were French commandos who landed in the early hours of the morning on the Pointe d'Esquillon. Their mission was to climb the rocky Estérel and blow up roads to prevent German reinforcements from moving west. They had been led to believe that the area was free of mines, but only hours before their arrival German sappers had laid a field across their course. Eleven out of a unit of 67 were killed, 17 badly wounded and the rest captured. Ten were rescued by the daring intervention of the Resistance.

German sappers had actually wired up charges to blow up every hotel, public building and monument in Cannes in the event of their withdrawal. The Carlton Hotel alone was sitting on 50 canisters of explosive, but it seems that a senior German officer relented at the last moment and revealed the whereabouts of the central detonator to the Resistance. It was in the wine cellar of the Hôtel Splendide.

Grenoble was retaken by elements of the US 6th Corps on 23 August, while the Germans put up a fighting retreat along the coast. Marseille and Toulon were liberated after two weeks' fighting, and on 1 September Nice, to which many of the German forces had withdrawn, was regained after stiff street fighting between the Germans and the Resistance fighters. On 12 September a Free French patrol moving north near Châtillon-sur-Seine ran into scouts from General Leclerc's French 2nd Armoured Division coming south. That emotional encounter meant the respective invasions of Normandy and Provence had linked up. Operation Dragoon was sewn up 77 days ahead of schedule.

Right, local children greet their liberators.

THE SUN CULT

For over a century British, American and European visitors flocked to the Côte d'Azur in search of status, health and pleasure, not to mention rare spiders and Roman antiquities. But after World War II the spotlight shifted to the French. Picasso moved to Antibes in 1946 and spent the rest of his life on the Côte d'Azur. The artists Arman, Klein and Raysse, all born in Nice, created the School of Nice, diametrically opposed to what was happening in the Paris galleries. Parisian bohemian stars like Juliette Greco began to visit St-Tropez in the footsteps of Colette, Poiret and Anaïs Nin.

The first Cannes Film Festival in 1946 attracted world-wide attention, publicising the Riviera as the land of the bikini. This was reinforced by Brigitte Bardot's 1956 film *And God Created Woman*, in which her unabashed sensuality and particularly her penchant for nude sunbathing scandalised the world. It popularised the sun worship which had started in the 1920s, as people began to associate health with a golden tan.

Even now the dangers attributed to sunbathing appear to have made little impact and sun-worshippers continue to baste themselves slowly on the sand, as if, in Françoise Sagan's words, they are "nailed to the beach by the forces of summer".

Sagan's highly successful novel *Bonjour Tristesse* also helped to popularise the region. With the advent of the post-war youth culture, and paid vacations for French workers, the Côte d'Azur entered the late 20th century. It was opened up to everyone, beyond the wealthy aristocracy that had frequented its glamorous hot spots for more than 100 years, and the show business people and shipping tycoons who dominated the scene immediately after World War II.

The Côte d'Azur was the quintessence of glamour: sun, sea, sand and sex with the added frisson of famous film stars who just might be, but never quite were, sunbathing

Preceding pages: 1953 Cannes Film Festival: Dany Robin, Kirk Douglas, Olivia de Havilland, Edward G. Robinson, and members of the festival's jury. **Left,** Brigitte Bardot arriving at Victorine Film Studios in Nice, 1959.

on the next *matelas*. But with a sun tan, a bikini and a pair of sun-glasses, who was to know the difference anyway. Here was a whole new swinging lifestyle that was emulated by millions, all hoping that two weeks on the French Riviera would somehow rub off, making them richer, more beautiful or at least more sun-tanned.

As Roger Vadim described St-Tropez: "It was the happy mixture of old and young, wealth and class. A person with no money could live like a millionaire and a millionaire could have fun living like a bohemian."

In her autobiography *With Fondest Regards*, Françoise Sagan captures the rapid change that took place in the formerly quiet

Suddenly St-Tropez was the "metropolis of illicit pleasures": "Germans, Americans, Italians and others think they're buying themselves enchantment as they pour marks, dollars and lire onto the blue carpet of the Mediterranean, a Mediterranean in which fish die from all the petrol, where the beaches are filthy by the first day of spring." She concludes nonetheless that St-Tropez has an indestructible beauty with its tonic winds, its peaceful yellow sun, and "the red-hued coastline with its intricate inlets".

An incident in Roger Vadim's autobiography typifies the period. "It was 1958. Tahiti beach in St-Tropez. One evening the sound of a Ferrari drowned out the crickets.

fishing port in the late '50s, "a village that triggers off a daydream." When she arrived in 1954 with a crowd of young, wild Parisians, they were the only young, wild people there; they found a scene of timeless calm with village women knitting and fishermen bringing home their catch.

But the very next year she describes "wild and disorderly groups of urban bathing beauties as they rush from street stall to street stall in search of a swimsuit, speed-boats and the rowdy screaming and shouting of young people who roar off in unruly disarray – all for the feeble purpose of lying on the sand five hundred metres farther down the beach."

The roar of a Mercedes 300 SL replied to the Ferrari. It was a duel." Roger Vadim and Gunther Sachs started up their cars positioned either side of a bend in the road with a huge parasol pine in the middle. Neither driver could see the other car and had to guess which way the other would turn at the tree. If they both found themselves on the same side of the tree there would be a head-on collision unless one of the drivers yielded. "It was a sort of Russian roulette with wheels," writes Vadim. He was driving the Ferrari, and the judges included Françoise Sagan, Christian and Serge Marquand and Marlon Brando.

In the second round the two cars came face to face and a split second before they crashed Sachs lost his nerve and plunged his Mercedes into the ditch. He wasn't hurt and the next day a crane hauled the car out; Gunther, who later became Brigitte Bardot's third husband, was very wealthy and could afford the damage. That evening he gave a celebration dinner at the Restaurant Tahiti; an enormous dish was served which turned out to be Serge Marquand decorated with mayonnaise and gherkins.

Just a typical day in St-Tropez when the world was young and not just anybody came to the Côte d'Azur in the summer. Vadim was an old hand, having spent previous visits

los hotel, pursued by the world's paparazzi who made sure the region stayed in the headlines.

Being the world's favourite holiday destination naturally took its toll; millions flocked every summer, renting anything from exclusive *pied dans l'eau* villas to caravans, from sailing yachts to surfboards, and from motocyclettes to Mercedes. The property market boomed. What began as merely good investment was rapidly exploited by developers and by the 1970s property prices were sky-rocketing, with luxury villas in areas like Californie and Super-Cannes commanding record prices from Arab oil sheiks and wealthy Europeans.

there with Brigitte Bardot, his former wife. It was here that they shot *And God Created Woman,* the film that made her a star. Bardot is still held largely responsible for starting the sun cult on the Côte d'Azur, and her signature pony tail, short gathered skirt, low-cut peasant blouse and flat shoes established a look imitated by young girls everywhere.

The Côte d'Azur, and St-Tropez in particular, remained immensely fashionable throughout the 1960s. It was here that Mick Jagger married Bianca at the luxurious Byb-

Left, aspiring starlet, Cannes. Above, Robert Mitchum, 1954.

What the French termed "caviarisation" began, as every rich globule on the coast began to connect up. Soon there was barely an inch of coastline left that was not built on. Vast marinas were constructed, and the coast became a mecca for boat owners everywhere. Every fat cat from Aristotle Onassis to Donald Trump had to have a yacht as big as a ferry moored in Antibes or Monte-Carlo.

Instead of mere luxury villas, huge apartment blocks rose everywhere. For a while it was a free-for-all, with ugly results. By 1980 the development had reached its zenith and the government began to crack down. B.B. also put her foot down, threatening to leave

BRIGITTE BARDOT

When the film *And God Created Woman* appeared in 1956 it made the young Brigitte Bardot a world-famous star and a sexual icon. "You are going to be the respectable married man's unattainable dream," her director-husband Roger Vadim told her.

It also put St-Tropez on the map and sun worship on every budding starlet's agenda. Today the film seems tame, but in 1956, when sexual union was represented by fireworks or waves crashing on to rocks, its nudity and love scenes caused a furore, particularly in the US. In 1957 it earned over $8 million, more than France's biggest export, the Renault Dauphine.

It was Bardot's 17th film, and hers was by no means a rags-to-riches story. Her parents were well-to-do: her father was an industrialist and her mother ran a clothes boutique in Paris. At 14, Brigitte, having done some modelling, was recruited as a cover girl for *Jardin des Modes* and *Elle*. Her parents insisted she could only be identified by her initials, "B.B."

Film-director Marc Allegret was developing a film-script written by a 19-year-old White Russian, Roger Vladimir Plemiannikov (known as Vadim). He asked Vadim to investigate the new *Elle* cover girl. While they made a formal visit to Brigitte's parents, the 15-year-old Brigitte and Vadim sneaked out onto the balcony together. Although the resulting screen test was a flop, Vadim and Brigitte soon became lovers, though

Vadim had to change his religion and wait until Brigitte was 18 before they could marry.

Enthusiastically promoted by Vadim, Brigitte was given a number of small parts in a series of mediocre films. Her fifth film, Anatole Litvak's *Act of Love*, starring Kirk Douglas, in which Bardot had a minuscule part, was promoted at the 1953 Cannes Film Festival. It was the opportunity Vadim had been waiting for. The United States aircraft carrier *Midway* was in Cannes to show the flag, entertaining the best known film-stars on deck: Edward G. Robinson, Gary Cooper, Lana Turner, Olivia de Havilland and Leslie Caron all paraded for the cameras, smiling and waving in time-honoured tradition. But the cameramen began to slip away, turning their backs on the stars and focusing instead on a slender girl in a raincoat who had not been invited on board. Brigitte let slip her coat to reveal a tiny little-girl outfit, tossed her pony-tail and smiled. The next day her face and figure were on the front pages of newspapers around the world.

She became an international star with a British film, *Doctor At Sea*, starring Dirk Bogarde, and caused a sensation with the press. When they asked her what wardrobe she had brought with her she replied, "Several nightdresses because I hope someone will take me out." Although the film was terrible, Brigitte's role received rave notices, and young girls everywhere copied her pony-tail and affected her famous pout.

Her movies became more and more daring, until *And God Created Woman*, which was such a *succès de scandale*. It was after this that Brigitte bought La Madrague, a large villa near St-Tropez. She has lived there ever since.

The presence of the most famous woman in France drew the tourists and an enterprising American tourist agency offered Riviera tours with the "possibility" of seeing B.B. bathing in the nude. Her fame attracted other celebrities and jet-setters whose presence transformed the tiny fishing port. St-Tropez has never been quite the same again.

Neither, indeed, has Brigitte Bardot. After three marriages and numerous love affairs she declared that she preferred animals to men. She began to devote her life to various animal causes, from saving the whales to rescuing her neighbour's donkey, and established her own animal sanctuary at nearby La Garrigue.

Since then, however, she has shocked the world again, first by marrying Bernard d'Ormale, a leading member of the Front Nationale. Then she published her controversial autobiography, which caused so much furore that her ex-husband and son tried to have it suppressed. ∎

Left, the young Bardot.

St-Tropez if the mayor went ahead with a new development scheme. She insisted that the town must decide who was the greater tourist attraction. The mayor backed down.

From 1980 new building was forbidden within 100 metres of the sea; high-rise apartment buildings were banned, and new ones limited to seven floors; nothing was to be built in designated "natural zones" of virgin woods and fields. In many areas new houses can only be built using traditional materials and methods.

The permanent exception to this rule is Monaco where skyscrapers cram the tiny principality like Hong Kong or Manhattan, the most recent of them built on landfill,

line offers to the visitor the same interest and pleasures as ever. It has a near-perfect climate resulting from its blessed geographical position nestling between snow-crowned mountains and palm-fringed sea. The scenery remains sensational, eclipsing even the most grotesque architectural mistakes. The same bare red porphyry rocks and glittering turquoise sea, silvery olive trees and fragrant broom greet new arrivals as they have always done. Matisse's "glaring festive light" still bathes everything in a luminescent glow that Matisse felt was so strong that no one would believe such intense colours were possible.

Inland the mountains are covered in laven-

Above, Monaco's high-rise prosperity.

often blocking light and views from older properties. Since many of Monaco's residents are domiciled there for tax purposes, nobody seems to complain.

Today, within the Alpes-Maritimes *département*, 94 percent of the housing stock is still located along the coast, although villages further and further inland are being enthusiastically restored. Of more than 300,000 residences, over a third are second homes. But, despite such unbridled development and the inevitable problems generated, in many essential respects this charmed coast-

der and broom, high mountain plateaus remain silent and windswept, and if the medieval villages are less desolate than they were, so much the better. The current wave of restoration has preserved many buildings which would otherwise be reduced to rubble. The more hedonistic latterday attractions still hold good; Scott Fitzgerald's "lost caviare days" endure for some. In Monte-Carlo the casinos still draw the gullible rich; the nightclubs of Juan-les-Pins continue to attract swarms of young people for whom a day on the beach, a good sun-tan, the latest fashion in beachwear (or even no beachwear at all), followed by a night of dancing, constitutes a perfect holiday. For the gourmet francophile, the area abounds in fine restaurants and top-flight chefs, and those of cultural aspirations cannot fail to be stimulated by a huge number of museums and art galleries. Sporting opportunities are endless, from water sports of every conceivable variety to skiing, golf or mountain-climbing. Even at the height of the summer season, it is perfectly possible to enjoy the Côte d'Azur, though you may need to be a little offbeat if you want to be alone.

The glamorous image of the Côte d'Azur undoubtedly remains. Perhaps what is most remarkable about the region is that it has, somehow, tenaciously hung on to its image

In fact business receipts now actually outweigh receipts from tourism. Traditional tourist attractions have been repackaged. Business tourism is very successful and there is a huge year-round conference trade. The region is second only to Paris in the number of new companies created. They relocate here, attracted by the climate, lifestyle and image of the Riviera, and take advantage of improved transport and communications systems – the second largest airport after Paris, and the densest telephone and telex system in regional France.

In particular, the high-tech sector has boomed with the development of the Sophia-Antipolis technology park and related pro-

and not gone slithering downmarket, the almost invariable fate of other popular holiday destinations.

Image, after all, is what it is all about, and it is the image of the Côte d'Azur that attracts not only 8 million tourists a year but swarms of business visitors, and entices companies to relocate here. Increasingly the Côte d'Azur is becoming the centre of the European sunbelt and a high-tech paradise along the lines of California's Silicon Valley. (Now the Provence-Alpes-Côte d'Azur region is formally twinned with California and the Var aims to become, somewhat dubiously, the "Florida of Europe".)

jects. The attractions are not hard to understand; the so-called "beach boffins" enjoy all the advantages of a high-tech working environment with in-house swimming-pools, good weather, pink, palm-fronded villas and frequent trips to the sea, not to mention reflective jogs round the Provençal countryside, newly landscaped for their convenience. Such developments result in strange anomalies; next to the 14th-century Chapelle Notre-Dame-de-la-Protection in Haut-de-Cagnes is the world's first fully computerised car-park; your car is shunted by computer 14 floors down into the bowels of the earth and automatically parked. It is a typical

Côte d'Azur conjunction of modern technology and ancient history.

But a "technological Eden" it is not. Despite such visionary developments, the Côte d'Azur can sometimes look as if it is approaching its zenith. Although the tourist authorities continue to talk in traditional terms about increasing the number of visitors, anticipating an increase from 8 million to 10 million a year, they do concede that it is important now to focus on "quality rather than quantity" and stimulate interest in art and culture as well as sun and sea.

There is now some recognition that to carry on regardless would be to risk killing the golden goose. The besetting problems of

the downfall of Jacques Médecin, the infamous mayor of Nice who was eventually brought to trial for corruption, has been considerable.

Nor was Médecin alone; throughout the region mayors and public officials have been indicted, and even imprisoned for corruption and underworld dealings. Hyères became known as the "Chicago of the Côte" after a series of bomb attacks and the mysterious assassination of a local official campaigning against corruption. The mayor of Cannes was brought to trial over a casino scandal and the mayor of Frèjus was investigated for financial irregularities. Politically the region is leaning further to the right with the Front

overcrowding and increasing pollution will eventually put off even the most weathered sun-worshipper. The early 1990s saw several disastrous seasons, with the Gulf War, fear of recession and a particularly ill-timed oil slick resulting in deserted beaches and empty restaurants. In 1994 major floods throughout the region caused severe devastation washing away bridges, roads, houses and several miles of railway track. The strength of the franc has discouraged many visitors, and the political fall-out following

Left, welcome heat on a St-Tropez beach. **Above**, unwelcome heat: forest fires are a constant threat.

National leader Jean-Marie Le Pen increasing his influence.

Pollution continues to be a volatile issue, and beaches now do have flags to warn bathers of excess contamination. Even so, there is a general tendency to try and minimise the problem rather than tackle it fundamentally. Toxic algae in the sea has become an increasing problem, due in part to yacht anchors damaging the sea bed, and new jetties and marinas affecting currents. According to the experts, the only real way to tackle it is to put an embargo on any further development and demolish nearly half of all the current developments.

Forest fires are another growing problem, with more financial resources being required every year to combat them; fire destroys between 30,000 and 50,000 hectares of land in the French Mediterranean every year.

While fire has always been a threat, the scale of the disasters has grown because incendiary material in the forests is no longer cleared by local inhabitants. Owners of forest land are now required to clear their own grounds and from 1 July to 15 October, the *période rouge*, no fire kindling is permitted in high-risk zones. Air surveillance is used to spot fires and fire-fighting technology has become increasingly sophisticated with water-filled planes, vaporised water hoses and motorbikes equipped with hydraulic pumps.

Appalling traffic means the coast roads are frequently choked, and car parking is always a nightmare. Transport remains the key to the development of the region, both for enhancing tourism and developing new business. A new airport is being built and a new métro system planned for Nice. An extension of the TGV is planned, though there has been controversy over the environmental effects of its routing. A relief autoroute further inland from the A8 is also planned to improve communications along the crucial Barcelona-Genoa Mediterranean axis and to connect the new technology parks like Sophia-Antipolis to the autoroute system.

But this plan, too, has run into local difficulties. While new companies are welcomed for their revenues and promise of employment, there is still some reluctance to provide facilities essential for their survival.

It remains to be seen whether the Côte d'Azur can juggle all its golden eggs successfully and retain its allure while exploiting it enough to survive. There are many contradictions in this richly endowed and over-exploited region of France. When a proud new villa-owner happily pays 2,000 francs for an ancient olive tree to be planted in his designer-landscaped garden, while centuries-old olive groves are ripped up to make way for new building, it is time to invoke the spirit of Renoir, who bought his land at Les Collettes with the express intention of preserving the grove of olive trees that had been growing there for centuries.

Right, crowded beach at Cannes.

WHEELING AND DEALING

Wheeling and dealing on the French Riviera doesn't mean just bicycle riding and blackjack. It is also the euphemism for a Mediterranean style of life that prompted Somerset Maugham to call Monaco "a sunny place for shady people".

It is endemic in both legitimate and illegitimate business sectors and evident in everything from cocktail party bravado and taxi-driver stings to corrupt commercial practices and crude political machinations.

If Maugham considered Monaco shady he must have thought Nice, not to mention Marseille, were pitch black. The fact is, everyone on the Côte d'Azur, from much-maligned Marseille to not-so-nice Nice and spick-and-span Monaco, wheels and deals to some extent.

Some people even get caught. Former Nice Mayor Jacques Médecin, who ran the town known as the Riviera's Big Olive like a personal fiefdom with just a little help from his friends, was fingered for financial shenanigans. He fled to Uruguay and was eventually extradited to serve a short prison sentence. Customs agents at the Nice-Côte d'Azur International Airport, who regularly pilfered from passengers' baggage, were themselves searched, confiscated and sent from the Big Olive to the Big Prison. A crop of croupiers at the Cannes casinos were nailed red-handed for helping selected "customers" to cheat.

A number of villas near Mougins lack patriarchs, including one formerly prominent Dutchman, because they are serving time for running dope. Drug-busts are so common that a haul of 120 illegal immigrants pushing heroin barely merited a line on the front page of Nice-Matin, the Riviera's monopolistic daily paper. Even a Monaco bank was shut down, with its bosses earning interest in the slammer, when it was discovered laundering drug money. Creating fraudulent bills, which has landed other members of the Nice political and business community in jail, and accepting bribes, are all a part of doing business in many Riviera communities. Try to work a deal with some local municipalities and you may find yourself allocating part of your budget to a local youth project, or some equally undefined cultural scheme, in order to get the contract. Try to pay your plumber with a cheque and you get a look that would block any respectable drain.

This type of activity occurs throughout the world, of course. But, like many other endeavours, it is much more prevalent on the French Riviera. The good climate, the glare from the morning sun or perhaps a plethora of *pastis* at sundown make everyone feel they can get away with absolutely anything. Something on the Riviera seems to encourage an abundance of excesses. A plumber in Valbonne was imprisoned because he tried to collect his bill in sexual favours rather than French francs.

Not everyone gets nailed, of course. A number of restaurants in St-Laurent-du-Var were burned down mysteriously and no one claimed responsibility or even explained why. The apprehension of a purse-snatcher or an arsonist would merit a front-page story because it happens so infrequently.

Typically, the wheelers and dealers will swear they don't cheat any more or less than the local priest and most are pretty straight (except when it comes to taxes, where the people on the Riviera perhaps play a little more with their returns than their northern brethren). But legitimate businesses complain on a regular basis that they pay hefty local taxes to support the Riviera's unceasing growth.

Naturally not all business is illicit. The Cannes Film Festival is just good-natured "stick a cigar in your mouth and sit on the Carlton terrace" business. Not all the yachts sold in Antibes go to drug-runners and some agents selling those 140 million franc upmarket homes on the Cap Ferrat are making an honest buck. The paparazzi in Monaco waiting to get a compromising photograph of the royal family are just doing a hard day's work. And people operating in seasonal businesses *need* that seasonal profit.

Tourism and high-tech: There is also legitimate big business on the French Riviera which generates more than $30 billion worth of economic activity. Tourism and high technology were two highly visible money-spinners and each sector brought in over $4.2 billion. But other traditional areas, from public works to perfume, remain important. The perfume business, for example, employs almost 3,000 people and exports over 50 percent of its sales. Tourism brings about 8 million visitors to the region each year and provides plenty of seasonal employment. But the down side has been the string of shoddy buildings and unattractive developments which line the coast.

The problem with tourism is that it remains concentrated between May and Octo-

ber, when events like the Cannes Film Festival and the Monaco Grand Prix set the pace. During the silly summer season it is rare to find a hotel, restaurant or service business which does not jack up the price a bit. This is the period when people like Ivana Trump will happily pay 250,000 francs a month to rent on Cap Ferrat.

There is a transformation in more than prices. The normally sensible people on the coast go crazy with the summer influx of Americans (who talk too loud), Brits (who are too polite), Italians (who wear their furs in July) and Scandinavians (who crowd like lemmings on the beaches). Riviera automo-

bile drivers, who tailgate throughout the year and take it very personally when a light turns red, get remarkably aggressive in the summer with visitors who do not know who has right of way.

Foreigners on vacation are, by nature, dumber than locals. They are prime targets for stings – usually unsophisticated purse-snatchings but also elaborate burglaries that bring back the delightful era of Cary Grant and Grace Kelly in *To Catch a Thief*. Thievery (check your purse – *now!*) is very much alive and well.

Yet nothing is more nonchalant than a local policeman's shrug when a foreigner comes in to report a crime. There is some improvement in the crime area, though – the forestry department have begun cleaning the carcasses of stolen cars out of the Esterel valleys, the traditional graveyard of many heisted vehicles.

What's worse is that much of the infrastructure, especially the road and sanitation systems, simply cannot cope with the surge of visitors during summer. By September, the Riviera can, and often does, look like a garbage dump.

The authorities are trying to spread some of the tourism to the hills and planning events throughout the year but they face a summer seaside tradition which has been alive and well since the 1920s. And most locals tolerate three months of heated hell and the invasion of the body-watchers because it has led to a proliferation of services and income they can enjoy all year round.

Indeed, about the only good tradition that has withstood the test of money and tourism is that most shops still close between noon and 2 or 3pm for lunch. Restaurants like Barale or La Mérenda in Nice still coolly close their doors during the high-flyer month of August.

Conventions and conferences: Business tourism continues to boom: the Acropolis in Nice and the festival hall in Cannes attract a huge variety of conventions and congresses. These include not just the Cannes film, television and music festivals but more "strategic" events like the International Duty Free Conference in Cannes and the annual insurance convention that takes place every September in Monte-Carlo.

There is growth everywhere. There is a new domestic airport in Nice and the international terminal has been renovated and extended. Combined traffic is almost 6 million passengers a year. The Arénas business complex ("Off the plane and into the office" is the promotional slogan) was created across from the airport almost overnight and is now one of the leading business sites in the South of France.

Drive along the coast and there is a commercial complex rising in Antibes-Golfe Juan and a cultural, convention and exposition centre under construction in Monaco, as well as a complex in Fontvieille that houses a host of new museums and even a subterranean railway station. There are now plans for further developments.

always – an address with a cachet like Cannes or the Cap d'Antibes, a sea view, isolation from neighbours and enough rooms and salons to invite guests during the season without getting in the way of each other," explained José Tauzia, a typical architect, interior decorator and landscape artist, based in Cannes.

Foreign business: Foreigners still like the place because of the sun. The Japanese bought the golf course in Valbonne and instantly made the green fees the coast's most expensive. Setting up business here is an attractive proposition. For one thing, there is an eager and wealthy local market that has not only attracted more banks and financial services

Property development, of course, is one area that remains ripe for exploitation. A foreign stooge will get taken not only by the real estate agent (there are more pages of real estate agents than restaurants in the telephone book) but also by everyone down the line – plumber, gardener, maid and electrician. They will pay exorbitant prices which can wreck the market for locals – who must then, of course, wheel and deal with even greater dexterity.

"The demands from clients are the same as

Left, apartments for sale in Cannes. **Above**, Jacques Médecin and friends.

than elsewhere in France; the Côte d'Azur now has the greatest concentration of French and foreign banks after Paris, but also many entrepreneurs.

For example, Lebanese businessman Nabil Boustany spent $300 million completely rebuilding the Metropole Palace Hotel in Monte-Carlo. "Every whim – from chocolates to diamonds, from a brasserie to royal cuisine, from a junior suite to your own apartment – can be satisfied under one roof," he boasted, claiming that despite the price the development is still considered a great investment.

Former Formula One race driver Fulvio

Maria Balladio chose tiny Monaco as the place to build his "Centenaire" cars – only 100 of them, selling for $500,000 each.

And in the land that helped form Picasso, Chagall, Matisse and Monet, art continues to be a lucrative commodity, with a proliferation of galleries and art dealers, many of them foreign, often situated in the smallest villages.

Technology transfer: The high-tech boom has produced an even more prosperous, budding business community. The Riviera has undergone a transformation, making technology a foundation of its economy. Today 40 percent of the high-tech revenue is generated by electronics and data processing with

an additional 20 percent of high-tech business coming from the chemicals and pharmaceuticals sectors.

The high-tech bandwagon began in the early 1960s when IBM created a telecommunications research laboratory in La Gaude and Texas Instruments located important research and production facilities in Villeneuve-Loubet. "The French Riviera is Europe's closest equivalent to California," said an IBM executive. It has progressed in the 1990s and numerous studies have been undertaken, by companies such as Coopers & Lybrand, to illustrate why the Mediterranean is *the* European place to invest.

But the Riviera is still perhaps best for self-employed professionals – like journalists, writers and consultants who choose to live and work there. While they generally refuse to acknowledge that they too are wheelers and dealers, they do create a diversity of nationalities.

However, all this business activity has taken its toll on the Riviera's infrastructure, one of the reasons that the current business thrust is to expand by pushing pan-regional projects in the Provence-Alpes Côte d'Azur region of France. One important project is "The High-tech Route of Southern Europe" aimed at improving communications, promoting technical cross-fertilisation and prompting a variety of cooperative projects at the regional and European level. The Riviera's high-tech sites have joined a strong and competitive technological network that stretches from Valencia in Spain to Liguria in Italy – around a sea becoming as renowned for science as sun.

People are, however, starting to question the direction of growth. There is debate about the wisdom of creating new autoroutes when many municipalities cannot even keep potholes filled. In fact, local uprisings have finally begun to limit the scope of many projects. In Valbonne, the mayor was told to "stop the massacre" when he proposed a vast building scheme.

There are also objections to a new ring road around the Sophia-Antipolis technology park and locals are questioning the wisdom of the new 25 km (16 mile) metro line planned to link it to Nice airport. A new TGV track has been planned to extend along the coast from Marseilles to Nice but this has met enormous opposition from local environment and resident groups and the project is now on hold. The new autoroute intended to relieve the A8 between Fréjus and Monaco and a new expressway to link Cannes and Grasse with the A8 has also met local opposition.

Even in the perched village of Peillon, back from the coastal frenzy, there is a poster reading "The back country must not be a victim of the coast's frenetic development." The big question remains: how long can the Riviera keep its goose alive and its golden eggs forthcoming?

Left, the Cannes Casino.

BEACH BOFFINS

There has been nothing more prominently touted in the evolution of the French Riviera during the past decade than Sophia-Antipolis, the high-technology park developed just off the autoroute between Nice and Cannes, that derives its name from the Greek words for wisdom and Antibes. "Sun, silicon and software" and "Silicon Valley South" are typical descriptions of the 6,200-acre (2,500-hectare) park with its constantly expanding mix of buildings, from high-tech pyramids to banal low-tech monstrosities, its natural forests and brand new road networks.

Brain power, the argument goes, works better in a good climate and since Sophia was founded by Pierre Laffitte (who became a senator) in the early 1970s, there has been a flood of companies, from Allergan to Zamboni, and self-employed individuals, from architects to zoologists, proving the premise that only fools or Eskimos prefer London or Stockholm.

Laffitte was inspired to build Sophia after a visit to Stanford University in California in the late 1960s. He wanted to duplicate the ingredients of Silicon Valley and create a technopole with a university, a strong infrastructure, good communications, established companies and high-tech start-ups in a pleasant environment.

Sophia grew quickly, not least because it became the focal point of the local government's efforts to diversify away from tourism and attract educational institutions, scientific ventures and high-tech industry. Aided by the national and regional governments (every politician is now claiming to have been behind the impetus of Sophia-Antipolis), Laffitte's vision became a combination of dream-come-true and nightmare.

In 1975, Sophia-Antipolis contained only five companies over an area which involved the communes of Antibes, Biot, Mougins, Vallauris and Valbonne. Rolling hills and greenery were more prominent than concrete. Of the 30 largest companies 70 percent are French-owned, 17 percent are American and the remainder are European with only one small Japanese research outfit.

Digital Equipment Corp. is the largest foreign firm on the site with a work force of over 1,000 people. The company bought and built on 50 acres (20 hectares) of land and its presence includes its world centre for telecommunications. Telecommunication is of major importance at Sophia since the European Telecommunications Standards Institute arrived. There are

<u>Right</u>, the Sophia-Antipolis technology park.

companies manufacturing fibre optic cable; France Telecom has installed its most advanced digital networks and software programmers are creating new services for the Minitel. A new university has been established, the Nice Sophia-Antipolis University, with students specialising in industrial economy, pharmacology, immunology and a variety of other disciplines.

But the infrastructure has not kept up with the advertisements and many locals feel the park is a development nightmare. Authorities, for example, did not always respect the edict to maintain a certain percentage of natural greenery and forests. And Sophia has stretched many local resources to the limit. Despite advances (such as the computerised touch-screen directional finders at the entrances to the park which were finally introduced in 1991), there are still numer-

ous complaints about parking, roads, housing costs and schools.

Relief looks unlikely to come from local government and development agencies whose internal politics have delayed simple improvements and inhibited the creation of a long-term plan. A new ring road around the park has met local opposition as have plans for a new 16-mile (25-km) metro line to link Sophia-Antipolis with Nice Airport. Companies, including Wellcome, Dow France, Allergan, France Telecom and Cordis, have banded together to form a "Club des Dirigeants" to resolve the problems. If the target working population of 25,000 by the year 2000 becomes a reality, then a future problem may well be the buses bringing tourists to stare at the latest manifestation of the changing Riviera. ∎

Our vision of the Riviera was first shaped by a handful of writers, most of all by Scott Fitzgerald and his portrait of life on Cap d'Antibes in the glittering 1920s. The French themselves have a different vision; the Riviera for them is not glamorised and mythologised as it is for the British or Americans. In 1927 the writer Colette moved into a villa in St-Tropez where she wrote *La Naissance du Tour*, set in the then unspoiled fishing village.

It wasn't until the 1950s, however, that a double impact did wonders for local tourism. In 1955 the 18-year-old Françoise Sagan had an enormous success with *Bonjour Tristesse*, in which Cécile, the spoiled teenage narrator, manipulates her father's love-triangle in a villa somewhere between Fréjus and Cannes. A year later, Brigitte Bardot's film *And God Created Woman* did the rest.

But British and American artists has long made the Côte d'Azur a port of call. The Americans arrived in France in the 1920s, in the aftermath of the Great War. A combination of reasons prompted their arrival: Prohibition, puritanism and the cultural wasteland that was then America. This, combined with the buying power of a strong dollar against a weak franc, meant that a poverty-stricken young writer could live very well on very few dollars and in luxury on a moderate income.

Scott Fitzgerald and Zelda first arrived in France in 1924, on the *Aquitania*, docking at St-Raphaël where they stayed at the Villa Marie in Valescure, the wealthy annex where villas and hotels are scattered over wooded hillsides overlooking the sea. They had found themselves with $7,000 in the bank and realised that, given their expensive lifestyle, it would not go far in Great Neck, Long Island, but they could live very reasonably in Europe for some time. "We were going to the Old World to find a new rhythm for our lives," Fitzgerald wrote, "with a true conviction that we had left our old selves behind forever." Initially, all went well and that June Fitzgerald wrote: "We are living here in a sort of idyllic state among everything lovely imaginable in the way of Mediterranean delights... I am content to work and become excruciatingly

Left, Colette. **Right**, Françoise Sagan.

healthy under Byron's and Shelley's and Dickens's sky."

They saw their wealthy American friends Gerald and Sara Murphy, who were living at the Eden Roc Hotel while their Villa America was being built. They had invited Gilbert Seldes and his new bride to spend a few days of their honeymoon at the Villa Marie. Seldes recorded the experience: "The road from their villa had been built for carriage traffic and there was one point at which it dangerously narrowed and curved. Every time, just at this

point, Zelda would turn to Scott, who was driving, and say, 'Give me a cigarette, Goofo'." In the terrified silence that followed, Fitzgerald was always able to give Zelda her cigarette, and manoeuvre the Renault around the narrow turn to safety. Clearly, not all of their old selves had been left behind forever.

The climate and relaxed lifestyle proved beneficial to Fitzgerald, who was able to unwind and concentrate on getting some work done on *The Great Gatsby*. Zelda, however, was not so happy. With Fitzgerald writing every day, she became bored and began a casual affair with a handsome young French aviator named Edouard Josanne. Everyone could see what was happening, it seemed, except Fitzgerald, and it was only when the Frenchman proposed marriage and Zelda asked Fitzgerald for a divorce that something was done. Fitzgerald asserted himself. Zelda acquiesced and Josanne departed, but the affair soured their marriage. Long after the event, Fitzgerald wrote in his notebook, "That September 1924, I knew something had happened that could never be repaired." The Fitzgeralds spent the winter in Italy and in April went to Paris.

In August 1925, they returned to the Riviera, staying with the Murphys at the now completed Villa America just below the lighthouse on Cap d'Antibes. The terrace of the

villa was the model for the Divers' in *Tender is the Night* (and incidentally was also used as the setting for the play *Hotel Universe* by Philip Barry). Gerald Murphy himself became the unwitting model for Dick Diver, the book's hero. The opening scene of the first edition of *Tender is the Night* (later moved to the second chapter) takes place on Garoupe Beach on Cap d'Antibes: the "bright tan prayer rug of a beach" which Murphy discovered and cleaned of its thick encrustation of seaweed.

Fitzgerald brought the Jazz Age to the Riviera; and gave a name to the frivolity, hedonism and arrogance of the rich young people who arrived daily on the Blue Train – people

like Dick Diver in *Tender is the Night*: "'I want to give a really bad party. I mean it. I want to give a party where there's a brawl and seductions and people going home with their feelings hurt and women passed out in the *cabinet de toilette*. You wait and see'." Fitzgerald was essentially writing about people like himself and Zelda, when he wrote: "One could get away with more on the summer Riviera, and whatever happened seemed to have something to do with art."

On their first sojourn on the Riviera Fitzgerald and Zelda dined with Sara and Gerald Murphy at La Colombe d'Or. There is a sheer drop away from the walls of the restaurant terrace and Murphy sat with his back to the parapet from which 10 stone steps led to a path. Isadora Duncan sat at another table and Fitzgerald went over to introduce himself. Seeing him kneel at the dancer's feet, and knowing by the way that Duncan ran her fingers through his hair that she had selected him as her partner for the night, Zelda, without warning, stood on her chair and threw herself into the darkness of the stairwell. She reappeared, with blood all over her dress.

In 1926 they settled into the Villa Paquita in Juan-les-Pins, but it was not large or comfortable enough for the Fitzgeralds so they moved to the Villa St-Louis, which was nearer to the casino and had a private beach.

They passed the Villa Paquita on to Ernest Hemingway and his wife Hadley who had to leave the Villa America because their son, Bumby, had contracted whooping cough and had to be quarantined. Everything was going well for Fitzgerald, but Hemingway and Hadley were less tranquil. They had been living in a *ménage à trois* with the rich American heiress Pauline Pfeiffer in Schruns, Austria. With Bumby in quarantine, the Hemingways were stuck in the Villa Paquita, but Pauline Pfeiffer, who was writing to Hemingway every day, suggested that, having had whooping cough as a child, she was not afraid of catching it again and proposed that she join them. Hemingway was enthusiastic and Hadley soon found herself again living in a threesome.

When the lease ran out, they all moved to the nearby Hôtel de Pinède. Hadley wrote: "Here it was that the three breakfast trays, three wet bathing suits on the line, three bicycles were to be found. Pauline tried to teach me to dive, but I was not a success.

Ernest wanted us to play bridge but I found it hard to concentrate. We spent all morning on the beach sunning or swimming, lunched in our little garden. After siesta time there were long bicycle rides along the Golfe de Juan." Hemingway set much of *The Garden of Eden* at La Napoule, which they visited on an automobile drive with the Murphys.

By June the Hemingways and Murphys had moved on to Pamplona and the Fitzgeralds were back in Paris. In August the Hemingways returned to the Villa America, all pretence of being happily married gone. Their return trip to Paris was their last together, divorce from Hadley followed and Pauline Pfeiffer soon became the second Mrs Hemingway. The

spent her winters in Menton with an elderly friend, Jinnie Fullerton. Touched by Katherine's plight, and hoping to convert her to Roman Catholicism, Connie Beauchamp invited her to move to Menton where the weather was warmer and installed her in a nursing home. The home was noisy and far too expensive and it was not long before she and Ida were being fussed over in Connie and Jinnie's Villa Flora on the outskirts of Menton.

Mansfield spent the four summer months in England with Murry, then in September 1920, she and Ida returned to Menton where they had arranged to rent the Villa Isola Bella, another of Connie and Jinnie's places which was built at the other end of their garden. Here

Fitzgeralds returned to the States, lured by Hollywood.

The New Zealand writer Katherine Mansfield moved to the Riviera to find relief from the tuberculosis which eventually killed her, going first to San Remo, on the Italian Riviera, in September 1919 with her husband Middleton Murry and her close friend Ida Baker. Murry returned to London where he edited the *Athenaeum*, leaving the two women to spend the winter alone. Katherine Mansfield's father had a cousin, Connie Beauchamp, who

Left, Ernest Hemingway. **Above**, Scott and Zelda Fitzgerald in 1932.

Katherine relaxed and wrote many of her best short stories: *The Young Girl, The Stranger, Miss Bull, Passion, The Lady's Maid.*

Two days after Christmas 1920 she wrote in her journal: "I went out into the garden just now. It is starry and mild. The leaves of the palm are like down-drooping feathers; the grass looks soft, unreal like moss. The sea sounded, and a little bell was ringing, and one fancied – was it real, was it imaginary? – one heard a body of sound, one heard all the preparations for night within the houses. Someone brings in food from the dark, lamp-stained yard. The evening meal is prepared. The charcoal is broken, the dishes are clattered; there is a soft movement on the stairs and in the passages and doorways. In dusky rooms where the shutters are closed the women, grave and quiet, turn down the beds and see that there is water in the water jugs. Little children are sleeping."

Having failed to convert her to Catholicism, Connie Beauchamp was rather hoping to have the villa for someone else, and since Katherine had grown dissatisfied with Menton, it was mutually convenient when on 4 May 1921 Katherine and Ida departed for a Swiss chalet, high in the mountains. Katherine Mansfield never again saw the Mediterranean. She died in January 1923.

One of the most prominent English writers

to settle in the South of France after the Great War was Ford Madox Ford who arrived with his wife Stella at St-Jean-Cap-Ferrat in the winter of 1922. After three days of freezing rain in Paris and sitting up all night in a second-class railway carriage they were astonished by the light and warmth of the south. Their villa had been lent to them by Harold Munro, the owner of the Poetry Bookshop in London, and they delighted in its simplicity and charm. Stella Bowen described it in her autobiography *Drawn From Life*: "You climbed to it by a rough mule track, or alternatively by long flights of stone steps of a giddy and exhausting steepness... The garden

terraces which overhung Villefranche harbour appeared to have been levelled and stoned up since the dawn of history. The villa only had three microscopic rooms in front and two behind. The only provision for cooking was the usual peasants' charcoal contraption, but there was electric light and the water was laid on... The front windows opened wide on to a great luminous sky with a Saracen fortress on the skyline opposite... Behind the villa you looked over Beaulieu towards Monte Carlo and Italy."

It was on a still winter night while walking among the ancient olive trees in Munro's garden, watching the lights of Villefranche reflected across the motionless water of the bay and surrounded by a great chorus of frogs, that Ford conceived and began work on his masterpiece, the war tetrology *Parade's End*. Ford was very afraid that his memory of the war and his creative powers "might have deteriorated" and wrote, "There remained then for me, under Munro's olive-trees, a final struggle with my courage... one day I sat down at Munro's grandfather's campaign-secrétaire – it had been on the field at Waterloo – I took up my pen: saluted St Anthony who looked down on me, in sheer gratitude for his letting me find my pen at all, and I wrote my first sentence." *Parade's End* is both Ford's most highly acclaimed work and – at four volumes – his largest. It is the basis for his reputation as one of the greatest novelists of World War I.

Aldous Huxley lived in the South of France from 1930 until 1937, when he moved to California believing that the climate would help his eyesight; his near-blindness had been a constant burden. Though he lived in the writers' colony of Sanary, near Bandol, he often visited friends in the Riviera or accompanied his wife Maria to Nice to get her red Bugatti fixed. It was in Sanary that he wrote *Brave New World*, and *Eyeless in Gaza* is set there: "The eye was drawn first towards the west, where the pines slanted down to the sea – a blue Mediterranean bay fringed with pale bone-like rocks and cupped between high hills, green on their lower slopes with vines, grey with olive trees, then pine-dark, earth red, rock-white or rosy-brown with parched heath..."

Huxley's neighbours included Thomas Mann who, together with other German intellectuals and writers, moved there in 1933 to escape the Nazis, and also Cyril Connolly who was writing his first and only novel, *The Rock Pool,* set further along the coast in Cagnes-sur-Mer and Juan-les-Pins. Connolly and his American wife Jean adored the South of France and spent the years before the war living an idyllic bohemian life, supported by Jean's small income and whatever Cyril made as a book reviewer for the *New Statesman.* They lived simply, surrounded by their ferrets and lemurs, drinking brandy before lunch (to Huxley's horror) and eating dinner with their fingers while reading beside the fire.

Connolly had lived in Cagnes in the 1920s after coming down from Balliol College, Oxford and *The Rock Pool* is in many ways a

cistus, the corrugations of sunshine on the bright Aleppo pines, held the whole classic essence of the Mediterranean." It is very much a 1920s book, as Connolly says: "It was a period when art was concerned with futility, when heroes were called Denis and Nigel and Stephen and had a tortured look... I think I may claim to have created a young man as futile as any."

Connolly's love of the Riviera is nowhere more evident than in his wistful memories in *The Unquiet Grave*: "Early morning on the Mediterranean: bright air resinous with Aleppo pine, water spraying over the gleaming tarmac of the Route Nationale and darkly reflecting the spring-summer green of the planes; swifts

roman-à-clef about his experiences among the English and American community there. In the book Cagnes becomes Trou-sur-Mer, but Juan-les-Pins, Antibes and the other settings all retain their proper names including the beach at La Garoupe: "This time he bathed at La Garoupe, floating on the waters of the wooded cove and looking across at the remote and snowy Alps beyond. It was his favourite beach: for him the white sand, the pale translucent water, the cicadas' jigging away at their perpetual rumba, the smell of rosemary and

Left, Katherine Mansfield. **Above**, Thomas Mann and his wife, who moved here to flee the Nazis.

wheeling round the oleander... armfuls of carnations on the flower-stall... Now cooks from many yachts step ashore with their market-baskets, one-eyed cats scrounge among the fish-heads, while the hot sun refracts the dancing sea-glitter on the café awning, until the sea becomes a green gin-fizz of stillness in whose depths a quiver of sprats charges and counter-charges in the pleasures of fishes."

Somerset Maugham bought a house on Cap Ferrat from King Leopold II of Belgium for $48,500 in 1926. He called it the Villa Mauresque, after its Moorish architecture and lived there for at least six months each year until his death in 1965. Here, served by a cook, a butler, a footman, a chauffeur, two maids and seven gardeners, he created the Maugham legend. His hand of Fatima trademark was painted on the gatepost and above the door through which passed many of the most famous people in the arts, letters and society of the time; his neighbour and friend Winston Churchill, Jean Cocteau, Noël Coward, Harold Nicolson, Ian Fleming, the Aga Khan and even a few famous women: Edna St Vincent Millay looked out over the Bay of Villefranche from the terrace and exclaimed, "Oh, Mr Maugham, but this is fairyland!" She was not intending to pun, but the fact was, Maugham was able to live with his lover on Cap Ferrat without the scandal this would have attracted in England.

However, political events were transforming Europe and by 1939 there was an anti-aircraft battery on Cap Ferrat and Nice golf course was covered with soldiers' tents. By the time the war ended, the Villa Mauresque had been badly damaged by a combination of German and Italian occupation, shelling by the British fleet and looting by the French. The Germans had drunk the contents of the wine cellar, stolen Maugham's cars and mined the garden, part of which had been destroyed by an incendiary bomb. After the American Seventh Army landing of 15 August 1944 the villa was used as a rest house for officers on leave. Undaunted, Maugham started again from scratch, restoring the villa to its former glory so that the gardens once again were filled with the chatter of rent boys, reprobates and royalty.

Among the most celebrated expatriate writers in recent times was Graham Greene, who moved to France to "escape the braying voices of the English middle-class." Greene lived quietly in Antibes, where it was his habit each day to leave his modest flat at the Résidence des Fleurs and walk to the gates of the Old Town. There, at Bernard Patriarch's café, he would buy *Nice-Matin* and a copy of *The Times* and then make his way to Chez Félix for lunch. He once wrote: "Since 1959, Chez Félix was my home-from-home. I found short stories served to me with my meal."

One of these was "Chagrin in Three Parts" which is to be found in his collection, *May We Borrow Your Husband?*: "It was February in Antibes. Gusts of rain blew along the ramparts, and the emaciated statues on the terrace of the Château Grimaldi dripped with wet, and there was a sound absent during the flat blue days of summer, the continual rustle below the ramparts of the small surf. All along the Côte the summer restaurants were closed, but lights shone in Félix au Port and one Peugeot of the latest model stood in the parking-rank. The bare masts of the abandoned yachts stuck up like tooth-picks and the last plane in the winter-service dropped, in a flicker of green, red and yellow lights, like Christmas-tree baubles, towards the airport of Nice. This was the Antibes I always enjoyed; and I was disappointed to find I was not alone in the restaurant as I was most nights of the week."

The short story which follows reads as if he simply transcribed the conversation of the two women in the restaurant. In the dialogue, he found a way to introduce the proprietor: "But before Madame Dejoie could reply, Monsieur Félix had arrived to perform his neat surgical operation upon the fish for the bouillabaisse…" Shortly before his death in April 1991 at the age of 86, Greene travelled to Switzerland for his health. In a letter to the Mayor of Antibes, Pierre Merli, he said: "I have always been very happy in Antibes. It is the only town on the Côte d'Azur where it was possible for me to live… I am going to keep on my apartment there in the vain hope of returning to it one day."

Left, the legendary Somerset Maugham.

Graham Greene's War

In 1982, the novelist Graham Greene caused a minor sensation when he took up the cudgels for Martine Guy, a friend's daughter who was living in Nice. In a booklet entitled *J'Accuse – The Dark Side of Nice*, he bitterly attacked Martine's husband, Daniel, for his behaviour in a long-drawn-out dispute over the custody of their children; he threw doubt on the way Daniel had got rich quick; and he accused local police and magistrates of corruption.

Nice, he said, was "the preserve of some of the most criminal organisations in the south of France." He concluded, sarcastically: "Of course Nice has its sunny side also, but I can leave it to the Mayor of Nice, Monsieur Jacques Médecin, to talk about that side of the city."

Médecin dismissed Greene's booklet as an "extraordinary hotch-potch of fiction and rumour" and made the absurd claim that the illustrious 77-year-old author was trying to "get some free publicity for himself". He called a meeting of Nice city council to decide whether to sue Greene. But in the end it was Daniel Guy who took Greene to court – and won damages from him and his publishers. Subsequent events showed that Greene's half-voiced suspicions about the mayor of Nice were well-founded: in September 1990, with the judicial authorities breathing down his neck and the taxman demanding arrears of £900,000, Médecin did a bunk to Uruguay.

The story of the rise and fall of Jacques Médecin is the stuff that novels are made of. His father, Jean, became mayor of Nice in 1928, the year Jacques was born; and he held the post until he died in 1966, when his son took over. The citizens had loved "*le Roi Jean*", and did their best to regard Jacques with equal fondness.

Like his father, he ran the city as though it were his own preserve and built up a large network of faithful, and often grateful, supporters. Questions began to be asked about his use of public money. Between 1983 and 1989 seven paramunicipal associations headed by Médecin himself (such as Nice-Opéra) together received some £100 million from the city of Nice, which they spent more or less as they wished. Médecin, nicknamed "Monsieur 10 Percent", set up a nexus of letter-box companies both in France and in the United States, where he passed himself off as "le Comte de Médicis" (*sic*). He even succeeded in spending up to six months a year away from Nice without the Niçois noticing or caring, mostly in his second wife's native California, where he owned considerable commercial and property interests.

<u>Right</u>, Graham Greene: a brave campaign.

By the mid-1980s, the storm clouds were gathering. Claudette Berke, who had fallen out with Médecin after representing his interests in the US, denounced Médecin's business practices. Médecin began lengthy libel proceedings. Berke told friends she was determined to reveal all. Early in 1989, just before the case was due to be heard, Médecin withdrew his suit. A few months later, Berke was found dead in her California jacuzzi. Cause of death: unknown.

Médecin also alienated Nice's large Jewish community. He made no secret of his far-right views, but an anti-Semitic outburst in 1990 proved too much for three Jewish members of his city council and they resigned.

After finally being forced to flee in 1990, Médecin wrote, in a letter to a friend which was read out before the city council: "I am now in a

position which few people, I suppose, have experienced before me. I am a dead man, yet I have the enormous privilege of being present at the kill and of observing from a distant planet what men and women who owe me everything are doing with my effects and my legacy." If by that time Graham Greene's animosity had turned to *Schadenfreude*, he could surely be forgiven.

Greene's campaign was finally vindicated when Médecin was extradited in 1994 and brought to trial in France, where he served a short prison sentence. There was a lot of political fall-out after his downfall, as Nice began to discover the extent of the corruption. Indeed, several more of the region's mayors have since been exposed for corruption and financial irregularities, further vindicating Greene's brave battle. ∎

Picasso's nymphs and sea urchins; the Promenade des Anglais seen from Matisse's balcony; Dufy's triangles of white sails on a blue sea; golden light through the olive trees of a Renoir landscape; Bonnard's red tiled roofs and palm trees from an open window; Léger's doves – the visual image of the Côte d'Azur has undoubtedly been created by the many painters who have been inspired by the intense light and colour of the region.

It is the Impressionists who first come to mind, because it was their business to paint light itself. Although best known for his waterlilies and studies of Rouen cathedral, Claude Monet also painted in the South of France which he visited for the first time with Renoir in 1883.

The "glaring festive light" was so strong that he feared the critics, who had not seen it for themselves, would be angered by his bright palette, even though he pitched his tones somewhat below the intensity of the real thing. He compared the light to the colours on a pigeon's throat or that of a flaming bowl of punch – shimmering, evanescent films of coloured light.

In 1888 he returned, staying in Antibes and Juan-les-Pins, where he relied upon tourist guides to show him picturesque spots as he did not know the region. By painting local beauty spots he also made his work more saleable as collectors liked to buy paintings of familiar places, rather like buying up-market postcards. He spent the winter and early spring in the south, as was the custom in those days. He only worked when the weather was good, believing that this was a landscape which demanded the sun. He exhibited his Antibes paintings at Theo van Gogh's gallery in the early summer of 1888, causing his friend, the poet Stéphane Mallarmé, to write to him in admiration, saying: "This is your finest hour."

It was not until old age that Auguste Renoir moved to Cagnes-sur-Mer. He was born in 1841 in Limoges and moved to Paris four years later. Claude Monet, Alfred Sisley and Renoir were all students together at the École des Beaux-Arts. Under the influence of Courbet, they tried to paint only what could be seen with the eyes as accurately as possible. They painted outdoors, and soon realised that the colour of objects changed with the lighting conditions. It was their attempt to capture this light that gave rise to Impressionism.

In 1889 Renoir suffered an attack of rheumatoid arthritis which forced him to spend the winter months in the south. He first

settled in Magagnosc, near Grasse, in 1899, then moved to Le Cannet in 1902. Hearing that a venerable old olive grove overlooking Cagnes was to be pulled up and built over, Renoir saved it from the developers to use as an outdoor studio. Finally in 1905 he decided to live there and had a modern house built for himself and his large family. He lived here for the rest of his life but not without some disturbance as hotel porters suggested his house as one of the sights to tourists and he was often disturbed by businessmen wanting him to paint their wives and children. Sometimes he did.

Illness and old age took their toll. By 1904

Preceding pages: Night Fishing at Antibes, 1939, Picasso. Left, Renoir's studio, Cagnes. Above, Little Road in Le Cannet, 1924, Pierre Bonnard.

he weighed only 7½ stone (48 kg) and found it difficult to sit. He used crutches to get about but by 1910 onwards even this was too painful and he became a prisoner of his wheelchair, his hands deformed and bandaged. His paintbrush had to be wedged in between rigid fingers and yet, day after day, he continued to paint. In his lifetime, he painted more than 6,000 pictures, making him almost as prolific as Picasso. Even in the last two painful decades he still painted an Arcadian wonderland of light and colour, naked girls bathing in shallow ponds, washed by the Mediterranean light. "I'm still making progress," he said a few days before his death. On 3 December 1919 as an assistant

1909 when he took a villa in St-Tropez. From then on he returned practically every year, staying in St-Tropez, Grasse, Antibes, Cannes or Le Cannet, where he rented the Villa Le Rêve. In 1925, shortly after marrying his model, Maria Boursin, with whom he had lived for the previous 30 years, he moved to Le Cannet permanently.

Garden inspiration: Le Cannet is a small village on a hill, which has now been engulfed by Cannes. There Bonnard bought a small pink house nestling high among the trees called Le Bosquet on the Avenue Victoria. The mountainside climbed above it, covered with olive trees where herdsmen tended their flocks of goats. He delighted in

arranged a still life for him, he uttered his last word: "Flowers."

Born in 1867 in Fontenay-aux-Roses, Pierre Bonnard's early career included furniture design, theatre posters and book illustration but from 1905 onwards he concentrated principally on painting, working in the Post-Impressionist manner which he quickly made his own. He studied at the Paris École des Beaux-Arts and came under the influence of Gauguin and Monet. But it was from Degas and his paintings of women at their toilet that Bonnard created his own "intimist" style of interiors.

Bonnard first discovered the Midi in June

his garden which was filled with plants and birds; mimosa in January, the flowering almond tree in spring and the fig tree in October. He made more than 200 paintings, his subjects including every inch of the interior of the house and the views from its window out across the red tiled roofs and palm trees of Le Cannet to the bay and surrounding mountains.

After the Impressionists, painters began to arrive in the south in droves. First came the Post-Impressionists such as Paul Signac, who painted a number of important works in the Riviera using the divisionist colour theory, or Pointillism, in which the picture is literally made up of coloured dots using the rainbow palette - colours that are found only in nature.

Then came the Fauves ("Wild Beasts"), known for their unnaturally bright and wild colours and deliberately unrefined painting technique: Henri Matisse, André Derain, Georges Braque and Raoul Dufy.

In 1908, Raoul Dufy spent the summer in close collaboration with Braque at L'Estaque, which caused him to abandon Fauvism for the Cézannesque palette from which he developed his mature style – his *Bâteaux à L'Estaque* can be seen in the Musée des Beaux-Arts in Nice. It is the work produced between 1926 and 1929 that makes us associate him with the Riviera. During this time he worked first in Nice and Golf-Juan, painting panoramic beach scenes and his characteristic views through windows. In 1927, he also made ceramics in the pottery town of Vallauris.

Between 1928 and 1929, he executed mural decorations for a semi-circular room in Arthur Weisweiller's Villa L'Altana at Antibes and did a number of paintings of Nice and Cannes. At the same time, he continued to design fabrics and make lithographs. The archtypical Dufy view remains a patch of pure blue sea, dotted with triangular white sails, as seen from a hotel window with a few palms neatly framing the picture. A deceptively simple and attractive picture, perhaps, but as Gertrude Stein said in 1946: "One must meditate about pleasure. Raoul Dufy is pleasure."

Greatest painters: Two giants of 20th-century painting are Picasso and Matisse, both of whom settled in the Riviera. (For details of Picasso's work, *see* pages 200–201.)

Henri Matisse was born in 1869 and studied law in Paris. Strangely, he showed no interest in art and during his two years of law studies did not visit a single gallery. He took a job as a clerk in a law office in St-Quentin where his family lived. It was not until he was 20 years old, and convalescing from an appendix operation, that he started to paint. The man in the bed next to him spent his time copying popular colour prints and Matisse asked his mother to buy him a paintbox. He began by copying prints and on leaving the hospital began taking lessons. Even after

such a late start, Matisse clearly felt that painting was his vocation. Against his father's wishes he gave up his secure job and moved to Paris where he enrolled in the Académie Julian. He failed the entrance examination for the École des Beaux-Arts and went to study with Gustave Moreau.

At the end of 1898 he and his new wife, Amélie, visited Corsica. He marvelled at the light and the climate of the Mediterranean. He wrote: "It was in Ajaccio that I became enchanted with the south." The paintings made in Corsica were his first attempts to escape the realist tradition; his colours and shapes are simplified and more evenly distributed. His compositions became bolder

and, most important, his range of colours was widened. Matisse, the great colourist, was beginning to emerge.

For Matisse, 1904 was a key year. He spent the summer in St-Tropez, where he was again exposed to the Mediterreanan light and there he met Paul Signac and Henri-Edmond Gross, both strict practitioners of Seurat's Pointillist technique. Matisse tried it, and though he did not respond well to such a systematic approach to painting, he produced some important work, particularly *Luxe, calme, et volupté* (now at the Pompidou Centre).

The use of the rainbow palette finally set

Left, *Antibes*, 1888, Claude Monet. **Above**, *La Baie de Nice*, 1918, Henri Matisse.

him free from the formal constraints of outline and into a realm of pure colour. Matisse could not abide the use of small even brushstrokes and soon gave up Pointillism, which only Seurat himself was able to use expressively. His paintings were now filled with luminous colours, often clashing. His *Portrait of a Woman*, done in 1905, was subtitled *The Green Line* because the line ran from the top of her forehead to the tip of her nose.

Colourful wild animals: Matisse and his friends Derain, Vlaminck, Manguin and Louis Valtat all exhibited together in Room VII of the Salon d'Automne in 1905. The critics were aghast and dubbed them "Fauves"; wild animals, and proclaimed

Matisse their leader. Fauvism lasted only three years in France, after which the artists went their own ways but traces of Fauvism always remained in Matisse's work even at its most decorative.

By now Matisse was well known and collectors such as Sergei Shchukin and Leo and Gertrude Stein were buying his work. It was shown in London, Stockholm, Moscow and at Stieglitz's famous 291 gallery in New York. Matisse was well off and able to concentrate entirely upon painting. His work consisted of colourful portraits, often of his daughter or wife, nudes, bathers and groups of nudes. The human figure was always an

essential starting-point for him, though he did sometimes paint a few landscapes. Cubism also made its impact on his work, and many of his figures have the "African mask" face of pre-Cubist Picassos.

Matisse's move to Nice at the age of 48 was to precipitate a change in his work because at no previous time in his career did his physical environment play so powerful a role in his art, or contribute so much to the appearance of the resulting paintings. The proximity of North Africa enhanced his interest in the exotic and resulted in the wonderful odalisque series.

But most of all it was the light. He had experienced the Mediterranean light many times before, most notably in L'Estaque where he and his old friend Albert Marquet spent December 1915 sketching and painting. He returned again in December 1917 and later wrote: "I left L'Estaque because of the wind, and I had caught bronchitis there. I came to Nice to cure it, and it rained for a month. Finally I decided to leave. The next day the *mistral* chased the clouds away and it was beautiful. I decided not to leave Nice, and have stayed there practically the rest of my life."

He first stayed at the Hôtel Beau-Rivage, 107 Quai des États-Unis, an extension of the Promenade des Anglais past the market and the old town. Here he had an uninterrupted view of the sea, the beach and the full trajectory of the sun. At least nine paintings made in this hotel room survive. "Most people came here for the light and the picturesque quality. As for me, I come from the north. What made me stay are the great coloured reflections of January, the luminosity of daylight." He rented a studio in the building next door and began painting.

When his hotel was requisitioned for soldiers, he moved his family to the Villa des Alliés in the hills which rise steeply above the old port of Nice, on the pass over to Villefranche. Here he took to painting landscapes and watching the dawn arrive. He wrote, "Ah! Nice is a beautiful place! What a gentle and soft light in spite of its brightness!" For the next three years he spent the summer travelling, then returned to Nice where he always stayed at the Hôtel Méditerranée at 25 Promenade des Anglais – now demolished. During the winter of 1918–19 he employed the 18-year-old model

Antoinette Arnoux, who was to figure in many nude and costume paintings made at the hotel, often posing in front of the huge windows with their decorative iron grilles, a palm tree silhouetted against the blue sea. A model, posed against a room interior, became one of his favourite themes and there are literally dozens from this period

The year 1920 saw the arrival of Henriette Darricarrère, who became Matisse's primary model for the next seven years. It was Henriette who entered most fully into Matisse's exotic odalisque fantasy and he painted her dozens of times in this role. Having painted and repainted his Niçoise model, and explored the limits of hotel inte-

his own collection of masks, fabric hangings and mirrors, so the studio had the lush atmosphere of an oriental bazaar. The period 1927–1931 was characterised by decorative odalisques in highly stylised settings

After a year-long visit to the United States in 1930, his style changed and he used more and more areas of flat tone. After a variety of models, in 1935 he settled upon Lydia Delectorskaya who remained his model and assistant for the rest of his life. In 1938 he moved to the Hôtel Regina in Cimiez, and it was here, being too disabled by arthritis to paint, that he began to work seriously at the paper cut-outs. "Cutting straight into colour reminds me of the direct carving of the

riors, Matisse now felt ready to become a resident, and took a large flat on Place Charles-Félix, in the old town, overlooking the old market and with an uninterrupted view of the sea, the Promenade des Anglais curving round to the west with its elegant rows of palms and the roof-tops of old Nice.

He remained in this building until 1938, posing his models against the window or using the spacious interiors. He loved the densely patterned wallpaper and introduced it into many of his paintings. To it, he added

Left, *The Green Line* and **above,** *Femme au Divan*, 1920, both by Henri Matisse.

sculptor," he wrote. He began his cut-outs at the age of 70 and was 84 when he did the last one. He made the medium his own, creating several important works: the famous "Jazz" series, which he executed betwen 1943 and 1944 at the Villa Le Rêve in Vence and his wonderful monochrome *Blue Nude* of 1952, which showed that all the subtlety of painting could be brought to this simple medium. Matisse died on 3 November 1954 at Cimiez.

Though the work of Fernand Léger appears throughout the region, particularly in the impressive museum devoted to his work in Biot, Léger always worked from the studio on Rue Notre-Dame-des-Champs in Paris that he first took in 1913 and retained until his death. He first visited Biot in 1949 with his former pupil Roland Brice to design their first ceramics together and the next year set up a small factory-workshop there which he visited until the end of his life on 7 August 1955. His intention was to find a way of using ceramics for monuments. Together with Brice, he found a method of accentuating the figures or abstract forms he was using by underlining them with black rings, a technique which enabled him "to house sun in my ceramic works and simultaneously to give a light, airy quality to the relief".

The large ceramic panel set in the terrace wall at La Colombe d'Or restaurant in Vence

only flat-roofed house on this part of the wall and in the 1930s a loggia was built on the roof with a terrace, to make an artist's studio. It was here that artist Nicolas de Staël spent the last six months of his life.

He arrived in September 1954 and began getting to know the town, making sketches and painting small-scale landscapes. He felt lonely, an "inhumane solitude"; he was 40 years old, cut off from his family and devoted every hour of the day to working on his outdoor terrace, from sunrise – which is the only time of day that Corsica is just visible, shimmering on the horizon, to sunset – when the Garoupe lighthouse on Cap d'Antibes begins its regular sweep across the seascape.

is a very good example of his success. The museum in Biot exhibits his monumental work to good effect, beginning with the 150-ft (45-metre) long ceramic originally designed for the Olympic Stadium in Hanover. But in his case there is no reason to believe that living in the South of France would have appreciably altered his work since, as he observed in 1942: "My work continues to develop and is in no way dependent on where I am situated geographically."

Inhumane solitude: On the corner of Rue de Revély in Antibes, close to the city wall next to the Grimaldi Museum, is a small 19th-century house that the road encircles. It is the

With de Stäel's work less is more: "I paint as I can and each time I try to add something by removing what encumbers me." He made 354 paintings in six months: "One has to get used to finishing more, without finishing," he wrote.

On 5 March 1955, he made a short trip to Paris where he saw a Webern concert. In the programme from the Théâtre Marigny he noted, "red, red/ochre violins." Upon his return to Antibes, he began work on a huge canvas, 20 by 9 ft (6 by 3 metres), designed to fit a wall in the Picasso Museum next door, in the room which nine years before had been Picasso's studio.

After preparing the canvas, and making preparatory sketches, de Stäel worked feverishly for three days on *The Grand Concert*, which was to be his *chef-d'oeuvre*. It is composed of two elements: a horizontal black piano to the left and a vertical cello to the right painted in ochre, but it is the background that causes astonishment. Behind the stage is a backdrop composed of 130 sq. ft (12 sq. metres) of bright transparent red paint, spread across the canvas in one bold gesture.

The day after completion, de Stäel wrote three letters, including one to his daughter, then, on 16 March 1955, "as a spiritual act, inoffensive, as it were, and undertaken in a

Paris, then in the early spring of 1949 settled in a *pension en famille* in St-Jean-Cap-Ferrat where the light and the sight of the Mediterranean released an explosion of new ideas in Chagall. They began looking for a house, something grand, as Chagall was always deeply jealous of Picasso and Matisse and in moving to their territory he obviously wanted to show the world he was their equal. "Chagall can't live in a house that has cow dung on the driveway," he said, despite the fact that, even then, there was very little cow dung to be found in Cap Ferrat.

They decided on a large furnished house called Le Studio, outside Vence, while they searched for a permanent place. Then in the

spirit of total goodness towards humanity", he threw himself to his death from the terrace which had been his studio for the past six months. *The Grand Concert* now hangs on the wall he intended it for, among a collection of his other works from the same period.

Chagall's return: After escaping to the United States for the duration of the war, Marc Chagall returned to France in 1948 together with his companion Virginia Haggard and their son David. They lived in Orgeval, near

spring of 1950 they moved into Les Collins. Unfortunately for Chagall, Henri Matisse lived further down the same road and not long after Chagall moved in the road was renamed Avenue Henri Matisse.

A long driveway lined with cypresses climbed up to the house, the terrace was shaded by vines and roses and there was a stand of eucalyptus in the grounds. From this studio, Chagall had views of the ancient walls of Vence, which later inspired a number of paintings, along with the Mediterranean Sea itself.

The influence of the Riviera is less obvious in Chagall's work than in that of other

Left, *Intérieuré à la fenêtre ouverte*, **1928, Raoul Dufy. Above,** *Women Running on the Beach,* **1922, Picasso.**

artists; he continued to paint fish climbing ladders and trees upside-down and his greatest inspiration remained the Old Testament. After seeing Matisse's chapel, he went to some lengths to find and decorate one of his own, but it was not until 1973, when he completed his Message Biblique Museum in Nice, that he achieved this aim, though many churches and chapels in the region contain examples of his mosaics.

Aimé Maeght, the art dealer, and his wife Marguerite lived nearby, though they had not yet opened their foundation, and it was not long before Maeght was Chagall's sole dealer. Chagall married Vava Brodsky and moved to St-Paul which remained his home

until 28 March 1985, when he died at the great age of 97.

New style: In the 1950s Nice produced its own school of artists: the Nouveaux Réalistes: Yves Klein, Arman and Martial Raysse, all from Nice; César, born in Marseille but settled in Nice, plus Ben Vautier from Naples and a group of associated artists: Tinguely, Niki de Saint-Phalle, Daniel Spoerri, Chubac, Rotella, Sosno and others. The Nouveaux Réalistes came as a reaction to American Abstract Expressionism and the more refined Parisian Lyrical Abstraction.

Born of Neo-Dadaism and experiments with Minimalism, the Nouveaux Réalistes

are united by a common appropriation of the material surfaces of contemporary life: paint tubes, trash, packaging, the contents of the industrial junk heap. Arman packed trash into transparent containers, freezing them in acrylic so they seemed set in aspic. He created a flock of birds, made from identical heavy-duty pliers, and exploded and deconstructed violins in every possible way including a violin and its case, neatly sliced like an onion and set in concrete.

César presented automobiles, compacted into neat cubes by a scrapyard. What the Nouveaux Réalistes also had in common was a light-hearted, easy-going approach to art: "Although we of the school of Nice are always on vacation, we are not tourists. That's the essential point. Tourists come here for vacations; we live in a land of vacations, which gives us the spirit of nonsense. We amuse ourselves without thinking of religon, art or science," wrote Yves Klein.

Yves Klein is the acknowledged leader of the movement. In 1955, when abstract painting ruled the world, Klein set up an easel on the Promenade des Anglais; gazing out to sea, he covered the canvas with blue pigment - one of his famous monochrome paintings - it was not abstract, it was real, literally just a canvas covered in blue paint. His *International Klein Blue*, or IKB as it is known, became his symbol, used over and over in different contexts. During his brief life, from 1928 to 1962, Klein astonished and irritated critics and the public with his radical inventiveness, particularly with his Anthropometries, in which he coated the bodies of nude models with paint, usually IKB, and either pressed them against the canvas or gave them directions to move their limbs or crawl. Some paintings were made before a live audience, with a 20-piece orchestra.

He worked on Cosmogonies in which the painting was shaped by the wind, rain and other natural phenomena, and made portraits by casting his subject in plaster. He worked with fire, sometimes combining the effect of fire with his Anthropometries. His stated aim was to sensitise the whole planet, to return to the state of nature in a technological Eden – as good an aim as any in an artist's paradise.

<u>Above</u>, Picasso Museum, Antibes. <u>Right</u>, Picasso and Françoise Gilot, Golfe Juan, 1948.

There still persists in the public's mind the notion that the Cannes Film Festival is a sedate affair, where the very best of world cinema is screened to the film critics so that they may report back on the state of the art, prizes are awarded by a jury composed of international alumni of the film world, judgements made, followed perhaps by a little lunch on the beach.

Nothing could be further from the truth. Of the 50,000 foreigners who descend on this small seaside resort every May, only 2,500 are journalists. Of the rest, there are the usual chancers, liggers, young hopefuls and fading starlets, but the greater majority are businessmen. They don't look like the businessmen you might expect to see in the City of London or on Wall Street, however.

Everywhere there are men in sharkskin suits, crocodile shoes, pony-tails and Hawaiian shirts that look like a nose-bleed on a road map. They lie around the hotel pool, sipping from Perrier bottles and murmur at each other, hoping that their dark glasses will mask the fact that they are watching the topless bathers.

Every so often, one of them will break off to do a quick calculation on a pocket computer. He will then say something like "But I get the satellite rights on this one," or something to do with a "four walls deal". They then shake hands on a movie deal, and say, "I'm sure we can get into bed on this one." But each party knows that the handshake will not be binding once they return to the real world and the balance sheets look a bit different away from the glare of noonday sun.

The origins of the festival lie in the French distrust of the Venice Film Festival. Mussolini had begun the Venice festival in the mid-1930s, and it soon became clear that it was simply an exercise in propaganda, with all the major prizes being awarded to the Fascist films. France proposed retaliation, with an international festival at Cannes set to begin in September 1939. However, the timing was not right. Mae West and Norma Shearer

arrived on the steamship *Normandie* to be greeted with the outbreak of war. They re-embarked almost immediately and sailed home again.

After this false start, the festival had its première in 1946, and was consciously designed to be part of the general optimism in a New Europe. In those days Cannes was still part of the playground favoured by the Riviera set. It was common to see the Aga Khan strolling into the screenings. One British critic records that as late as 1955 he was

invited into a small private screening of *The Cranes are Flying*, only to discover that he shared the auditorium alone with Picasso and Jean Cocteau.

Throughout the 1950s it was possible to fit everyone involved with the festival onto a small motor-boat and all go for an outdoor lunch on the nearby Île Ste-Marguerite. It was also common for the jury to include illustrious members of the Académie Française; one particular member gave an opening speech in which he said he was delighted to return to watching cinema since the last film he had seen had been in 1913.

The festival may have been small in those

Preceding pages: spectacular Cannes. Left, Elizabeth Taylor, a veteran visitor. Above, guests arriving at Cannes party.

days, but it still attracted its share of publicity and scandal. An English starlet, Simone Silva, made history by ripping off the top of her bikini and thrusting her talents into the surprised arms of Robert Mitchum, who just happened to be strolling nearby. There also happened to be a corps of press photographers present, and the pictures were duly printed world-wide, leading to the horror of the American leagues of decency and to general increase in interest in the festival. And Brigitte Bardot made such an impact on the festivals of 1955 and 1956 that there were complaints about her hogging the limelight, much as there were in 1991 over the appearance of Madonna.

it seemed more of a gesture of solidarity with the revolutionaries and a demand for more publicity for their own films, than any serious political gesture. Nonetheless the mayhem caused the festival to be cancelled that year. The following year, Robert Favre Le Bret, the president of the festival, exercised his usual diplomatic skills and began the Director's Fortnight, a sidebar event for new and off-beat films which were not eligible for the main competition. It continues to this day, along with other extra sidebar events which have subsequently developed.

The best film in competition each year is awarded the Palme d'Or. Outside Hollywood, it is the highest award a film can gain.

It was in 1959 that the festival began to take on its modern crowded aspect. There was a large American presence for the first time. They had realised that Cannes was a perfect opportunity to set up a European shop window for American products, and very soon the *marché* was established, showing films to the world's distributors and journalists outside the official festival.

In 1968, moved by the spirit of *les évènements* in Paris, the stage at Cannes was invaded by Jean-Luc Godard, Claude Chabrol, François Truffaut and many other of the younger talents of the French New Wave. Their demands were unclear, indeed

It confers upon the film considerable prestige, but this is usually the limit of its effect. Only an Oscar can have a noticeable effect upon the box-office take. In recent years, a quality film such as *The Mission* is a good example of a movie which gained the Palme d'Or but did not live up to the makers' hopes at the box-office.

Like the Oscar ceremonies, the awarding of the Palme d'Or is also prone to vested interests, in-fighting, and the general muddle and compromise which always attends the workings of any jury. In 1984, the competition included both Robert Bresson's *L'Argent* and Tarkovsky's *Nostalgia*, two films of unquestionable excellence. The Palme d'Or went to a lesser work, Imamura's *The Ballad of Narayama*, with the other two films being forced to share a specially created prize, the Grand Prix de Création.

Cannes today is all about excess – excessive posing, excessive indulgence and excessive spending. Cannes has never been a real town at all. The Croisette, or main promenade along the shore, with its rows of *grande luxe* hotels, was created largely to please the English taste for the Riviera in a more gracious age. Even the beaches are false; sand is imported to cover the pebbles and is duly raked over each morning by minions from the hotel opposite. Each section of the beach

Clint Eastwood must be seen in. The harbour becomes a forest of masts and silver rigging. There is very little serious nautical activity from these yachts other than a good deal of posing in Armani, designed scuba gear by their owners.

Recently there has been an imposing three-masted galleon of antique design moored near the harbour mouth. Even this is a fake. It was brought here to publicise Roman Polanski's *Pirates*. When the film failed to find favour, the film's main prop was left where it was. Perhaps it was intended as a warning to all. But its presence is simply one more instance of the artificiality which predominates everywhere.

is privately owned by its nearby hotel and the visitor will pay heavily for lunch in the restaurant at the back of the beach, or for the mattresses and parasols invitingly laid out near the water. Few complain since everyone is on expenses.

Even the harbour, the oldest part of the town, has a suspect air about it. No-one ever sees a *bona fide* fishing vessel land its catch there. This may not be surprising since during the festival it becomes jammed with every kind of non-fishing boat from small pleasure-cruisers to the sort of yacht that

Left, star line-up. **Above**, paparazzi opportunity.

The main films in competition used to be screened at the Grand Palais, a magnificent old cinema with a marble foyer and one of the best projection systems in the world. Since each film was usually a brand new print, and the projection was pin-sharp, the viewing often took on an almost hallucinatory quality. It was like watching a moving, three-dimensional piece of sculpture.

Alas, the numbers of people clamouring to get into the relatively small cinema meant that a larger venue had to be built. Some years ago, a hideous piece of neo-brutal architecture emerged down near the harbour, designed by a British architect whose name is now mercifully lost to history. It was immediately nicknamed "*Le Bunker*". And while it contained many screening rooms of various sizes, nothing, sadly, quite matched the quality of the old Palais.

Finding the way around inside takes years of practice, since much of the interior resembles a glass maze. The deep stage between the front row and the screen betrays the true nature of the building. It was not designed as a cinema at all, but as a conference centre. Cannes has become a conference town.

Entering the screenings, however, takes many years of assiduous reporting for quality newspapers before the lucky journalist is allotted the coveted *pastille d'or* (gold spot)

The doormen at Cannes seem to be recruited from the lower ranks of the French riot police. A frustrated critic was once spotted trying to take a flying leap over the phalanx at the door. He failed and was led away in disgrace.

The year that the bunker was built saw a riot outside its portals. It was not, in fact, the local citizenry protesting at the hideousness of the building, but merely some medical students protesting at a cut in grants. Huge squads of riot police were deployed, outnumbering the students by three to one. They duly let off some CS riot gas, which has the effect upon innocent bystanders of feeling as if they have inhaled a mouthful of wood

on his press card. This, when waved at the doormen, will allow entry into most, if not quite all, the screenings, many of which begin at 8.30 in the morning.

For the novice hack with a lesser entrance card, life can be tiresome. As always with French officialdom, the golden rule is: Yes, it might be possible… but first there must be drama. A stout "*Non*" from a doorman barring your way is often the opening round in a vicious battle. Protestations that you do indeed have the right card, and the auditorium is half-empty, usually produce a shrug. A little barging often produces the desired result, although this has to be done carefully.

splinters. The sight of several indignant film critics being held down on the ground by the determined *flics* will long be cherished by film directors who believe that this is their proper fate.

The debarred critic can always take refuge on the Rue d'Antibes, the main shopping street, inland from the Croisette, and running parallel to it. Apart from the inordinate number of expensive lingerie shops, there are also half a dozen multi-screen cinemas, and film companies from all over the world hire them to show their films around the clock in the hope of attracting distributors and exhibitors. Hopping from screen to screen, without checking what is on, can often yield surprise catches. Many critics hope to increase their reputations by spotting unsung masterpieces and recommending them to a distributor; Bob Swaim's *La Balance* was discovered in this fashion.

There also used to be unlimited screenings of hard-core pornography, although these have been banned in recent years. They could always be counted on to keep the most jaded hack awake. It was even reported one year that a whole row of Chinese, identically clad in blue denim, were discovered at one of these screenings, politely laughing into the palms of their hands. This was in the days of Chairman Mao, and there was much specu-

The jaded gossip does the circuit, as does the warm white wine. The Japanese party is noted for the lavishness of the gift given to each invitee. The Australian party usually involves debauchery at a barbecue on the beach. A New Zealand party one year was notable for a girl who turned up in an official capacity wearing nothing but a carefully applied coat of green paint. Since the evening was far advanced, everyone thought she was wearing a leotard and so the effect went for nought. But there is always the feeling that, somewhere else, there is another party going on, to which one has not been invited, and which is much, much better than this one. It is not so.

lation about what their official report would look like once they returned to Peking.

Then there are the parties. It is possible for the poorer journalists to survive at Cannes simply by party-hopping, if they do not mind existing on a diet of canapés. The parties are thrown by distributors, exhibitors, public relations companies, producers, national film bodies – in fact, everyone who wants to make sure that everyone else knows they can afford it. No-one enjoys them. The same faces turn up at each one.

Left, Roman Polanski's abandoned pirate ship. **Above**, behind the scenes.

Every year, there will come a point at three in the morning when some over-indulged producer will raise his head from the pool of liquor on the café table, and announce that he had just had the brainwave of making a film set at the Cannes Film Festival. It would be about a struggling young film company with a hot starlet, touting a brilliant script around town to all the money men. And it would capture the intensity, the sheer white heat of this creative chaos.

Most years, the idea will lie there on the table where it belongs. For the chaos of Cannes is not to be captured. It is pure, formless anarchy.

"My accent has a touch of garlic," says the film actor Charles Blavette in his book of memoirs, *Ma Provence en Cuisine*. The remark is not surprising coming from a native of the Midi. In no other part of France are the characteristics of a regional culture so closely bound up with food.

Characters in the films of Marcel Pagnol, for example, not only put down their cultural markers by using quaint Provençal expressions and speaking with thick southern accents, but often refer to local dishes and the ritual of making them. Indeed, the lilting words for many such specialities – *bourride, bouillabaisse, ratatouille, rouille* and *ailloli*, for example – might almost have been designed so that Pagnol's favourite actors could wrap their tongues around them.

The cuisine of the Côte d'Azur does not differ much from that of Provence, except that it is a little more fish-orientated and offers the added attraction of Nice's idiosyncratic specialities. It was forged centuries before the Côte d'Azur became a string of seaside resorts, at a time when transport was difficult and people needed to rely essentially on local ingredients. Its most famous – and most often traduced – dish, the fish stew *bouillabaisse*, often used to be cooked on the beach or the boat after the catch. Many different kinds of Mediterranean fish both great and small – whose kaleidoscopic hues before cooking have inspired more than one painter – should go into *bouillabaisse*, each providing its distinctive flavour.

There are no hard and fast rules about which fish are mandatory, though there seems to be a consensus that no *bouillabaisse* worthy of the name can do without *rascasse* or conger eel. Other ingredients include olive oil, onions, garlic, tomatoes, fennel and saffron. *Bouillabaisse* usually comes in two courses (first the broth, poured over croûtons, then the fish) and is served with *rouille*, a fiery chilli-laced version of the garlic mayonnaise *ailloli* (or *aioli*). Spiny lobster in *bouillabaisse* is regarded by purists as his-

torically unsound and the grated cheese that is often served with the dish is a naff and relatively recent innovation; above all, it makes little or no contribution to the flavour. Be warned: a good *bouillabaisse* makes an ample meal on its own (and so it should, given the price it commands).

Fish soup, which when properly prepared consists of more or less the same ingredients as *bouillabaisse*, but sieved to remove the bones, is equally filling; once again, the grated cheese can be dispensed with. In

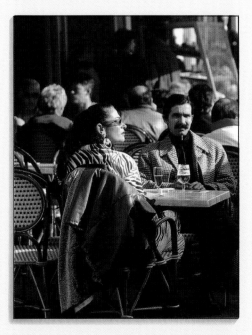

bourride, another delicious fish stew, *ailloli* is used to thicken the cooking liquid at the last moment, producing a creamy and perfumed sauce to go with the fish (which is sometimes filleted). An ubiquitous dish on Côte d'Azur menus is fennel-flavoured grilled *loup* (sea bass), which is often overcooked and dry. Grilled fresh sardines with a squeeze of lemon are a better bet. On no account miss sampling that most delicately flavoured of Mediterranean fish, red mullet (*rouget*), best cooked very simply.

In the old days, it was difficult for people living in the hinterland to get hold of fresh fish, so on Fridays they tended to make

Preceding pages: market olive display. **Left,** Café des Arts, St-Tropez. **Above,** Cours Saleya café, Nice.

dishes using salt cod (*morue*). If salt cod sounds dreary, you will probably change your mind after tasting *brandade*, a rich, aromatic blend of that ingredient, olive oil, garlic and (usually) potato. Poached salt cod is often the centrepiece of a *grand ailloli* or *ailloli garni* (sometimes it is called just *ailloli*), a cold dish that is marvellous on a hot summer's day.

Ailloli is just a sauce, of course, but like *pistou* (of which more in a moment) it has also come to denote a whole dish. In addition to the salt cod and garlic mayonnaise, it consists of cooked vegetables (potatoes, French beans, carrots, small local artichokes), hard-boiled eggs and, sometimes, cold

south of France garlic "is used so carefully that it rarely leaves its usual unpleasant mark."

The exact meaning of "its usual unpleasant mark" eludes the present writer. But if the classier restaurants on the Côte d'Azur are careful in their use of garlic, that is not the way it is eaten by the locals: they rub it enthusiastically into croûtons, pound it into *ailloli*, pile it into meat stews, strew it chopped on baked *tomates provençales* – indeed, in restaurants all over the world the term "*à la provençale*" or "*provençale*" tells customers to expect lashings of garlic. Garlic also goes into *ratatouille*, that resonant mixture of tomatoes, onions, courgettes, peppers and aubergines which can range in quality

poached snails. Curnonsky, self-styled "Prince of Gastronomes", rightly urged his readers not to eat *ailloli* at midday unless they were able to "doze off after lunch, for those who partake of it generally have an irresistible urge to take a nap."

A word here about garlic. Gone, fortunately, are the days when most British regarded garlic with distaste and a Pelican book on herbs written in 1949 could write: "Anyone who travels in Italian buses might be forgiven for deciding never to grow this evil-smelling plant." But there are lingering reservations even today: a pocket guidebook recently published in Britain notes that in the

from the practically inedible to the sublime.

A dish that combines so many vegetables is symptomatic of the way the cuisine of the Côte d'Azur revels in the ingredients which the region produces best, whether they be vegetables, fruit or herbs. Local sun-gorged tomatoes taste of the sweet fruit they really are (surprisingly, in view of the important role they now play in the cuisine of the Côte d'Azur, tomatoes were initially viewed with suspicion and became widely used there only from the 19th century on).

The luscious, almost caramelly flavour of melons from Cavaillon is unrivalled. The taste of fresh figs belies their dull appearance; startlingly complex and not too sweet, the fig is sometimes exploited in meat dishes. Most households boast several pots of lovingly watered basil. Aromatic rosemary, savory, fennel and thyme grow wild on the parched hillsides. The herbs and other vegetation of the *maquis* are ideal food for the sheep that graze there: the lamb of the Côte d'Azur is justly celebrated.

But, on the whole, meat does not feature prominently in local cuisine – until recent times there was little available - though *daube*, a wonderfully rich-flavoured beef stew, is a great favourite. In his book, Blavette gives a recipe for it: a large quantity of shin is put for 24 hours in a marinade of red wine, bay leaf,

Lactarius deliciosus, or saffron milk cap), are highly prized on the Côte d'Azur. Thrushes and blackbirds are regarded as very tasty by locals, who still hunt them. But under French law they can no longer be served in restaurants. Tinier birds that Blavette recalls eating with relish, such as the robin and the cirl bunting, are now, fortunately, protected even from hunters.

This taste for our smaller feathered friends is an Italian trait. Italian culinary influences are strong on the Côte d'Azur, partly as a result of considerable immigration from Italy in the early part of the 20th century. They are particularly noticeable in Nice – though the proudly individualistic Niçois would deny it.

thyme, pepper, zest of an orange, cloves and grated nutmeg, then cooked gently for five or six hours with salt pork, a calf's foot, garlic, onions, tomatoes and pork rind. He recommends using even a very good burgundy like a Pommard in the dish, remarking that "what you put into the casserole you'll find in your plate."

In the Niçois version of *daube*, dried *cèpes* (mushrooms) add a further distinctive flavour. All wild mushrooms, and especially *cèpes* and *sanguins* (the aptly named

Left, Nice *marchand*; the makings of bouillabaisse. **Above,** Côtes-de-Provence vineyard.

The Comté de Nice (Nice and its surrounding area) has been French only since 1860. Before that it was part of the Kingdom of Sardinia, which also included Savoy, Sardinia and Piedmont. From a culinary point of view, Nice straddles several cultures but has retained its own special character.

The best way to get an idea of what Niçois food is all about is to stroll through the old quarter of the city, which is packed with small food stores. Cheese shops are stacked high with Parmesan and mature Gouda (both are used grated in cooked dishes) as well as local cheeses like fresh *brousse* (often made from ewe's-milk) and the rare *tome de Rouré*.

Tubs of capers and salted anchovies serve as a reminder that it is in Nice that the finest version of *anchoãade*, a sauce served with vegetables in the same way as *ailloli*, can be sampled (it contains not only anchovies, olive oil and garlic but capers, unlike its cousin found along the Côte to the west).

Alongside slabs of salt cod you may see large, curiously emaciated fish that seem to be screaming (their open "jaws" are in fact the gill-bones of the beheaded fish): this is stockfish, the wind-dried cod that goes into *estocaficada*, a pungent fish stew that is Nice's proudest speciality. Shops displaying fresh pasta and gnocchi often also sell the strange cuttlebone-shaped *panisses*, made

charcuterie that can only excite admiration - your gaze may even be returned by the spectacular *porchetta*, a boned, stuffed and reconstituted roast piglet which is cut into huge slices from the back end. Greengrocers always have a good stock of fresh basil, handfuls of which go into that truly wonderful Niçois soup, *pistou* (though *pistou* strictly refers to the paste of pounded basil, garlic and Parmesan that is usually added to the minestrone-like soup at the last moment).

Baby courgettes, with their orange-yellow flowers still attached to one end, form the basis of a subtle gratin called *tian*. The flowers alone are also sometimes stuffed with a rice-based, Parmesan-flavoured mixture.

from chickpea flour, deep-fried and served with salt and pepper. Chickpea flour, a peculiarity of Niçois cooking, also goes into *socca*, a very thick, tasty pancake sold in chunks by street vendors.

Other snacks that can be eaten on the move in Nice and in many resorts along the coast are *pissaladière* (a cousin of pizza consisting of black olives, cooked onions and anchovy spread on a bread dough base) and *pan bagnat* (a small round loaf cut in half and stuffed with the ingredients of *salade niçoise* - tomato, hard-boiled egg, anchovy, tunny, spring onion, cucumber and green peppers).

There is a wide range of Niçoise

Also on sale in markets and at greengrocers all along the Côte d'Azur is *mesclun* (or *mesclum*), a mixture of baby salad plants which includes all or some of the following: rocket, dandelion, lettuce (Cos, oak-leaf), watercress, chicory, radicchio and chervil. *Mesclun* has been something of a success story: it is now common, if not *de rigueur*, on the menus of restaurants all over France.

With its wealth of top-quality ingredients the Côte d'Azur should be renowned for its restaurants. So it is, up to a point. If you want to splurge, you cannot go wrong. The Louis XV, in the Hotel de Paris in Monte-Carlo, combines the peak of luxury with sublime food and towering prices. Roger Vergé's Le Moulin de Mougins and Jacques Maximin's eponymous restaurant in Nice offer similar fare in more relaxed surroundings.

All three establishments offer some dishes which reflect or reinterpret local culinary traditions, as is the fashion nowadays. Problems begin to arise when it a question of choosing restaurants in the middle or lower price ranges. Chancing one's arm with a village bistro or tiny restaurant tucked away in some Cannes or Nice backstreet may not be too hazardous. But as soon as you decide to eat on or near the beach, or in some otherwise fashionable location, an apparently honest establishment can turn out to be

taste in your mouth, it is a good idea before leaving to browse round a street market or food store and stock up with the kind of preserved or dried staples which any good kitchen requires and which are more expensive and/or of inferior quality at home. There is a wide range of olives available, the best being the tiny black Niçois olives marinated for six months in thyme and bay leaf. These are available in jars from Alziari in Nice, a firm celebrated for its smooth and subtly flavoured olive oil, unquestionably the best on the Côte d'Azur.

Other possibles for your shopping-bag include fragrant local honey, crystallised flowers from Grasse, dried cèpes, Parmesan

a tourist trap. Our advice is to consult one of the specialised food guides like the Michelin or the Gault-Millau (many hotels have them at reception). Otherwise, you may find yourself paying through the nose for watery, overcooked ratatouille, thin tasteless fish soup, *bouillabaisse* that is little more than a fish soup – at five or six times the price - with a few flakes of fish and a couple of fish bones in it, and a bottle of Côtes-de-Provence rosé that produces instant heartburn.

To ensure that your stay leaves a pleasant

Left, a tempting stall on St-Tropez waterfront.
Above, dining *al fresco*, St-Tropez.

cheese, anchovies in glass jars (better than in tins), and maybe a bottle or two of good Côtes-de-Provence (Ott, Jas-d'Esclans and Château Minuty are reliable growers), or that rare and surprisingly strong port-like Niçois wine, Bellet.

But there is one widely available product which, once you are back home, can conjure up memories of those lazy holiday meals more powerfully than any other, when for example spread on warm toast or used as a stuffing for hard-boiled eggs: *tapenade*, a smooth purée of capers, black olives and anchovies with olive oil, plenty of pepper and a little thyme.

PLACES

From the world-famous beaches of the Côte d'Azur to its Provençal heart, here we explore the region in depth. From the ancient stones of Roman ruins to the villas of present-day inhabitants fully equipped with swimming pools and satellite dishes, we look at every aspect of this rich and complex area – its past, present and future.

The contrasts are legion: the cool clear waters of the Golfe de Giens, the ultra-chic beach clubs of St-Tropez, the glitzy heights of Cannes and the medieval charms of its old town, Le Suquet, the millionaire yachts of Antibes' Port Vauban and the fabulous Grimaldi Picasso collection. Other facets include the perfumes of Grasse, the high-tech industry of Sophia-Antipolis, the pulsating beaches of Juan-les-Pins, the exclusive luxury of Cap d'Antibes, the art galleries of St-Paul-de-Vence, the street markets of Nice and its stunning modern architecture. Here too are the exotic gardens of Cap Ferrat, the fishermen of Menton, the sophisticated hotels of Beaulieu, the winding streets of ancient fortified towns, the rococo facades of Monaco, the celebrated perched villages of Éze and Roquebrune and the remote secret places of the mountains.

Play *boules* in the village square or roulette in the Casino; eat three-star *nouvelle cuisine* or a *pan bagnat* on the beach; windsurf for recumbent admirers or wander a lonely hillside; investigate medieval villages or watch dolphins at play, sunbathe by the pool in isolated splendour or head for the shore.

Whatever your inclination, the Côte d'Azur encompasses such a variety of landscapes, culture and facilities that every whim can be satisfied. And if all you want to do is spend your entire time sea-gazing, no beaches are better designed for the purpose. You can rent a parasol-shaded *matelas* for the day and only rise for an ice bucket of Provençal rosé and *moules marinière* in the beach restaurant. Should your activities stretch to the need for a good book, this Insight Guide will certainly assure you of plenty to read.

Preceding pages: jardin exotique, Éze; yachts in Antibes; the terrace of a mansion in Nice. **Left**, Menton harbour.

HYÈRES

One of the longest established and most southerly of the Côte d'Azur resorts is **Hyères**, although it is often viewed as an unfashionable and slightly shabby cousin of the "real" Riviera towns of Cannes or Nice. This unfair reputation has its seeds in Queen Victoria's flippant patronage of Hyères in 1892, for no sooner had hotels and palm-lined avenues been built in honour of Her Majesty and her entourage than she decided to move on to Cimiez, rendering the town *passé* almost overnight.

However, the French never ceased visiting Hyères-les-Palmiers, and it has long been a centre for the seriously *sportif*, who take advantage of the subtropical climate to sail, scuba-dive, windsurf and water-ski. There are now three vast leisure ports and 22 miles (35 km) of beaches to be sampled. The town is not wholly reliant upon tourism and is surrounded by vast greenhouses cultivating early fruits such as strawberries, peaches and kiwis as well as ornamental plants, rare flowers (orchids in particular) and potted palms. Close by are many good vineyards which thrive in excellent growing conditions. The busy atmosphere of the modern town combines charmingly with its backdrop of faded *belle-époque* grandeur, the setting for Joseph Conrad's atmospheric last novel *The Rover*.

The distinctive colonial feel of Hyères has meant that it has also been popular as a location with French film-makers. Man Ray's *The Mystery of the Château of Dice* was filmed in 1929 in the villa of the modernist architect Mallet-Stevens. In 1930 Charles de Noailles produced the first film of Jean Cocteau, *The Blood of the Poet*, here and the same year risked excommunication for financing Luis Buñuel's *L'Age d'Or*.

More recently, in 1982, François Truffaut made *Finally Sunday!* in Hyères using black and white film and the eclectic mix of seaside town architecture to create a mood of tension and claustrophobia. The town continues to link itself to experimental cinema and has held an International Festival for young cinema for 20 years.

Pause for coffee under the plane trees of the **Place de la République**, before setting off on the steep climb through the twisting medieval streets of the old town built on the Castéou hill, and up to the ruins of the 14th-century **château**.

Close by is the **Church of St-Louis**, who recuperated here in the 13th century when the now disused port of L'Syguade was a base for returning crusaders. This calm, elegant church is an example of a successful marriage between Italian Romanesque style and Provençal Gothic.

Entering the **Vieille Ville** through the 13th-century gate, you will find yourself in the Rue Massillon, named after the great preacher of the court of Louis XIV who was born in the nearby Rue Rabaton. On the left is the **Collegiate Church of St-Paul**, with an interesting Gothic nave and Romanesque belltower. In the **Place Massillon**, a food market is held each morning, and Arab

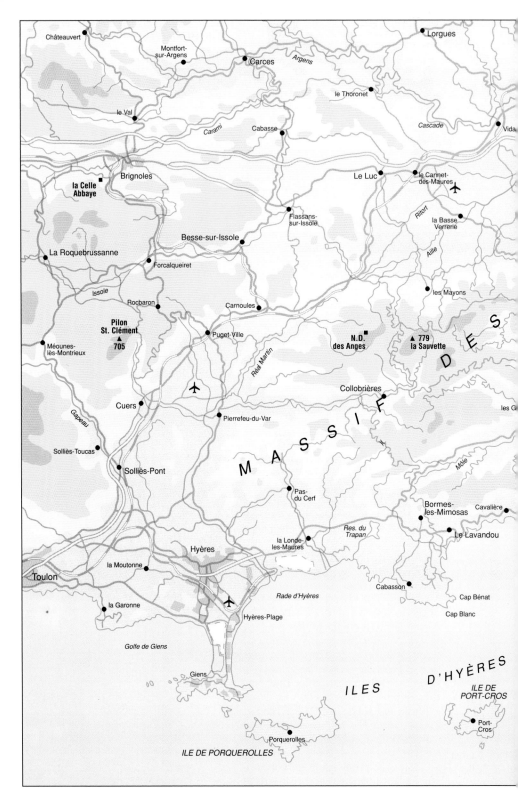

Châteauvert

Montfort-
sur-Argens

Carces

Lorgues

Argens

le Thoronet

Cascade

Vida

le Val

Carami

Cabasse

Brignoles

Le Luc

le Cannet-
des-Maures

la Celle
Abbaye

Flassans-
sur-Issole

Ritort

la Basse
Verrerie

La Roquebrussanne

Besse-sur-Issole

Aille

Forcalqueiret

les Mayons

Issole

Rocbaron

Carnoules

N.D.
des Anges

▲ 779
la Sauvette

D
E
S

Pilon
St. Clément
▲
705

Puget-Ville

Réal Martin

Méounes-
lès-Montrieux

Collobrières

les G

Cuers

Gapeau

Pierrefeu-du-Var

M
A
S
S
I
F

Môle

Solliès-Toucas

Pas-
du-Cerf

Bormes-
les-Mimosas

Cavalière

Solliès-Pont

Res. du
Trapan

Le Lavandou

Hyères

la Londe-
les-Maures

la Moutonne

Toulon

Cabasson

Cap Bénat

la Garonne

Rade d'Hyères

Cap Blanc

Hyères-Plage

Golfe de Giens

Giens

ILES

D'HYÈRES

ILE DE
PORT-CROS

Port-
Cros

ILE DE PORQUEROLLES

Porquerolles

130

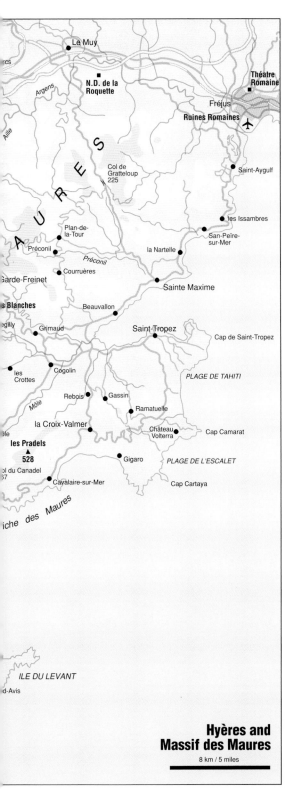

Le Muy

rcs

N.D. de la
Roquette

Argens

Théâtre
Romaine

Fréjus

Ruines Romaines

Aille

Col de
Gratteloup
225

Saint-Aygulf

les Issambres

Plan-de-
la-Tour

San-Peïre-
sur-Mer

Préconil

la Nartelle

Préconil

Courruères

Garde-Freinet

Sainte Maxime

Blanches

Beauvallon

egilly

Grimaud

Saint-Tropez

Cap de Saint-Tropez

les
Crottes

Cogolin

PLAGE DE TAHITI

Rebois

Gassin

Môle

Ramatuelle

la Croix-Valmer

Château
Volterra

Cap Camarat

le

les Pradels

528

Gigaro

PLAGE DE L'ESCALET

ol du Canadel
67

Cavalaire-sur-Mer

Cap Cartaya

iche des Maures

ILE DU LEVANT

d-Avis

**Hyères and
Massif des Maures**

8 km / 5 miles

and Provençal delicacies can be bought. The square is overlooked by the 12th-century **Tower of St-Blaise**, last remnant of a Knights Templar command post, set up in Hyères after the town gained royal status with the blessing of Charles I of Anjou.

Continue up the pretty Rue Barbacane and walk through an arch and Romanesque house to Rue Paradis, where a calf-achingly steep track snakes past the **Parc St-Bernard**, a garden of Mediterranean flowers and plants, to the castle.

The panoramic view from the castle's turrets provides a strong sense of the geography and history of the town. Over to the east are the dark curves of the Massif des Maures, while in the south you can see over Les Oiseaux peak and the Costebelle hill to the Giens peninsula and the islands of Hyères.

The American novelist Edith Wharton fell in love with the view when she first visited Hyères with André Gide in 1915. She returned after World War I and wrote that she was ravished by "views of land and sea such as were never seen before".

The château has its foundations on a Greek defence wall from the 4th century BC when a Greek trading-post called Olbia was founded on the coast at Almanarre which was later to become the Roman town of Pomponiana. Fragments of pottery, spears and statues have been excavated from Almanarre and can be seen at the municipal museum. The castle was established by the Lords of Fos and passed to Charles I in 1257. In the 16th century Charles IX was brought here by his mother Catherine de Medicis and was enchanted by the profusion of orange blossom trees. In 1662 the castle was pulled down during the wars of religion. Without its stronghold the importance of the town was drastically reduced in favour of Toulon.

Round the castle is the **Rue Victor Basch**, a road cut through layers of slate. Here is the unremarkable house where Robert Louis Stevenson convalesced and whose words, "I was only happy once - that was at Hyères," are immortalised on a blue plaque.

The street curves down to the **Rue Edith Wharton**, named in honour of her efforts to restore the ruined castle of St-Clair and its garden. Bernard Berenson pronounced the old Clarisses convent and its views to be "sheer paradise… with the incense-like fragrance of the pines and cypresses and the artistic beauty of the rocks." Other literary figures to visit St-Clair were William Gerhardie, Robert Norton, Sinclair Lewis, Kenneth and Jane Clark, H. G. Wells and Aldous Huxley.

Another famous inhabitant of old Hyères, with a tomb in the grounds of St-Clair, is Olivier Voitier, the 19th-century naval officer who discovered the statue of the *Venus de Milo*, now in the Louvre, when on a maritime campaign in Greece.

The road back into modern Hyères passes a pink house with a bridge across to the upper road which would look perfectly at home in Lisbon, and then down a delightful spiral rampart. The large number of clinics and convalescent homes are evidence of the contin-ued belief in the health-giving properties of the town's situation and the local *Source de la Vierge* whose waters were enjoyed by Tolstoy who took a winter "cure" in Hyères in 1860.

The modern town has its own attractions with many Moorish-style buildings, such as **La Tunisienne** in the Avenue de Beauregard, **La Mauresque** in the Avenue Jean Natte, and the sea-side neo-baroque rotunda tourist office in the Avenue de Belgique-Hyères. You can see just-married couples jostling to pose for the wedding photographer against the tropical plants and flowers, the peacocks and the ornamental lakes of the **Olbius Riquier Gardens**. For beaches, head for Hyères Plage or the isthmus of Presqu'île de Giens and the long sandy expanse of La Capte. Safe shallow waters make it very popular in summer.

The approach to **La Tour Fondue**, where ferries and glass-bottomed boats leave regularly for the Hyères islands, is by the tow roads on the peninsula of Giens either side of the Marais Salins

Moorish influence in Hyères.

des Pesquiers, the coast's only working salt marsh. In Roman times this strange narrow strip was probably still an island and briefly became one again in the great storms of 1811.

At the foot of the tower, which the young Napoleon re-established as a stronghold when he was an artillery officer at Toulon, happy day-trippers with hampers and gaggles of divers congregate. It is a half-hour trip to the beautiful and densely vegetated **Îles d'Or**, also known as Iles d'Hyères, so called because of the Mica or "Fool's Gold" which sparkles in the sand and rocks of the islands.

François I granted the right of asylum to convicts provided they would live on the islands and protect them against corsairs and pirates. However, the criminal underclass flooded the islands and turned to piracy themselves, rewarding the king's generosity by trying to capture one of his ships.

The three small islands have been **Ferry ride to** unable to escape the troubles of the **Porquerolles.** mainland for in 1793 the British landed on Porquerolles and blew up the fort, and in August 1944 American troops landed on the islands of Port-Cros and Le Levant to fight off German batteries.

Porquerolles, so called because of the wild boar that once roamed here, is the largest and most popular of the islands. It offers the most amenities for families, pleasure-craft owners and the less intrepid while its white sandy beaches and woods of pine heather, eucalyptus and myrtle remain remarkably unspoilt. Porquerolles has been protected from developers by State ownership, with a large conservation area established in 1972.

The island's village, also called Porquerolles, has a strong colonial flavour in the simple style of its houses, built by the military in the mid-19th century. The small village church has a wooden Stations of the Cross carved by a soldier with his penknife. Inexpensive lunches can be enjoyed at one of the many restaurants around the main square. Alternatively, hire mountain bikes (beware of uncomprising seats) or

the gearless *classique* and set off with a picnic to the lighthouse or beaches on the north or south coast.

Climb the **lighthouse** to enjoy dramatic views of the hills of Le Grand Langoustier to the west, St-Agatha's fort to the south as well as the cliffs of the south coast, the Hyères roadstead and the Maures Massif.

Port-Cros is more rugged and quiet and is worth a whole day's visit. The island is named after the hollowed-out *(creux)* shape of its harbour. Explore the island by walking through the Valley of Solitude to the only hotel in the National Park of Port-Cros. The Manoir d'Hélène is named after the heroine in Melchoir de Vogue's novel *Jean d'Agrève* which is set on the island. It was here that D. H. Lawrence is supposed to have met the Englishwoman whose confessional post-coital conversation inspired *Lady Chatterley's Lover*. Continue to **l'Estissac Fort**; the botanical path is overgrown with wild flowers whose scent accompanies you down to the sheltered beach and turquoise waters of La Palud.

Île de Levant is a strip of barren rock only 5 miles (8 km) long and 1,300 yards (1,200 metres) wide. Bare all at the nudist village and beach of Héliopolis which used to be the "Mecca of Naturism". The nudist colony was founded on the island (once inhabited by Lérins monks) in 1931 by the doctors Gaston and André Durville who urged their patients to enjoy the physical and psychological benefits of "the childlike liberation of nakedness". Since it has become acceptable to take off your swimsuit on many beaches around the Mediterranean, the island has lost some of its *risqué* reputation, but is still popular with dedicated nudists. There is not much of the island to explore as most of Levant is owned by the navy, but there is the strange sight of shopkeepers, estate agents and waiters going about their daily routine in a G-string or less.

Exploring the Massif des Maures: The oldest range of mountains in Provence is the **Massif des Maures**, separated from the Estérel range by the valley created by the Argens river; the mainly **Golfe de Giens.**

Schistous rock was originally part of the huge Tyrrhenian massif which once included Corsica and Sardinia. The name of *Maures* is not an allusion to the Moors (Saracens), who occupied the area for more than a century and who were finally driven out in AD 973, but to the Provençal word *Maouro* which describes the dark density of the cork oak, chestnut and pine forest.

The glorious views and abundance of flowers and plants such as yellow gorse, flowering lavender and wild roses are enjoyed by drivers, walkers and cyclists who use the Massif's towns and points of interest to shape their route through the mountainous forest, stopping en route for a meal, a coffee or a night.

La Garde-Freinet is the capital of the Maures and full of left-overs from the 1960s, as you will notice drinking in the bar of Claire Fontaine, watched by a large signed photo of John Wayne, or hanging out in the *Brasserie le lézard*.

In the 19th century the town produced more than three-quarters of France's bottle corks and the oaks are still farmed every 8 to 12 years with a yielding life of 150 years. The light, impermeable and elastic outer bark is cut in strips by a knife from the cork oaks, leaving a clean red-brown trunk. The cork is then broken up, steam-cleaned and pressed into moulds of the desired shape. As well as being made into tiles and stoppers many cork craft ornaments are on sale at the Rue St-Jacques or on display at the disused St-Eloi chapel at the entrance to the village.

The Rue St-Jacques caters for the tourists from the coast with local antiques, pottery and ornamental flower shops. There is also some exquisite but expensive jewellery made from the local blue and green serpentine stone.

The Saracens are credited with building the castle on a high point to the northeast of the village, but it is now thought that it may be of a slightly later period. Some have attributed it to Count William who spared many Saracen prisoners and who, in return, taught his farmers how to roof their houses with flat tiles, how to make use of the oak

Street in Collobrières.

trees for cork and resin and, probably, the secret of *marrons glacés*, chestnuts crystallised and preserved in a sugary syrup, now the main local industry.

The road to **Collobrières** is dedicated to fire-fighters who died in 1971, and the large areas of blackened and twisted trees are evidence of the constant forest fires, sparked spontaneously by thoughtless visitors, or, as some locals think, by arsonists. Throughout the forest fire-fighters can be seen carrying out their daily duties of strimming down the undergrowth and creating fire-blocks. There are points all along the route for cars to stop and admire the breathtaking views of the Maures or simply to let an impatient hill-farmer overtake in his van. Tracks and paths are clearly marked for groups of hearty walkers in plus-fours and heavy boots.

Before reaching the village one can take a detour to the eccentric Merovingian priory of the **Notre-Dame-des-Anges**, which shares its high point with a large communications tower and transmitter mast. The 19th-century

chapel is filled with offerings made by pilgrims who have climbed to the spot where a statue of the Virgin Mary was found by a shepherd in the 11th century. Babies' bonnets and pictures of the sick being cured cram the dark chapel and, more mysteriously, two stuffed alligators hang from the ceiling.

Much more aesthetically pleasing is the **Chartreuse de la Verne** which is southeast of Collobrières. The Carthusian Charterhouse stands by a spring on a plateau overlooking the holm oak and chestnut forest. Most of the structure was built in the 17th and 18th centuries, after which it was abandoned by revolution-fearing monks, but the blue-green serpentine cloisters and four restored monks' cells reveal medieval origins.

While tourists are welcome to walk through the beautiful semi-ruin, remember that the Charterhouse has been occupied by nuns from the order of Bethlehem since 1984.

The centre of **Collobrières** is not the attractive main square with its Spanish feel, or the main boulevard with its grand mercantile houses, but the extensive bouledrome by the river. Nearby is the **Confiserie Azuréenne**, attached to the delicious-smelling factory famous for its chestnut sweets and purées. There are often long queues here, so it is worthwhile taking advantage of the less expensive chestnut delicacy stalls on the way out on the D14 road.

The Maures corniche: White, sandy and relatively uncrowded beaches can be found just a short walk down from the scenic coastal road of the D559. The main resort of this corniche is **Le Lavandou**, whose name recalls the lavender fields on the banks of the Batailler. It is now a resort catering mainly for the teenage holiday market and the owners of pleasure-craft although it does still function as a fishing port. It is a mixture of nightclubs, bars, cheap hotels and leather jacketed *mecs* on motorbikes.

The main square next to the marina is named after the composer Ernest Reyer who lived in the town in the 19th century. From here ferries leave regularly **Café in La Garde-Freinet.**

for the Hyères islands. The town's best point is its sandy beach with a long, tree-lined promenade; quieter beaches can be found at the less built-up and much smaller resorts of **St-Clair**, **Aquebelle**, **Cavalière** and **Pramousquier**.

To the west of Le Lavandou is **Cap Benat**, France's equivalent of Camp David, with most of the beaches inaccessible by car but possible on foot. The rocky promontory with its two ruined castles is a military training ground leading to the official summer residence of the President.

Visit the delightful **Bormes-les-Mimosas** for a tantalising flavour of Provence. Take the road from Le Lavandou through an avenue of eucalyptus and mimosa. The coral-coloured houses nestle on the steeply sloping roads, one of which is aptly called *rompi-cuou* - the neck-breaker. The beach at L'Estagnol is a wide bay fringed by parasol pines.

In the **Place St-François** is a statue of Francesco di Paola whose visit to the town was said to have miraculously ended an outbreak of plague. In the chapel of St-François there is a monument to the landscape painter Jean-Charles Cazin whose works are on display both in the town hall and in the small Museum of Bormes. At the top of the town there are excellent cafés and magnificent views of the coast and the forest of Dom spread out below. Nearby is a marina, with a capacity for 800 yachts, and three attractive beaches.

It is worth stopping at the beach of **Rayol-Canadel-sur-Mer** at the base of the Pradels range, flanked by two pinewoods sheltering it from the *mistral* winds. The village sits in a natural amphitheatre in the wooded hillside.

Cavalaire-sur-Mer is a town built for the convenience of yacht- and boat-owners. It has mooring for 1,200 yachts, good shops, a post office, doctors and a long sandy beach. You can catch a ferry from the new port for the Hyères islands or for the market on Wednesday in the Place Jean Moulin. Here you can savour an abundance of regional produce: honey from the forest, olives, olive oil, *saucisson* and the essential local rosé.

Rooftops of Bormes-les-Mimosas.

ST-TROPEZ

Like Hollywood, **St-Tropez** ranks among an élite handful of place-names to have achieved practically mythical status. To large numbers of French, the myth is still one of the *ne plus ultra* of summer chic. To others, St-Tropez typifies over-commercialism and vulgarity. Needless to say, the reality is somewhere between the two, and varies in any case according to the season.

Crammed with between 60,000 and 100,000 visitors in July and August, in winter St-Tropez's population returns to a placid and neighbourly 6,000. Though obviously not for those in search of rustic serenity, at least in summer, a visit to St-Tropez can be considerable fun, taken in the right spirit, and preferably equipped with a generous budget. Perhaps the best approach is to that of the town as a sort of Mediterranean extension of the Left Bank of Paris, with all that this implies in terms of parking problems and expense.

St-Tropez's original attraction was based on the beauty of the dusky pink and ochre houses of the old town, its position on the southern curve of its large, sheltered gulf, and the climatic conditions which contribute to its beautiful, clear light. Uniquely on the French Riviera, St-Tropez faces north, so that the quayside cafés receive the famous golden evening light, as well as the bay's stunning sunsets.

As neither railway nor major trunk roads passed through the town due to its peninsular position, it escaped the late 19th-century development of earlier resorts such as Juan-les-Pins and Cannes. Its restricted road access is now a mixed blessing, since the advent of the famous summer traffic jams the length of the D98 to the blocked roundabout at Le Foux, and, sometimes, the whole way round the bay to Ste-Maxime. (The times absolutely to be avoided on this road are late morning until early afternoon, and between 6 o'clock and 10 o'clock in the evening.)

St-Tropez is named after Torpes, a Christian Roman centurion, steward of the Emperor Nero's palace at Pisa who, according to legend, was beheaded for his faith and cast adrift with a dog and a cock in a boat which eventually drifted to the site of the present port. The early town was sacked and its population killed or dispersed by Saracen raiders who occupied the region in the 7th and 9th centuries. In the 15th, St-Tropez was ceded to a Genoese nobleman, Raphaël de Garezzio, with rights tantamount to those of a republic, and was populated by a number of Genoese families, some of whose descendants remain today.

The citadel overlooking the town dates from the ensuing period of well-organized security, provided by an elected "town captain" and defence force; the current *bravade* ceremony which takes place in June every year, involving musket firing and 16th-century uniform, commemorates the successful repulse by Tropeziens in 1637 of a raiding force of Spanish galleys.

By the late 19th-century St-Tropez was primarily involved in tuna fishing,

shipping wines from the region to Marseille and Toulon, and making corks from the bark of the local oaks, while a handful of large houses outside the town had been restored or constructed by prominent individuals such as Napoleon III's minister Émile Ollivier, who retired to the château of La Moutte, in whose grounds his tomb stands, "seeking only peace, but finding delight".

In 1887 the writer Guy de Maupassant arrived in St-Tropez aboard his boat *Bel Ami* and found it "a charming, simple daughter of the sea" with "sardine scales glistening like pearls on the cobblestones." It was the painter Paul Signac, however, who, sailing into the port on his yacht in 1892 and falling in love with the light, acquired a small house overlooking the beach of Les Graniers and began to attract friends and painter acquaintances: Matisse, Bonnard, Camoin, Dunoyer de Segonzac. In 1927 the novelist Colette moved to her villa La Treille Muscate. She was followed by 1930s *beau monde* such as the couturier Paul Poiret, the writer Anaïs Nin, and after

the interruption of World War II, when the long Pampelonne beach was used for the Allied liberation landings, by the first of the St-Germain bohemian stars, Juliette Greco.

In 1959 Roger Vadim shot *And God Created Woman* in St-Tropez, with the sex-kitten Brigitte Bardot wreaking havoc around the old port, and the floodgates of the town's modern showbusiness invasion were opened. The *yé yé* industry – pop stars led by Johnny Hallyday and record magnate Eddie Barclay – followed the film world, and in 1969 the opening of the luxurious Hotel Byblos marked a turning point in the transformation of the hitherto simple fishing village into a fully paid-up jet-set destination. It only remained for the masses to follow, and the seriously rich to move out of town to luxurious and secluded villas, or the staterooms of their substantial yachts.

The St-Tropez season starts around the beginning of April, peaks in the frenzy of the national holiday month of August and continues until the end of

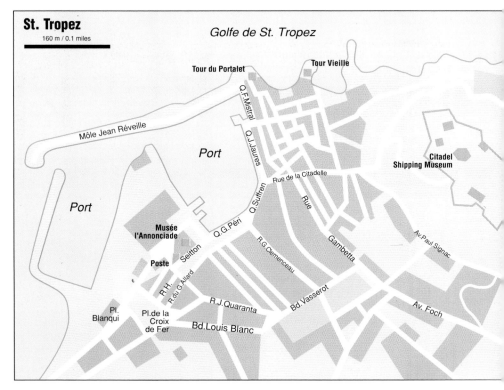

the fashionable Nioulargue yacht-racing week in early October. The quiet winter months are interrupted by a substantial mini-season around Christmas; many shops and restaurants close during the off-peak period.

The centre of St-Tropez is the old port (which has been undergoing restoration), enclosed by the long stone **Jean Reveille jetty** extending outwards from the squat, round 15th-century **Portalet Tower**. Along the **Quais Frédéric Mistral** and **Jean Jaurès** are the fashionable cafés, notably the all-red Sennequier, formerly a pâtisserie and still famed for its nougat, and, stern to the quay, the great yachts – futuristic white plastic gin palaces or gleaming teak classics – with uniformed crews and, increasingly, non-sailing corporate charterers. Distributed throughout the old, and adjacent new, ports is a wide range of craft, from vintage sailing yachts to the long, spearhead-shaped, V8-engined, offshore "cigarettes" that drone across the bay at 60 miles an hour (100kph). Between the new port and the small sea-front heliport is a huge, continually packed car-park, with a small shaded area for dogs with bowls of water and an attendant, financed by the Brigitte Bardot Foundation.

On the west side of the old port is the **Museum of the Annonciade**, a 16th-century former chapel attractively converted to house a large and excellent collection of paintings and sculptures, donated by the Tropezien philanthropist Georges Grammont, by artists who have lived or worked in the town. The Annonciade's collection constitutes one of the most important assemblages of early and mid 20th-century French art outside Paris. Signac is represented by a rotating collection of 10 watercolours and five oils, and other high points include works by Van Dongen, Matisse, Seurat, Bonnard, Rouault, Utrillo, Dufy, and Charles Camoin, whose 1925 game of *boules* in the Place de Lices is one of the most atmospheric of the scenes of St-Tropez itself.

A little way beyond the Annonciade is the **Quai Suffren**, with its bronze

View of Golfe de St-Tropez.

statue of one of St-Tropez's most illustrious adopted citizens, the Bailli de Suffren, whose late-flourishing nautical career ended with a famously successful Indian campaign in the 1780s and the command of the French navy. De Suffren's name was retrospectively applied to the 10th-century square tower just behind the Quai Mistral, used along with a similar building in Ste-Maxime by the Knights Templar to protect the gulf's settlements from the North African Barbary pirates whose raids plagued the region until the 15th century.

The so-called **"Corsairs' House"** behind the church dates from 100 years later; it is unclear whether its fine Renaissance doorway and carved stone balustrade were ever actually used by pirates. In the centre of the old town, St-Tropez's 19th-century Italian baroque parish church, with its typical Provençal wrought-iron campanile, contains statues of the town's patron saint both headless and recumbent, plus menagerie, in his boat, invariably festooned with votive offerings of flowers and hearts.

A block away is the attractive town hall and all around the lovely narrow stone streets, those nearer the port lined with smart shops and restaurants, those further back residential and surprisingly quiet and unspoilt even in August. In the old *quartier* of **La Ponche**, reached through the 15th-century stone Revelen gate-tower, the small remaining corps of Tropezien fishermen keep their boats and in a few cases sell their catch fresh from small garage/stalls. Nearby is the charming medium-priced Hôtel La Ponche with its popular terrace restaurant, and around the corner the similarly elegant Yaca Hotel with a lovely ivy-surrounded central pool and patio. La Ponche and Le Yaca (then known as L'Aioli) were the first hotels, in the pre-Byblos 1950s and '60s, to accommodate the Sagans and the Vadims, and both have managed to update their facilities and decor (and prices) with great taste, retaining the charm of the lovely old buildings.

Other points of interest in the centre of St-Tropez include the 15th-century

Repairing a fishing boat in the old quarter of La Ponche.

semi-ruined **Jarlier tower**, the 16th-century **Chapelle de la Miséricorde** with its blue, green and gold tiled belfry, and the pretty old **Place des Herbes** with its morning vegetable and fish market. Best of all, though, is the general effect of the little streets, warm pastel walls enlivened by pots of geraniums (once put on the window ledge to keep out mosquitoes) and glimpses of oleander or bougainvillaea peeking from walled gardens.

Ten minutes from the centre, overlooking the whole bay from its grassy, pine-dotted hillock, is the triangular **Citadel**, surrounded by an extensive wall and dry moat, and patrolled by peacocks. Apart from the superb view from the ramparts, the maritime museum within the Citadel offers displays of torpedoes (the town still possesses a torpedo factory, moved from Toulon after World War II) and of maps, uniforms and guns relating to the 1943–45 Resistance and Liberation. Below the Citadel, on the opposite slope of the hill from the town centre, is the cemetery,

its rows of white headstones outlined strikingly against the blue of the sea it overlooks. Another excellent view is available from the 16th-century **St Anne's Chapel**, 15 minutes' walk via the road which also passes the St-Tropez wine cooperative.

St-Tropez itself has very limited beach areas, being centred around the port: the famous golden beaches are on either side of the town, and, in the case of the biggest, Pampelonne beach, 2 miles away in the commune of Ramatuelle. Most of them are occupied by a series of beach "clubs" which are usually not clubs at all, but concessions rented by their proprietors from the local council and offering their bars, restaurants, parasols, loungers, and some cases shops, hairdressers, and tenders to pick up customers from their offshore yachts, to anyone who is willing to pay for these services.

This is not to deny they can seem as cliquey and exclusive as clubs, with different social sets patronising different establishments. Beach life tends to

The fashionable Sennequier café.

ST-TROPEZ STYLE

St-Tropez is a barometer of style, a sort of summer alternative to Paris, just as ski resorts such as Mégève are winter ones. Fashion professionals have always patronised it, combining holidays with studying the market. Daniel Hechter showed his first collection in town in the early 1960s, and more than 30 years later top names such as designer Jean-Paul Gaultier or London-based retailer Joseph Ettedgui still make a point of visiting regularly to hang out at the fashionable Sennequier café by the port and see who's wearing what.

Getting the measure of the St-Tropez look is deceptively complex. Informality has always been the keyword – but *studied* informality; St-Tropez is certainly not a place to go if you don't want to bother about what you look like. On the other hand, one should never underestimate the democracy of French public life: just when it seems a certain restaurant must be reserved exclusively for golden-limbed 22-year-olds in leather jackets and white lace shorts (and that's just the men), along

comes a couple of elderly hippies in bulging denim and pony-tails to take the best table. And since everyone stares at everyone else all the time anyway, it doesn't seem to matter whether it's out of contempt or admiration.

Retro fashion means the Bardots and Vadims still represent the height of chic. And, though there are convertibles and buggies by the dozen, it's hard to think of a modern vehicle – Porsches being as 10-a-centime as they are – that would outclass a 1960 MGA or Citroën DS *décapotable* in the traffic jam along the D98 today. Harley-Davidsons have hardly changed since then anyway, and if there's one quintessentially Tropezien accessory, it's a Harley.

Some long-established boutiques, such as Vachon on the Quai Suffren, are still doing good business with silk shirts, stretch dresses, T-shirts – all the things the Parisians need. "Lots of people come here immediately they arrive to get their holiday outfits," Vachon's manager will tell you, "they look ridiculous in their Paris clothes, they've brought all the wrong stuff..."

These days, of course, shops such as Vachon face plenty of competition. All around the old port, in chic little shopping streets, and in the increasing number of mini-malls, the cream of European *prêt-à-porter* is available in season – many shops close in winter. Hermès has long been established with its own shop; the Hotel Byblos shop sells Yves St-Laurent; Joanna sells John Galliano, Dolce & Gabbano and Sybilla, while Uomo deals in Gianni Versace, Thierry Mugler and Claude Montana for men.

Perhaps the most surprising thing is how fashionable St-Tropez remains. Like much of the Côte d'Azur, it tends to be dismissed as overcrowded and over-rated, but for a lot of people (usually the ones with the yachts and the private villas) it has remained as chic as ever. They still want to be seen in St-Tropez. Supermodels such as Naomi Campbell and Elle Macpherson stroll barefoot and casual, but never unrecognisable, through the Place des Lices. Roger Moore is glimpsed canoodling on a yacht. Elton John flies in for a day by helicopter to buy a property like his friend, George Michael.

Major villa properties sell for anything between £2 and £5 million (US$5–8 million), fully equipped with pools, helipads, mature olive trees and serious security. Luxury yachts are chartered at around £13,000 ($20,000) a day – then, if the beach scene palls, you can take off for a really expensive lunch offshore. ■ **Night life.**

begin late morning, proceed to a leisurely lunch at the restaurant and peak during the post-prandial mid to late afternoon lazing time.

The beaches actually forming part of St-Tropez are: to the west of the town centre the **Bouillabaisse**, showing signs of a return to fashion after a decade of decline, with its new Golfe Azur establishment; the simple little local beach, a favourite of native Tropeziens, **Les Graniers**, just below the Citadel; the slightly larger **Plage des Canebiers**, overlooked by Bardot's villa, La Madrague; and on the eastern edge of the peninsula and now rather crowded, **Les Salins**.

Along the great golden sweep of the **Plage de Pampelonne**, the concessions, from north to south are: Tropezina; Tabou-Plage; Tahiti-Plage, a big long-established showbiz favourite including a hotel and shops; Bora Bora and the very chic Moorea; La Voile Rouge, home of topless nymphettes and a rockstar/Hollywood ambiance; the new Sun 77 with its teenage offshoot Hysteria;

the quieter Force 7 and Le Club du Planteur; the naturist Le Blouch; Club 55, the oldest (founded in 1955 by the de Colmont family) and classiest of the concessions; Nioulargo, with its traditional and Indo-Chinese restaurants; La Plage des Jumeaux, noted for excellent Provençal cuisine; fashionable L'Epi-Plage; La Cabane Bambou; Tropicana, another showbiz favourite with excellent local cooking; and La Bastide Blanche, which is accessible only by boat and therefore relatively quiet and exclusive.

At anchor off the shore of Pampelonne are the dozens of major yachts and the smaller craft used for the very Tropezien custom of sailing out for lunch to yet another exclusive restaurant - the Mas du Langoustier on the island of Porquerolles, for example.

If the duo of Sennequier and Le Gorille (named after its proprietor's hirsute torso), and the other lesser quayside cafés are St-Tropez's supreme breakfast and coffee haunts, they are rivalled in the evening by the cafés on the **Place des**

Handy water transport.

Lices five minutes' walk away. Under the five rows of big plane trees, illuminated by long strips of light bulbs, hundreds of people play *boules*, still occasionally in the traditional celebrity teams hosted by the Eddie Barclay set, stroll, sit on benches, or in the case of younger holidaymakers, on motorbikes and scooters.

This is the night-time centre of the Harley-Davidson cult still led by Johnny Hallyday (you can rent Harleys complete with fringed leather mudflaps by the day for a couple of thousand francs in St-Tropez). The terraces of the Brasserie de la Renaissance, successfully relaunched by the Colmont family of Club 55, and of the old favourite Café des Arts, with its crammed, jolly bistro interior, are excellent places to dine well at a medium price with a view over the fascinating bustle.

Elsewhere around town, a thoroughly Parisian range of restaurants buzz with diners till midnight. At the foot of the slope housing the Byblos Hotel, Michel Rochedy's smart Le Chabichou offers specialities such as pig's trotter stuffed with lobster and peach soup with an excellent Beaumes de Venise wine; Le Chabichou's cooking is generally regarded as the most refined in town, along with that of the restaurants of the elegant, exclusive beach-front Résidence de la Pinède (specialities include pigeon with green lentils, truffles and bacon) and the wildly flashy new hilltop Château de la Messardière (iced potato soup with truffles).

All of these restaurants, incidentally, operate also as de luxe take-aways, with a catering service for opulent dinner parties in the villas in the hills outside town. Around midnight, queues start to form outside St-Tropez nightclubs, which range from the exclusive and glamorous Caves du Roy at the Hôtel Byblos, with its Ancient Egyptian theme decor, and the classic 1960s favourite Papagayo, to the Pirate's Studio, a sort of VIP French karaoke joint, and Le Bal, a favourite on the gay and supermodel circuit.

After a heavy night at one of these

The golden stretch of Pampelonne beach.

establishments, it is worth remembering that the most revivifying of hangover cures, a gentle sea excursion, is not only available to boat-owners. The regular ferries that leave the old port for Port Grimaud, Ste-Maxime and St-Raphaël offer a delightful and relaxing run across the bay.

To arrive at St-Tropez in this manner not only entitles you to the classic and most enchanting view of the old town, but can also be two or three times as quick, from Ste-Maxime for example, as a similar journey spent sweating in a semi-stationary car.

Inland from St-Tropez, the gently rising terrain is dominated by vineyards. Viticulture accounts for 40 percent of the agriculture of the region, and the St-Tropez peninsula is an important part of the Côtes-de-Provence *appellation contrôlée* area. Running through this region, the "Route des Côtes-de-Provence" (maps and details available from all local tourist offices) is a signposted itinerary passing by some of the most important individual *domaines*, all of them open for visits and sales, such as the elegant Napoleon III **Château de Minuty** with its family chapel, surrounded by cypress, mulberry and eucalyptus, and the **Château de Barbeyrolles**, its neighbour just outside the village of Gassin.

The interior of the peninsula is dominated by the three beautiful hilltop villages of **Gassin**, **Ramatuelle** and **La Croix-Valmer**, their old stone centres rising above the surrounding oak and beech woods to command superb views of the sea, and on a good day, far back to the north, glimpses of snow on the peaks of the lower Alps. In and around them are opulent holiday homes and, in their centres, pretty, chic, tree-shaded restaurants offering a slightly more secluded alternative to those of St-Tropez.

Gassin, the most elevated of the peninsular trio, is an exquisite little town with a 16th-century church and town hall, a pretty central square planted with African lotus trees and surrounded by a warren of tiny roads and alleys, and a circular boulevard with magnificent

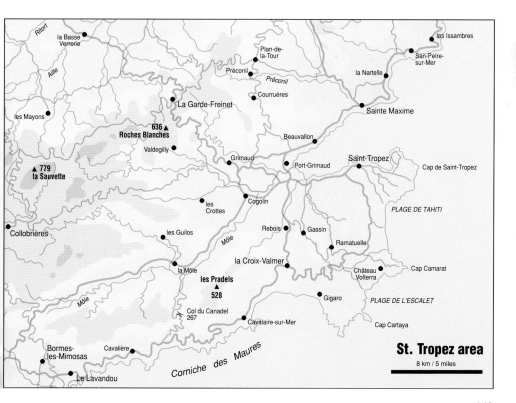

St. Tropez area

8 km / 5 miles

views over the entire gulf. Gassin's position was its early *raison d'être*; as a look-out post, from the 10th century manned by Knights Templar, who did not, however, prevent a Saracen raiding party in 1394 carrying off 33 of the village's inhabitants.

The Saracens are said to be responsible for the name (from *Rahmatu 'llah*, Arabic for "God's Gift") of Gassin's neighbour, **Ramatuelle**, which also retains two 10th-century doors in the remains of its fortifications from its Saracen occupation. Other significant episodes in the village's martial history include the unusual and apparently effective use of hives of bees hurled from the ramparts to repel a Royalist siege in 1592, and during World War II, its role as a point of contact for the Resistance with Allied submarines, attested to by a monument near the cemetery.

Another pretty, tile-roofed, flower-bedecked village of narrow, winding streets, Ramatuelle is also noted for its annual summer jazz festival and, especially, for its theatre festival, both held

in an open-air auditorium on the southern slope of Ramatuelle's hill. The theatre festival, named from its inception in 1985 after the famous actor Gérard Philippe who is buried there, was disassociated from his name on the request of his daughter due to what she regarded as "over-commercialisation". Just outside Ramatuelle, a further magnificent view is available from the road running past three ruined oil mills known as the **Moulins de Paillas**.

On the southern slope of the peninsula, looking down across vineyards, reed-beds and pine groves towards Cavalaire Bay, the village of **La Croix-Valmer** contains few vestiges of its Roman past. Its name, however, is believed to derive from the legend whereby the Emperor Constantine, while passing en route to Italy, was persuaded by the vision of a cross in the sky to convert to Christianity.

For the most part dating from the late 19th century, La Croix-Valmer also contains some striking modern buildings, including the parish church. In addition to its role as a centre for vacation homes, it is an important wine-producing centre. It is a good place to spend a day following a wine tour; as a winter resort in the 19th century, it used to claim the benefits of its healthy climate – and maintains the tradition these days by specialising in a "grape" cure.

West of St-Tropez, just before the coastal plain begins its long mutation into the hills of the Massif des Maures, sits the larger town, equal to St-Tropez in population, of **Cogolin**, General de Lattre de Tassigny's headquarters during the 1944 battle to liberate Provence. Although possessed of a pretty old centre with 16th-century church, numerous green marble doorways and vaulted passageways, Cogolin is also a working town; in addition to wine, it produces furniture, naval armaments, hand-woven fine wool carpets, fishing rods and clarinet mouthpieces from the surrounding reed beds and pipes carved from the roots of local mountain heather.

Its seaside extension, 3 miles (5 km) from the town, comprises a good, sandy beach and a large marina, with 1,800 **St-Tropez golden boy.**

berths, which attempts perfunctorily to echo the style of Port Grimaud, its near neighbour.

Across the gulf from St-Tropez, **Ste-Maxime** is a prosperous and pleasant resort of 8,000 inhabitants with a modern 750-berth leisure port and a pretty seafront marred only by the traffic passing along its main coast road. The centre is occupied by the massed red, blue and green striped sun-shades of the main beach, the pastel bulk of the casino, with an art deco bas-relief of swimming girls, and well-kept gardens of palm trees, mimosa and oleander.

Just behind the centre, the old town is pedestrianised, if busy in the summer; on its edge is the cool, immaculately kept 19th-century parish church and a square 16th-century defensive tower, now a museum. The town contains a number of modest hotels retaining a distinct and non-conformist character: the pleasant, old-fashioned Les Palmiers, with its promenade terrace and old leather armchairs and also the idiosyncratic 1920s mini-palace of La Résidence

Brutus. Cherry Beach is the chic choice and further on Plage des Eléphants is a bit more affordable.

Six miles (10 km) behind Ste-Maxime, in the foothills of the Massif des Maures, by the small **St-Donat park**, a privately-run **Phonographe Museum** houses a curious collection, displayed in an amiable jumble as in a bric-a-brac store, of 350 assorted antique record players, barrel organs, and other mechanical music-makers, including an 1860s clockwork songbird.

Just as the Massif de l'Estérel, to the north, acts as a buffer against the urbanisation of the coast between Cannes and St-Raphaël, so the great wild bulk of the **Massif des Maures** counterbalances the St-Tropez build-up. Indeed, until the seaside boom at the beginning of the century, the presence of the Maures kept the coastline isolated and undeveloped for centuries.

The Maures are among the areas of the Riviera worst afflicted by brush fires, however, and long stretches of the roads which wind north through the low hills

One of St-Tropez's famous sunsets.

above Ste-Maxime pass acres of sinister, fire-blackened, dead trunks, protruding from the thistle, thyme and broom scrub. Patrolling fire engines and look-out points are a common sight in summer and occasionally the big yellow Canadair flying boats which alight on lakes and scoop up tons of water to deposit on the burning forest.

Inland from the Gulf of St-Tropez, the massif rises gently - its highest peak, La Saurette, is a modest 2,500 ft (780 metres) – dotted with the familiar fortified villages. **Grimaud**, 10 minutes' drive from its scene-stealing new offshore **Port Grimaud**, is a typical and beautiful example, flower-decorated and immaculately maintained by what appears to be a population containing an inordinate proportion of Range-Rover-owning architects. The name of the village derives from that of Gibelin de Grimaldi, a knight who was given lordship of the area in the 10th century as a reward for his part in the expulsion of the Saracen occupiers; the name is also that of the Monégasque royal family.

Modern-day Grimaud, clustering around the ruins of its medieval castle, contains an impressive small Romanesque church, St-Michel, once used by the Templars, after whom the lovely arcaded street nearby is named, an old square with *boules* pitch and huge micocoulier tree, and no shortage of chic and pretty hotels, one of the prettiest being the small, traditional Coteau Fleuri, with its flower-packed garden and wonderful terrace view.

At the northern perimeter of the Massif des Maures, the land levels off, vine-covered, peaceful and still dotted with medieval-centred villages, until it reaches the first slopes of the Lower Alps. This is the heart of the Côtes-de-Provence wine appellation, whose capital, if such a thing existed, would be the small town of **Les Arcs**. Here, the **Maison des Vins**, down on the main road, provides copious information and sampling facilities for the many *crus* of the region, while its restaurant offers hundreds of bottles, often at good prices, to accompany a traditionally-based but still very imaginative cuisine.

Les Arcs' medieval village, known as the **Parage**, is as lovely as any in the region, winding down the slopes of the hill on which stand the remains of the Château de Villeneuve.

The former château complex, with its watch-tower and flat stone assembly-point, is now occupied partly by exquisitely pretty little houses, tiny olive-shaded squares, and partly by the very beautiful hotel/restaurant the Logis du Guetteur, with its vine-draped terrace and shuttered bedroom windows looking out over the vineyards beyond the town. Diners tired of exquisite views may opt to eat inside the Logis restaurant, which is the stone vaulted former dungeon of the castle, now made un-medievally comfortable.

Among the vineyards to the north of Les Arcs is the **Chapel of Ste-Roseline**, a former abbey of which chapel and cloisters remain. The recently restored chapel contains two Giacometti sculptures and modern stained-glass windows, and the relics of Ste Roseline still attract pilgrimages, six centuries later.

A game of boules.

PORT GRIMAUD

Inhabitants of Port Grimaud like to ask visitors jokingly if they have ever visited St-Tropez –"you know, that little village across the bay." The implication of the newer resort's fame is by no means all hyperbole: it now rates as one of the most popular tourist attraction in France, averaging over a million visitors a year – not bad-going for a town which 25 years earlier did not exist.

Port Grimaud, furthermore, is the creation essentially of one man, the Alsace-born architect François Spoerry, whose world reputation was made by this little Provençal Venice, and who went on to consult on similar schemes in New York, Louisiana, Mexico and Japan. Spoerry's idea for Port Grimaud was nurtured in the 1950s at his parents' holiday home along the coast in Cavalaire. "I found it dreary to have to get up in the middle of the night, if there was a storm, and go to the port to secure our boat's mooring." He determined to design a leisure port, with yacht-owners primarily in mind, on the model of Venice, where the "ground floor" of the buildings serves as a reception area and mooring for the owners' boats and those of traders and delivery men.

In 1962 Spoerry obtained a stretch of marshy land by the mouth of the little river Giscle at the end of the Gulf of St-Tropez in the commune of Grimaud. The area was a mosquito-infested sand-pit, and it took Spoerry four years to obtain building permission for a project widely regarded as crazy. The earliest houses went for as little as 150,000 francs; 25 years later they were fetching between 10 and 20 times that.

Spoerry's guiding principles were those of what he describes as *architecture douce* (soft architecture). Buildings, he believes, should be unassuming, human in scale, and functional, and should avail themselves of local traditional materials and techniques. He therefore designed Port Grimaud in the traditional local style with terracotta tiled roofs, and facades painted in the wonderful shades of ochre and cream that characterise so many Provençal villages.

Every house has a waterfront and boat mooring – later "streets" have small front gardens with lawns and trees – and access roads at the rear permit vehicle access for deliveries, but not in theory for parking.

It's meant to remind you of Venice.

Movement between the 2,500 houses, two squares, 30-odd bars and restaurants and several dozen shops is on foot, via the little wood or stone-clad bridges connecting the little islands, or by the small electric powered boats used as runabouts.

Port Grimaud is an impressive achievement and in many places extremely pretty, but ultimately it is a stage-set. The French, German, Italian and British owners of the huge yachts moored outside the houses are absent for a large part of the year, consigning their properties to resident caretakers.

If the development lacks the soul of a true Provençal village, however, its manifest convenience attracts buyers, including François Spoerry himself. The buildings are acquiring a patina of age, and cigales have begun to chirrup in the main square, adding that quintessential Midi sound-tract to the pastiche.

The town council of Grimaud, meanwhile, has been planning a major extension to the site, to be designed jointly by François Spoerry and the equally famous modern urbanist Ricardo Bofill, with an eye on the year 2020. By that time, they confidently assert, the Var will have become "the Florida of Europe". ∎

ST-RAPHAËL/FRÉJUS

If the Fréjus/St-Raphaël region is rather overshadowed by world-famous neighbours such as St-Tropez to the west and Cannes to the east, it is by no means totally eclipsed. Economically and demographically, the area is booming - the local population, rate of employment and small business sector all grew substantially in the 1980s and 1990s.

In Fréjus, it possesses a visible Roman architectural heritage of national importance as well as a medieval centre the equal of any on the Riviera. And the wild forested hills of the Massif de l'Estérel, by ensuring that a large tract of the interior remains undeveloped, has assisted this easternmost part of the department of the Var (which surrounds the Alpes-Maritimes just south of Cannes) to retain its reputation as the green *département*. Even the coast, while built-up and crowded in summer, is relatively lightly so.

The Fréjus/St-Raphaël conurbation may be reached inland from Cannes via a sprint down the A8 autoroute (*la provençale*), a slightly longer but still brisk drive along the pretty winding Route Nationale 7 just south, or via the Corniche de l'Esterel road (N98) which twists along a narrow strip between the sea and the steep red rock edges of the massif. The corniche road, and the railway line it approximately accompanies, pass beside a succession of coves, small beaches and villages surrounded by a scarcely interrupted fringe of villas, hotels, restaurants and campsites: in July and August the traffic is heavy, if not as bad as in the Ste-Maxime–St-Tropez stretch further to the west. To one side rear the red porphyry peaks of the **Pic de l'Ours** and the **Pic du Cap Roux**. To the other, the sea is dotted with little islets, forming part of the same ancient rock mass.

At the eastern edge of the Massif de l'Estérel, just beyond Cannes, is **La Napoule**, in effect a sea-front extension of the mimosa centre and Cannes-satellite, Mandelieu. La Napoule possesses three sandy beaches, a leisure port, a magnificent view across the Golfe de Napoule to Antibes from the top of St-Peyré hill (a half-hour climb from the centre) and the **Château de la Napoule**, an arts foundation set in a (visitable) converted medieval castle filled with the idiosyncratic sculptures of the American artist/philanthropist Henry Clews, whose grandson Christopher now runs the château.

The series of increases of building density which follow along the coast – for this is what the formerly separate villages have become – are distinguishable from each other by features such as a 19th-century soap factory turned château at **Théoule**, or a deeper than average natural harbour in the former Roman port of **Agay**, where there is a lovely bay shaded by pines and red cliffs. Just beyond Agay, covering the long slope of the hillside above the wide beach of **Dramont** (a key landing-point of the American 7th Army in August 1944), is a development which symbolises the nadir of the rampant over-build-

ing of the 1970s and '80s, but which may also represent its belated check. **Cap Estérel**, a vast, self-contained concrete "Provençal village" of holiday apartments, centred around a pair of stadium-sized, screamingly blue swimming-pools, was obliged to stop construction in July 1991 when the Nice regional tribunal revoked building permission, a landmark decision in an area long milked with impunity by French hotel and property companies.

As in even the most densely touristed places, however, oases of calm subsist, surprisingly near to the beaten track. At **Boulouris**, a resort of pine-shaded villas just outside St-Raphaël, the **Plage D'Arène Grosse**, tucked behind the garish hotel complex of Le Toukan, is a pleasant spot to sip an evening apéritif and watch the pin-prick shimmer of lights on the far-off dark bulk of the St-Tropez promontory. A sea-front walk here, similar to the Chemin des Douaniers (Customs Officers' Path) across the bay at St-Aygulf, is also pretty and (relatively) quiet. The gardens of a

series of large, elegant villas stretch down to the edge of the path, with their umbrella pine and yuccas. On the benches against the walls, elderly couples sit looking out to sea, and the occasional dog races in and out of the gentle waves lapping on the flat rocks and little stretches of sand.

Even the earliest citizens of **St-Raphaël** came looking for sea air and relaxation. They were wealthy Romans from the important naval and military settlement of Fréjus, and they built terraced villas decorated with mosaics close enough to enjoy the restorative properties of the sea; the same motive is as strong as ever today. One of the first buildings you encounter on entering the town along the coast road is the big white Centre de Thalassotherapie (seawater cures). Next to it is a modern Palais de Congrès (conference centre) and the serried ranks (1,800 berths) of the new yacht harbour, observed from a couple of hundred metres offshore by the two distinctive rocks, the **Lion de Mer** and the **Lion de Terre**, which

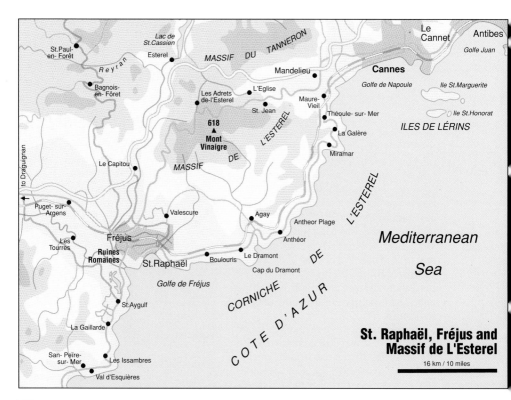

St. Raphaël, Fréjus and Massif de L'Esterel

16 km / 10 miles

explain St-Raphaël's occasional description as the "Town of the Lions".

A little further on, along the **Boulevard du Général de Gaulle** and the **Promenade de Lattre de Tassigny**, are the luxury shops and the handful of turn-of-the-century hotels and apartment blocks which lend the town its air of a little Cannes. Curlicued art nouveau balconies, the moulding painted pistachio and cream, look out over the tall palms which line the raised promenade.

At the end of this sweep of passable Riviera elegance stands the **Casino**, in front of the dome of the late 19th-century church of **Notre-Dame-de-Victoire**, the two main features (with a large pink block of flats characteristically obscuring both) which mark out the town if approached from the sea. The Casino shares its evening roulette and *chemin de fer* rooms with a new all-day *bandits manchot* (one-armed bandit) salon, where paisley bow-tied attendants supervise the 98 machines recently authorised for installation. It represents St-Raphaël's most recent mass

tourism phase, as well as the town's heyday of bourgeois gentility, and its earliest origins, too, as the Casino site was occupied by the first Roman settlement.

In the Middle Ages, the settlement was sacked by the Saracens; it was re-inhabited by monks from Marseille, placed under the protection of the Knights Templar and subsequently attracted a small fishing and agricultural community. In 1799, Napoleon entitled St-Raphaël to one of its rare entries in the history books by disembarking there on his return from Egypt.

In the 1860s the celebrated Parisian journalist Alphonse Karr moved along the coast from already-crowded Nice and began to invite down the advance guard of metropolitan intellectual trendsetters (including writers Alexandre Dumas and Maupassant, and composers Berlioz and Gounod) who, rapidly augmented by rich English, made St-Raphaël a fashionable resort. In 1864, the arrival of the railway provided a major boost (the modern station with its

Notre-Dame-de-Victoire and the Casino, St-Raphaël.

abstract stained-glass roof panels is still a magnet for the younger end of the summer clientèle over a century later).

The so-called "old port" in front of the Casino is another construction of the late 1800s. It is now home to a small fishing fleet, a number of pleasure-craft, the occasional visiting naval vessel, also small, and the regular ferry service to Ste-Maxime and St-Tropez. (The 50-minute journey to the latter is the pleasantest, and in August the fastest, way of getting there.) The fishing boats' daily catch is on sale between 7.30am and midday at the wood-beamed fish market on the **Place Ortolan**. Close beside, the simple traditional restaurant La Bouillabaisse, with its check tablecloths and ivy-covered terrace, is an excellent place to consume good value bouillabaisse and langoustes.

Running along two sides of the square port basin, the **Cours Jean-Bart** with its stone benches and double row of big plane trees is the night-time centre for strolling and sitting at café terraces consuming beers, lurid ice-cream confec-tions and cocktails. Entertainment is provided in the high season by the usual panoply of itinerant pavement artistes, street performers, Senegalese fake Louis Vuitton pedlars, and, in some of the cafés, resident entertainers on Yamaha keyboards. At its western end, marked in summer by a plastic reproduction 18th-century Venetian fairground car-ousel, the bustle of activity merges with that of Fréjus Plage, which is much the same minus any trace of the architec-tural grace of the Cours Jean-Bart.

St-Raphaël is not a town of monu-ments. Traces of its Roman past are restricted to a substantial collection of amphora in the **Musée Archéologique**, most of which have been obtained by local diving teams from the sea. The museum also contains prehistoric mate-rial as well as documents and photos of the 19th century, Alphonse Karr memo-rabilia, and so on.

In the pretty, but minuscule, old town, nestled five minutes' walk behind the old port, the 12th-century **Église St-Raphaël**, from which the town took its

St-Raphaël beach.

name, provides a link with the period of the Knights Templar. The small, plain, single-nave church was used as a fortified refuge in case of attack by pirates, as its military-looking watchtower may suggest.

In the leafy hillside suburbs to the north and east of the town centre are the Edwardian-Provençal villas surrounded by gardens built for the early moneyed English visitors. These are concentrated particularly around the suburb of **Valescure**, with its large golf course whose perimeters feature an increasingly common Riviera combination – golf facilities and holiday flats – in developments such as Valescure's Résidence Le Birdie.

If present-day signs of St-Raphaël's medieval past are limited, and of its Roman past virtually non-existent, the reverse is true of **Fréjus**. The larger town (40,000 inhabitants as opposed to St-Raphaël's 30,000) retains extensive remains from the period during which it was second only to Marseille in size and importance as a Roman military port. Its medieval centre bears even more visible and impressive testimony to its status in the early Christian world; Fréjus was a bishopric as early as AD 374 and remained one until 1957 when the diocese was merged with that of Toulon. Though Fréjus lost its maritime functions in the 10th century as the sea receded, it has responded to the demands of 20th-century tourism by acquiring two offshoots radically different in style from the old town, and both closer to St-Raphaël.

Fréjus Plage is a 1960s and '70s development of apartment blocks and hotels running the length of a fine flat sandy beach bordered to the east by the old port of St-Raphaël and to the west by the new yacht basin of Port Fréjus. Its attractions are by day quite simply the beach, which is separated from the accommodation by the quadruple line of parked cars along a beach-level promenade, and by night the numerous cafés, shops and stalls which stay open, and thronged, until 1 or 2am, along with two discotheques. Fréjus Plage thus constitutes the newer, brasher end of a con-

tinuum which reaches its "classiest" point a mile east on St-Raphaël's Promenade de Lattre de Tassigny.

Port Fréjus, whose new harbour was inaugurated in 1989, is a mixed-investment development designed to provide accommodation for 10,000 people and mooring for 700 yachts of up to 100 ft (30 metres). Its first constructions, rather hopefully described as "neo-Palladian", are six- and seven-storey apartment blocks set on wide, concrete quays with restaurants and shops at ground level. If Port Fréjus is symptomatic of the dynamic and expansionist future, it also aims to relate to the conurbation's ancient past. Port Fréjus is at the mouth of the original Roman port, which was connected to a second basin inland beside the settlement of Forum Julii by a broad, half-mile long canal. The aim is to re-excavate this channel as the final stage of Port Fréjus and thus to return to Fréjus town the sea access it lost to Saracen depredations and silt.

Fréjus was founded by Julius Caesar as a stopping place on the route (the

Aurelian Way) heading ultimately to Spain. It was rapidly expanded into an important military port by Augustus Octavius, and at its Roman zenith had as large a population – around 40,000 – as it has today. Its Roman remains are no less interesting for being dispersed throughout the town. Just beyond the enclosed remains of the **theatre**, for example, a sizeable chunk of Roman wall sits incongruously in the middle of a council housing estate. The 2,500-capacity theatre is largely destroyed, but the low remaining section is used, with scaffolding benches, for concerts.

Major Roman remains include the base of the western citadel, known as the **Butte St-Antoine**, which connects via a partly-ruined wall to the stump of a tower, the "**Lanterne d'Auguste**". This structure once held a flame marking the entrance to the port, and at night was the anchor point for an iron chain across the canal which denied access from the sea. Other important remains are the **Porte d'Orée**, a decorative arched entrance, probably once to the baths, the **aqueduct**, which once supplied the whole city with running water from the river Siagnale 25 miles (40 km) away, and of which a large and impressive section straddles the road at the junction between the N7 and the autoroute *péage* link, and the **arena**, just outside the centre of the town.

The Fréjus arena, half resting against a grass knoll, has suffered from centuries of stone looting, and is neither as large nor as sumptuous as those at Nîmes or Arles, being designed for a simpler, lower-class audience, primarily soldiers and townspeople rather than the rich or elevated. Its huge sandstone arches loom out of the bushes and lawns of a small park just outside the old town centre, as though they have survived years of mortar attack unbowed. The arena is in regular use for rock concerts and, several times a year, corridas. Fréjus is, in effect, the most easterly outpost of bullfighting in France, although its taurine life is not booming, like that of Nîmes, but rather in the same state of decline – diminishing audiences, poor quality **Fréjus** *corridas* – as its fellow seaside bull- **fountain.**

fighting town, Les-Stes-Maries-de-la-Mer further down the coast. The final substantial Roman remains, the large, level area of miscellaneous masonry known as the **Plateforme**, of which the only intact item is a vaulted subterranean water reservoir, are scheduled for excavation and fuller display.

The old central area of Fréjus has considerable charm, particularly by contrast with the brashness and the crowds of summertime St-Raphaël and Fréjus Plage. This is due partly to its handsome architecture and partly to its slightly elevated position, looking out over the flower and fruit smallholdings of the flat Plaine area to its west. At the centre of the old town is the **Quartier Episcopal**, a medieval complex comprising the 12th-century, double-naved **Cathedral**, the small stone **baptistry**, one of the oldest in France dating originally to the 5th century, and the lovely two-storey **cloister** with its ceiling composed of 1,200 little square painted wooden tiles. Visits to the baptistry and cloister must be conducted, and are worth

waiting for, as both are fascinating, particularly the tall, narrow, sombre octagonal baptistry with its separate entry and exit doors, octagonal baptismal pool and dolium for liturgical oil. The cloister, by contrast, with its white marble columns, central tile-roofed well and laurel bushes, is pretty and sunny. The collection of Roman and early Ligurian tiles, mosaics and sculptures in the archaeological museum off the cloister includes the fine double-faced head of Hermès, discovered in 1970, which Fréjus has made its symbol. In front of the carved door to the baptistry and the facade of the **Hôtel de Ville**, formerly the Bishop's Palace, which adjoins it, the **Place Formigé** is used for public entertainment in the summer – a military brass band plays on a tree-shaded podium there on Sunday mornings.

Round the corner, the larger triangular **Place Paul Albert Février** contains the prettiest open-air restaurants, though not necessarily those with the best cuisine; nonetheless, tables can be hard to obtain by 9pm in summer. The Saturday

12th-century cloisters, Fréjus.

market (local peaches and roses a Fréjus speciality) takes place on the square. The other main centre of café life, the **Place de la Liberté**, with its fountain and four big plane trees, is the best place for coffees, mid-afternoon beers, apéritifs and midnight café-cognacs. Much later Fréjus closes down, and you have to head down to the sea-front.

The streets and alleys surrounding the pedestrianised medieval centre and the Rue Jean Jaurès, which circles downhill through town bearing a constant stream of traffic, are extremely pretty, with numerous ornate doorways, cats peering through lace curtains and geranium-clad windowsills. A brief pause at the Tourist Office at the beginning of the Rue Jean Jaurès to pick up a free copy of the leaflet *Fréjus, Ville d'Art et d'Histoire* is recommended: the publication contains good, concise photographic details of the best facades and doorways to look at in the old town.

An enjoyable stroll just outside the town centre might also take in the lovely 1906 **Villa Marie**, now the public library, in its garden, and the slightly older Palladian style **Villa Aurélienne**, set in an even finer small park. Ten minutes' drive outside town on the N7, the small circular chapel of **Notre-Dame-de-Jerusalem** was designed by Jean Cocteau in 1961 and the beautiful cool, blue and pastel murals inside are among the poet's last work.

Two other architectural curiosities just outside Fréjus are connected with the town's continuing military tradition – it is home to 3,000 men of the Fourth and Twenty-First Marine Regiments, who formed the core of the Daguet Battalion sent to the Iraqi border in 1990–91. Both buildings acknowledge the role of troops from France's former colonies. The **Missiri mosque** is a replica of the Soudan style of Northwest Africa, while a **Buddhist pagoda** commemorates France's Vietnamese operations.

The interior of the Massif de l'Estérel is easily explored by car, with walks of between half an hour and an hour and a half on scrub-surrounded paths to reach the panoramas available from the tops

Roman remains, Fréjus.

of the main peaks: the **Pic de l'Ours**, **Pic d'Aurelle** and **Pic du Cap Roux** via the D37 out of St-Raphaël; further inland **Mont Vinaigre**, with its old watch tower, via the RN7. Both roads wind prettily through a landscape of low but massive hills, with open stretches of scented thyme, thistle broom and eucalyptus interrupting the wooded expanses of cork oak and chestnut.

By the side of the RN7, in the lee of the forested Mont Vinaigre and a couple of miles from the simple and attractive village of **Les Adrets**, is the **Auberge des Adrets**, an 18th-century former coaching inn once patronised by the local highwayman Gaspard de Besse.

Further inland, the D837 road through Les Adrets crosses the autoroute and shortly afterwards arrives at the **Lac de St-Cassien**, an extensive stretch of water, still relatively wild in aspect but heavily patronised by fishermen, picnickers and dinghy sailors in summer. Northwest of Fréjus, the N7 main road follows the valley of the River Argens through flat, flower and vegetable culti-

vated fields, gradually climbing through vineyards – this is the eastern extremity of the region of the Côtes-de-Provence appellation and rockier olive, pine and oak groves.

The most substantial villages on the way to **Draguignan**, the former departmental capital 20 miles (30 km) inland from Fréjus, are **le Muy**, with its medieval centre and 16th-century parish church, and **Trans**, with its unusual little 18th-century town hall, perched on the edge of the deep boulder-strewn bed of the small River Nartuby, and its dubious distinction of possessing the only McDonald's in the region. **Draguignan** itself is the biggest army base in France. It is a solid, pleasant country town with several attractive hotels (including the extraordinarily preserved Grand Hôtel Berton, with its dowdy but intact 1930s to 1950s interior decor) and a beautiful old centre around the market place with a 17th-century Tour d'Horloge. Just beyond Draguignan is the Pierre de la Fée (the Fairy Stone), a huge dolmen.

Massif des Maures.

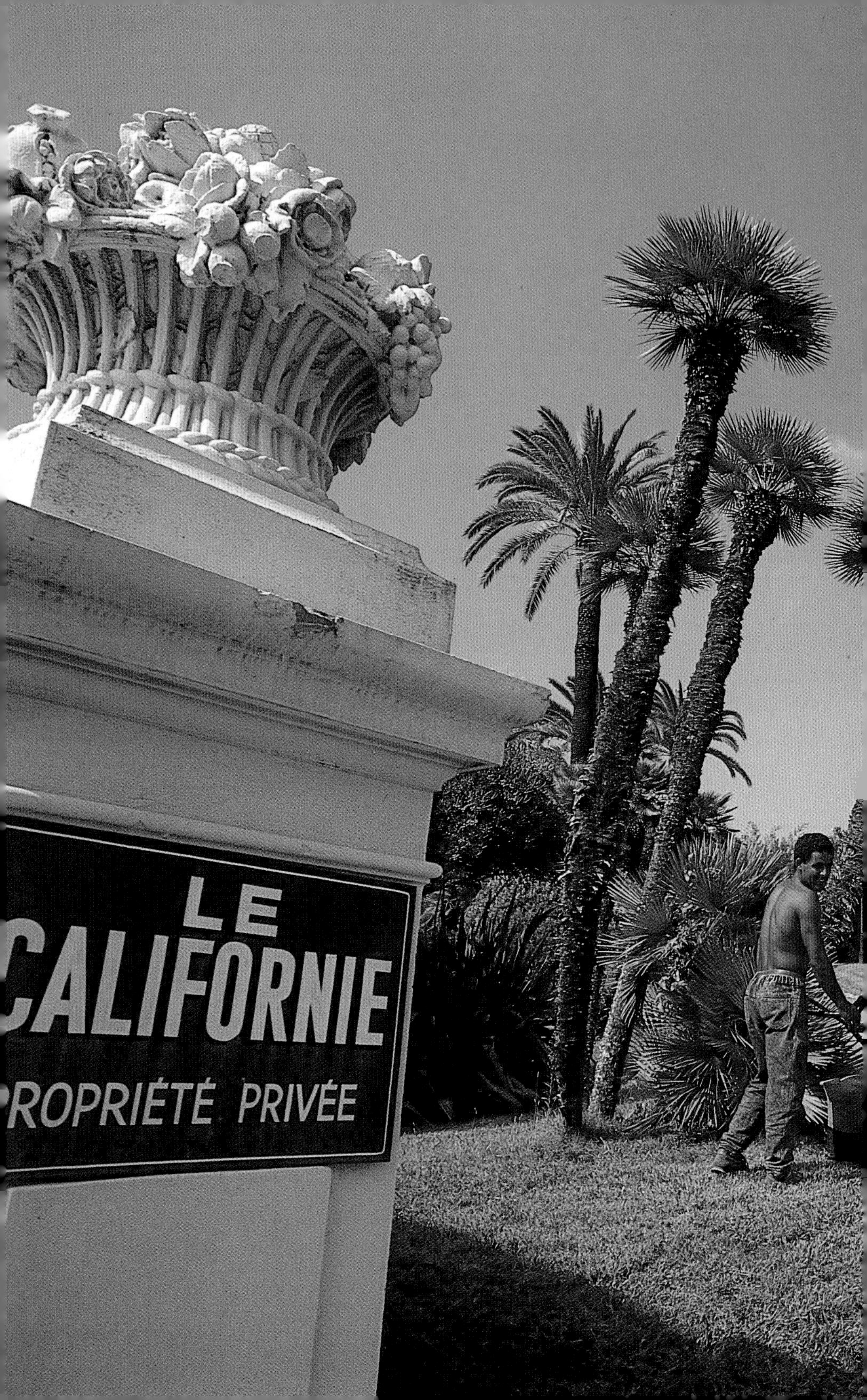
LE
CALIFORNIE
ROPRIÉTÉ PRIVÉE

CANNES

"Cannes: Côte d'Azur. Some gleaming town of rose and white, there where the Alps like elephants come down to kneel beside the calm and azure sea. On the sky and the water lies a hard glaring glaze of gold. The Mediterranean, level and smooth, lips the shore with a slow rise and fall of sound like the breath of a sleeper – a gentle insistent rhythm – brushing the beach with sound. The cactus clumps (aloes) like spiky octopi. The palms that stud the Croisette at Cannes with tignasse tufts and thick pineapple stems. At night the pale dark peppered with stars like the finest of silver tinsel. The last soft red streamers of the sunset faded behind the gray silhouette of the Estérel, and from the jetty I saw the green trees and the red roofs of the houses that mount the little hill to the square Saracen town grown somber and black above the silver blue-gray water of the harbor, where the little boats were neatly moored in a fringe about the shore: above the boats was the low avenue of lindens and along between their trunks were the lights of the shops."

– Edmund Wilson, *The Twenties. From Notebooks and Diaries of the Period.* Cannes, 1921.

Cannes has undoubtedly developed since Edmund Wilson recorded its charms, but the surprising news is that in a changing world where the character and soul of lesser oases have been swept away in a tide of mass tourism, Cannes sparkles miraculously as a jewelled survivor of a bygone age.

Skirting the skies above Cannes, sumptuous summer palaces still glitter like golden eggs. Here there is a hidden lane – the road to Heaven on Earth – which hardly figures on some maps; a bumpy corniche endowed with hundreds of what the French call chicken-nests, and we know mundanely as potholes. Here is the best view of the city of stars, along the **Corniche du Paradis Terrestre** or, one level higher, on the **Che-min des Collines**. But it is precisely to deter *hoi polloi* that the road has been left unpaved. Much of the wealth up here is Arabian and royal, and you might think their owners would be satisfied with such residences worthy of *A Thousand and One Nights*, but no. If you can afford to live in neighbourhoods with names like **Super-Cannes** and **Californie** you have to think big. Twin marble palaces built in the early 1980s for two brother princelings who never spent a night in them were demolished and resurrected as apartments in classic Palladian style for sale at over £3 million each, including individual swimming-pools. Disgracefully, there was but one, shared, helipad.

Keeping up with the high-rollers takes on new meaning here, where you may find yourself rubbing shoulders with the likes of the Gulf sheikh who frittered away a world-record £8.8 million in one binge at roulette. Certainly, the extent of Cannes' dependence on Arab money has its place in history. When King Fahad ordered a total exodus of holi-

daying Saudis from the Riviera there was such a scramble they only just squeezed aboard two chartered Airbuses. Cannes may seem Elysium to those fleeing the crushing heat of the desert, but neither have its attractions gone unnoticed by the world's hedonists, who have been beating a path to its beaches and casinos since the 1920s. Long before that, even, British royalty and nobility were drawn here like iron filings to a magnet.

Nothing has devalued Cannes' aura of glamour, sophistication or exclusivity. The pristine **Croisette**, with its haughty palms and flower-beds manicured 12 months of the year by 130 full-time gardeners, is the most internationally-recognised of all seafront promenades, yet not one advert for fast food or tanning cream has been allowed to sully its Edwardian elegance.

True, a new Hilton now stands in place of the old Palais des Festivals, where Vadim launched Bardot. But the wedding-cake facade of the **Carlton Hotel** only a few yards away has barely changed in over 80 years, complete with its twin pepper-pot cupolas modelled on the breasts of La Belle Otero, a famous courtesan of the period. It symbolises Cannes just as much as Big Ben does London, its name a synonym for comfort and grace.

A minor breach of these tasteful standards was noted when the city twinned itself with Beverly Hills to celebrate its links with the film industry. But nobody was really scandalised and life quickly reverted to what passes for normal out on the Carlton Terrace, where even pet poodles have their own Hollywood-style Doggies' Bar. Sighs of relief were heard when another twinning operation took place, this time with London's Royal Borough of Kensington and Chelsea. Cannes is most definitely not Tinseltown-on-Sea. At heart it is a sweetly modest provincial resort, more like a sub-tropical Hastings if anything, with about the same number of inhabitants (around 75,000). The difference is that it is as cosmopolitan as Paris and almost as rich in terms of personal

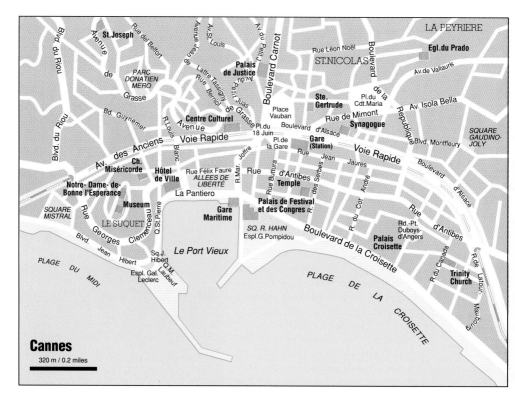

Cannes

320 m / 0.2 miles

wealth, for many of these residents are Parisians with second homes.

It guards some delightfully down-to-earth secrets nevertheless. Take, for instance, the fishing boats, or *pointus*, with their nets piled up in the **Old Port** within hailing distance of the vast concrete bunker of the **Palais des Festivals**. The dazzling white hulls, shining brass and polished teak of greater vessels sharing this little basin dwarf them, and the fishermen themselves are becoming fewer and fewer each year like an endangered species, now that 7,000 registered craft are based in these waters.

These status symbols belong to some of the world's richest individuals, or corporations. Yet the *manja pei* (literally, "fish-eaters") still chug past them to bring in their catch in the early dawn. Strange Mediterranenan fish with names like *rascasse, rouquier* or *blavier*, some of which have poisonous, spiny fins and are best enjoyed in a bouillabaisse on the quay, flip and flop as they have always done.

The rose-tinted night.

The last vestiges of the fishing village of pre-Victorian days can still be seen from the **Quai St-Jacques**, and in a little lane no wider than an ox cart only a minute's walk away you can still find *coquillages* spilling from the fishmongers' open-air displays.

Time has not changed these salty scents, nor can it the smell of chickens roasting in a coating of Provençal herbs that wafts down the lane. **Rue Meynadier**, always a boisterous pedestrian thoroughfare, is where Le Tout Cannes shops for the best home-made pasta, the freshest cheese, and the most mouth-watering delicacies its master *traiteurs* can produce.

Around the corner in the **Marché Forville** smallholders from the back country bring their produce to market proudly marked with the name of the village of origin instead of some new-fangled notion of a "sell-by" date. Nobody has to ask. It is always dew-fresh. Their clamorous cries and good-natured banter fill a pitch half the size of a football field with their twanging Provençal accents.

This festival predates the film festival by 100 years. Long before the stars lived in Beverly Hills its French twin's roots were firmly established in the dark red earth of the Midi. Here they run a continuous performance – a free spectacle for the eyes, ears and nose.

They say the Duke of Windsor, when he was Prince of Wales, deliberately gave his bodyguards the slip on one of his many visits to Cannes in the 1930s. There was panic, of course, and for hours they scoured all his favourite haunts: the casinos, the *boules* pitch on the **Allées de la Liberté**, the restaurants of the **Rue Félix Faure** and the flower stalls facing them, all in vain. Friends and courtiers combed the best hotels, the beaches and boutiques of the fashionable **Rue d'Antibes**.

Finally, someone had the wit to eschew the ritzy side of life and investigate the market and the Old Port. There, in the back lanes, he found the future King of England sitting in the sun outside a tiny *auberge*, eating sea urchins in garlic sauce. Pleased with himself for his few hours' freedom as a commoner, the Prince looked up and said (according to local history, which must have had a reporter present): "Cannes is like a beautiful woman. Charming, but full of secrets." How much *aïoli* he had consumed by that stage is certainly not recorded.

This is the oldest part of town, **Le Suquet,** still with secret alleys, passages and half-hidden *auberges* and bistros. Its hill and its moorings date from Roman times (they named the site Canoïs Castrum because of the reeds and canes growing there). The landmark **Tower** at its summit dates from the 11th century, however, and was built by the monks of Lérins to guard against Saracen attack. From the **Place de la Castre** you can appreciate its commanding view all along the shore and back to the hill of La Californie, but to get this far is an achievement. These cobbled lanes are steep and narrow and the temptation to emulate the Prince has spelled the ruin of many a latter-day photo expedition.

Another secret Edward must have

The pristine Croisette.

remarked upon lies in the city's residential streets away from the front. Mrs Simpson took sanctuary in a villa here when the King was preparing to abdicate, and they planned to move into one of their own which they rented on a 10-year lease but never took up because of the outbreak of war.

Now, these same bourgeois houses built at the turn of the 19th century are nervously lying in wait for the century to turn once again. They do well to veil their charms behind sentinel palms and wisteria-entwined pergolas, for like the fishermen they too are a dying species. They are the last bastions of the *belle époque*, under siege in a less-mannered age when site values are appreciating faster than the properties standing upon them. The approach of the third millennium has brought soaring land prices in these desirable neighbourhoods and no matter how sweetly they evoke a lost chapter of history, it counts for little with unsentimental property developers who are changing the face of Cannes remorselessly.

Closing a deal?

How it has changed. Three roads with fishermen's houses, the tower of La Castre and an inn serving bouillabaisse were all there was to Cannes before a chance incident altered its destiny late in 1834. Fatigued after six years as Lord Chancellor of Great Britain (where among other achievements he championed the abolition of slavery), Henry, Lord Brougham, resigned and set off from London with his sickly daughter Eleonore in search of a mild climate on the Riviera, where the British were already making their presence felt in increasing numbers.

He intended to go to Nice, travelling in a six-horse berlin as far as the River Var which then formed a formidable frontier between Provence (France) and the Kingdom of Sardinia (Italy) - though this stretches the imagination today, looking at the unremarkable trickle that skirts Nice airport. However, he found more than a raging torrent barring his way. Soldiers refused to let him through as cholera had broken out in Provence. They forced him to turn back, first to

Antibes which displeased him, then to Cannes where an inn which had previously accommodated Victor Hugo and Pope Pius VII proved more to his liking. Brougham was so captivated by the countryside that within a week he had bought a plot of land and built the **Villa Eleonore** to the west of Le Suquet along the Fréjus road. It still stands, tastefully converted into flats, on Avenue Docteur Picaud.

So began the Anglicisation of Cannes. Other rich and influential British visitors soon followed, encouraged to find an alternative winter retreat to Nice where an "inferior class" was establishing itself, and a highly cultivated society took root. Quite literally, it seems: they even had their new villas' lawns relaid annually with turf brought from England by boat. Brougham extracted one million francs out of King Louis-Philippe – 33 times the town's municipal budget – to fund a new harbour where it could dock.

Royalty was not far behind. Though Queen Victoria did not disdain Nice, it was here, 18 miles down the coast, that her sons Leopold, Duke of Albany, and Edward, Prince of Wales, discovered the more entertaining aspects of Riviera life. Poor Leopold, who was a haemophiliac, vaguely remembered for having introduced croquet to the coast, died after falling down stairs at Cannes' Cercle Nautique. Edward (later King Edward VII) on the other hand is hugely famed for having indulged his appetite for gambling, tobacco, food and sex.

Cannes today still has streets that bear the names of Sir Walter Scott, Lord Byron, Shakespeare and Milton. A much-praised hospital called Sunnybank administers to resident English-speakers' medical needs. La Côte d'Or, in the Rue d'Antibes, purveys everything from bacon and kippers to kedgeree and curry paste. The Cannes English Bookshop, in the same street, takes care of more cerebral requirements.

Brougham died in 1868, two years before the railway came to town and spelled the end of an idyll. A statue of him stands in the **Allées de la Liberté,** **Read all about it.**

not far from another, of Edward VII, as if emphasising the diverse roles which the British have played in the city's history. Today the whole area turns into a flea market every Saturday morning.

What of Cannes today: its conventions and congresses, its beaches, its shopping, its "Season"? Everyone knows "the Festival": two star-spangled weeks in May when the movie world turns this dowager resort into a painted lady, starlets cavort topless on the sands and big deals are clinched by moguls clenching big cigars in their even bigger teeth. The images are the same every year and their ritualism would be dismissed as quaintly amusing but for the revenue – around £3 million – the event generates.

Casual it may seem, but behind the scenes a huge effort goes into ensuring that those 50,000 people visiting this affair, with all its hype and hoopla, are not disappointed. Those golden sands, for instance, are raked and disinfected fastidiously every day, and on the private beaches are groomed to perfection before the *beau monde* gathers for cocktails beneath pastel-coloured parasols.

Likewise the floral arrangements. The municipality grows 400,000 bedding-out plants a year and out on the Croisette they are replanted every spring, summer, autumn and winter. Notice, too, how the streets are mercifully free of parking meters – scrapped years ago in favour of "pay and display" ticket dispensers powered by solar energy. Cleaning crews on motorbikes with high-pressure vacuum pipes are meanwhile supposed to eliminate that other pavement peril left behind by dogs, not always successfully.

Nature also deserves an Oscar in Cannes' success story. In February and early March mimosa spreads yellow fire across its hills. Boughs of mauve wisteria snake around its old ochre facades in April. Gardens burst with oleander pinks in summer and for much of the year splashes of purple and red bougainvillaea everywhere are taken almost for granted.

Lord Brougham's mild climate has

Cannes street chic.

not changed much despite global warming. October to January is usually dry and rewardingly sunny and when it does rain it rarely sets in for days. Even in the off-season it is possible to sit outdoors to sample the mountains of seafood available along the Rue Félix Faure, where the restaurants tuck in together like pearls on a string.

The city has more than its share of sophisticated Riviera socialites who will shop only in the designer boutiques of the Rue d'Antibes – Rodeo Drive, if you must – or at the exclusive haute couturiers of the Croisette, which serve as clubs for the fashion-conscious 12 months of the year. Entrance is free, but please bring your traveller's cheques. This city does not nurture its image for the faint of heart or light of pocket.

Even out on the street everyday citizens seem dressed to kill, from miniskirted *Cannoises* who carry pet Yorkies like fashion accessories to traffic wardens in periwinkle blue uniforms stalking anyone failing to appreciate the nuances of high-tech parking.

The Season, of course, puts a great strain on the city from mid-July until the end of August and many find the crush intolerable, though thousands of other masochists love it here then. The sand disappears under the press of near-naked bodies. "Full" signs go up in restaurants and hotels. The thermometer soars and the hot *mistral* wind can blow to disastrous incendiary effect.

Yet there are three dates which should be marked in everyone's diary as moments of light relief: Bastille Day (14 July), Assumption (15 August) and Liberation Day (24 August). At night, crescendoes of fireworks and classical music burst around the Croisette in a spectacular summer celebration lasting half an hour, provided free by the city council. Each show is different, involving tons of explosives launched from barges, and if you don't have your own personal yacht as a vantage point (some coming into the bay are the size of cross-Channel ferries) there are alternatives. Exceptionally, the beach restaurants which normally close at night offer superb dinners and a front-row seat under a sky that suddenly erupts in a storm of light. Or for a dress circle view you could retreat inland to a hill and watch the pyrotechnics while listening to the music on local radio.

One admirable viewpoint is **Place Bellevue** in the old village of **Le Cannet**, worth a visit for its good-value restaurants and intriguing little lanes where several musical evenings are a big draw in summer. It's a short ride by No. 5 bus. Originally Cannes formed part of the commune of Le Cannet, and the little village still insists on the definite article prefixed to its name.

Across the bay lie the pretty **Îles de Lérins**, noted more for daytime than nocturnal delights though a summer *son et lumière* show on **Ste-Marguerite** is a rewarding excursion and a glass-bottomed boat, *Nautilus*, skulks around its waters at night with its giant underwater searchlights illuminating the seabed. The mysterious Man in the Iron Mask was held prisoner here in Fort Royal from 1687 to 1698. Every day, boats leave regularly for Ste-Marguerite and the

Dining out in Le Suquet, the oldest part of town.

176

smaller island of St-Honorat from the Gare Maritime alongside the Palais des Festivals. Most holidaymakers head for Ste Marguerite where they roam around trying to find a place to picnic in the peace and quiet denied them on the mainland. They are more likely to find it on **St-Honorat**, 437 yards (400 metres) wide and mainly covered by parasol pines, eucalyptus trees and cypresses. St-Honorat has an impressive ecclesiastical history commencing with the monastery originally founded by St Honorat in the 5th century. Ste-Marguerite is named after St-Honorat's sister, who founded a nunnery there.

For hundreds of years St-Honorat was the centre of religious life for the whole of Southern Europe, and was so powerful that it owned much of the land along the Mediterranean coast, including Cannes itself. At one time 3,700 monks lived on the island, and the monastery was responsible for the training of many important bishops, including Ireland's St Patrick. But its wealth meant it was subject to constant raids from pirates, as well as papal corruption, and its decline was inevitable.

The 11th-century tower of the fortified monastery remains, with a chapel and cloisters, and of the seven chapels originally scattered across the island, the Chapel of the Trinity at the eastern end of the island still celebrates mass. In 1869 it was bought by the Cistercians, who built a new monastery on the site of the old one. The museum and church are open to visitors but mainly it is the private domain of the monks who grow lavender, grapes and oranges and are pleased to sell their own honey and Lérina liqueur to visitors.

This is the last secret. Out here on a fine summer's day only the distant jet-wash of planes making their final approach to Nice airport reminds you that the centuries have marched on. It is a negligible price to pay, because a sound as old as time, the *kriii-kriii-kriii* of the cicadas, quickly reasserts itself to convince you that here you have indeed found that elusive prize: a true little corner of Heaven on Earth.

The St-Honorat, remains of 11th-century monastery.

ANTIBES AND PLATEAU DE VALBONNE

Cap d'Antibes has secured its legendary status through the work of Scott Fitzgerald and its popularity with American expatriates in the 1920s and '30s. Although it is sometimes hard to imagine the original attraction of the quiet beaches and clear sea as one sits in a traffic jam in the middle of Juan-les-Pins with disco music blaring and beach shanty towns rising on all sides, it is still possible to discover and understand its special charms and sample its undoubted luxuries.

It must be said, however, that its real pleasures remain reserved for the rich with their *pied dans l'eau* villas, hotels and private beaches, from which they can contemplate the sea in the same exclusive calm enjoyed by Scott and Zelda, forgetting the milling crowds outside. The coast itself is nearly always crowded, and venturing on to a public beach should be done with people-watching firmly a priority; inland the popular towns of Vallauris and Biot also draw crowds of visitors to their craft workshops and glass factories. But even here within a very few miles of the coast the roads are quieter and one can seek respite in charming towns such as Valbonne, Mougins and Mouans-Sartoux. The region is famous for its flower production, in particular roses, carnations and anemones.

Antibes itself is surprisingly untouristy; its venerable history gives it a gravitas which is undeterred by waves of tourism, and the old town offers many instructive sights. Ultimately Antibes is a yachting town, with **Port Vauban** the true centre of Mediterranean yachting. Its inner harbour is home to several hundred vessels and the outer port shelters some of the world's most prestigious yachts on a wide *quai* known as "millionaires' row". The presence of these yachts, and the considerable crew and services required to support them, means that Antibes functions all year round, and is not as limited to seasonal

visitors as are other parts of the coast. Graham Greene, who was a longtime resident, always preferred the winter. In *May We Borrow Your Husband?* he wrote: "Then Antibes comes into its own as a small country town with the Auberge de Provence full of local people and old men sit indoors drinking beer or pastis at the *glacier* in the Place de Gaulle. The small garden, which forms a roundabout on the ramparts, looks a little sad with the short stout palms blowing their brown fronds; the sun in the morning shines without any glare, and the few white sails move gently on the unblinding sea."

The area of interest in Antibes is really quite small so you would be well advised to park in one of the multi-storey car parks as soon as you enter the town (do not forget to keep your ticket with you as you need it to pay before reclaiming the car). A good free map is available from the Maison du Tourisme on the **Place Général de Gaulle**. This used to be the Place Macé and the Maison de Tourism is in what was once the

Grand Hotel and home of the Municipal Casino which opened in 1911.

Antibes, now the third largest town on the Côte d'Azur, began life as the Greek city of Antipolis, "the town opposite", facing the earlier settlement of Nice. The Greeks held only a narrow stretch between the sea and the present **Cours Masséna**; it was a narrow enclosure filled with warehouses and only one gate, entered opposite the present **Hôtel de Ville** on the Cours Masséna at the Rue Pardisse.

The settlement traded with the Ligurian tribes along the coast but did not allow them to enter the city so all dealing took place outside the city walls; the covered market is still located on the Cours Masséna at roughly the same spot. But nothing more, save the name and a few objects in the museum, remains of this distant period.

The Romans, in their turn, built an important city at Antibes and the ruins of the baths, the aqueduct, the circus and the theatre stood until 1691 when Vauban used the stones to construct his massive fortifications. Vauban's ramparts were demolished in 1898 except those which constituted the sea wall; today the **Promenade Amiral de Grasse** runs along the ramparts, beginning at the **Bastian St-André** in the south. This now houses the excellent archaeological museum; two huge barrel-vaulted rooms with a well organised display of Greek, Etruscan and Roman pottery and exquisite examples of Roman glass. The remains include a large collection of amphora, stacked as if in the hold of a Roman galley.

The original Roman camp was built on the ruins of the Greek acropolis, on a terrace overlooking the sea; in the 12th century the **Grimaldi Château** was built on the same site. Many of the Romanesque features remain, including arched windows and the square tower which dominates the old town, though the building was reconstructed in the 16th century. Some of the tiny inner doorways have very attractive carving. The château is now the home of the Picasso Museum and contains a remarkable,

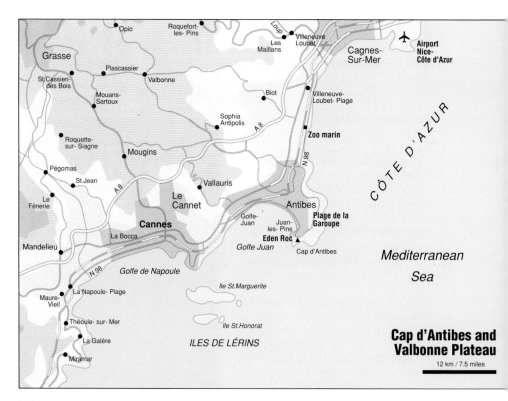

Cap d'Antibes and Valbonne Plateau

12 km / 7.5 miles

unified collection of more than 50 works Picasso executed there in 1946, when he was offered the keys to the château to use as a studio.

He painted solidly for five months, revitalised after spending the war years restricted to his Paris studio. The light and intense colour of the south were immediately incorporated into his work in a series of drawings and paintings of fish, sea urchins, goats, stars and the sea shore. He was captivated by the antiquity of the Mediterranean. Standing on the terrace of the ancient castle the site of a Greek acropolis, a Roman castrum, the residence of the Bishops of Antiboul and the 16th-century Grimaldi, he invented a mythological cast of characters to inhabit his drawings and paintings: a faun, often playing the double flute of antiquity, a bearded centaur (undoubtedly himself) and a beautiful nymph, sometimes dancing with a tambourine (Françoise Gilot).

The paintings and drawings of these figures eventually resulted in a major work, *La Joie de Vivre*, which symbol-

ised his entire stay in the château. The fishermen provided another source of inspiration, as they had done before the war in his huge painting *Night Fishing at Antibes*. Some of these, such as *Man Gulping Sea Urchins* are on canvas and later x-ray photographs revealed that Picasso, holding the keys of the château, had raided the storerooms and painted over what he regarded as mediocre 19th-century paintings. It was also here that Picasso painted the *Antipolis Suite*, a series depicting highly stylised, pared-down nudes, often reclining.

In an unusual act of generosity, Picasso left virtually everything to the museum in which they were created. Now on display are 27 paintings, 44 drawings, two sculptures, 50 engravings (mostly from the Vollard Suite) and 75 original ceramics – a major collection and in fact the first permanent collection devoted to the work of a living artist. It is supported by works of tribute by other artists, photographs and documentation.

The museum also has one of the larg-

Port Vauban and Fort Carré.

est collections of the work of Nicolas de Staël, who lived in Antibes and also painted in the château. There is an important collection of the modern Nice School of César, Arman, Spoerri, Klein and others. Provision is made for the blind with paintings reproduced in a form of braille (with braille explanations alongside).

The château was bought by the city of Antibes in 1925, and founded as the **Museum of Art, History and Archaeology**. Among its numerous Roman artefacts is one which gives an evocative glimpse of Antibes' past – the charming 3rd-century Roman stela to the slave child, a dancer named Septentrion, whose Latin funerary inscription reads: "To the Manes of the Child Septentrion aged twelve who at the theatre at Antibes on two days danced and gave pleasure." On the terrace overlooking the ramparts is a series of sculptures by Germaine Richier, César and Miró, in a fragrant Mediterranean garden with the sea providing a dramatic backdrop.

To the north of the château is the old cathedral, the **Church of the Immaculate Conception.** The square Romanesque bell tower is a converted 12th-century watchtower but only the east end remains of the original 12th-century building, the west end being 17th-century rebuilding. The 1710 doors are worth noting. The old town gate with its two round towers on the Cours Masséna survives. The Orme Tower now houses the **Musée de la Tour**, a museum of popular arts and traditions, concentrating on 18th- and 19th-century costumes, furniture and objects.

The ramparts continue past the cathedral to the Vieux Port. Below is the small **Plage de la Gravette**, a sheltered sandy beach, separated from the Vieux Port by the Quai H. Rambaud. From the ramparts there is a gateway to the **Rue Aubernon** where there is a regular flea market. Just around the corner, opposite the gate to the old fishing port, at 50 Boulevard d'Aguillon, is Restaurant Chez Félix, the old-fashioned bistro where Graham Greene took his lunch and often found inspiration. The restau-

The ubiquitous baguette, lunch on the sea wall.

rant remains unchanged, its decor determinedly unpretentious, with flowery tablecloths and a motorcycle parked at the bar. And there is the same proprietor, who will always show you the fish you have ordered before it is cooked.

On the other side of the old port is the massive yacht harbour of Port Vauban, and the imposing mass of the 16th-century **Fort Carré**, where Napoleon was imprisoned fror a time. The old town of Antibes quickly outgrew its medieval walls and expanded inland. The grid of old lanes between Rue James Close and the bus station are worth exploring; here life continues much as it has always done, with washing hanging from windows, pots full of geraniums, and children playing games between the ancient stone walls of the narrow streets.

The **Place Nationale** is the home of the Musée Peynet, whose delightful, somewhat coy drawings have made him a cult figure. In the Place Nationale and many of the narrow streets leading to the cathedral there are lots of restaurants, so this is a popular place to stop for lunch after the morning market (arrive not long after midday to be sure of a table).

Cap d'Antibes is still very much the preserve of those fortunate enough to have villas there, but as a result it has retained much of its charm, and rewards exploration. There is a public beach with golden sand stretching from the **Pointe de l'Ilet** down to the **Port de la Salis**; although not large, it is the only sandy beach this side of the Cap apart from the tiny Plage de la Garoupe. Most of the beach clubs here suffice with wooden decks built out over the rocks, the lack of sand compensated somewhat by the clear waters this far out.

The famous **Plage de la Garoupe** is more of a reference to a beach than anything else. Scott Fitzgerald's description of the "bright tan prayer rug of a beach" is most accurate in calling it a rug, and a fairly moth-eaten one at that. Had Gerald Murphy, the original for Fitzgerald's hero in *Tender is the Night*, known the fate of his quiet little cove he may have been more inclined to cover it

Antibes, the old town.

RIVIERA YACHT-WATCHING

Luxury yachting has always been part of the Riviera legend but in recent years it has become a fully-fledged industry, vital to the region's economy. Nowhere else on earth is there so much extravagant floating real estate in one place. While some harbours – like Cannes or St-Tropez – see the traditional *pointu* fishing boats go happily about their business alongside sleek luxury vessels, the many new ports designed exclusively for private yachts have made the Riviera the uncontested world centre for a new type of craft, dubbed the "megayacht" – fully crewed private vessels over 120 ft (36 metres) long.

Riviera harbours are open to anyone wishing for a closer look at the lifestyles of the rich and famous. Between the Italian border at Menton and the port of Marseille 127 nautical miles (235 km) to the west there are 130 of these harbours, totalling over 52,000 moorings. French Riviera ports shelter a third of the world megayacht fleet of about 3,500 yachts. Yachting occupies 1,500 local businesses, including many small craftsmen and tradesmen, and

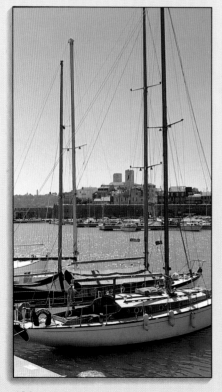

provides 6,000 jobs, not including crew.

Monaco was Aristotle Onassis's favourite harbour, and remains the permanent home-port of his compatriot Stavros Niarcos's *Atlantis*, a vessel of cruise-ship proportions. But Antibes' Port Vauban is the true centre of Mediterranean yachting. The inner harbour is home to several hundred smallish vessels (under 120 ft) but the IYCA (International Yacht Club of Antibes) outer port, built to shelter Adnan Kashoggi's Italian-built 270 ft (80 metres) *Nabila* is now the home of 20 of the world's most prestigious megayachts, berthed with their sterns to the wide quay known as "millionaires' row".

Famous names still frequent Riviera ports but, except in a few cases (terrorism and taxman *oblige*), with cautious discretion. Some of the more flamboyant owners, however, make no secret of their possession and the name of a yacht is often a clue to who her owner could be.

The costs of running one of these boats often means that an entire offshore company is set up to own and manage the vessel, which partly explains the majority of British-flag yachts on the Côte d'Azur. Some of the owners are indeed British, but many are not and are only attracted by British tax law which, given the nation's maritime tradition, is more favourable than in other European countries.

If a taste of the seafaring life sounds tempting, a used 60-ft (18-metre) displacement model can be had for about £1 million. If you want something with a bit more speed or cabin space you should be thinking in the neighbourhood of £3 million. Today, yachts worth more than £20 million are not at all uncommon and you should count on 10 percent of the boat's value as the cost of annual upkeep.

Chartering offers a cheaper solution for those on a budget and the American dollar is the trading currency. For about $4,000 a day you can hire a modest yacht, but if you plan on sailing farther afield or throwing large parties on board you'll need a bigger model at up to $20,000 a day. Prices include yacht and crew but not berthing fees, fuel, food or drink. Sailing is perhaps an overstated term for the activities of many of these yachts, since they seem to spend more time quay-side than they ever do at sea. Sometimes it seems as if their sole purpose is to host ostentatious cocktails on deck for the entertainment of spectators on shore. On the Côte d'Azur more than anywhere else, a yacht truly is a hole in the water you throw money into. ■

A yacht's name often gives a clue to the owner.

up with rocks than painstakingly remove all the seaweed, as he did in the 1920s. Today wooden sundecks on stilts extend the tiny beach out over the rocks with beachclubs charging for the use of a mattress.

In 1923, Gerald and Sara Murphy stayed with Cole Porter in a rented villa on the Cap, then moved to the Hôtel du Cap. "Right out on the end of the Cap there was a tiny beach," wrote Murphy, "the Garoupe – only about forty yards long and covered with a bed of seaweed that must have been four feet thick. We dug out a corner of the beach and bathed there and sat in the sun." The Murphys' constant companions that summer were Picasso and his wife Olga, who liked the area so much that they decided to take a villa in Antibes.

The Murphys decided to settle there and bought a villa with a huge garden just below the lighthouse, naming it the Villa America. While the villa was being remodelled, Gerald was clearing the beach of seaweed at the rate of eight square feet a day. One of the first visitors from the Hôtel du Cap to use it was Rudolph Valentino.

Between the beach at La Sallis and Garoupe, is the rocky outcrop of **Pointe Bacon.** From Garoupe you can walk out to the rocks at Cap Gros, following the cliff path. The **Pointe de l'Ilette** is the southernmost point of the Cap with spectacular rocks and another lighthouse sweeping the night sea.

The coast between here and the **Musée Naval et Napoléonien** is the preserve of the **Hôtel du Cap-Eden Roc**, the most glamorous hotel on the Riviera, popular today with Cannes superstars, including Madonna. It is expensive, of course, but can be visited for drinks or a day at the pool. You can drive in, use the free undercover parking, and stroll through the parasol pines to the restaurant and terrace bar.

It was originally built by the founder of *Le Figaro* newspaper, supposedly as a home for impoverished artists and musicians, but in 1863 was taken over by Russian princes who transformed it into a hotel. It was one of the first luxury

Villa entrance, Cap d'Antibes.

hotels on the Riviera and has always attracted shoals of celebrities, but it remains most famous for being the setting of Fitzgerald's *Tender is the Night*. The Murphys stayed here in 1923 and persuaded the owner to open during the summer, thus launching the Riviera summer season.

Sipping an Americano cocktail on the 1930s-style terrace with its elegant white railings and yellow cushions, watching the colour-coordinated yellow buoys bobbing about in the sea below, is the essence of luxury, as is swimming in the organic, shaped pool cut into the rocks (where mad Zelda used to dive). It is as good a way as any to appreciate the enduring allure of the Côte d'Azur.

Dominating the skyline of the Cap is the **Phare de la Garoupe.** The lighthouse itself is of recent date, since the retreating Germans dynamited the old one in 1944. The chapel next to it, **La Chapelle Notre-Dame-du-Bon-Port**, however, is old, with two naves, one 13th and one 16th-century. Despite its setting amid luxury villas, it is still used by the local people and feels like a small village church.

For centuries seafarers have left votive offerings in the church which now resembles a Portobello Road junkshop of naïf paintings, drawings and medals. To the right of the entrance, low on the wall is an extraordinary drawing of a wrecked car, smoking in a ditch. Its owners pray to God for their survival but unfortunately for their future prospects they are kneeling right in the middle of the road. In front of the chapel is a viewing platform; looking east you can see as far as Cap St Erasmo in Italy and to St-Tropez to the west.

Not far from the chapel and lighthouse, on the Boulevard du Cap, and a fairly easy walk from the public beaches of Antibes or the Casino end of the Plage de Juan-les-Pins, is the **Jardin Thuret**, with its collection of exotic trees and plants, many of which have been successfully introduced to the region. Right next door is the Villa Thenard, where the Grand-Duke Nicholas of Russia died in 1929.

Plage de la Garoupe. Only the beach is missing.

Back up the D2559 to Juan-les-Pins, there is a marina at **Port Gallice** and the tiniest of sandy beaches reaching out to the **Port du Croûton**. The sheltered sandy beaches of **Juan-les-Pins** reach almost this far down the Cap and stretch the full length of the town, providing plenty of space for a frenetic beach life of intensive sunbathing and shoreline promenading; the palpable pleasures which for many visitors fulfil their expectations of the Côte d'Azur. This is also the place for nightlife with its casino and throbbing discos, and lots of people-watching pavement cafés. In July an annual jazz festival is held under the famous pines.

Between Juan-les-Pins and Cannes is **Golfe Juan**. The bay is famous for Napoleon's ill-fated return from exile on Elba in 1815. He apparently met the Prince of Monaco on his way to reclaim his own throne after the Revolution and said to him, "Monsieur, we are in the same business." Napoleon headed north with his troops through the rough terrain of the Alps to Paris. The path he took, via Grasse, Sisteron, Castellane and Digne is now commemorated as the **Route Napoleon**.

On the way into Golfe Juan there was once a strip of 1930s villas, jammed in between the railway and the coast road to Antibes, facing the beach; now predatory tower cranes menace the buildings, and the old villas near the port are being torn down, their gardens uprooted, and in their place is a row of high-rise apartment blocks which will eventually stretch all the way to Juan-les-Pins. The kilometre-long beach, however, remains the same with its elegant line of palms, golden sand banned to dogs, and with a seductive Cap d'Antibes shimmering across the bay.

The part of the old fishermen's port at Golfe Juan which faces the enclosed harbour has not changed much; the traffic on the coast road has always been busy and the fact that the old port is cut off from the main town by the railway tracks has preserved it. After the war Picasso and Françoise Gilot had an apartment overlooking the boats. It was on

the beach at Golfe Juan that Picasso met Susanne and Georges Ramié, owners of the Madoura pottery in Vallauris, an event which was to transform the fortunes of the inland town.

Vallauris is less than three built-up kilometres from Golfe Juan and the coast, and resembles a seaside town with rest homes, private hospitals, and a tourist strip, except in this case, the souvenirs are pots. Vallauris has always been a potters' town, a tradition begun by the Romans and continued by Italian potters fom Grasse, but its fortunes declined drastically and did not improve until Picasso began patronising the Madoura pottery workshop. His output was prodigious, 2,000 pieces in the first year which required a whole team of people to prepare and fire. The pottery was permitted to make limited edition copies of his plates and vases, which they still do, and his presence attracted other artists, including Chagall.

Today Vallauris is one of France's largest pottery centres and virtually the whole of the Rue Clemenceau from the museum to the edge of town is lined with pottery shops. Behind them are the kilns and workshops that produce the pottery, open to the public when in operation (though not at weekends).

A wide variety of pottery is for sale, some of it good value, although sadly much of it is dull and occasionally ghastly. Basic terracotta cooking-pots are worth buying, and the Galerie Madoura is still the best place to shop for high-quality, though expensive pots. There are other crafts available including wickerwork, glass and woodwork, the most interesting is a shop specialising in perfume flasks made from rare woods. There is a small private pottery museum, with a kiln, and a variety of presses and mixes for treating the clay. The "Picasso experience" is fully exploited with photographs and even a wax model of the master at work.

The Vallauris Museum is housed in the château, originally a 13th-century Lérins priory. It is entered through a courtyard shaded by a huge lime tree, with a 1985 Riopelle mosaic on the **Potter at work in Vallauris.**

190

wall. The château was rebuilt in the 16th century and has a round pepperpot tower at each end in the Renaissance style, unusual in Provence. There is also a splendid Renaissance staircase. Of the priory, only the Romanesque chapel survived intact. It is a fine example with barrel vaulted ceiling and round arches.

In 1952, at the request of the town, Picasso decorated it with a huge composition called *War and Peace* painted in his studio on hardboard panels which would bend to follow the curve of the roof. It is by no means Picasso's best work and is not improved by the fact that he neglected to prime his surface so the dull brown of the hardboard shows through the large fields of white paint and scrubbed brushwork. The colours seem to have sunk into the boards, sapping the painting of its vitality. It is worth seeing but *Guernica* it is not.

Picasso's *l'Homme à l'Agneau* in Vallauris.

The museum also contains other work by Picasso: a collection of lithographs on the ground floor and a display of ceramic work, mostly glazed plates and dishes with a few larger painted jugs, produced in a limited edition by the craftsmen of the Madoura pottery to Picasso's designs. Although they carry the usual themes of the bullring, owls and faces, these, too, lack a certain vitality, the touch of the master perhaps. But there are some very good photographs by André Villers of Picasso in Vallauris.

The museum also has six rooms containing the work of Alberto Magnelli (Florence 1888–1971), including some of his important early abstract works from 1914.

Because Picasso saved the town's principal industry, he was made an honorary citizen. In 1950 Picasso in turn presented Vallauris with a life-size bronze statue, *Man Holding A Sheep*, which stands outside the church in the Place Paul Isnard.

Picasso regarded it as an important work: "I did this statue in a single afternoon, but not until after months of reflection and I don't know how many sketches... It was much too weak; it wouldn't hold. The statue began to stagger under the weight of the clay. It was

dreadful! It was threatening to collapse at any moment. I had to do something quickly… We took lengths of cord and lashed *l'Homme à l'Agneau* to the beams. I decided to cast it in plaster immediately. And it was done that same afternoon. What a job! I'll never forget it… I had intended to go back to it, to work on it again. You see those long thin legs, and the feet, just indicated, scarcely separate from the ground? I would have liked to model them, in keeping with the rest. I didn't have the time…"

Picasso connections in the area abound. If you head inland from Vallauris, picking up the D35 to Mougins, you should visit the small chapel of **Notre-Dame-de-Vie** on the way, taking an easily missed turning east on the D3. The one-way lane winds up the hillside and the chapel is reached when the car-park appears on the left, immediately after the sign to the chapel. The 17th-century chapel has an outdoor porch and is on a beautiful site overlooking Mougins. The area is popular for walking and to the south on the same lane, is an entrance with parking to the Parcs de Mougins which border the Parc Départemental de la Valmasque. It is beautiful forest land and very popular for weekend picnics.

Picasso spent the last 12 years of his life in the neighbouring Villa Notre-Dam-de-Vie; it remains extremely well protected, not open to the public or visible from the road, much like most of the expensive villas in this area. The house was a former *mas*, converted before the war into a luxurious villa by Benjamin Guinness, who also paid for the restoration of the chapel.

Mougins itself was also "discovered" by Picasso, along with Francis Picabia in 1936 and they were followed shortly after by Paul Eluard, Man Ray and Jean Cocteau. It is a pretty hill town, surprisingly small, with wonderful views of the Mediterranean, surrounded now by a rash of more recent housing, including some discreet but sumptuous villas. Today Mougins is best known for its restaurants, in particular Roger Vergé's

17th-century chapel of Notre-Dame-de-Vie, near Mougins.

Moulin de Mougins and his famous *"cuisine du soleil"*.

Even if you forswear more serious gourmandising, Mougins is a pleasant place for a stroll and a drink. The site has been occupied since Roman times, and during the Middle Ages was owned by the Abbey of Lérins. All that remains today of the original ramparts is a 15th-century fortified gate, called the Saracen Gate, which originally had a portcullis. The church, L'Eglise St-Jacques-le-Majeur, was begun in the 11th century but has been heavily restored. The bell tower is open to the public; the key is available from the Museum of Photography round the corner. Here there is a good collection of photographs of Picasso by Lartigue, Villiers, Doisneau and others.

Between Mougins and Grasse on the N85 is **Mouans-Sartoux.** The village was reconstructed in the 15th century on a grid plan like nearby Valbonne, with five streets in each direction and space for a pretty square outside the church and facing the castle. The chapel has huge buttresses on its northern side facing the Château Mouans-Sartoux, which has round towers on each corner. There is also a small formal garden and an old well in the middle of a lawn.

It was from this castle that Suzanne de Villeneuve offered obstinate resistance to the Duke of Savoy in 1592 during the War of the League. He destroyed her castle and sacked the village despite the convention signed by the Duke who was in retreat. Enraged, she pursued him, overtaking him at Cagnes. Seizing the bridle of his horse, she reproached him in front of his whole army. Embarrassed, the Duke had 4000 écus indemnity counted out to her on the spot and she returned to rebuild her ruined town.

The Château is now a centre for modern and contemporary art, **L'Espace de l'Art Conoret**, one of the regional venues selected by Jack Lang, the former socialist minister for culture. Next to the car-park is a small chapel with a naïf carved typanum over the door featuring a nativity scene with church, shepherds and dozens of sheep.

The Provençal pastiche of Sophia-Antipolis.

Sophia-Antipolis – or, to give its full name, Parc International d'Activités de Valbonne Sophia-Antipolis – covers an enormous area of the Valbonne plain; miles and miles of new roads have been laid, sympathetically following the gentle contours of the wooded hills.

The development, which accommodates scores of high-tech companies, is much more than just a green-site technical park; it also includes housing, shopping, schools and research institutes, many of them in futuristic modern buildings – horizontal cylinders, mirror pyramids and more.

The Parc is continuing to expand, and a metro link to Nice airport is planned. The success of Sophia-Antipolis reflects the region's determination to become the Silicon Valley of Southern Europe, though the site of eager young American executives jogging along the landscaped roads has an inescapably bizarre quality.

As a result of the Sophia-Antipolis development, nearby **Valbonne** has seen its population increase dramatically. It was laid out in the 16th century by the Lérins monks, on a strict grid four blocks wide and 10 blocks long.

In the centre is a beautifully proportioned arcaded square shaded by old elm trees. The church, built on the river bank just outside the grid, began life as part of an abbey founded by the Chalais order who built it on the shape of a Latin cross. The abbey was taken over by the Lérins and the present building finally became the parish church. Sadly, the building has been very badly restored. The adjoining convent is also being restored by the commune.

The road between Valbonne and Opio passes through pleasant green and shady woodland, shielding an abundance of luxury villas and hotels. **Opio** is a bijou little village, well maintained with painstakingly restored houses and neatly trimmed hedges. Here you can visit the Roger Michel olive oil mill, where you can see the olive-crushing in operation, and buy a variety of olive oil-based products.

Returning to the coast from Valbonne along the D4 is the ancient town of **Biot.** Although tourists are encouraged to visit its potteries and glass making ateliers, parking provision is poor, and you would be well advised to park instead at the foot of the hill near La Verrerie de Tines, one of the glass factories for which Biot is famous, and walk up the hill to the Port des Tines.

The climb, in any case, is a more authentically medieval way to enter the town; a rather run-down cobblestone ramp takes you through the 16th-century Port des Tines and into the old walled village. Here the narrow lanes and *ruelles* house the citizens of Biot in quiet retreat from the tourist-oriented main streets and shops; truly the very best part of Biot.

The Rue de Mitan has a number of untouched examples of medieval shops and the entire quarter has a charm which is missing from some of the more popular hill towns. The Rue Plus Basse, the Rue Basse, the Rue du Mitan and Rue des Orfèvres all run parallel, connected by steep steps that climb the hillside. The closer you get to the church, the

Poodle power.

older the streets and houses become. The Rue de la Vieille Boucherie still has its old butcher's shop with ceramic tiles and metal meat racks hanging in the street outside.

The village centre is the Place aux Arcades, originally the Roman forum, for this was a Roman town. It has two long 13th- and 14th-century arcades either side of an oblong plaza; one later doorway is dated 1579. The 15th-century church leads off the east end of the Place aux Arcades and has one very unusual feature: because of the slope of the ground, the visitor is immediately faced with a flight of 20 steps, leading down into the nave. It is built upon the foundations of an earlier Romanesque church, and rebuilding continued from 1470 until 1655, when the lateral chapels were completed. The old cemetery, just a few streets to the north, is also well worth a visit.

In the Rue St-Sébastien are all the potteries and glass shops, along with cafés, tourist information and a small **A fête at Biot.** local history museum; it is often the only part of Biot visitors ever see, which is a pity.

At the foot of the town, on a small hill, is the National Fernand Léger Museum, conceived by Madame Nadia Léger and the present director George Bauquier and purpose-built to hold Léger's work and archives. It contains a complete cross-section of over 300 works executed between 1905 and 1955. It suffers from the usual problems of "estate museums" in that Leger's greatest works are scattered among the major museums of the world. Though he kept examples of all periods of his work few of them were among the very best.

It would take a retrospective exhibition to show the full range of his achievement and this museum is of the most interest to those who already know his work. Still, there are enough of his early post-Cubist paintings to show his importance, and his gigantic ceramic panels and mosaics exhibited on the exterior walls of the building are a spectacularly colourful sight burnished by the strong sun of the Midi.

PICASSO COUNTRY

Pablo Picasso was the greatest artist of the 20th century: he broke new ground in painting, sculpture, lithography, engraving, pottery and book illustration. He is an all-pervading presence, a bench-mark against which all 20th-century work is measured.

Every phase of his work has been tremendously influential; indeed it has been said that anything painted since the war can be traced back to Marcel Duchamp or Picasso. His sad Blue Period portraiture and wistful Rose Period style have both been widely copied, ultimately by sentimental chocolate-box artists. His Cubism and collages began a line of development from

Schwitters, Miró, Léger, Ernst, Dubuffet, Motherwell, Nevelson, Rauschenberg and the Pop artists to Arman and the School of Nice. De Kooning's women, early Pollock, the work of Henry Moore, Victor Pasmore, Hans Arp, Elizabeth Frink, all show the influence of Picasso.

From day one his life attracted legends. On 25 October 1881, the midwife attending his birth gave him up for dead and turned her attentions to his mother. But his uncle, Don Salvador, blew cigar smoke in his face, thus making the baby cry and saving him from suffocation. It is a classic story of Picasso triumphing over all odds.

His first 10 years were spent in Málaga, where his painter father taught art. His father encouraged his talent until the decisive moment when,

in Picasso's words, his father was so impressed with the work of his 13-year-old son that "he handed me his paint and his brush and never painted again." Picasso entered the La Longa school of art in Barcelona where he skipped the beginner's course. To take an advanced course in classical art, he had to submit a project file within a month. The other students earnestly began their month-long preparations but Picasso handed in his file of far superior work the very next day. A child prodigy, he graduated at the age of 14.

By 1896 he had his own studio and was exhibiting regularly – but the world centre of art was Paris. He took his first studio in Montmartre in 1900, painting life in Paris: old age, loneliness, poverty, and using mostly blues and greens – his "Blue Period". In 1905 he began painting circus acrobats and jugglers – the "Rose Period". By 1907 he made a major breakthrough with *Les Demoiselles d'Avignon* which was essentially the first Cubist painting with the picture plane distorted into flat slabs and the faces simplified into African masks. He and Georges Braque took Cubism to the limit, painting the subject-matter from all angles simultaneously, then went their separate ways. Picasso developed many sides of the technique, from collage to the distortion and abstraction, which irritated so many early critics.

Picasso's love affair with the Riviera first began in 1920 when he spent the summer at Juan-les-Pins; the beach there inspired him to create a series of monumental neoclassical nudes. But it was not until after the war that he moved there permanently. In the pre-war years, he often spent his summers there, returning to Paris for the winter season. In 1923 he painted harlequins in Cap d'Antibes. In the summer of 1924, he painted a series of large still-lifes at Juan-les-Pins and spent most of 1926 and 1927 at Juan-les-Pins and Cannes, working chiefly on etchings, and he continued to visit until 1939 when he made a hurried retreat to Paris as war broke out.

He had been living in Antibes working on a major painting, *Night Fishing at Antibes*, a very large work, 6 ft high and over 10 ft wide (2 by 3 metres), a format he used only for important subjects. This painting summed up many of his feelings about the Riviera, a luminous nocturnal seascape with the fishermen and their boats illuminated by white acetylene lamps – a common sight in the Mediterranean. It turned out to be more of a leave-taking than a summing-up for he was not to see the Riviera again for six years. Picasso openly refused to collaborate with the Nazis during the Occupation of France.

In 1946 he left Paris to settle in the Riviera for good, going first to Antibes. Here was the same intense light and warm Mediterranean lifestyle as his native Spain, to which he could not return while Franco remained in power. He responded to the clear silhouettes of the mountains, the hard shadows and bright luminous colours. Though he rarely painted a traditional landscape – his paintings are almost always populated – he responded to the familiar. At Vallauris in 1953, for instance, he painted 13 variations of a view of the elecricity transformer near his house. These post-war paintings have a freedom he could not find in his Paris studio. He felt at home and remained in the region for the rest of his life, leaving only for short visits.

Picasso country is a very small area, a few square miles between Antibes and Cannes, though he moved constantly within this area. He and Françoise Gilot, whom he met in 1943, spent the summer of 1945 at the Villa Pour Toi, facing the fishermen's harbour at Golfe Juan, but it was not until the following year that he acquired his first property in the south. He exchanged a still-life for a house in the village of Menerbes, which he gave to Dora Maar, his companion of many years.

In the early summer of 1946, Picasso and Françoise Gilot returned and Picasso was given the keys to the Grimaldi Palace to use as a studio. He donated most of the work to the museum, including the delightful *La Joie de Vivre*.

He and Gilot moved to Vallauris, to La Galloise, a "small rather ugly house", as she called it, and Picasso began his experiments with ceramics, evolving new techniques of glazing to suit his unusual needs, and single-handedly reviving the town's fortunes. It was there between April and June 1954 that Picasso painted his famous series of more than 30 drawings and paintings of Sylvette David, a young English girl who worked next door to his studio on the Rue de Fournas. Sylvette herself posed for the paintings, causing him to paint her in every conceivable style from naturalistic to highly abstract Cubist variations (his portraits were usually done from memory). Her long neck, thick blonde hair held high in a pony-tail, straight nose and sloping shoulders created a fashionable, much copied style *à la Picasso*. The pony-tail, introduced the year before by Bardot, became all the rage.

After Picasso's relationship with Gilot broke up, he lived alone for a time at La Galloise, painting interiors. The break-up, however, released a flood of energy; the 80-odd drawings made between 1953 and 1954 of the artist and his model; the old artist always in the act of creation, painting the young model. It was to be a recurring theme.

Picasso began living with Jacqueline Roque,

whom he married in 1958. In 1955 he moved from Vallauris to La Californie, a large, ornate turn-of-the-century mansion overlooking Cannes. The space caused him to invent the term *paysages d'intérieur* for the series of interiors he painted, driven by an urge to fill the echoing empty rooms.

In 1958 he was again on the move and bought the huge Château Vauvenargues near Aix-en-Provence but this move from the Riviera did not last long and in 1961 he returned, to Mas Notre-Dame-de-Vie, on a hill overlooking Mougins surrounded by terraces of cypresses and olives and named after a nearby chapel.

He remained prolific to the end. During his last five years, he created over 1,000 works of art: drawings, paintings and graphics. His Riviera

period was perhaps his most obsessional; he would take a theme or a new medium and work at it until it was exhausted. The astonishing productivity continued until, on 8 April 1973, Picasso died at Mas Notre-Dame-de-Vie, at the age of 92.

Today Picasso is a constant theme on the Côte d'Azur. Antibes has a major museum in the Château Grimaldi, with a superb collection of work painted there and donated by Picasso. Mougins has an exhibition of photographs of the artist, including works by Lartigue and Doisneau. Vallauris has his *War and Peace* in the château museum and the sculpture of *L'Homme à l'Angeau* in the centre of town. Sometimes it seems as if every town or village is anxious to claim some connection with the master. ∎

Two aspects of Picasso: <u>left</u>, *The Doves* (1957) and, <u>right</u>, *Jacqueline with Flowers* (1954).

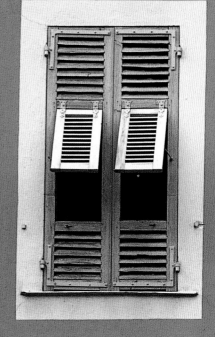
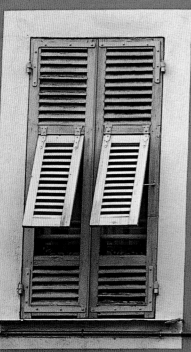

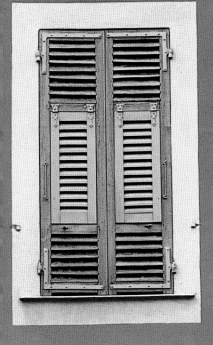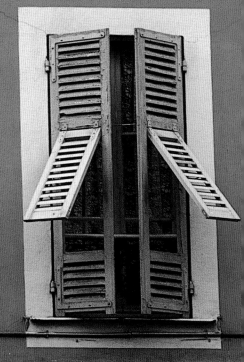

GRASSE AND THE LOUP VALLEY

The ancient town of Grasse is an excellent place to appreciate the acute contrast between the Côte d'Azur and its bucolic hinterland. The town is set on a fabulous site, cradled by sheltering hills and surrounded by flowers, and with splendid views all the way to the sea. Beneath its palm-fronded terraces, elegant pink villas decorate the hillside, sloping gently down to the highly populated valley below, thick with executive housing and high-technology parks. Here the desired synthesis of modern technology with the peace and beauty of the countryside seems entirely possible.

Beyond Grasse are craggy mountains terraced with lavender, meandering river gorges, and the medieval villages of Provence. Within only a few miles spectacular drives and walks are possible. The Gorge du Loup, in particular, makes a wonderful excursion, leading you rapidly into an altogether more elevated universe of alpine pastures and mountain mists.

It is the centre of the perfume industry, and at almost any time of year the air is laden with fragrance; golden mimosa flowers in March; in early summer there are acres of roses waiting to be picked and lavender to be processed; in the autumn the tiny white stars and heavy perfume of jasmine appear.

As well as being a base for the major fragrance manufacturers, Grasse is the hub of an idyllic industry of small flower farms and perfumeries. These days, Grasse concentrates more on processing raw materials from other countries, but it is still possible to see vast mountains of rose petals, vats of jonquils and spadefuls of violets and orange blossom waiting to be processed each morning.

The flowers must be picked early, when the oil is most concentrated and delivered immediately. It takes enormous quantities of blooms to produce even the tiniest amounts of perfume; about 1,650 lb (750 kg) of roses for just 2 lb (1 kg) of rose "absolute", about 8,820 lb (4,000 kg) for 2 lb (1 kg) of essential oil.

Of the basic methods of extracting the scent, two of the oldest are still in use today. They are described in exquisite detail in Patrick Süskind's sinister and compelling novel, *Perfume*. Steam distillation is now mainly used for orange blossom; flowers and water are boiled in a still and the essential oils extracted by steam. A more expensive method, mainly used for jasmine and tuberose, is *enfleurage*; the flowers are layered with lard which becomes impregnated with the scent and is then washed out with alcohol. More modern methods include extraction by volatile solvents.

The highly-trained perfumers of Grasse have been world-famous for centuries. Each "nose" can identify and classify hundreds of fragrances, and working rather like a musician, blends together different "chords" of scent to create a harmonious combination that will radiate around the body in a slow process of diffusion that the French know as *sillage*.

Preceding pages: shuttered lives. Left, negotiating the medieval streets of Grasse. Right, nose at work.

Grasse has a venerable past; between 1138 and 1227 it was a free city, allied to Pisa and Genoa, and governed by a consulate, like the Italian republics. It became a bishopric in 1243 and remained so until 1791, thus becoming a focal point for local power. Its most famous cleric was the 15th-century Bishop Isnard de Grasse who was head of the monastery of the Lérins Islands.

The town was annexed by the counts of Provence until 1482, when Provence was united with France. Grasse continued to trade with Italy, importing animal skins and selling linen and leather goods. Grasse leather was of very high quality, characterised by its greenish hue, caused by treating it with myrtle leaves. In the 16th century, the fashion for perfumed gloves (masking, along with pomanders and handkerchiefs, the undesirable smell of the populace) was introduced by Catherine de Medici. This encouraged the perfume industry in Grasse, but it was not until the 18th century that tanning and perfumery began to develop as separate trades.

Grasse is a very satisfying town to visit; there is much of historic interest to see and perfumeries abound, but it does not feel like a touristy town. It has a working feel to it, the main square full of real shops, selling cheese, buckets and brushes and washing machines instead of Provençal lavender bags, though these are to be had if you want them.

In the architecture of Grasse the influence of the Italian Renaissance is clear; as the city guide points out, "It is to Genoa that the city is indebted for its austere medieval facades, for its Renaissance staircases, for its houses furnished with arcades…"

The town walls were not demolished until the mid-19th century and so, as in Edinburgh, the buildings crammed within the walls were extended vertically; the majority are six storeys high, even in the narrowest of alleys, many of which are dark medieval tunnels reeking of garbage and poverty (a side of Riviera life rarely encountered by the tourist). The southern part of the old town houses many Algerians, bringing

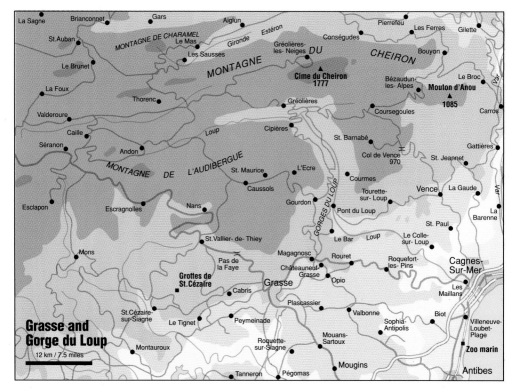

Grasse and Gorge du Loup
12 km / 7.5 miles

a lively street life and Arab music to the lanes and squares.

The **Place Cours** is a good place to begin a tour of Grasse; a number of museums flank a charming terraced garden full of fountains and waterfalls. Here is the **Musée International de la Parfumerie**, housed in an elegant 18th-century mansion, where you can witness the entire history and manufacture of perfume, see a beautiful collection of related items from exquisite perfume bottles to Marie-Antoinette's travelling case. Best of all is the greenhouse garden of Mediterranean and sub-tropical perfumed plants.

A little further down is the **Fragonard perfume museum** and, opposite, the **Villa-Musée Fragonard**, the 18th-century villa where Fragonard, who was born in Grasse, lived with his family for some years before the Revolution. The museum contains drawings and etchings, and two self-portraits by Fragonard as well as copies of the famous panels made for the Comtesse du Barry which are now in the Frick Collection, New York. There are works by other members of his family and other documentation. The building is surrounded by a charming formal garden.

On the corner of the Boulevard du Jeu de Ballon is the **Musée de la Marine**, the beautiful 18th-century former town house of the Pontèves family. The museum commemorates the life and career of Amiral de Grasse (1722–88) who was born locally in Le Bar and played a decisive role in the American War of Independence at the Battle of Yorktown, Virginia, the final battle of the campaign against the British. The museum contains flags and memorabilia, and has a delightful garden with neatly trimmed hedges surrounding roses and small lemon trees, and a pair of cannon captured from the British.

The **Place aux Aires** is long and narrow, with shady trees and an 18th-century fountain facing the 1781 six-storey Hôtel de Ville, with its slightly incongruous portico of pillars supporting a balcony. The square dates from the 14th century but the row of arcaded buildings which is its pride and joy are

Street games in Grasse.

wealthy family town houses from the 16th and 17th centuries, mostly six storeys with shutters and washing hanging from the windows, giving a rather Italian feel to the scene. A market is held in the square every morning.

Turning south, down the narrow steps of the Rue des Fabreries, you encounter the remains of a 14th-century mansion on the corner of the Rue de l'Oratoire. The first two floors are rusticated in the Italian Renaissance manner and there is a very fine two-arched window on the third floor, below which runs the line of corbels for a missing balcony. You could be in Lucca or Florence.

As you continue along the Rue de l'Oratoire, you reach the 14th-century **Église de l'Oratoire** with its 14th-century doorway and window, though the bright yellow ochre paintwork on the walls makes the building look much more recent. Everywhere you walk, there is evidence of great age in the buildings, with blocks of stone and fragments of arches peeking through the now flaking rendering.

Return to the Place Jean Jaurès and make a right down the very narrow and rather creepy Rue Répitrel to the **Rue Mougins-Roquefort** where a 14th-century double round-arched window survives. It has Italian Renaissance corbels and, like many of these buildings, was obviously originally arched on the ground floor. Further down, close to the cathedral and contemporary in date is a 13th-century house.

The **Place du Petit Puy** is the centre of the medieval town. Facing the square is the **Cathedral of Notre-Dame-du-Puy**. It has a very high nave with a ribbed vault supported by four enormous 12th-century pillars, scarred and worn, evidence of the burning of the building in 1795 when it was transformed into a forage store. View the nave from the west door looking straight down to the altar. It was altered considerably in the 13th century and remodelled in the 17th century.

The classic Italian Romanesque facade now has a double staircase by Vauban, architect of the ramparts of Antibes, in a failed attempt to give this crude and powerful building a touch of 17th-century elegance. The ground-floor side windows were restored this century; they had been previously cut into by insensitive "modern" windows at a higher level.

The interior features some interesting works: a rare religious painting by Fragonard; *The Washing of the Feet* (1754), in the south transept, and three works by Rubens on the south wall of the nave: *The Crown of Thorns, the Crucifixion* and *St Helen in Exaltation of the Holy Cross,* painted in Rome in 1601. There is a triptych attributed to Louis Bréa, and some interesting reliquaries and church treasure.

Outside there is a good view of the south transept from the Place St-Martin, and through a tunnel to the Place Godeau the Bishop's Palace forms the other side of a small square. Arrow slits in the palace are aimed straight at the north doorway of the church. The Palace once had an elegant three-arched loggia in the Italian manner but this was mostly infilled in later years, leaving only the passage through from the Place Godeau. The group of buildings is completed by a good tall 12th-century square tower in red tufa.

To the east of the Bishop's Palace, on the Place du 24 Août, is a solitary clock tower, the remains of the 13th-century consulate (law courts).

Rue J. Ossola has another former townhouse of the Villeneuve family, with parts dating to the 14th century, below which is a 14th-century passage leading to the ramparts, and on the Rue Mirabeau are the two townhouses of the Clapiers de Cabris family, one 17th-century and the other, now the **Musée d'Art et d'Histoire de Provence**, built in 1771. The museum has a good collection of regional crafts including ironwork, ceramics and furniture, and a library of Provençal documents.

Gorge du Loup: The area around Grasse is traditionally dependent on the flower industry, and a good way to take in a number of interesting villages is to follow the Gorge du Loup north. At **Le Bar**, a pair of cannon, captured by

The high vaulted nave of the Cathedral of Notre-Dame-de-Puy.

Amiral François de Grasse from the British, stand either side of the door to l'Amiral restaurant on the Place F. Pault. De Grasse (1722–88) was born in the 16th-century castle of Le Bar and played an important role in the Battle of Yorktown, the final battle in the American War of Independence, after which Rue Yorktown is named. Le Bar is a centre for walking and itineraries are available in English from the Syndicat d'Initiatif located in the strange *donjon* in the middle of the village. The Gothic church has been extensively remodelled but has fine door panels by Jacotin Bellot, who carved the choir stalls in Grasse. There is an extraordinary 15th-century painting of *La Danse Macabre* (The Dance of Death) in the nave.

Pont de Loup, at the south end of the Gorge du Loup, is like an Alpine village with palm trees. The village is framed by mountains on either side with spectacular views, making it a good place for walking tours. It is dominated by the remains of a railway viaduct, blown up by the Germans in 1944 and never re-paired; great ruined monoliths rise hundreds of feet over the houses and trees.

Gourdon, one of the most dramatic *villages perchés* of them all, is still relatively inaccessible, though the new road to it is an easy ride in comparison with the steep mountain track the peasant with his mule used in centuries past. The approach gives a stunning view of the village with its sheer drop of several thousand feet below the castle walls.

Today only the castle's living quarters have survived and where the tower once was, is now laid out a formal French garden, providing an almost surreal contrast between the neatly trimmed low hedges and topiary and the wild backdrop of the surrounding mountains. The castle has a museum containing some very interesting (and valuable) armour: suits of plate armour, chain mail, broad swords, rifles and various types of ordnance. All of the rooms have huge fireplaces, even the private chapel, certainly necessary because Gourdon is a cold and rugged place for much of the year. On the upper floor is a large and

The perched village of Gourdon.

exceptionally good collection of naive painting, including a Henri Rousseau portrait with an excellent Proustian moustache.

The Gorge du Loup itself is glorious and terrifying by turns, tunnelling through the rock, past magnificent waterfalls and over bridges from which you can peer down to the river rushing far below. The footpaths along the gorge are very well maintained with steps cut in the steeper parts.

Beyond are the Clues (gorges) de Haute Provence, a barren remoter region which comes into its own in the winter skiing season. **Gréolières** to the west is on an alpine slope, remote and quiet, the hillsides dotted with violets and spring flowers. Eleven miles (18 km) beyond is **Gréolières-le-Neige**, the nearest ski resort to the Mediterranean. Turning east you will come to **Coursegoules**, a pretty town of muted terracotta stone nestling protectively against the bare rock of the mountain side, surrounded by sheep pastures and tinkling bells. Surprisingly it is not tumbledown

and deserted as you might expect; indeed, there is a considerable amount of new building – basic apartments, not tourist villas – and a lively school housed in a beautifully-restored old building. Remote as it may seem, Coursegoules is only 10 miles (16 km) from Vence and the excellence of the roads means local people can commute to the coast. The next village is **Bézaudun-les-Alpes** which has a fabulous view of the Montagne du Chiers and is equally well-maintained and prosperous.

Beyond Bézaudun, the road becomes more exciting; the rusting hulks of cars halfway down the mountainside and skidmarks burned into the road at every blind turning add a frisson to an already discomfiting mountain drive. Here the D8 meets the D1 which leads back to the coast. An alternative route from Grasse follows the D2210 to **Tourette-sur-Loup**, clinging to the rock between two deep ravines. To the west of the village are great expanses of sheer rock, and at the cliff edge are troglodyte houses carved from the living rock. Today

Tourette-sur-Loup.

Tourette is an important centre for violet production, supplying Grasse perfumeries and the factories manufacturing candied violets in Toulouse.

The village is in an ideal defensive position, and began life occupied by Ligurian tribes. In 262 BC, the Romans established an observation post there: "Turres Altae", which became corrupted to "Tourette".

The Romans left in AD 476, after which the village suffered the same series of invasions and massacres that befell its neighbours. The Saracens were responsible for fortifying the site. In 1387, Tourette came into the hands of the Villeneuve family, where it remained until the French Revolution when the Villeneuves fled, never to return. The Black Death, the Wars of Religion and the Revolution all took their toll and by 1944 the population had shrunk to 850. Today the revitalisation of the area has resulted in a population of over 3,000.

The old village is quite amazingly crooked, with no two windows alike or a straight line anywhere, and the twisting streets feel completely enclosed until a cool, dim little alley unexpectedly emerges on to a windblown mountain panorama. The horse-shoe-shaped Grand Rue is lined with art galleries and craft shops but is not over-commercialised, and there are medieval shops, now private houses, and numerous interesting doorways still visible.

In the centre of the village a very formal Hôtel de Ville looks rather out of place. It incorporates an 11th-century watchtower, and has a pleasant courtyard with a tinkling fountain. The 11th-century church has been rebuilt on and off from the mid-16th until the 18th century and has a simple stylised Virgin and Child over the front door. To the north of the village is the chapel of St John with recent naive wall paintings.

A little further along the D2210 is **Notre-Dame-des-Fleurs**, a perfume museum and restaurant, "Château des Aromes", offering a delightful way to appreciate the pleasures of perfume. The 19th-century **château** was built by a Grasse perfumer on the remains of an 11th-century Benedictine monastery,

and behind the facade on the ground floor are the monks' cells and private chapels, all beautifully restored. The large chapel has a high vaulted ceiling, a 16th-century Provençal font, and stunning modern stained-glass windows high in the walls. Through the massive oak-studded door at the back is a recently discovered sarcophagus with the skeletons of 9th-century monks. The small chapel is a charming odd little niche with an 11th-century stone virgin and vestigial Romanesque columns.

The restaurant in the magnificent old chapter house, hung with tapestries and huge iron candlebra, specialises in perfumed dishes. The museum exhibits include a history of perfume, and a collection of copper vats, presses and bottles. Most beguiling of all is the garden, a terrace with a great variety of aromatic plants and herbs, gloriously fragrant in the sun, overlooking cool fountains, orange trees, figs and roses, and an impressive park full of modern sculptures. The coastline of Cap Ferrat is visible beyond.

The deep ravine of the Gorge du Loup.

CAGNES, VENCE AND THE VAR VALLEY

The coastline between Antibes and Nice is perhaps the most exploited on the Riviera, although the beaches themselves are often unappealingly pebbly. Inland the property development from Cagnes to Vence is almost equally unbridled, and St-Paul-de-Vence is claimed to be the most visited village in France after Mont St-Michel.

Popularity should not dissuade anyone from visiting this area, however – it is entirely justified. Both St-Paul and Vence are of enormous historical interest and the area has long been a thriving artistic centre; St-Paul, for example, is home to the Fondation Maeght, one of the world's great art museums.

Try and avoid visiting at peak times, but otherwise grit your teeth and anticipate the pleasures to be had once you have found a parking space. And only a few more miles inland to St-Jeannet and the Var Valley, the roads are much quieter, and you can find yourself in relatively sleepy Provençal villages which seem light-years away from the coastal cacophony.

Still on the coast, the N7 highway closely resembles a Hollywood-style strip of neon lights, hoardings, gas stations and huge drive-in supermarkets (well worth checking out, nonetheless, by anyone with serious shopping to do). The view is dominated from all directions by the **Marina-Baie des Anges**, at **Villeneuve-Loubet Plage**, a much reviled piece of modern architecture, built in the 1970s.

Actually it is by no means out of place, its curving terraces echoing the sea waves and the mountains behind. Easiest access to the marina, sardine-packed with hundreds of magnificent yachts, is from the N98 coast road. Next to it is the Hippodrome race-track, and on the other side is Marineland, a big marine zoo with dolphins, sea-lions and whales to be seen.

The original medieval village of **Villeneuve-Loubet** is just off the N7,

east of the river Loup. Surprisingly it still has an authentic feel to its steep narrow lanes and lived-in ancient buildings which resist gentrification with layers of cement and pebbledash. They huddle at the foot of the château, restored in the 19th century and now private property. The path round the château walls gives a good view out to the Baie des Anges.

There are two museums. The **Musée Militaire** specialises in the two world wars, as well as the colonial wars in French Indo-China (Vietnam) and Algeria. Particularly recommended is the **Fondation Auguste Escoffier** (Museum of Culinary Art), housed in the great chef's birthplace, a few steps up the hill from the main square. Exhibits include an old Provençal kitchen; gleaming copperware and kitchen utensils; Escoffier's own inventions, like his device for making breadcrumbs; a roomful of mouthwateringly beautiful old menus; some wildly imaginative examples of sugarwork, including a haywain and a model of a Loire château; Escoffier's

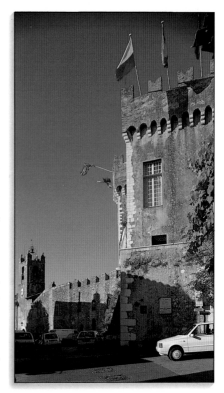

own hand-written recipe book and, touchingly, the master's last *toque*. There is also an excellent selection of old photographs, including a number of Dame Nelly Melba, for whom Escoffier invented the Peach Melba while he was chef at the London Carlton Hotel. And there are a couple of gratifyingly good pâtisseries in the square below.

Surrounded by a tangle of freeway intersections is **Cagnes-sur-Mer**, which divides into three very distinct parts: the modern seaside resort of Cros-de-Cagnes, the modern town of Cagnes-sur-Mer with its shops, supermarket, public park and a good covered market (mornings only), nestling at the foot of the hill, and the celebrated old town of **Haut-de-Cagnes**, crowned by its 14th-century château.

The history of the town begins with the monks of Lérins, who founded an abbey at Saint-Véran in the 5th century, now the site of the Hippodrome. By the 14th century Cagnes became a Grimaldi possession and subject to the constant turmoil of the Middle Ages. It has al-ways depended on agriculture for its economic survival, notably olives, vines and flowers. By the 19th century Mentonnais fishermen had settled on the coast, and the town thus developed between coast and castle. Today it is an important artistic centre, a popular tourist destination, and particularly noted for its flower production. Every spring the Exposition Internationale de Fleur takes over the town, château and the Hippodrome.

The world's first fully computerised car-park marks the entry to the old town; a typical Côte d'Azur conjunction of modern technology and ancient history. Nearby is one of the oldest buildings, the **Chapelle Notre-Dame-de-la-Protection**, a bijou 14th-century structure erected as protection against plague and pestilence and containing some beautiful 1530 frescoes. There is a large open-sided porch with a wide view south over Cagnes-sur-Mer to the Mediterranean and Nice airport. A narrow, hidden path curves round the outside of the apse and down the hillside.

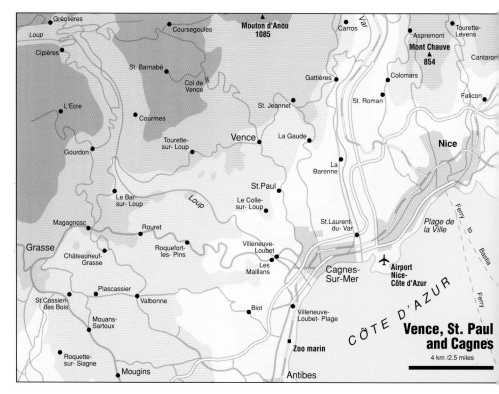

If all you see of Haut-de-Cagnes is the château and main square it would be easy to dismiss it as irredeemably touristy, but in fact, like so many of these over-visited villages, most of the populace continue their lives as they have always done. The steep, winding streets and tiny squares are as carefully tended as their own living-rooms, decorated with terracotta pots of flowering jasmine and geraniums. Fig trees and wisteria overhang tantalisingly from roof gardens and the traditional garden *potagers* serried beneath the ramparts are still zealously cultivated.

The restaurant row of Haut-de-Cagnes is Montée de la Bourgade. Steps to the left lead to the Rue du Portis Long, a lane following the inside of the ramparts through a continuous barrel vault past the ground floors and basements of the buildings – pleasantly cool and medieval in the heat of summer. You can also follow the outside of the ramparts by leaving through one of the many medieval gateways. Cagnes has many 15th- and 16th-century houses and there are some Renaissance houses with arcades near the castle.

L'Église St-Pierre is worth a visit to see the Grimaldi tombs and Gothic nave. Place de l'Église features a number of jettied, or overhanging buildings, most unusual for this area. There are squares on either side of the **Grimaldi Château**; the Place du Château is filled with cafés and nightclubs, and to the north looks out over distant and frequently snow-covered mountains. A medieval archway will take you through to the Place Grimaldi and the entrance to the **Musée Grimaldi**.

Within is an unexpectedly cool and pleasant open courtyard shaded by tall trees, with flags flapping three floors above; fortified outside walls meant this was the only source of light and air. The Musée Grimaldi is the very best sort of provincial museum: local history and artefacts, bad local paintings housed in wonderful rooms and, amidst the clutter, one or two absolute gems. A detailed history of the olive and its importance to the region includes a collection

he curving rraces of Marina-Baie es Anges.

of old olive presses and implements. There is an excellent fireplace, an old well, a magnificent ceiling, and red brick floors polished to a glassy patina by centuries of feet.

You can ignore all the paintings except for those in the Suzy Solidor collection. In the 1930s singer Suzy Solidor had a famous nightclub, the Vie Parisienne, in Paris. She was a modern young woman with bobbed hair who moved in artistic circles and had the brilliant idea of having her many artistic friends paint her. In the end, she had 224 portraits of which 47 are on display here. It is fascinating to see so many artists approaching the same subject: an excellent Van Dongen of Suzy in a sailor suit; Foujita's gold-leaf panels surrounding an oriental-looking Suzy with adoring dog; a colour wash Marie Laurencin; a Lydis treating her as a Vargas pin-up; a naïf Kisling; an odd, rapidly executed Francis Picabia; drawings by Raoul Dufy and Jean Cocteau; and the jewel of the collection, a Tamara de Lempicka nude of her with a Cubist cityscape background. The Lempicka alone is worth the admission charge. On the top floor is the **Musée d'Art Moderne Méditerranéen**, dedicated to artists who have worked on the Côte d'Azur.

The building itself, a solid square keep built as a prison in about 1300, has been disgracefully treated and takes some sorting out architecturally. It has been described as the finest specimen of a medieval stronghold in this part of France but at some point large modern windows have been cut through its great walls, some even cutting away the machicolations which are the castle's finest feature.

The main hall has a 17th-century ceiling by Carlone representing the fall of Phaeton, but this has been heavily restored. This is because in 1815 the castle was occupied by Piedmontese soldiers who, lolling on divans, amused themselves by successfully firing at the head of Phaeton.

In the 1920s, Cagnes became a popular bohemian haunt for artists, and was the setting for Cyril Connolly's only

Roof-top technology, Cagnes today.

novel, *The Rock Pool*, in which the town becomes Trou-sur-Mer. He describes the louche doings of "the doomed tribe" of failed artists, "the mysterious jungle atmosphere… intense nocturnal life… where the hopelessness of the struggle was admitted with fatalism, yet where all fought on."

A rather more celebrated local artist is Auguste Renoir, and his house in the suburb of **Les Collettes** is a wonderful place to visit. It is surrounded by a magnificent olive grove: five and half acres of 300-year-old olive trees, spread out across the hillside with superb views of the old village of Haut-de-Cagnes, the Mediterranean and Cap d'Antibes – a view which has, of course, changed dramatically since Renoir's day. There is no admission charge to the grounds which provide a welcome haven of shade on a hot summer's day. The house itself is now the Renoir Museum; Renoir spent the last 12 years of his life there and the building still feels like a private home. Nine of the rooms are open, including his two studios, still filled with memo-rabilia: his easel, his wheelchair. In the small studio is his palette, a square of white ceramic, wiped clean after use, so that he could see the pure colour as it would look on a white canvas. Not for Renoir the heavily encrusted kidney-shaped wooden palette of the stereotype artist. Even the bathroom is on view, with a wonderful tub and, low on the wall next to the bidet, a small ceramic tile of a nude, probably by his son Claude.

There are 10 original paintings by Renoir in the museum, including a large sketch for *Les Grandes Baigneuses* in which he roughs in the form with cross-hatch pencil work over the paint. There are also drawings, busts and other work. They are interspersed with reproductions, often quite crude ones, which give the museum a homely feel.

On the way between Cagnes and Vence is the small but perfectly forti-fied town of **St-Paul-de-Vence,** now one of the region's main tourist spots, besieged today by coach parties which invade its tiny streets and buy St-Paul embossed T-shirts and Provençal lav-

errasse à agnes, as *enoir saw it 1905.*

ender bags. If you drive straight to Vence in the high season you will have ample opportunity to examine St-Paul's fortifications from the traffic jam which extends all the way down the D36.

Parking is always a problem here so expect to leave your car outside the town if you drive at all; the Café de la Place just outside the main (north) gate is a good place to stop for coffee and watch a *boules* game.

The circle of ramparts, built in 1536, remains unbroken. A walk round them gives a good view of the surrounding countryside studded with dark cypresses and azure swimming-pools, as well as a better sense of life in St-Paul than a walk down the Grand Rue provides; glimpses of bougainvillaea-filled gardens and treasured terraces hint at an insider's life beyond the stout wooden doors visible from the street.

A cannon captured at the Battle of Cérisoles in 1544 defends the north gate, la Porte Royale, where a machicolated 13th-century tower houses the tourist centre. The gate opens straight on to the Grand Rue, a narrow crooked street which runs the full length of the village passing Place de la Grande-Fontaine with its pretty urn-shaped fountain. Many of the the 16th- and 17th-century houses bear coats of arms and are now "artists'" ateliers. Some of the medieval shops survive, usually as private homes; look out for a wide arch, beneath which is a doorway and an adjoining window. The window has a large marble sill which used to be the shop counter, a direct descendant from the Roman shop.

The church (La Collégiale de la Conversion de Saint Paul) was begun in the 12th century and has an 18th-century bell tower. Among its treasures is a painting attributed to Tintoretto of Ste Catherine of Alexandria, at the end of the north aisle. Also displayed is a 13th-century enamel virgin and child and the shoulder blade of St George enclosed in a curious silver reliquary (visible upon payment of 1 franc).

Across from the church is the donjon, a tower which completes a pleasing group of buildings; it now contains a

La Colombe d'Or restaurant, St-Paul-de-Vence.

museum of local history in tableaux of wax figures – more endearing than it sounds. Much more interesting, however, is an exhibition of photographs of celebrities taken in St-Paul: Garbo, Mitchner, Brynner, Loren, Lancaster, Cocteau, Sartre and de Beauvoir, Baldwin and Belafonte all on vacation. Many are caught off guard, Catherine Deneuve in a girlish Provençal dress, Gene Wilder and Gilda Radnor getting married, Minister of Culture Jack Lang in designer suit. The rich and famous really do come to St-Paul, most often to eat at the still celebrated **La Colombe d'Or** restaurant.

In the 19th century, the village of St-Paul declined and it was not until the 1920s that it was "discovered" by a group of artists which included Bonnard, Modigliani, Soutine, Signac and others who used to gather in a café which has now become La Colombe d'Or; they paid for meals and rooms with paintings and sculptures and the Roux family proprietors assembled an enviable and now priceless collection of art. The dining-room walls are adorned with works by Picasso, Braque, Miró and Matisse, the garden wall features a huge brilliantly-coloured Léger mosaic, there is a Calder mobile and a Braque mosaic dove by the cypress-sheltered green swimming-pool and works by Dufy, Chagall, César and more at every turn. The hotel itself is charming, cosy even, a feast of warm terracotta, bright ceramic tiles, painted wooden ceilings and burnished wood. Dining outside on the terrace is one of the pleasures of Provence; sampling the 15 famous hors d'oeuvres and the Grand Marnier soufflé an essential – if expensive – experience.

There are further riches close by; within easy walking distance of the village, on La Gardette Hill, is the **Fondation Maeght**, a world-class museum of modern art, with a sculpture garden full of works by Miró, Giacometti, Calder and many others.

A short drive up the D2 is **Vence**, a delightfully civilised town, perched high on a rock promontory, surrounded by rose farms and orange groves which are

St-Paul-de-Vence, small but perfectly fortified.

THE FONDATION MAEGHT

Visiting the Fondation Maeght outside St-Paul-de-Vence is a bit like finding London's Tate Gallery set in steep pine woods. It is a world-class museum of modern art, housing not only exhibition galleries but a library, residences and artists' workshops, as well as an entrancing sculpture garden. The foundation itself has an ever changing exhibition, but the permanent collection is very strong in Miró, Braque and Giacometti, and examples of their work are always on display. Giacometti's attenuated club-footed bronze figures stride across the central sculpture court and are the most photographed pieces in the collection. There is art everywhere; even the door handles were designed by Miró.

Behind the gallery is the Joan Miró labyrinth: a series of connecting spaces designed by Catalan architect Josep Luis Sert, who also built the main galleries. Each of the big humorous sculptures has its own special setting, in water or silhouetted against the sky. Miró made the ceramics at the foundation workshop and the large concrete pieces were built *in situ*.

Children adore the Pol Bury, which is easily missed, tucked in a little space between the café and the chapel. The chapel itself was also built by Sert; it contains Georges Braque's beautiful *White Bird on a Mauve Background* (1962), a delicate stained-glass panel set high above the altar. Below it is a large 15th-century Spanish Christ strongly carved from an ochre wood which contrasts well with the Braque panel. There is a Léger ceramic on the outside wall.

The tiny chapel building was actually the first building on the site, erected in memory of the child of the founders of the museum, Aimé and Marguerite Maeght. Aimé came from Nîmes, where he had shown some aptitude for engraving, and he met Marguerite in Cannes. They married and set up in business together with an electrical goods shop which was very successful. Marguerite indeed had such an instinct for business that she once said of herself, "If I were cast up naked on a desert island, I'd make money."

During World War II many Jews fled to the relative safety of the South of France, bringing with them art works to sell. The Maeghts seized the opportunity and replaced the electrical appliances with paintings. The supply of work was increased when Pierre Bonnard, who lived in Le Cannet, noticed Aimé's engravings and asked for his assistance. Because Marguerite's father ran a grocery business, they were able to make judicious swaps of scarce wartime provisions for art works. Bonnard then introduced his new friends to Henri Matisse in Vence, another artist in need of groceries.

Within 10 years the Maeghts, famous for their wheeling and dealing, had risen to extraordinary prominence in the art world. Their Paris gallery represented, amongst others, Matisse, Miró, Giacometti, Kandinsky, Braque, Chagall and Calder.

Following the tragic early death of their child, the Maeghts decided to build a chapel in his memory, which evolved into the foundation. Maeght was an art dealer who did something no art dealer had ever done before: he created a museum in his own name, paid for entirely by himself and filled with art from his own extensive stock.

At the inauguration in 1964, André Malraux, the Minister of Cultural Affairs, said: "Here something has been attempted which has never been attempted before: to create, instinctively and lovingly, the universe in which modern art might find both its place and the other world once called supernatural."

Outdoor sculpture at the Fondation ■

sheltered by the mountains to the north. Its gentle climate has made it popular, especially with invalids – D. H. Lawrence died here in 1930 – and has resulted in property development scarring the surrounding hillsides.

Such popularity has its advantages; today Vence provides excellent food shopping for fresh fish, vegetables and pâtisserie, as well as a market twice a week, and it is always pleasant to stroll round its leafy squares and ancient streets. It has a chequered history. It was occupied by the Phoenicians and the Gauls, savaged and ruined by the Saracens and the Lombards before the Romans named it Ventium and made it an important religious centre. Vence converted to Christianity early, a change usually attributed to St Trophime. The first Bishopric was founded in Vence in AD 374 and the town quickly grew to become an important regional centre. Bishops remained until the outbreak of the French Revolution when Bishop Pisani fled the country; the see was never restored.

Much of the history of Vence has been the conflict between the power of the bishops and that of the Villeneuves, because the lords of Villeneuve-Loubet shared seignorial rights over the town with the church. Vence won a great victory in the Wars of Religion against the Huguenots, but it suffered horribly from the Black Death in 1572.

Vence drifted into steady decline so that by the beginning of the 20th century it was half-deserted with many houses in ruins and a population of a mere few thousand, mostly in the new parts of town. Tourism and sun-belt industries have transformed it into a bustling centre of more than 15,000 people.

Before you reach the old town, you pass through the Place du Grand-Jardin, and Place du Frêne with its huge ash tree planted in 1538. The medieval centre of Vence is very picturesque and once you get away from the souvenir sellers, the lanes and alleyways are little changed from previous centuries – except that many of the lanes in the northeast side of the old town now have light and air

Below, Place du Peyra, Vence. **Right**, Chagall mosaic in Vence's Old Cathedral.

where they end at the town ramparts; the walls have been cut down to waist height so that now there is a mountain view instead of a prison-like wall.

The ramparts were built in the 13th and 14th centuries and used to have a broad walk running along the top. In the northern section, this promenade still exists where it has become Boulevard Paul André. The south section of the ramparts has been repeatedly pierced to make shops along Avenue Marcellin Maurel. Vence has retained its town gates: the 13th-century Signadour Gate incorporated into a defensive tower; the round arched Porte d'Orient pierced through in the 18th century (the date of 1592 refers to a battle during the Wars of Religion); the 14th-century Portail Levis which once possessed a portcullis and opens on to Rue de la Coste, one of the oldest lanes in the town; Le Pontis, built in 1863 by literally driving through the medieval houses. Most impressive of all is the Portail du Peyra built by Good King René who died in 1480. It is much restored and in the 17th century

an imposing square tower was added to its side.

The entrance through Portail du Peyra leads past a small fountain to the Place du Peyra which has a grand and ancient chestnut tree shading the cafés. Place Godeau, named after the famous poet Bishop, is outside the cathedral and was once the cemetery. Today it is a pleasant place to stop for a drink. There is a granite Roman column in the centre of the square and some fine old houses: a 13th-century house with a two-arch Romanesque window, and another dated 1524. Many of the windows and doors in Vence have suffered from modernisation though some old iron-nail studded doors and a few medieval shop fronts have survived.

The 15th-century watchtower rises next to the church, which is entered from Place Clemenceau, the old Roman forum, where there is a flea market held every Wednesday. The cathedral has plenty of interest to see even though its outline is virtually hidden by later buildings. Buried in its outside walls on the Passage Cahours are reused Roman stones bearing inscriptions, mostly of a commemorative nature, one to the goddess Cybele and the ceremony of the Taurobolium, in which a bull was sacrificed to the gods, and another to Lucius Veludius Valerianus, decurian of Vence and his wife Vibia.

The church is 10th-century, though what you see was built between the 12th and 15th centuries. It was the site of the Temple of Mars in Roman times but the first Christian building was the Merovingian church of the 5th century. The first Bishop of Vence, St Eusebius, was in office in the year 374 and he must have adapted the Roman temple for Christian worship. It is a building of great antiquity.

It consists of a nave with four aisles. The roof is carried on immense square pillars, lacking in ornament. The two side aisles were roofed over in the 15th century by a wide gallery which looks down into the nave through a row of arches, built to accommodate an enlarged congregation. Either side are two more aisles, which contain the chapels:

Portail du Peyra, one of the ancient gateways of Vence.

one, which is said to contain the body of St Veran who died in 492, uses a carved Roman sarcophagus as both tomb and altar. Other Roman figures can be found in the walls, one in the pillar before the chapel of St Veran.

In 1499, at the same time as the roofing of the aisles, a tribune was added at the west end, housing the choir on a gallery high above the door. This contains the 51 famous wooden choir stalls imaginatively carved by Jacotin Bellot of Grasse who began work on them in 1455 and finished them 25 years later. He carved animals and plants and recorded the everyday life of the people and clergy, sometimes not at all reverently. The church also has a wonderfully carved wooden door taken from the destroyed prévôté or chapter house. It is from an earlier date than Bellot's work but may be by the same master who carved the lectern housed in the choir. In the baptistry there is a mosaic design by Marc Chagall of Moses in the bulrushes.

Throughout the church there are ex-quisite examples of Carolingian carving incorporated in the wall and columns, taken from the previous church. Outside the city walls is the **Château de Villeneuve,** which has been renovated as an exhibition space for modern art.

The other church of interest in Vence is quite different: **the Rosaire,** designed by Henri Matisse between 1947 and 1951. The architecture now clearly shows its origin in the 1950s, indicating perhaps that Matisse was more at home with the fine arts, though its most original element, the chapel's ultramarine and white tile roof still looks superb. The yellow-and-blue stained glass, based on a leaf motif, works very well with the simple wall decorations chosen by Matisse: instead of frescoes he painted his designs for the walls on uniform white tiles, specially made for the building. Unfortunately quite a few on his Stations of the Cross wall cracked when the building settled.

The drawing itself is confident and strong, remarkably so considering Matisse's advanced age and terrible ar-

One of Vence's tree-shaded squares.

thritis during its creation. Many of the original drawings for the project are on display and well worth examination. Of the greatest interest are the details: the candlesticks on the altar and the confessional door – an assemblage of wooden shapes painted white echoing the traditional perforated doors in medieval churches. The road was renamed Blvd Henri Matisse in his honour.

From Vence the road climbs to **St-Jeannet**, towered over by the great **Baou de St-Jeannet** like a huge headland (*baou* is the Provençal for rock). In fact it is an ancient coral crag that did once look down upon the Mediterranean, many aeons ago. It has inspired many painters, among them Poussin, Fragonard, Renoir and Chagall. The village of St-Jeannet nestles on a terrace at the foot of the Baou. In some lights the village looks no more than a natural outcrop of the rock; at other times the rock itself looks like a craggy château.

At one time St-Jeannet was famous for its grapes and wine but today production is concentrated on flowers. However, locally-produced wines and jams are sometimes available for sale in the village – and if the shop is shut you may find them left outside with a little box for payment.

St-Jeannet is a town of quiet courtyards, arched doorways and sloping lanes of stone steps. On a pleasant square with a four spout fountain, is the Chapelle St-Bernadin, built in 1666 and lit by only three recent stained-glass windows. Behind the church is a wonderful panorama from a small platform partly covered by an old archway with thick beams. It is amazing to see how the narrow terraces below accommodate carefully tended *potagers*, parked cars and even swimming pools,

St-Jeannet has a number of good restaurants making it a good place to stop for lunch – before or probably after, a climb. There is a path to the top of Baou St-Jeannet which starts from the Auberge St-Jeannet and takes about an hour each way. There is a spectacular view of the French and Italian Alps from the viewing platform at the top.

The craggy outcrop of Baou de St-Jeannet.

Gattières, further along the D2210, is a working perched village with steep streets filled with washing lines and barking dogs. The ancient buildings are there but covered in pebbledash or rendering, making it an interesting contrast to many other self-consciously picturesque villages with virtually identical housing stock.

South of St-Jeannet, on the D18, is **La Gaude**, a small lively village built high above the River Cagne; it is the nearest village to the massive IBM Research and Study Centre on the D118 to St-Laurent. When Breuer's IBM centre was built it was highly praised for harmonising with the landscape – as well as two giant Y-shaped blocks supported by concrete pillars can. Now the area has become heavily built up and the IBM architecture no longer looks so modern or interesting.

Le Broc is another classic perched village, this time high on a rock overlooking the River Var. The view is extraordinary because the scale of human intervention on the landscape comes as a shock; the Var has been straightened out like a canal in a gigantic feat of engineering, taming it and binding it with freeways and industrial zones on either side.

Nearby is **Carros**, perched on a rock, commanding a bend in the river. A new town has been built down on the flood plane called **Carros-le-Neuf** which is also worth a visit. The city centre is familiar enough, with high-rise flats and shopping malls, but the scale is miniature and the streets curve and wind. Part of the residential area hugs a ridge like a hill town and the houses imitate a higgledy-piggledy medieval hill town with funny dead end lanes and squares making parking almost as difficult as in the medieval originals.

Returning to the coast, take the D118 to St-Laurent-du-Var, the higher of the two corniche roads following the Var. There are spectacular views over the Var Valley and and a chance to see the phenomenal industrial development that has taken place beside the river and all the way to Nice.

Human intervention on the landscape: the view of the Var valley from Le Broc.

NICE

Rain or shine (and there is much of the latter), the man up the ladder on the seafront at Nice has been standing immobile on the top rung for years now. Precariously poised, with an artist's palette in his left hand and a brush in his right, he is attempting to paint a palm tree while feathery shadows of a real one creep across his canvas.

You may think this odd – even more so when you realise the artist's work will never be completed. For the twist is he himself is the focal point of a painting within a painting, an artistic joke which never fails to cause merriment among Nice's visitors.

Whoever painted the man up the ladder has done more than transform the outside wall of an Indian restaurant from a banal stretch of white plaster into a witty set-piece tableau of life along the Baie des Anges. Nothing better serves to symbolise the *savoir vivre* of the Niçois, their very un-French ability to laugh at themselves and their delight in taking the visitor by surprise.

Welcome, then, to a carnival town where not everything that meets the eye is as it seems, from painted pigeons that are surely the only ones in the world not to leave droppings, to *trompe l'oeil* doorways and windows that don't need oiling or cleaning.

Un-French? Certainly. Nice has officially been part of the French Republic only since 1860; before then it was part of Italy. Local jokers, however, like to dispute even this, saying that for 62 years up to 1990 Nice was the personal fief of the Médecin men – first Jean, then his son Jacques – both of whom ruled as mayor and left indelible marks.

Jacques was a man up a ladder if ever there was one, and no mean political artist either. When he tumbled and fled in 1990 his downfall closed just another chapter in the city's see-saw history of changing management which began in 350 BC with the Greeks, who named it after the goddess, Nikea ("she who brings victory"), and variously saw in power Romans, counts of Provence, dukes of Savoy and kings of Sardinia. As a tug-of-love baby, the "Maid of Provence" certainly had a turbulent upbringing, and was a ward of the Italian court for most of 500 years.

Today Nice is essentially French but its character and temperament remain Italian, with constant reminders that the frontier is still just 25 miles away. However, it is rightly proud of its own language, Nissard, its own surrounding "county" of the Alpes-Maritimes and its cuisine, which goes much further than just a famous salad.

It is now a unique city of western, medieval and oriental influences, a provincial metropolis that is the richest, most attractive tourist centre outside Paris. Nice is France's fifth-largest city with the second-busiest airport (after Paris), and is rapidly becoming a business and cultural centre to be reckoned with as well.

It was the British who invented the name "Riviera". They laid the foundations for its present-day capital and were

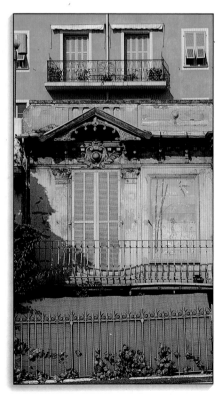

certainly in no doubt about its being the brightest jewel in the river of towns sparkling all the way from Cannes to Monte-Carlo.

A thriving English colony subsequently developed. Well-heeled British *fainéants* and aristocrats and retired army officers zealously set about turning Nice into a kind of sanitised Bournemouth, with hotels called Westminster and West End in a sector they named Newborough.

Indeed it is an English clergyman, the Rev. Lewis Way, whom we must thank for the Promenade des Anglais, which remains the main thoroughfare of the city. He was a skilled missionary with remarkable powers of persuasion who talked his flock into providing construction work for men thrown out of work by a severe frost which killed the area's orange trees in 1821.

By 1887 when poet Stephen Liégeard first named the coastline the Côte d'Azur, Nice had already expanded to the size of Cannes today, and was regularly attracting over 25,000 winter visitors, mainly by train. There were shops selling trinkets made of olive wood inscribed with the words "Nice", and "*Je reviendrai*" – forerunners of today's "Nice is Nice" T-shirts and "*J'aime la Côte d'Azur*" bumper stickers.

There was an air of prosperity, electric lighting in the streets and, naturally, guidebooks. "Nice is a home for the millionaire and the working man," one proclaimed. "The intermediate class is not wanted. Visitors are expected to have money, and if they have to look at pounds, shillings and pence had much better remain at home."

The Promenade des Anglais, the little coastal road that was then used by about 100 English families and their carriages, has today become one of the most clogged thoroughfares in France. It is an eight-lane highway, 3 miles (5 km) long, on which only the aggressive survive, and you need to be alert. Watch your window, too, if you stop at the lights in summer. Resplendent with marching palms and flowerbeds, the Prom (even the French call it that) has a concealed automatic watering system

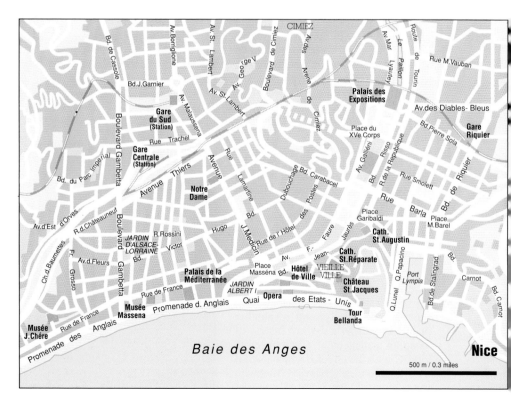

and the sprinklers are liable to turn your car into a jacuzzi if your reflexes aren't sharp enough.

Today's scene on the Promenade des Anglais is very different from its 19th-century counterparts. When Henri Negresco's palace first opened its doors in 1913 they pointed north: 150 years after Tobias Smollett introduced sea-bathing here it still had not dawned on anyone that the future of tourism lay in hotels with their resplendent fronts, not their backs, to the sea.

The famed **Negresco** remains the crown of the Promenade; it is a national monument where visiting heads of state still occupy entire floors, and the flamboyance of the exterior is only eclipsed by the jewels within. This was where Scott Fitzgerald stayed and although you won't find a Diamond as Big as the Ritz there is a crystal chandelier by Baccarat with 16,309 stones and weighing more than a tonne, designed originally for the Tsar.

There are a number of fine museums clustered around the Promenade des Anglais. These include the **International Museum of Naïf Art** in the Château Ste-Helène on the Avenue Val Marie with its collection of 600 works from 27 countries, and the **Musée des Beaux-Arts**, a *belle-époque* villa built for Russian royalty at 33 Avenue des Baumettes, mainly devoted to 19th-century painting. Here too is the **Musée Masséna** at Rue de France 65 , a mixed bag including École de Nice tableaux and regional artefacts.

Also worth noting on the Promenade itself is the active **Ruhl Casino** and the very passive former **Palais de la Méditerranée**, now undergoing much needed restoration.

The seafront: The locals' sunny disposition derives from an ability to use the **beaches** every day in summer, in the grinding halt between noon and 3pm. The 3 miles (5 km) of curving seafront may be disappointingly pebbly, but they are clean, like the sea, and run right through the heart of town. For a quick dip, there is nothing wrong with the public beaches (there are 80 free show-

The Negresco Hotel.

ers), but 15 private establishments offer excellent facilities at half the price charged down the coast at Cannes. One favourite is **Opéra Plage**, which claims to be the oldest in France, run by the same family since 1906, just a towel's shake from the old Opera House and the man up the ladder.

Where the English Prom crosses the Atlantic is known as the **Quai des États-Unis;** here is the small but delightful Dufy museum. Traffic barrelling down the Prom vanishes into a tunnel in front of the old Opera House and emerges in the port area, a long-neglected side of Nice which, with its disciplined quays lined with terracotta and ochre buildings, bobbing yachts and excellent restaurants, is the epitome of the Mediterranean harbour.

For a city whose history depends so much on the sea **Lympia** is disappointingly bereft of tourist attractions, its main attribute being the bathing rocks on its eastern edge from which you can see the Corsican ferry glide by. However, all this may rapidly change as a new jetty is planned which is expected to attract cruise ships, and a revival of fortunes is anticipated in their wake.

An overview: For the best overview of what is not really a very complicated city you should have a car and drive up to the ruined fort of **Mont Alban**, approached through 140 acres (345 hectares) of municipal forest on **Mont Boron,** a good place for picnics. It is easy to see how the city has evolved in three different parts, with the **Paillon River** in the middle. Don't bother searching for that on a map: it is only a trickle and the entire river-bed has been covered over with the new promenade, roads, parks, and hanging gardens hiding a bus terminus and car-park. Here is the new **Acropolis** convention centre decorated inside and out with the work of contemporary artists, the **Musée d'Art Moderne et Contemporain** and the **"Promenade des Arts"**. It is a masterpiece of municipal planning, and whatever they say about Jacques Médecin this city is his living monument. Look for Avenue Félix Faure and Boulevard Jean Jaurès.

Nice's beachfront.

To the west is **Place Masséna**, the modern heart of the city, with its neo-classical red colonnades. This is the new town, with shops, hotels, and an extensive pedestrian zone housing smart boutiques with all the big designer names. **Avenue Jean Médecin**, a wide thoroughfare lined with plane trees to the north of Place Masséna, is the main business and shopping street. The **Jardin Albert I** is a refreshing oasis of fountains and from here you can take a mini-train for sightseeing.

To the east of the Paillon is the old town, signposted either as **Vieille Ville** or Vieux Nice. This has to be the *pièce de résistance*: a cracked basin of russet, yellow, pink and beige earth tones. You are now entering the Painted City, where the municipality is breathing new life into the 13th century.

The renaissance seems to be working all right, though the task may seem equivalent to the cleansing of the Augean stables in this warren of pedestrian alleys. There is always a remarkable busyness about the place. For all its medieval seductions, scaffolding is a perpetual hazard and ladders and buckets of paint are being winched away with bewildering urgency in a society more at ease with the Midi spirit of *farniente*. Look up and admire facades adorned with *trompe l'oeil* and frescoes, especially at the so-called Adam and Eve house in **Rue de la Poissonnerie**; the "Pistone" building in **Rue du Marché**; No. 20, **Rue de Malouat**; No.27, **Rue Benoît Bunico**; and in **Rue Pairolière**, where the "Maison de la Treille" (the house with a climbing vine) inspired one of Raoul Dufy's pictures. The showpiece is the **Palais Lascaris** (No.15 Rue Droite), a 17th-century mansion now completely restored as an elegant museum, complete with pharmacy and a splendid open staircase in the Genoese style.

The streets become darker and narrower the further in you go, with intriguing scents and smells coming from the doorways. As you advance through the labyrinth look at the lintels, some of which are inscribed with dates and in-

cantations; INTERNA MELIORA – "Inside it's Better" – hangs over a former brothel, now a crowded used-book store on **Rue Place Vieille.**

The 18th-century **Place Garibaldi** echoes the style of Place Masséna; nearby is the church of St-Martin-St-Augustin, where Garibaldi was baptised and Luther celebrated mass.

Place St-François is the morning fish market. **Rue Miralheti** is the place to sample classic street food such as *socca*, a delicious chickpea pancake not found anywhere else in France. **Place Rossetti** across from the painted facade (1650) of the **Cathédrale Ste-Reparate**, the city's patron, is the spot for ice-cream or coffee; admire the cathedral's bell tower and beautiful roof of coloured tiles. After years of neglect, it is all coming back to life again as the city's magnificent homogenous heart.

The markets: The promenade between the old city and the sea is known as **Cours Saleya**; famous residents like Matisse, who lived at the end of the Cours in a big yellow house (No. 1: it has snarling faces of plaster lions protruding from it), and Chagall loved the city and their work fills the museums.

It was from his third-floor window in the Vieille Ville that Matisse painted those cheerful little pictures of the blue sea, the palm trees and the houses with green shutters. He surely painted the market that is still held in the Cours, 655 yards (600 metres) long, separated from sea by the **Ponchettes** on one side and from the older part of town by the palace of the Sardinian kings, now the **Préfecture**, to the north. Don't miss the famous flower market open all day, or the fruit and vegetable market which vanishes at noon. On Mondays there is a large flea market; although bargains are unlikely there is bountiful variety of antique furniture, china and linen.

Artistic heritage: Nice has made an impressive contribution to the history of art; it first produced a school of primitive painters in the 15th and 16th centuries; it was home to the Van Loos in the 17th; Rodin worked here in the 19th and it has given its name to the modern

Shopping in the Place Masséna.

École de Nice centred around Yves Klein, Arman and César. This was born in the Vieille Ville and some of the best young artists of modern France now have their ateliers on **Rue Droite**, so named not because it is straight but for the fact that it directly connected the two main gates of the old city. As long ago as 1764, Tobias Smollett observed high society taking its *passeggiatas* along the Cours; one wonders what he would have made of the new lift shafts for the underground car-park, cunningly tricked out with paintings of market stalls with striped awnings, reflecting the bustling morning scene. It is so hard to distinguish fact from fiction, disguise from decoration.

Don't go looking for the **château,** by the way; it is just a trick of the tongue to match all this *trompe l'oeil.* One has not existed since the illegitimate son of James II razed it in 1706 on the orders of Louis XIV, thus sealing the fate of a citadel that was more than 2,000 years old. In its place on the 300-ft (90-metre) high hill are gardens, playgrounds, an artificial waterfall and a couple of discreet snack-bars – all very welcome on a hot day, but it's the panoramic views that attract people. There is a lift from the end of Quai des Étas-Unis.

Cimiez is most easily reached from the Boulevard de Cimiez. Here the Romans built their Cemenelum to compete with rival Greek Nikaïa down the road. It is noted for its recently excavated Roman ruins, including baths and the amphitheatre which is often used for festivals; the Archaeological Museum; the Chagall Museum (Avenue Dr Ménard), specially designed to house Chagall's masterpiece, *Messages Bibliques,* and the biggest single collection of his work. Most popular is the recently restored **Musée Matisse**, a 17th-century Genoese villa which cunningly conceals a new gallery wing beneath. It houses Matisse's personal collection, with works from every period, as well as the vases, shell furniture and Moroccan wall-hangings – even the giant cheese plant, which he so often included in his paintings.

Sculpture on the roof of the new art museum.

Once-fashionable Cimiez still has intimations of empire. The crowned heads of Europe – Britain, Sweden, Denmark, Portugal, Belgium and the entire Russian Imperial Family – once wintered up here in nine "palais-hotels" modelled on the ghastly Regina Palace, opened by Queen Victoria in 1897. In the western suburbs, on boulevard du Tzarewitch, you can find evidence of a once-thriving Russian colony, the finest **Russian Orthodox Cathedral** outside Russia. Its five green-and-gold onion domes pleased Tsar Nicholas II himself. Services are held in Russian.

Nice is nice: Nice might miss its castle but not much else. Despite being top dog in the holiday league with 8 million summer visitors and a comparatively small resident population of not much more than 400,000 it hasn't allowed its character and unique ambiance to be subsumed into soul-less skyscraper blocks. The newly-expanded airport still has orange trees in its car-park. Coconut-icing villas hide among the olives and parasol pines on the hills overlooking the Baie. Tunnels of plane trees on the main streets, Boulevard Victor Hugo and Avenue Jean Médecin, lead to shaded squares and fountained gardens. Downtown, the *fin-de-siècle* glory of the buildings, all of uniform height and rococo charm, sings to you in friezes, frescoes and domed arpeggios. The city has a human scale. Nice really is nice.

It is a real gutsy town with its own gutsy wine (Bellet, whose vines were planted by the Phoenicians who founded Marseille), a commercial life based on more than just its flower industry and a cultural richness second only to Paris. It is also surprisingly efficient and clean, equipped with automatic loos with piped muzak, spotless bus shelters and public phones which actually work. There are 40 wardens employed to prevent vandalism in its 750 acres (300 hectares) of public greenery, and 280 gardeners who start work at 5am daily.

Nice also has all the Identikit street furniture common to other big conurbations of the Fifth Republic, plus bendy buses to negotiate the corners, the **Three miles of pebbly beaches.**

Galeries Lafayette (a kind of French John Lewis), C & A, Habitat, and yes, even a couple of McDonald's.

And for all its Mediterranean *laissez-faire*, Nice is developing into a highly modern city: the Acropolis conference centre, in the middle of town, with a 2,500-seat auditorium – the biggest in France; the Arénas business centre opposite the airport; the expensive and carefully landscaped Haliotis sewage plant; and, on the way to the airport, the Parc Floral, the world's largest conservatory with seven different climatic zones.

There should be more to come. Other major projects include an ambitious métro system linking the northeastern edge of the city with the airport in the southwest, eventually branching inland and on to the Sophia-Antipolis science park 12 miles (19 km) away. There is plenty of action too. Its opera, concert-orchestra and international jazz festival are famous. Carnival has become a safer event now that the confetti is made of small bits of coloured paper rather than lumps of hard plaster (confetti once meant anything from small sugar-coated sweets to rotten eggs, flour, plaster, chickpeas, to egg-shells filled with soot and sand). The practice of throwing flowers became separated from the main event, and the Battle of Flowers is now an established attraction in its own right.

The Cours market in the Vieille Ville is perhaps the best place to take the pulse of Nice, a complete antidote to the pace of life on the other side of the Paillon. The performance is never-ending, though it is transformed dramatically with the firing of a mid-day gun, which is the time to discover that the pigeon you thought was painted was not. To the sound of clattering wings, the scenery changes miraculously as gangs of sweepers armed with brooms and high-pressure hoses march in and the market is cleaned up. Chairs and tables come out. Hardly a piece of ground is left unoccupied as the stage is set for a bravura performance of Niçois life. The whole place is turned into a sea of happy people absorbing the scene unfolding before them.

Cours Saleya flea market.

CAP FERRAT AND THE GOLDEN TRIANGLE

The area known as the **Corne d'Or** – Golden Horn or Golden Triangle – which includes Cap Ferrat, Beaulieu and Villefranche is very different from the Côte d'Azur to the west. The terrain changes dramatically beyond Nice, from wide bays to dramatic towering cliffs. Every view is dominated by the mountains, giving it a grandeur that would be impossible to spoil – though thankfully, apart from in Monaco, no one has really tried.

The famous corniche roads are spectacular, snaking one above the other round the mountain side. Along the cliff top, the **Grande Corniche** follows the old Roman road, the Via Aurelia, to Italy, and was built by Napoleon for military purposes. After passing through La Turbie it descends at Roquebrune and ends at Menton. The Lower Corniche road, **la Basse Corniche**, built in the 18th century, emerges from Nice at the old Port Douanges, then winds its way around the Cap de Nice, offering spectacular views across Villefranche Bay to the high ridge of Cap Ferrat.

The traffic is worse on the Basse Corniche than the higher roads, but it is well worth it for the views. The Moyenne Corniche is the most recently built of the roads. All the corniche levels are connected by roads, and there is also a railway running along the coast.

Villefranche-sur-Mer is a surprisingly unspoiled little town, given its proximity to Nice and the fact that the American 6th fleet used it as a base until the French left NATO. Villefranche was founded in the 14th century as a customs-free port by Charles II of Anjou and British and American ships still use its wonderful harbour, which is one of the deepest in the world.

The town itself is well restored but not bijou; there is plenty of authentic laundry hanging from the balconies and inquisitive matrons leaning from their windows to gossip across the narrow streets. The entire town of citadel, port and old streets has retained an homogenous, medieval character.

The huge 16th-century stone **Citadel of St-Elme** dominates the bay and looks impregnable enough to still fulfil its original function, though the deep dry moat is now used, intelligently, as a car-park. It is like an enormous quarry, with sheer walls set at an angle for greater stability and tiny watchtowers and viaducts crossing on slender pylons.

There is a bridge over the moat entrance to the citadel, marked by what used to be a drawbridge in a portal dated 1557. Now the giant iron-studded doors to the fortress have an incongruous modern letterbox. Within the walls are housed the town **Mairie**, the chapel of St-Elme, and several museums.

The Henri Goetz-Christine Baoumeester Museum is a collection of about 100 minor works by Picasso, Han Hartung, Picabia and Miró, all of which were gifts to the couple. Volti was a resident of Villefranche and the Volti Museum has a good collection of his monumental smooth figurative sculp-

Preceding pages: the bay of Villefranche from St-Jean-Cap-Ferrat. Left, terracotta ues of Villefranche harbour. Right, Villa Kerylos, Beaulieu.

tures, most of them female, some of which are displayed outside in the main courtyard of the citadel. The citadel also contains the museum of the 24th Batallion of the Alpine Light Infantry.

The old town of Villefranche nestles in the protection of the citadel, very Italian in its architecture and atmosphere; along the front of the old Port de la Santé the houses have a cheerful, faded air, each facade a different colour ranging from terracotta and ochre to rose and magnolia with the shutters painted half a dozen different shades of green. There are lots of attractive little bars and restaurants along the quay and in the alleyways leading to it. On the Quai Courbet is the tiny 14th-century **Chapelle St-Pierre**, with a candy-coloured facade and interior decorated by Jean Cocteau, who spent his childhood in Villefranche.

Many of the houses in the old town are built on the Italian model with large arched loggias on the ground floor, most of which have subsequently been filled in. The area around the church features the steepest, most winding streets and twisted houses. The church itself is 18th-century Italian baroque, with an early 14th-century origin of which little can be seen. It features many religious statues, including one of Jesus and another of Mary, both with electric halos.

The town seems to specialise in *trompe l'oeil* wall painting: usually windows, often with cats in them. There is a good window with cat on the **Place de la République**, a charming little square with a large shady pine tree in the centre and houses dating from the 17th and 18th centuries. In one instance the eye is deceived by a chapel with an entire *faux* Pisan Romanesque facade, which has what appears to be a genuine Pisan-style doorway dated 1590, right next door to the American Navy judo school on the Rue de l'Église.

The main street of the old town is the **Rue du Poilu**, which leads to the tiny Place du Conseil, from which there is a good view of the harbour and Cap Ferrat. Starting from the Place du Conseil is the celebrated 13th-century **Rue Obscure**.

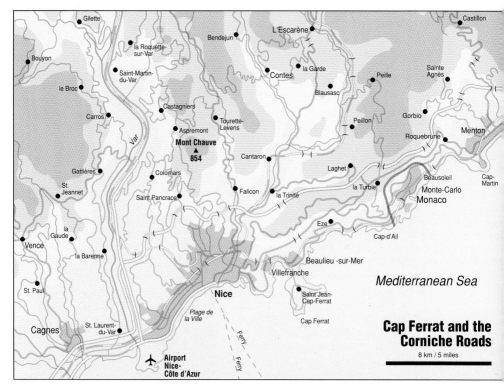

Cap Ferrat and the Corniche Roads

8 km / 5 miles

Steps lead down to an arched passage which has changed little since it was built; the street is almost entirely composed of covered passageways which the inhabitants could reach from back doors or intersecting streets and squares. Here the inhabitants would shelter whenever the town was bombarded, which, given its strategic position and excellent harbour, was often.

Where the Rue Obscure crosses the **Rue de l'Église** is perhaps the most picturesque spot in the town. The blue waters of the harbour glint through an arch at the end of the street.

The turning off La Petite Corniche for **Cap Ferrat** is marked, significantly, by a shop offering electronic surveillance systems and 24-hour personal security. This is a very expensive, very private place but well worth a visit, if only to see how the other 3 percent live. A 6-mile (10-km) road right round the Cap offers glimpses of luxurious villas and magnificent gardens, all secreted behind high hedges and serious gates.

The **Musée Ephrussi de Rothschild**

is a good example of how they used to live. Seventeen acres (7 hectares) of gardens spread right along the crest of the Cap with wonderful panoramic views on all sides. The pink-and-white *belle-époque* villa was built to house the personal art collection of the Baroness Ephrussi de Rothschild and includes a magnificent variety of mainly 18th-century furniture, porcelain, carpets and paintings. The ceilings were specifically designed around her Tiepolos.

The grand salon leads out on to a marble terrace with views to each side of the Cap and down to the gardens. They are perfect for gentle strolling, through the cactus grove, the Japanese garden, the Italian sunken garden with grotto, even a temple of Diana; all, it must be said, looking somewhat neglected. But sitting under the deep green shade of the umbrella pines, cooled by gentle breezes, looking out to an aquamarine sea, it is easy to understand the appeal of such a perfect place. It is an appeal felt more strongly perhaps by latter-day visitors than the Baroness

Musée Ephrussi de Rothschild, St-Jean-Cap-Ferrat.

herself, who didn't get around to visiting the mansion between World War I and her death in 1934.

Cap Ferrat has the reputation of having the most pleasant climate on the Riviera and it was for this reason that Leopold II, King of Belgium, bought it. (He also bought the Congo, making Belgium one of the world's major colonial powers.) On the peninsula he created a large park, Les Cèdres, with a palace for himself and three houses, one for each of his mistresses, one of which, La Radiana, was recently up for sale for £9.5 million. With so many mistresses at hand, Leopold was concerned that he might die without absolution, so in 1906 he built a house near his palace for his confessor Monseigneur Charmeton.

It was this house, set in 8 acres (3.2 hectares) of terraced land, that Somerset Maugham bought in 1926. He called it the Villa Mauresque because Charmeton had it designed in the Moorish style. It is possible to visit the gardens of **Les Cèdres**, which has more than 15,000 rare plants set in 35 acres of woodland overlooking Villefranche Bay. There is a zoo in what used to be a lake on the estate, which is very popular for its daily chimpanzees' tea-party.

In 1938, the Duke and Duchess of Windsor arrived on the Riviera, adding even more cachet to the already exclusive Cap Ferrat scene. They rented Sir Pomeroy Burton's villa where the duke dug the garden and the duchess kept house. The Duke insisted that his guests refer to the duchess as Her Royal Highness, despite a strict edict from Buckingham Palace that she was not permitted to use such a title.

Soon the Cap was home to industrialists such as Singer, the sewing machine magnate, and show-business glitterati like Charlie Chaplin. Later residents included Edith Piaf, David Niven and Otto Preminger. More recent residents have included the Rolling Stones, who lived there as tax exiles, and Tina Turner. Despite the predominance of private estates, a great deal of the natural beauty of the peninsula, which includes some of the oldest olive trees in France, can

Interior, La Radiana, a villa built for Leopold II's mistress.

still be seen. There is a 6-mile (10-km) footpath all around the headland, most of it following the cliff edge or at sea level itself. It is clearly marked: approaching from Villefranche, it begins at Passable Beach and continues to St-Jean-Cap-Ferrat. Another promenade extends from the harbour at St-Jean-Cap-Ferrat around the Fourmis Bay to Beaulieu-sur-Mer.

The village of **St-Jean-Cap-Ferrat** consists of little more than a beautiful yacht harbour, once home to fishing boats, lined with a few old houses and cafés, with a small residential area extending up the hillside. There is a one-way system in and out of the village and parking is often difficult. On the very tip of the Cap is the exclusive and fashionable **Grand Hôtel du Cap Ferrat**, which is set in wonderful gardens at the water's edge.

Just the other side of the isthmus is **Beaulieu-sur-Mer**, a town with a slightly more refined air to it - the Cheltenham of the Côte d'Azur. Here beach clothes anywhere other than the beach

are still rather frowned on, though all that is changing rapidly.

It always seems to be warm in Beaulieu, which claims to have the best climate on the coast, protected from the north wind by a great rock face. It is thus a popular retirement town, with many elegant rest homes and genteel hotels surrounded by softly waving palm trees, neatly clipped hedges and carefully weeded gardens. It is quietly stylish if a little old-fashioned, with shops offering goods of the highest quality.

It also boasts some of the best hotels on the Riviera; the Russian and British gentry spent their winters in Beaulieu, which used to be one of the most fashionable of the Riviera resorts. The elegant turn-of-the-century luxury hotels known as the Riviera Palaces, in which they stayed are still there, surrounded by beautiful, well-tended gardens.

The **Promenade Maurice Rouvier** extends along the sea front and follows the coast of Cap Ferrat all the way to St-Jean-Cap-Ferrat, past villas and hotels with beautiful gardens. In the town the

High society.

walk goes through formal flower gardens flanked by park seats looking out to Fourmis Bay.

One of the few remaining indications that Beaulieu-sur-Mer is an old town is the 11th-century Romanesque chapel near the old fishing port. It has a fine round apse and round arches and was sympathetically restored in 1960. Also worth a visit is the **Villa Kerylos**, a complete reconstruction of a Greek villa with marble columns and cool courtyards open to the sky and sea, housing a large collection of mosaics, frescoes and antique furniture.

Further along the Basse Corniche, the Commune of Èze has built a resort on the seafront of its land called Èze-Bord-de-Mer with its own private beach and Club Nautique. Just before Monaco is the secluded Cap d'Ail, a luxury retreat of private villas and hotels.

Èze itself is accessible from the Moyenne Corniche. It is possibly the most *perché* of all the perched villages, with steep lanes, tiny twisting alleys and crooked steps. The rock upon which

Èze is built is so sheer that very little fortification was ever needed and there are only two gates to the town.

The **Rue du Barri** climbs up steps, tunnels under houses and meanders over them. There are wonderful features to be seen at every turn; here a cluster of medieval chimneys, there a Romanesque window or tiny rooftop garden. Some of the houses are still ruinous but on the whole the standard of the restoration has been very zealous; indeed, with very few residents remaining, the entire place is like a bijou museum, most of it given over to small shops, galleries and restaurants. From the terraces there are superb views of the surrounding cliffs and out to the Mediterranean.

Èze has almost ceased to exist many times, and its beleaguered past reflects the history of the region very well. For some of its history Èze has been nothing but a charred, empty ruin, at other times it has risen to become a great power. It was a Ligurian settlement later fortified by the Phoenicians and developed by the Romans, who established a harbour in the bay below. After the Romans came the Lombards, who in AD 578 murdered the inhabitants and burned the town to the ground. The Lombards held Èze until AD 740, when the Saracens appeared, enslaving any inhabitants they could capture and murdering the rest. It was they who built the first castle in Èze.

Èze was one of the last strongholds of the Saracens; they were not driven from Provence until 980. Naturally they razed the town when they left. After the Saracens things could only get worse; it was taken and retaken over and over, first by the Guelphs, then by the Ghibellines, then by the House of Anjou and the Counts of Provence. Èze was continually burned to the ground, its inhabitants tortured and starved into submission. It suffered from the plague and was devastated by fever, burned by lightning and toppled by an earthquake. In the 14th century it was finally bought by Amadeus of Savoy, whose family retained control until the entire area was ceded to France in 1860.

During the Middle Ages, Èze became

Wedding in Èze.

244

a centre of piracy, and vaulted passages and storerooms were built to hide the booty. A particularly nasty massacre took place when the French army of Francis I, aided by the Turkish fleet, launched an attack in 1543. The Turks were under the command of the corsair Barbarossa, known as Redbeard. Accompanying him was Gaspard de Caïs, a native of the area who, for a price, had agreed to turn traitor to his friends and kinfolk.

Yet again Èze was put to the sword. Street by street, the inhabitants were sytematically slaughtered. Such fortifications that could be destroyed were levelled and the castle was blown to pieces with its own store of powder. The town was looted and then burned. A new Èze slowly grew from the ruins. The castle, however, was dismantled in 1606 on orders of King Louis XIV. The earthquake of 1887 did more damage to the town and the lightning of the terrible storm of May 1887 split what remained of the town walls. The village was abandoned and by the 1920s was almost completely depopulated.

A 1921 guidebook to the area (*The Riviera of the Corniche Road* by Sir Frederick Treves) reported: "It is a silent town and desolate. On the occasion of a certain visit the only occupant I came upon was a half-demented beggar who gibbered in an unknown tongue."

Today there is little left of the castle, which is now surrounded by the **Jardin Exotique**, a fine collection of cacti and succulents. The church was rebuilt in 1765, though a 16th-century font remains. The 14th-century White Penitents' chapel on the **Place du Planet** should not be missed; it has an unusual 1258 Catalan crucifix with Christ smiling. Other features of the village include the narrow path to the coast favoured by Frederich Nietzche as he conceived *Thus Spake Zarathustra*.

The only pirates encountered today in Èze are those selling furry animals, handmade pottery, and Provençal fabric as wave after wave of tourists invade the village in centuries-old tradition. The views of the sea from the summit of Èze are spectacular.

The steep, twisting streets of Èze.

MONACO

Monaco's fiercest critic was Katherine Mansfield, who labelled it *"Real Hell,* the cleanest, most polished place I've ever seen". She preferred her home in sleepy Menton to this "procession of pimps, governesses in thread gloves - Jews – old, old hags, ancient men, stiff and greyish, panting on the climb, rich fat capitalists, little girls tricked out to look like babies".

Today Mansfield might be charged with ageism, racism and snobbery or just plain unfairness. "Rich fat capitalists", for example, are now quite sleek through working out in Monte-Carlo Golf Club. And Monaco boasts an idyllic natural setting, glamorous residents, Americanised culture and international cuisine. Yet Mansfield's repugnance does strike a chord, at least with ordinary visitors. Society runs like clockwork: toy-town guards seem to be everywhere; and multilingual signs tell visitors not to walk around "bare-chested or barefoot".

"To live in Monaco, all you need is good taste and a lot of money," proclaims the principality's *Society* magazine. Money is essential but good taste is optional, even a liability. In short, everything – except perhaps Monégasque citizenship – is available at a price. The writer Anthony Burgess, who was a long-term resident, once called Monaco "the most uncultivated community I've ever come across."

Mere creativity cannot compete with financial talk. Residents have the highest per capita income in the world. Given its size, Monaco arguably has the greatest ratio of banks in the world. Its status as a tax haven has led to Monaco's claim to hold $25 billion in deposits, 60 percent belonging to non-residents. In fact, out of a population of 30,000, only 6,000 residents are Monégasques. Of the rest, 40 percent are French, 17 percent are Italian and 5 percent are British.

This pocket handkerchief of a country could fit neatly into New York's Central Park. Monaco's critics call it a princely theme park where fairy-tale lifestyles are shrewdly sold. The principality's tourist board boasts of *"Monaco – un rêve, une réalité"*. Writer Jeffrey Robinson pokes gentle fun at the nonchalant vulgarity of the Monaco jet set. "On a grand yacht, a Chinese waitress lays a buffet for 20 guests who will shortly be leaving on a two-hour cruise to nowhere, burning 40,000 francs worth of gasoline in the process."

The current ruler, Prince Rainier III, rules like a Medici who has been on a marketing course. Monaco's independence is guaranteed by France but Rainier is nonetheless worried that Monaco will be dragged into the European Community. With the advent of the single market, Monaco's future is in jeopardy. The harmonisation of value-added tax would mean the end to Monaco's most lucrative source of revenue as would the possibility that European Union citizens might lose their tax-exempt status.

Still, Rainier is optimistic that Monaco can become "a financial outpost", the Hong Kong of the Mediterranean,

Preceding pages: Monaco Casino. Left, Monégasque chic. Right, a princely theme park.

with its own tax system and political status. The Grimaldi are survivors.

Sea, skyscrapers and mountains form concentric circles around the headland that is Monaco. A looming crag, the Tête de Chien, is the backdrop to Monaco-Ville, the medieval quarter built on Le Rocher. The Rock is flanked by two harbours, the artificial Port de Fontvieille to the west and the original Port de Monaco to the east. From here to Monte-Carlo stretches the dull Condamine quarter, an area in which *belle-époque* villas are fast giving way to high-rise sprawl. Monte-Carlo, perched on a skyscraper-studded hill, has been dubbed "Manhattan-sur-Mer" or "Las Vegas-Plage".

Princely sights: From the Place d'Armes it is a short but steep walk up to the **Palais des Princes**, Rainier's official winter residence. The walk, linking the port and the palace, leads through medieval gateways. Until 1863 the gates to the old town were closed at night, much to the annoyance of sociable Monégasques. The final arch, La Rampe

Major, opens on to Palace Square, known as *Placa d'u Palaci* in Monégasque, an obscure Provençal-Genovese dialect. The square is dotted with old cannons, some presented by Louis XIV to the Grimaldi Dynasty.

The salmon-pink palace was pale yellow until it was redesigned by Princess Grace. When Prince Rainier's red and white diamond-spangled banner is flying, the Prince is in residence and the Palace is closed to the public. Rainier claims that people feel more secure when he is "at home" rather than on his Mont Agel farm in the French foothills behind Monaco. Visitors who arrive at 11.55 will see the changing of the guard, a daily ceremony performed by the Prince's French *carabinieri*. The Constitution forbids the use of Monégasque guards, a precaution designed to prevent a coup d'état. Depending upon the season, the *carabinieri* are dressed in winter blue and red-striped uniforms or in dazzling white.

The State Apartments are sumptuous recreations of palatial 17th- and 18th-

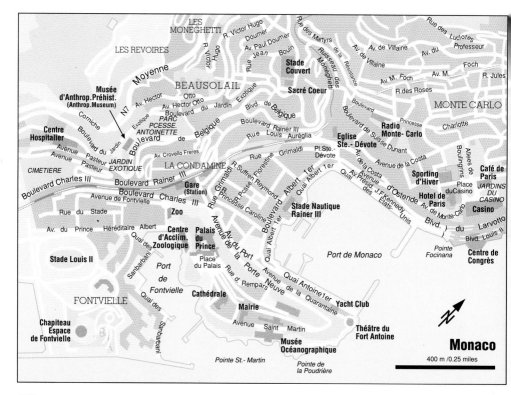

Monaco

400 m /0.25 miles

century decor. The Cour d'Honneur, an Italianate quadrangle, forms the backdrop for concerts. However, the most appealing room is the Chambre d'York, where the Duke of York, George III's brother, died. He was on his way to visit a mistress in Genoa when he was taken ill off Monaco. Here, reported Horace Walpole, "the poor Duke of York has ended his silly, good-humoured, troublesome career in a piteous manner." Still, he chose a bedchamber with a frescoed ceiling, Venetian furniture and a gilt-encrusted, canopied bed.

From outside the palace, there are fine views over the **Port de Fontvieille**, a hugely successful development. Built on 30 acres (74 hectares) of reclaimed land, it half-heartedly combines highrises with Provençal colours. Also down below is the Parc de Fontvieille, the Princess Grace Rose Garden and the Terasses de Fontvieille, a new complex including several museums; the Prince's collection of vintage cars, a **Musée Naval**, and a **Musée des Timbres et des Monnaies** (Stamps and Coins).

In the 1970s Prince Rainier realised that he had to expand Monaco's economic base so created this quarter as a home to non-pollutant light industry, especially perfumes and electronics. These industries now produce 30 percent of state revenue while value-added tax provides 50 percent and, contrary to popular belief, gambling brings in less than 5 percent. As Rainier says: "Nowadays we probably have as many gardeners as croupiers." In fact, the proliferation of gardeners and gendarmes is proof that Monaco is a civil servants' paradise.

Monaco-Ville: From the Palace, a stroll through the old quarter leads to the cathedral and exotic gardens. This area is a labyrinth of covered passageways, tiny squares, fountains and tangerine-coloured facades. Rue Basse has old porticoed houses with carved lintels and vaulted cellars. But in the height of summer it is hard to appreciate the architecture since the quarter is given over to tawdry tourist trinkets, including Princess Caroline T-shirts, Prince Rainier

Monaco from the Corniche road.

mugs and Princess Stephanie's albums. The **Cathedral** dominates a rocky spur, like the figurehead of a boat. The clinical white building was built in 1884 on the site of a medieval church. Designed in neo-Romanesque style with Byzantine flourishes, it is at once majestic and oppressive. The greatest treasures lie in the Chapelle des Princes, the Grimaldi burial chamber. Princess Grace's tomb is nearby, adorned with fresh pink roses. Above is a series of lovely paintings, including the St Nicolas altarpiece by Louis Bréa, the great Niçois artist.

Just outside the cathedral are the lush **Jardins St-Martin**, descending to the sea. Tiers of Aleppo pines and yellow agaves wind around the headland. The gardens are dotted with 18th-century turrets and medieval fortifications. In these manicured and neatly-labelled gardens, bossy signs forbid the feeding of goldfish and cats. In fact, the goldfish are fat enough already and the teams of watchful, uniformed gardeners are a definite cat-deterrent. Visitors who stop too often are virtually taken in for questioning. From here the Avenue St-Martin leads to Prince Albert's grandiose **Oceanographic Museum**. In summer, a tourist submarine plies the waters down below.

Known as the Navigator Prince, Albert is the best-loved of previous sovereigns. He dedicated his life to the oceans and this "temple of the sea" is his memorial. The undoubted star is the aquarium, a surreal home to weird species: secretive crabs called *dromies* hide in sponges clutched in their back legs; *Bernard l'Hermite* travels with a sea anemone permanently lodged on his back; the noble female octopus waits weeks for her eggs to hatch on her tentacles; as soon as her offspring are born, she dies, exhausted.

One of the most startling sights is not a fish at all but a model of a live coral reef taken from the waters off Djibouti. Children are drawn to the huge tank of *catsharks* and *black-tip reef shark,* which constantly circle a wrecked boat alive with yellow and blue surgeon fish. It is a sobering thought that every morning

The love of money.

the aquarium occupants devour over 8,800 lbs (4,000 kg) of mussels, sardines, seafood cocktail and spinach.

From Monaco-Ville a short bus journey or steep walk leads to the equally surreal environment of the **Jardin Exotique**. These tropical gardens are set just below the Moyenne Corniche. The former mayor of Monaco likens the scene to the Hanging Gardens of Babylon, exotic praise for gardens on the same line of latitude as Vladivostok. Naturally, it is Monaco's balmy climate that fosters plants normally found in Madagascar or Southern California.

Landscaping the cliffs was a mammoth feat of engineering, taking 20 years to complete. The result is breathtaking: tiered gardens are interlinked by high footbridges and canopies of vegetation; secluded spots are formed by pergolas and arbours; an ornamental pond is enclosed by jungle-like greenery. To weed the gardens specialists have to be suspended in parachute harnesses over the cliff. The stars are the fierce-looking cacti and succulents, in particular those

on the path known as the Valley of the Candles.

Amongst the 8,000 species of plants are Mexican yuccas, Peruvian monster candles and Moroccan euphorbia that grow up to 49 ft (15 metres) high. Prickly pears, red aloes and downy-eared elephant ears climb up the rocky vaults. The most striking plant is the Mexican echinocactus: it resembles a spiky hedgehog and is better known as "mother-in-law's pillows".

At the foot of the Jardin Exotique is a series of strange caves known as the **Grottes de l'Observatoire**. A precarious descent through the garden is followed by slippery steps leading down to the bottom of the caves. All around are stalagmites and stalagtites, ice-blue pools and natural sculptures. The majestic Grande Salle resembles the inside of a cathedral, with Romanesque pillars and baptismal fonts. The galleries are impressive for their silence, broken only by the faint dripping of water.

Builder prince: Between Monaco-Ville and Monte-Carlo is the portside busi-

The Hong Kong of the Mediterranean.

ness area known as **La Condamine**. The railway brought prosperity but lemon groves were supplanted by villas and now skyscrapers. Not for nothing is Rainier known as the Builder Prince. A minuscule studio can cost in the region of 1.5 million francs. Rainier defends his record: "If I build, then I'm a spend-thrift. If I don't, then what's to become of the working classes?" Princess Grace complained that one couldn't sunbathe on the beach after 3pm because of long shadows cast by the skyscrapers. In short, no one claims responsibility for Californian-style patios, hexagonal sky-scrapers and a disfigured skyline.

However, the **Port de Monaco** is striking enough, particularly if filled with magnificent cruise liners. From the golden years of the 1950s onwards, Ar-istotle Onassis's boat *Christina* was moored here and often welcomed Prin-cess Grace aboard. The 1960s and '70s saw the jet set take to water, with or without Greek shipping tycoons.

Here, Charles Revson, the cosmetics tycoon, dreamed up new products on his opulent *Ultima II*. Times have indeed changed: Donald Trump had his boat impounded for failing to settle debts. Current visitors are more likely to be bored Italian industrialists or South American gamblers.

In the right company, and with the right income, **Monte-Carlo** is still a name to conjure with. However, the only magical area is the Place du Casino and the Square Beaumarchais. As well as the Casino and the Salle Garnier, this golden square boasts the Hôtel de Paris, the Café de Paris and the Hôtel Hermit-age, haunts worth visiting for their ar-chitecture as well as their atmosphere. Until the building of the Place du Ca-sino, the steep-sided Mont Charles hill was known as a "desert riddled with insalubrious caves". In 1886 the new railway brought aristocratic visitors to gamble in a *belle-époque* setting – and the rest is history.

The **Hôtel de Paris** has a delightful setting, overlooking the lush Casino gardens, the Café de Paris and the sea. Built in 1864, this inspirational hotel set

Monaco Grand Prix.

the tone for the rest. It was designed with unbridled extravagance and borrows from an earlier rococo style. Exquisite details include the gracious rotunda with its fan-shaped portico, the curvaceous cupolas and the facades decorated with bare-breasted figureheads. The interior is equally captivating, with caryatids adorning the reception rooms and restaurants.

Alain Ducasse, one of the world's top chefs, presides over the Louis XV restaurant, following in the footsteps of the great Escoffier. The Louis XV is a neo-baroque concoction with cream and gold decor surpassed by a frescoed ceiling. Here, Ducasse pampers the privileged with Italo-Provençal cuisine. Guests include Sophia Loren, Ringo Starr and Roger Moore, all of whom have apartments in Monaco. The Salle Empire restaurant is equally luxurious, decorated with frescoes of bathing nymphs. On its opening night in 1866, the restaurant served caviare and pink champagne, and little has changed since then. Le Grill rooftop restaurant appeals to the

informal, younger set, including Boris Becker, Bjorn Borg and Princess Stephanie. Still, this motley crew of sportsmen and stars pales in comparison with the procession of grand dukes, royals and statesman who once peopled the hotel. After losing her last 100,000 francs in the Casino, Sarah Bernhardt made a failed suicide bid in her suite here. In more recent times, Onassis retained a suite for his special house guests, including Winston Churchill and his pet parrot. Here, Churchill and Lord Beaverbrook once polished off a bottle of 1815 cognac before breakfast.

In 1943 the Hôtel de Paris was occupied by the Gestapo. In theory Monaco was neutral but Rainier's grandfather supported the Vichy régime. Goering and Himmler used the principality as a place for laundering war spoils. The hotel manager feared for the loss of his finest wines and cognacs so concealed them in a crypt at the bottom of the cellar. The other bottles were drunk but his cache remained intact. It is still the deepest hotel wine cellar in the world

Palais des Princes.

GRIMALDI INC.

If Monaco is now referred to as Grimaldi Inc, it is thanks to the business acumen of the present ruler, Rainier III. The Grimaldi are Europe's oldest reigning family and the last constitutional autocrats. The male line has twice died out but then sovereignty has passed through the female line. Yet the throne is never totally secure.

This old Ligurian family from Genoa were exiled during the medieval political struggle between Guelphs and Ghibellines. The Grimaldi clan found a new power base in Monaco in 1297 and have ruled there ever since. Legend has it a woman wronged by Rainier I put a curse on the Grimaldi line, denying them lasting happiness.

Until the French Revolution, the princes lived on taxes levied on wine, lemons, tobacco, shipping and playing cards. Menton and Roquebrune formed part of Monaco until 1848 and their loss reduced Monaco's territory by 94 percent. However, the creation of Monte-Carlo by Charles III delivered Monaco to grand tourism, which flourished until the reign of Louis II, Prince Rainier III's grandfather. Rainier's mother,

Princess Charlotte, was the fruit of Louis' liaison with a washerwoman he met in North Africa. Rainier, educated in England and Switzerland, is the first prince to have been born in Monaco and is also the first full-time sovereign. After acceding to the throne in 1949, Rainier set about running Monaco as a business empire, reducing its dependence on gambling.

Rainier's marriage in 1956 to the Hollywood star Grace Kelly brought a new glamour to Monaco, and her tragic death in a car accident in 1982 was a great blow. Grace's legacy lies in the Americanisation of Monaco, from the business ethos to the sophisticated social life, from the street names to the shopping malls. The Gallerie du Sporting is typical Monaco franglais, in keeping with Rainier's mixed marriage. The greatest crisis of his reign was in 1962, when President de Gaulle, trying to stop French citizens settling in Monaco to avoid paying French taxes, sealed off Monaco's borders until Rainier conceded the issue. Still, except for unlucky French citizens, Monaco remains a tax haven.

In 1997 Monaco celebrated 700 years of independence with great celebrations: musical concerts, sports events, boat races and an historic Grand Prix with classic cars, one of Prince Rainier's passions. Plans for further developments include an extension of the Fontvieille complex to include a new conference centre, a new deep-sea jetty and further offshore developments.

However, the fortunes of the principality are far from secure. The possibility that Monaco may be dragged into the European Union presents a major threat, especially if EU nationals lose their tax-exempt status. The 1990s saw a significant drop in tourism and disastrous losses for the casino business. Like the rest of the Côte d'Azur, financial scandals began to emerge.

Nor did the Grimaldi family escape disaster. Princess Stephanie's sad trail of broken romances (and failed careers) finally resulted in a particularly unsuitable liaison with her bodyguard. Princess Caroline, the eldest, has not escaped the Grimaldi curse. In 1990 her second husband, Stefano Casiraghi, was killed while competing in the World Offshore Boat Race, leaving Caroline with three children and huge debts. After Grace's death, Caroline assumed most of her mother's cultural duties but is tired of being Monaco's First Lady – but Prince Albert, Rainier's heir apparent, shows no sign of marrying. Despite his playboy tastes, Albert has been perfectly groomed to inherit a £200-million fortune. ■

Rainer III: victim of a woman's curse?

and boasts a "champagne alley" with bottles dating back to 1805.

Outside the hotel is a bronze statue of Louis XV on horseback. The gleaming fetlock has long been stroked by gamblers in search of luck. At the end of the facade is a secret bronze door adorned with a mirror. It conceals a lift which leads to the Casino via a secret passageway. During his time as owner of the Casino, Onassis installed the system so that no one would witness the jubilation or despair on the faces of gamblers returning to their suites.

The **Café de Paris** was once an equally glamorous location. It was built in 1865 but acquired an art deco interior in the 1920s. The overall effect is seaside Edwardian, with a delicious peaches and cream facade adorned with a fan-shaped portico. Floral mosaics and stained-glass designs lend sophistication to the interior. However, the Café's claim to fame is linked to the womaniser, Edward VII. Legend has it that Escoffier was preparing a special dessert which accidentally caught fire. Edward's companion was Suzette and the *flambé* was christened *crêpe suzette* in her honour.

Just around the corner on Square Beaumarchais is the **Hotel Hermitage**, the loveliest of the *belle-époque* hotels. It also lays claim to being the most discreet, not that anywhere with gold-encrusted cupids and rococo guests should be so bold. It has a dramatic setting above the port and opposite the Rock. Built in 1890, the hotel indulges in soft lines and sensual sculptures. With its understated elegance, the glass-domed Jardin d'Hiver is the ideal winter garden. Light is filtered through a stained-glass sunflower, a cool scene complemented by lush ferns and wrought-iron balconies.

The Casino: Terraced gardens and fountains lead down to the green-domed Casino and the sea. Amongst the lushness are pineapple-shaped palms, ferns and figs, jacaranda and magnolia. The Casino was created by Prince Florestan, the founder of Monte-Carlo. The Prince wanted a world stage for Monaco arts and, having lost Monégasque territory

The Grimaldis at the Monte-Carlo opera.

to France, also needed to generate new revenue. Inspired by the success of aristocratic tourism in Baden Baden, he realised that good health and gambling were a winning combination.

The early attempts were unsuccessful but the Casino's luck changed when François Blanc, a talented fraudster, bought the concession. He was helped by the arrival of the railway and by his European gambling monopoly. Business boomed in the *belle époque*.

If the Casino was losing heavily, a black cloth was placed over a table as a sign of mourning. Occasionally, lucky gamblers would "break the bank". If so, the coffers were ostentatiously refilled since Blanc shrewdly realised, "One winner always attracts a crowd of losers." One lucky loser was a bankrupt Pole who tried to commit suicide. With admirable sense of public relations, the Casino gave him a room in the Hotel de Paris and presented him with a ticket home. Cunning not charity was the name of the game.

But Lord Salisbury, Queen Victoria's long-serving prime minister, was refused admission to the Casino, having come to the Riviera without his passport. "You see, I'm the man who issues them," was not considered a good enough excuse.

World War I brought the end to grand tourism and Monte-Carlo faced competition from casinos in Cannes, Menton and Nice. In 1951, soon after Prince Rainier came to power, Aristotle Onassis took over the Casino. While Onassis wanted to maintain the Casino as a glamorous preserve, Rainier wanted to open up Monaco to bourgeois tourism. After a showdown in 1962, Rainier wrested control and made the state the principal shareholder.

Today, the Casino retains much of its old glamour as well as its strict rules. A sign by the Casino forbids ministers of religion or Monégasques to enter the *salles de jeux*. If the Grimaldi attend an opera in the Casino's Salle Garnier, they have to enter through a side door.

The Casino is decorated in exuberant *belle-époque* style. Daylight filters

Residents have the highest per capita income in the world.

through stained-glass domes and windows; bronze lamps are held aloft by sculpted nymphs.

To admire the architecture, one should come in the late afternoon but for atmosphere only the late evening will do. In the *salons privés*, serious bets are laid by cigar-smoking gamblers with glazed expressions. Games include roulette, craps, blackjack, baccarat and *chemin de fer*. Spectators eddy from table to table and sound is reduced to low murmurs and sliding chips. No one drinks; gambling is the only addiction.

The entrance staircase boasts a sculpted palm, welcoming one to the Salon des Palmiers and the summery feel of the Casino. Yet the *salons ordinaires* are disappointing. The slot machines seem out of place beside gilded mirrors, chandeliers, cut flowers and Fragonard paintings. In the plush Salon Rose bar, gamblers play on space invaders; on the ceiling, sculpted nudes puff cigars, a reminder that this was once the smoking-room. Just off these public rooms is Le Train Bleu, a chic restaurant modelled on the famous train that brought high society to the Riviera.

The *salons privés* are only private insofar as there is a second admission charge. That said, stakes are much higher and non-gamblers are discouraged by the door manager's penetrating gaze. This is no mere doorman but someone with a photographic memory for matching faces to gambling history. The most famous of these "physiognomists" was Monsieur le Broq, who claimed to have memorised over 60,000 faces. The Casino's main "bank" can also be made to vanish down a trap-door in the event of a hold-up.

In the *salons privés* there is a high ratio of croupiers to clients. The croupiers are Las Vegas-trained and form the most powerful lobby in Monaco. When workers went on strike in 1968, the croupiers were the only ones who picketed in Cadillacs. John Addington Symonds had little good to say of the breed in 1866: "The croupiers are either fat, sensual cormorants or sallow, lean-cheeked vultures, or suspicious foxes."

High rollers at the casino.

In the 1970s many of the major players were Arabs. Adnan Khashoggi and Prince Fahd played for $2 million bets and insisted on playing alone. The Casino encourages the maximum number of players to spread the risk so was not pleased by the Arabs' dramatic winnings. To save its skin, the Casino made a deal: the Arabs could play in private at any time of day or night but had to stay until 6am and stop then, whatever the outcome. The Arabs tired and the Casino won.

Nowadays, the big gamblers tend to be Italian or South American. According to Raoul Bianchieri, the head of SBM: "There are big fortunes in South America, and they are gamesters by temperament." Because of his power in Monaco, Bianchieri is known as "the other prince". Gianni Agnelli used to be an *habitué* here but confessed to Rainier: "I can't allow myself to do it any more." If the Fiat workforce knew of their boss's gambling habit, Agnelli would have been in a weak position in calling for union wage restraints.

From the Casino, a period lift leads to Le Cabaret, a kitsch restaurant and floor show. Couples are tucked into pink velvet alcoves. The main lighting is provided by bare-breasted Amazons, lamps swathed in gold lamé below the waist. Between courses, artistes perform compulsory card tricks at one's table. After the cabaret, diners are photographed, presented with a plate of chocolates, then expected to dance. For less exhibitionist diners there is Les Privés, a discreet restaurant-bar overlooking the sea.

The **Salle Garnier**, situated in the Casino complex, is the prestigious setting for opera, ballet and concerts. It was here that Diaghilev's *Ballets Russes* once performed to great acclaim. Monte-Carlo has a noted orchestra which stages summer concerts in the medieval Fort Antoine. Monaco has the most sophisticated nightlife on the Riviera. The Red Cross Gala is the society event of the year, an occasion for the richest society ladies to flaunt their jewels. It is held at the Monte-Carlo Sporting Club, not a sports club at all. According to Prince

Princess Stephanie in happier times.

Albert, a bobsleigh champion, "to be a good Monégasque, you have to be sporty." The major event is, of course, the Grand Prix. This dangerous circuit involves 78 laps around the port, the Hermitage Hotel and the Place du Casino. The timing is perfect: it takes place immediately after the Cannes Film Festival so there are still plenty of stars around.

Stirling Moss, who won three times, loved the atmosphere. "When I was racing, I'll never forget looking at a beautiful young girl with pale lipstick who was always sitting in front of Oscar's bar. Every time I passed, I blew her a kiss. This sort of thing is only possible in Monaco."

During the Monte-Carlo season, evening is the time for dazzling displays of wealth. Stretch limousines ferry bronzed and bejewelled celebrities between the Hôtel de Paris, the Casino and Jimmy'z, Monte-Carlo's fashionable night spot. Boris Becker and Princess Stephanie dance under the stars at Parady'z nightclub. This is what the Monaco public relations department would have one believe. But these are troubled times for the Principality, which celebrated its 700th year in 1997. The Grimalidi family seems beset by tragedy and scandal, there has been a significant drop in tourism, and gaming scandals erode the carefully polished image.

Private snapshots of Monaco differ too. The ultra-discreet set do not stir from security-conscious apartments. In the Salle Garnier, a world-weary tycoon feigns an interest in the latest cultural offering and wonders why Princess Caroline always selects such obscure operas. Next door, in Le Train Bleu, a *grande dame* toys with her caviare, briefly leaving the table to place a losing bet on number 22, her lover's age.

Visitors listen to a Mozart recital in Fort Antoine, the open-air theatre. Monégasque bank clerks and shopkeepers watch their football team play Marseille. A bored croupier polishes his buttons. An Italian tourist wonders how a slice of Parma ham and melon can cost 300 francs. "*Monaco – un rêve, une réalité.*"

The glittering Port of Monaco.

MENTON

"Nowhere else have I felt such complete happiness," declared Franz Liszt of Menton. Sheltered by mountains, **Menton** basks in an enchanted setting with 300 days of sun a year. In this tropical greenhouse, Mexican and North African vegetation flourishes in a climate at least 2°C warmer than in Nice. *Belle-époque* villas aside, one could easily be in Sicily. But in the 19th century Menton's charm was as a winter sanatorium rather than as a hot-house. Royal visitors such as Queen Victoria and Edward VII helped Menton acquire a reputation as the most aristocratic and anglophile of all the Riviera resorts.

Nowadays the dowager-like image has softened: Menton is cosy rather than genteel, anglophile rather than aristocratic. But even this image is *passé*, since Menton has more young people than any other Riviera town. Certainly, the presence of Italian executives and trippers has revived the town, especially since the joining of Menton with Ventimiglia in 1993, as the European Union's first joint urban community, when frontier posts, municipal and business activities were combined.

Foreign history: Originally Genovese, Menton became part of the Principality of Monaco in 1346 and by and large remained a Grimaldi possession until 1860. However, the Grimaldi astutely placed Menton under the protection of the rising political powers, a form of opportunism still practised by the present Monégasque rulers. In succession, Menton became a Spanish, French and Sardinian protectorate. Given such a cosmopolitan past, it is hardly surprising that Menton can feel so deliciously foreign.

In 1848 Menton rebelled against high Monégasque taxes on oil and fruit. Along with Roquebrune, the town declared itself a republic but this was shortlived and in 1861 Monaco sold both towns to France. This coincided with the beginning of grand tourism and Menton was one of the first health resorts to benefit, thanks to the favourable publicity generated by Dr Bennet. The English doctor promoted Menton's mild climate as perfect for invalids so British and Germans flocked to winter there.

Sights: Set just behind the seafront, the sweetly-scented **Jardin Biovès** is a natural introduction to flowery Menton. Facing inland, one's eye is drawn to the gentle gradations of colour and height: lush pink borders and serried ranks of palms and citrus trees that fade to distant mauve hills. The lemon trees are carefully decorated with fairy lights. In the evening glow, the park's cosy prettiness envelops passers-by in a cloying embrace.

A voluptuous tone is set by a reclining nude statue and by a fountain dedicated to the "goddess of the golden fruits". Nearby, boughs of sharp Seville oranges and sweet Genovese mandarins intermingle with the Mentonnais lemon, the town's trademark. This oval-shaped lemon, introduced in the 14th century, is noted for its gorgeous scent and unacidic flavour. The Mentonnais boast

that it keeps for months longer than its common Portuguese rival.

During the spring *Fête du Citron* the park looks good enough to eat. The fruit, moulded into such shapes as boats and cathedrals, attracts 300,000 visitors every year. When not pressed into promoting the tourist industry, the Menton lemon can be sampled as a refreshing *citron pressé* – at Parisian prices, of course. Menton's sweet aftertaste conceals very sharp marketing.

Overlooking the park is the splendour of the Palais de l'Europe, once the city's grand casino and now home to the helpful tourist office. The present Casino, facing out on to the seafront, is a staid affair, reduced to seaside cabaret, sedate *thés dansants* and low-key gambling. As if in disapproval, St John's Anglican church turns its back on the Casino. The church provides retired British expatriates with spiritual counselling, fêtes and free library books. In the afternoon, elderly visitors congregate on the **Promenade du Soleil** to enjoy the sea views. Along the seafront are

vestiges of *belle-époque* villas, epitomised by the charmingly dilapidated Le Pin Doré and similar pastel-coloured hotels. Many of the finest villas have been converted into chic flats or homes for retired French civil servants. Below the Promenade du Soleil sun-seekers stretch out on boulders or on pocket handkerchiefs of sand.

Nearby, genteel dowagers sip afternoon tea in the George V's *salon de thé*. The solicitous service is reminiscent of an expensive nursing home. Here, life is meted out not in coffee spoons but in ice-cream scoops. Yet in keeping with the changing times, the cafés cater to both ends of the social scale, serving anything from chilled Chablis and bouillabaisse to hot dogs and Coke. In general, however, Menton's sea views are more memorable than the cuisine.

At the eastern end of the Promenade, the *belle-époque* quarter merges into Vieux Menton, the pedestrianised old town. The **Marché Couvert** provides **Menton's** the quirky link between the two quarters. The market, topped by a decorative **Festival.**

Lemon

clocktower, is adorned with comical sculpted faces. The profusion of lemons, figs and artichokes is a match for the market's green, yellow and brown ceramics.

Fishing: Rue des Marins, beside the market, is still the centre of Menton's small but thriving fish trade. As the only medieval guild to have survived on the Riviera, it retains a symbolic importance in local eyes. The trade, still passed from father to son, is based on small fry such as sardines and anchovies. In spring, anchovies are attracted to Menton's warm water and by May the season is underway. May is also the traditional time for salting and storing. Sardines, still fished from February to April, are eaten fried with lemon or in a spicy *omelette de poutines*.

Restaurants around the market are a good place to sample the local fish dishes, including *stockfisch*, spiced with garlic and white wine before being flambéed in cognac. A typical accompaniment to fish is *fleurs farcies*, courgette flowers stuffed with cheese, tomatoes and garlic. Aromatic *Côtes-de-Provence Blanc* is a good wine choice.

Beside the Marché Couvert is the Place du Marché, with its flower stalls doing a brisk trade in young lemon trees and cacti. Next door is the **Place aux Herbes**, a charming arcaded square. Ignore the antique shop, lavender stalls and North African trinket-sellers. Instead, focus on the chestnut trees, fountain and statue, best appreciated from an outdoor café. Place du Marché leads to the bustling **Rue St-Michel**, Menton at its most commercial. Avenue Félix Faure and Rue St-Michel provide ample opportunity to stock up on designer luggage, Provençal herbs and lemon-scented soap.

Seen from the old fishing harbour, Vieux Menton is stacked on the hillside, framed by rugged mountains and shimmering reflections. The finest coastal views are from the Empress Eugénie jetty: Cap Martin, the millionaires' enclave, lies to the west, with Bordighera, the Italian resort, to the east.

Viewed from the port, the clustered

Vieux Menton stacked on the hillside.

towers of the **Cathedral** and two chapels appear inseparable. From Quai Bonaparte, steep steps lead to a pebble-mosaic courtyard of striking Italianate design. Just above is the pink and ochre cathedral, flanked by two steeples. It was begun in 1619 by Honoré II of Monaco but its facade and atmosphere are essentially baroque. Inside are several heavily-restored chapels which were damaged in the 1887 earthquake. Just outside is the Place de l'Église, the setting for Menton's celebrated *Juillet Musicale* and August Festival of Chamber Music. This sunken square has excellent acoustics, framed by the cathedral and chapel yet open to the sea on one side. The unexpected blend of intimacy and sea views has also made it a sought-after film location.

Next door, the apricot-tinged **Chapelle de l'Immaculée Conception** is a much creamier affair. It was built in 1687 for the White Penitents, a lay confraternity who sought to return to a simpler faith. The 1887 earthquake damaged the church but after a restoration in 1987 it is now the city's pride and joy. Depending on taste, the baroque interior is garish or exuberant. It is lit by old coaching lamps but locals gaze up at the *lanteron* to appreciate the natural light. The *pièce de résistance* is the ceiling representing Heaven, a Mediterranean paradise with golden figures and blue skies. In the Hôtel de Ville, Cocteau's pastiche of a Mediterranean marriage shows the same *joie de vivre*.

The cathedral quarter, dating from the 16th century, is the oldest part of town. It is also the poorest, populated by Algerian and Moroccan immigrants as well as Mentonnais craftsmen. Renovation has yet to make an impact on this warren of vaulted brick and cobbled streets. Ramparts from the old fortress have been incorporated into existing buildings. Blind alleys end with tiny stone houses decorated with drying peppers. Inside one, a family sorts through a sack of pungent olives; a canary sings out of tune.

After running the gauntlet of the lavender sellers on Rue St-Michel, reach

Mentonnais fishermen, the only medieval guild to have survived on the Riviera.

the Bastion on the seafront. This fort was built in 1636, when Menton's Spanish rulers feared a French attack. The orange-brick bastion now houses the **Jean Cocteau Museum**, in homage to the painter and poet who once lived locally. Cocteau himself oversaw the restoration of the fort, designing the mosaic flooring and the bright tiling on the four turrets. He donated numerous works to the museum but sadly did not live to see the opening in 1967.

The ground floor, formerly the arms store, contains brilliantly-coloured abstractions, powerful self-portraits and *Judith and Holopherne*, Cocteau's first tapestry. Matisse loved it, praising this depiction of seduction, murder and flight as *"la seule vraie tapisserie contemporaine."* As an artist, the eclectic Cocteau dabbled in tapestry, ceramics, photography and scuplture as well as painting. Throughout the museum are examples of his beautifully crafted jars influenced by Greek, Hellenic and Etruscan designs. The upper floor, once the guards' room, still contains its original

vaulted ceiling and brick oven. The highlight is the *Innamorati* collection, a series of love paintings inspired by the lives of Provençal fisher folk. With the sea beating against the bastion walls, the atmospheric setting is reminiscent of the Cap Ferrat tower where Cocteau worked.

Cocteau fans will head inland to the Hôtel de Ville to see the **Salle des Mariages**, designed by the artist in the 1950s. Cocteau's touch is evident in the Spanish chairs, the mock panther-skin carpet and the lamps shaped like prickly-pears. As for the murals, Cocteau's inspiration was the Riviera style at the turn of the century, "a mood redolent of art nouveau villas decorated with swirling seaweed, irises and flowing hair".

On the wall above the official's desk, Cocteau depicts the engaged couple trying to read the future in each other's eyes. The mural is full of Provençal symbols, from the sun and swirling sea to the woman's Mentonnais straw hat and her fiancé's fisherman's cap. Cocteau humorously gives the fisher-

View of Menton and the sea.

man a fish instead of an eye. The mural on the right features an exotic Saracen wedding, a reference to earlier Riviera settlers but also a pretext for a colourful ceremony and extravagant emotions. The bride and groom set off on a white horse amidst rejoicing, sorrow and mystery. Three wise friends bear gifts; a slave girl dances; a jilted girlfriend is comforted by her vengeful brother; a mother-in-law glowers; a gypsy guides the newlyweds towards the future.

Cocteau's aim was to "create a theatrical setting… to offset the officialdom of a civil ceremony". In this he succeeds, bringing wonder and an epic dimension to a dreary register office. Cocteau watched his adopted son get married in this very room. Since then, Menton has become a recherché wedding location, not just a joke to *"épater les bourgeois"*.

From Menton it is a pleasant stroll to **Garavan**, a chic garden suburb with the most exotic vegetation in France. At the turn of the century Garavan was in its heyday, a haunt for high society. Glam-

orous villas with matching landscaped gardens were *de rigueur*. Today, despite encroaching high-rise developments, *belle-époque* villas and art deco follies still survive. Sadly, many luxuriant gardens can only be glimpsed through *chien méchant* signs.

The high inland road to Garavan is more appealing than the route along the seafront. From the cathedral, climb the winding Rue du Vieux Château to the **Cemetery** on the hill. The Italianate cemetery, built over the ancient citadel, spans four terraces, each devoted to a different faith. The tone is set by a smiling marble angel which looks set to soar over the *vieille ville*. The cemetery is noted for its foreign graves, a cosmopolitan cast-list of 19th-century celebrities who stayed longer than intended. Aubrey Beardsley, the illustrator, is joined by Webb Ellis, the founder of rugby. Nearby are graves of consumptive English girls who made a vocation of dying poetically. Cats sun themselves on Prince Youssoupov's tomb, unafraid of Rasputin's murderer.

The **Place du Cimetière**, just outside the cemetery walls, is a popular place for expatriate picnics and gossip. Count on sharing views of the **Vieux Port** and Garavan's modern marina. In the distance are signs for *"Frontière"*, proof that the wooded headland beyond is, indeed, Italy.

From the square, **Le Boulevard de Garavan** leads past terraced gardens and villas hugging the coast. Rooftop villas are draped with mimosa, bougainvillaea, lentisks and giant cacti. Number 13, a *belle-époque* mansion built into the old city walls, is surrounded by olive and lemon groves. Next-door is an art deco villa with magnificent views of the old port. *"Attention aux chats gentils,"* a sign on the Villa Rayons et Ombres, is presumably a cover for pit bull terriers.

Several public paths lead down through lemon groves to the Garavan seafront. One such path, Sentier Villa Noël, leads to the **Jardin Botanique Exotique**, Menton's most successful park. This lush botanical garden was laid out by Lord Redcliffe, the Gover-

Menton Casino, a staid affair of *thés dansants* and cabaret.

nor of Malta, in 1905. The last owner, the retiring Miss Campbell, continued to introduce plants from Asia, Africa and America, making this the most tropical garden in France. It now resembles a cultural melting pot.

Japanese cane bamboos and African succulents compete with Australian eucalyptus and Brazilian bougainvillaea; Arabian date trees and Canary palms dwarf Mexican yucca and Iranian pistachios. The fruit trees smell quite delicious: as well as *citrus amara* and *citrus blanco* lemons, there are also mandarins, bananas, oranges, figs and dates. Even succulents like the deep red aloes look distinctly edible.

Yet Menton's Jardin Botanique does not neglect quieter, more Provençal charms. Sweet-smelling myrtle, rosemary and thyme flourish, as do evergreen lentisks, drooping lilies and a riot of roses. One intimate patch contains an ordinary rockery, except that no rockery is ordinary in Menton. A balmy climate helps but these plants seem to have been raised on anabolic steroids.

Virtually next door is the **Olivaie du Pian**, Garavan's public park. It was once part of a Spanish estate but is now a wild olive grove. This variety of olive, *le cailletier*, has been grown here for over 2,000 years and stands out for its stocky trunk and succulent black olives. Some of the gnarled specimens are hundreds of years old. By day, the olive grove is a ball park but on summer nights it is an open-air stage.

On the far side of the park is Rue Blasco Ibañez, named after the Spanish novelist who lived in exile here. Shunning the military dictatorship in Spain, Blasco Ibañez settled in the Riviera in 1923. His villa, **Fontana Rosa**, is a piece of self-indulgence, heralded by ceramic portraits of Balzac, Cervantes and Dickens on the gateway. Surrounding the villa is the Spaniard's **Jardin des romanciers**, a further tribute to his favourite novelists. The grounds, planted with cypress and Mediterranean shrubs, reflect a pastiche of classical and art deco styles. A couple of follies take centre stage, adorned by sculpted *putti*,

Salles des Mariages, designed by Cocteau, now a recherché wedding location.

kneeling angels and busts of novelists. Mosaics represent Mediterranean fruit and flowers. It may be kitsch but it is fun. The ceramics have just been restored to their former splendour.

A short but steep walk along Avenue Ferdinand Bac leads to **Les Colombières**, arguably the most romantic gardens on the Riviera. The writer and artist Ferdinand Bac longed for an authentic Mediterrranean garden, planted with Provençal herbs, box borders and clumps of yews. The shaded terraces are punctuated by ornamental pools, fountains, classical urns and baroque statues. In fact, the hill-top location and the giant black cypresses closely resemble a French Tuscany.

But if the gardens are Italianate, the exuberant villa defies description. Decorated by Bac in 1926, it borrows freely from Hellenic, Roman and Oriental traditions. A colonnaded atrium contains frescoes of the Ulysses myth while the art deco music room is covered with murals of the nine Muses. In the grounds, a Moorish-style pavilion contains Bac's tomb. Although the villa and grounds are untended, the neglect adds romance to this lush wilderness.

From Les Colombières, steps cut down to the the Boulevard de Garavan and a turning right leads to **Avenue Katherine Mansfield**, the writer's retreat. The street boasts *belle-époque* villas, from the stuccoed *La Favorite* to *Chrisoleina*, a turreted folly. Before Garavan station, a sign indicates Mansfield's **Isola Bella**, a disappointingly small, lemon-coloured villa with a disfigured view. Despite suffering from tuberculosis, Katherine wrote some of her best work here, including *The Daughters of the Late Colonel*, an essay on genteel frustation. By contrast, she found Menton liberating, "a heavenly place" with "no division between one's work and one's external existence". Life was centred on "my pale yellow house with its mimosa in a slightly deeper hue." Soon after moving in to the villa, Katherine wrote: "When I die you will find Isola Bella in poker work on my heart."

Menton, popular for health benefits.

Mansfield would not have approved of the ugly high-rise sprawl on Garavan seafront, just around the corner. Nor would she have liked the tacky seafood restaurants lining the quayside. (She admired her maid's knack of turning any dish into an artistic still life, "the fish with its huge, tragic mouth stuffed with parsley.") For more stylish cuisine, follow the *Italie 1,000 metres* sign.

On Promenade Reine Astrid, just before the border, is **Villa Serena**, Menton's last major garden. Menton is famous for its gardens, many of them planted by English residents. Others worth visiting include nearby **Serres de la Madone**, which was designed and planted by Lawrence Johnston, and has a magnificent collection of palms and tropical plants; and the botanical gardens at **Val Rahmeh**, the Mediterranean outpost of the Paris Natural History Museum.

From Menton, a brisk walk west along the seafront leads to Carnolès. This dull suburb is worth visiting for one site alone: the **Palais Carnolès**, once the Grimaldi summer home is now Menton's major art museum. This pink and white palace is encircled by parasol pines and 50 different varieties of citrus trees. In 1640 Prince Honoré II built a summer house in the olive groves but Antoine I remodelled it on the Grand Trianon. The well-restored palace mostly displays works bequeathed by Wakefield Mori, an eclectic English collector.

The museum's strengths lie in the Italian *Quattrocento* works, 16th-century portraits and modern Riviera landscapes. Amongst the ancient art, the Italian and French madonnas take pride of place. Louis Bréa, often called "Provence's Fra Angelico", is the only home-grown star of this period. The soft and spiritual *Virgin and Child* shows his delicate touch. The rest of the Niçois school cannot compete with the expressive *École de Leonardo* madonna presented here. The ground floor displays a rotating collection of modern art, including Kisling's *Paysage à St-Tropez* and Sutherland's *La Fontaine*, a glowing composition of fountain and leaves.

nd the mildest limate on he Mediteranean.

From Carnolès or Menton, a short drive north leads to the **Monastère de L'Annonciade** and arguably the loveliest views from Menton. By car, take the Avenue de Sospel and turn left into the Route de l'Annonciade. Alternatively, walk along the Chemin du Rosaire, a steep but delightful walk which, until 1936, was the only way of reaching the monastery. The path winds uphill through pine trees and spiky yellow agaves; small shrines represent the stations of the cross.

The path and the monastery were created by Isabelle de Monaco after her miraculous cure from leprosy. Apart from an interruption during the Revolution, a Franciscan community has lived here ever since. Inside the chapel is a bizarre collection of votive offerings, from boats and crutches to a Zeppelin fragment and a strip of parachute from the 1991 Gulf War. The monastery is perched among cypress and olive groves. From its terrace of swaying eucalyptus trees there are coastal views towards Italy, Corsica and Cap Martin.

A few miles west of Carnolès lies **Roquebrune-Cap Martin**, an historic commune sandwiched between Menton and Monaco. In the 1840s, the medieval village of Roquebrune was practically deserted and the wooded headland of Cap Martin was the preserve of sheep and cows. Before the turn of the century, however, Cap Martin was discovered by richer flocks, from Queen Victoria to Empress Eugénie. *Belle-époque* villas sprang up among the olive groves and Cap Martin remains the preserve of the rich today.

From Roquebrune station on the coast it is a short drive or an arduous climb to the medieval village. Steep staircases with vertiginous views lead up the reddish-brown cliff to **Roquebrune**. The distinction between castle and village only evolved in the 15th century. Before then, the whole of Roquebrune was a *castellum*, a fortified 10th-century settlement which remains unique in France.

The path finally emerges in Rue de l'Église, beside the parish church. Ste-Marguerite, originally Romanesque, was

The rooftops of Roquebrune, a unique fortified settlement.

heavily restored in the 18th century and looks classical. The facade is apricot-coloured, like much of Roquebrune, and overlooks a sweet Marian shrine. The welcoming interior is bathed in a soft pink glow.

But the village's vocation is for tourism, not for the priesthood. Lavender, honey and carved wood sculptures are Roquebrune's icons, in summer at least. Yet despite being overpriced, over-crowded and over-restored, Roquebrune remains a magical place. The apricot houses, chiselled out of the rock, over-hang tiny squares and blind alleys. Narrow passageways burrow through a labyrinth of vaulted archways.

The geranium-covered walls present a misleadingly decorative picture. This ancient *castellum* was supremely functional. The château battlements commanded views of Mont Agel, Monaco and the coast; there were only two entrances, both heavily guarded. If invaders broke through the defences, they were quickly backed into cul-de-sacs and bombarded with boulders. As the

oldest castle in France, Roquebrune was the prototype feudal château for centuries to come.

Roquebrune was built by the Count of Ventimiglia as a means of keeping the "Saracens" at bay. After a long struggle between the Genovese and the Counts of Provence, Roquebrune became a Grimaldi possession and remained so for five centuries. The grim **château**, situated on Place Ingram, is largely 13th century, although it was heavily restored this century by Sir William Ingram. The locals were outraged when the Englishman added a mock medieval *tour anglaise*. From the battlements there are magnificent views of the coast.

Rue Grimaldi, the main street, is marred by cute gentrification and craft shops. But even here, the eccentricity and friendliness of the traders sets Roquebrune apart. An artist with an *atelier* readily discusses local history or produces photos of himself dressed as a Roman centurion. Ever since 1467, when the Virgin saved the town from the plague, 500 Roquebrunois have re-en-

Paintings for sale at Roquebrune.

acted scenes from the Passion every August. A sculptor carves angels and virgins out of olive wood, boasting about his discovery of *"le plus vieil homme de l'Europe"* in a local cave. Certainly, Roquebrune is riddled with prehistoric remains. Although the most famous caves, the Grottes du Vallonet, are still being excavated, major finds are predicted.

Before leaving, stroll down Rue Grimaldi to **Place des Deux Frères**, named after the square's twin crags. In 1890 the square came into being when a huge outcrop was split to create an access road. The result is a success, a release from the slightly claustrophobic feeling of Roquebrune. La Grotta bistrot enjoys views of the château above and the Côte below. Be prepared to share a table with an American bee-keeper, Swiss banker or French artisan, all Roquebrune residents.

From Roquebrune, it is a pleasant, leisurely downhill stroll to **Cap Martin** and the coast. The prettiest route leads along Rue Souta Riba, a narrow, vaulted

path edging round the outside of the village. Views through firs and pines reveal privatised Roman statuary in discreet villas. Soon after Souta Riba joins the Chemin de Menton there is a huge gnarled olive tree, reputedly over 1,000 years old. Further on are a couple of chapels, the dilapidated St Roch and the rural de la Pausa, which was built in 1462 as a plague offering. Faded frescoes of olive groves and angels cover the walls.

By the time the path reaches Avenue du Danemark, suburbia is underway. On Avenue Paul Doumer the Roman **Monument de Lumone** is a redeeming feature. These arches and mosaics are all that remain of the Roman settlement on the cape. Although its olive and lemon groves have receded, Cap Martin is still lusher and less spoilt than Cap Ferrat. However, none of Cap Martin's *belle-époque* villas are open to the public and most bask in smug, celebrity cool. Name-droppers have a field day on Cap Martin but it is unwise to label all its grand residents as slavish followers of fashion. Designer Karl Lagerfeld lives on the Cap both to service Monte-Carlo fashion victims and to be close to the Grimaldi family. Fragrant Coco Chanel wafted in to entertain German officers during the war. Empress Eugénie liked to play the *grande dame* here but presumably Greta Garbo didn't come for the company. Churchill and Le Corbusier came for the painter's light. Empress Sissy of Austria wintered here after a bad case of *fin-de-siècle* blues. W. B. Yeats came, and died, for reasons of ill-health.

The highlight of the cape is the **Promenade le Corbusier**, a lovely coastal path running west to Monaco and southeast around Cap Martin. The path crosses an olive grove and then hugs the shore. Willows, sea pines and white rocks typify this stretch of coast. The walk towards Monaco passes Le Corbusier's beach house, just before the Pointe de Cabbé. The architect drowned here in 1965 but had the foresight to design a splendid memorial to himself in Roquebrune cemetery. Cynics label this a supremely Cap Martin gesture.

Left, the coast from Roquebrune. **Right**, religion – the British prefer Anglican protection.

PERCHED VILLAGES

For the adventurous prepared to explore further than the coast, a whole new world awaits: high mountain plateaux, plunging gorges, clear sparkling rivers and, crowning the most inaccessible craggy peaks, the justly famous *villages perchés.*

A number of these perched villages, such as Ste-Agnes, Gorbio and Peillon, are only a few miles inland, and yet provide a stark and welcome contrast to the urbanised coast. Even villages further into the mountains, such as Utelle, Lantosque or Luceram, can easily be visited in a day, since the roads are good, if often steep, and rarely busy.

However, it can be particularly pleasant to find a hotel and stay overnight in these beautiful mountains, to fully appreciate the pristine air and star-studded night skies, and to wake up to a deep silence broken only by cow bells. Spring, when the flowers are at their most beautiful, is perhaps the best time to enjoy these unspoilt regions, but during the summer they can provide a cool, refreshing break from the coast.

The perched village of **Falicon** is close to Nice and well worth a visit. It was the setting for Jules Romains's novel *La Douceur de la Vie,* and was also where Queen Victoria liked to stroll and take her afternoon tea whilst staying in Nice; an event commemorated by a restaurant called Au Thé de la Reine. The old village is very small, filled with covered passages and twisting lanes and is characterised by a series of picturesque little *placettes*, one of which has a rare perpendicular staircase leading to a raised front door. There is a baroque church dating from 1624.

Peille and Peillon, in the valley of the Paillon river, are both superb examples of *villages perchés*, all the more so for their proximity to Nice. One has barely escaped the tangle of the city's industrial suburbs when these ancient craggy places rise up impossibly elevated above the valley floor.

It is surprising that **Peille** is not better known. It is a large, almost completely medieval village, with a wonderful variety of features and views. There is parking either end of the town, which is traversed by the Rue Centrale. There are two very old quarters, both of which were founded in the 11th century.

Don't miss the Place André Laugier, where there is a pair of 13th-century doors, one Romanesque, one Gothic, and a pair of matched Gothic windows. Behind this is the Place du Mont Agel, surrounded by very old houses, with a Gothic fountain in the centre. The Rue Lascaris leaves the square through the loggia of the ancient palais, and out to a viewing platform. From here, a short path leads to the cemetery and the war memorial. The view extends all the way to Cap d'Antibes.

All the roads leading from Place du Mont Agel are worth exploring: Rue du Moulins has double round-arched windows, probably 15th-century, Rue de la Turbie leads down stone steps under an arch to a charming square housing a small museum of local history.

Preceding pages: village women enjoy a joke. *Left,* a typical Alpes-Maritimes hilltown. *Right,* remains of a massive Roman trophy visible through the streets of La Turbie.

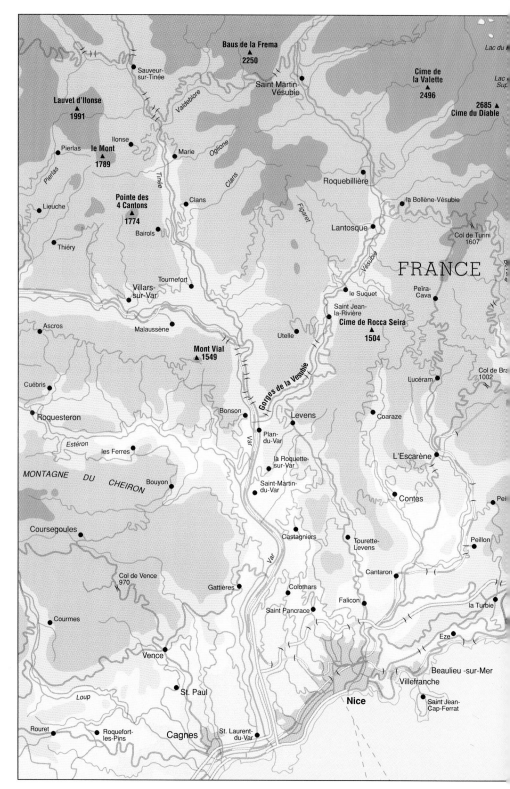

Baus de la Frema ▲
2250

Cime de
la Valette
▲
2496

2685 ▲
Cime du Diable

Lac du

Lac
Sup

Sauveur-
sur-Tinée

Saint Martin-
Vésubie

Lauvet d'Ilonse ▲
1991

Ilonse

Pierlas

le Mont
▲
1789

Marie

Oglione

Roquebillière

la Bollène-Vésubie

Lieuche

Pierlas

Tinée

Clans

Pointe des
4 Cantons
▲
1774

Clans

Lantosque

Col de Turini
1607

Thiéry

Bairols

Figaret

FRANCE

Villars-
sur-Var

Tournefort

le Suquet

Peïra-
Cava

Ascros

Malaussène

Saint Jean-
la-Rivière

Cime de Rocca Seira
▲
1504

Utelle

Cuébris

Mont Vial
▲ 1549

Col de Bra
1002

Lucéram

Roquesteron

Bonson

Levens

Coaraze

Estéron

les Ferres

MONTAGNE DU CHEIRON

Bouyon

Plan-
du-Var

la Roquette-
sur-Var

L'Escarène

Coursegoules

Saint-Martin-
du-Var

Contes

Pei

Var

Castagniers

Tourette-
Levens

Peillon

Col de Vence
970

Gattières

Colomars

Cantaron

Courmes

Var

Falicon

la Turbie

Saint Pancrace

Eze

Vence

Beaulieu-sur-Mer

Villefranche

St. Paul

Nice

Saint Jean-
Cap-Ferrat

Loup

Rouret

Roquefort-
les-Pins

Cagnes

St. Laurent-
du-Var

Gorges de la Vésubie

Vésubie

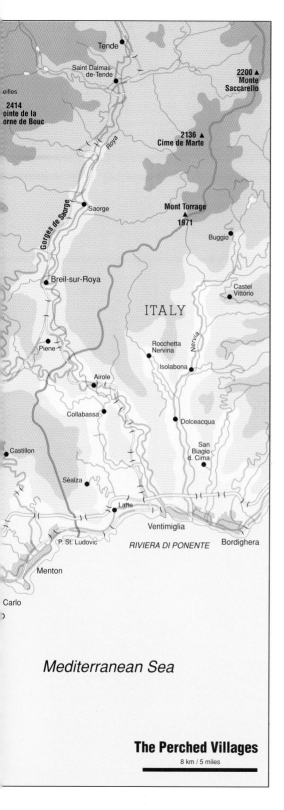

The finest feature is the large Église Ste-Marie, set at the head of the village and created from two adjoining chapels, the oldest being 12th-century. Two buttresses span the road, and a slender Romanesque bell tower dominates the village. A picture to the right of the altar shows Peille in the 16th century.

On the side of Montée St-Bernard next to the church are the ruins of a 14th-century castle, part of the original fortifications of the town which were mostly pulled down during the revolution. A very old part of the town lies directly below the castle, across the main road, consisting of very steep stone stairs and covered alleys. The Hôtel de Ville on Rue Centrale is housed in an 18th-century chapel, which has an interesting domed roof.

Nearby **Peillon** is regarded as one of the most beautiful of all the perched villages. Approaching from the main road it seems impossible to believe that 2 miles (3 km) will be enough to reach its dizzy heights amongst the olives and pines. As the French memorably put it, *"Peillon marque l'extrémité du monde habité."* Its charm is in the entire ensemble, the fantastic position, the winding main "street", which would be better described as a staircase, and the superb views from the square at the top. As you enter the village from the small square shaded by plane trees, there is a fragment of an old archway to the left, part of the springing is still visible. There is also a tower of white stone, very clean and well restored.

A number of houses have open top floors in the Renaissance manner. Its narrow streets have very steep stone steps through vaulted tunnels and sometimes as many as four front doors leading from someone else's basement. Footpaths start at the end of the village leading to Peille and La Turbie through the wonderful wooded mountainside.

La Turbie, high above Monte-Carlo, is one of the most magnificent sights of the Côte d'Azur but more easily accessible from the Provençale autoroute, leaving at the La Turbie-Monaco interchange. The autoroute is spectacular on this stretch, spanning great ravines and tunnelling through mountains. The name La Turbie comes from the Latin, *tropaea*, trophy, and it is named after the Trophy of Augustus, a huge Roman monument erected to commemorate the conquest of the 45 Alpine tribes who had been attacking Romanised Gaul. Augustus himself, the first of the Roman emperors, led the campaigns in 15 and 14 BC. The trophy was built between 13 and 5 BC, probably using the enslaved Alpine tribesmen as labour.

The structure was originally 165 ft (50 metres) high, and even now, 115 ft (35 metres) are still standing after 2,000 years. It consists of a large rectangular base supporting a cylindrical core of 24 huge Doric columns, some of which remain, their load bearing supports now visible. The columns once supported a masonry tower, surmounted by a stepped cone roof, topped with a giant statue of Emperor Augustus as the conquering general.

A nine-line inscription framed by two winged victories exists on the front face, the longest intact Roman inscription to come down to us from antiquity. From the 7th to 10th centuries its upper parts were used as a watchtower during the period of barbarian raids, and parts of its masonry were reused in ramparts to stave off the Saracens.

In the Middle Ages, the Lérins monks destroyed its statues because they were pagan. In the wars between the Guelphs and the Ghibellines, during the 12th and 13th centuries, the villagers took refuge in its passages and stairways. In 1706 it was partially destroyed because of its strategic location and later Louis XIV ordered the destruction of the "castle", not wishing any fortification to fall into the hands of the Dukes of Savoie. The ruins became a quarry and most of the town of La Turbie is built from the very stones which gave it its name. Only one other similar trophy is known, that of Trajan at Adam Klissi in Rumania, making this of particular interest.

It is set in a lovely clifftop park, ideal for picnics. There is a fine museum, displaying the many bits which have been unearthed from the monument,

A hill village at the turn of the century.

1913. COTE D'AZUR - SAINT-JEANNET — Vieille Rue

with a large scale model of how it originally looked, very useful for understanding the present remains. From the cliff is a spectacular view over the Mediterranean and to Monte-Carlo below. Yachts and speedboats go about their business and tiny cars crawl along the winding roads, but on the days when formula-one racing cars are in Monte-Carlo for the Grand Prix, the throaty roar is deafening, even 1,500 ft (450 metres) up.

The town is small, built in a quarter circle with two surviving town gates, one of which is best seen from the gardens of the Trophy, and many old buildings from the 11th and 13th centuries, particularly lining what used to be the Roman Via Julia which led to the Trophy. The baroque 18th-century church is built from stones taken from the Trophy and has attractive bands of coloured tiles on its cupola. The village is utterly charming with a wealth of odd little architectural details embedded in its ochre walls and vaulted arcades, large terracotta pots of geraniums and bou-

gainvillaea, its narrow cobbled streets dominated by the vast monument, so large in scale as to be almost surreal in its presence.

Just north of Roquebrune and Menton are a group of hill villages which are just far enough from the bustling coast to have escaped the crowds. It helps that the villages lie at the end of tortuous roads and are literally hidden in mists. Not for nothing are residents of Ste-Agnès and Gorbio known as *les nébuleux*, the mist-dwellers.

Gorbio sits high on its hill looking out to the Mediterranean, amongst the olives which provided its livelihood until the 19th century, when its inhabitants turned to tourism, catering to the growing-numbers of visitors from Menton. It is famous for its narrow arched streets, and for its snail procession, *la procession aux escargots*, which, disappointingly, is not actually a promenade of snails, but a festival celebrated by the White Penitents when the streets are illuminated by oil flames lit in a multitude of snail shells.

Medieval walls and doorways of La Turbie.

Although close to Menton, **Ste-Agnès** belongs to medieval Provence, a landscape at once Mediterranean and mountainous. As a quaint *village perché*, Ste-Agnès is the most attractive in the area. Its eagerness to send visitors away with souvenirs rather than memories is the only jarring note.

En route to Ste-Agnès, the familiar olive and lemon groves merge into Provençal *maquis*. As the land climbs to 2,296 ft (700 metres), the olives disappear; sturdy juniper, pine and fir trees jut over the crags. By Ste-Agnès the mists and the temperatures fall, particularly in the early morning. "*Je vais me noyer dans la brume*," ("I'm off to drown myself in the fog,") is almost a cheery greeting in the village.

It is not clear how Ste Agnès acquired her sainthood. One legend has it that she was a Roman empress who sought refuge from a storm in a local grotto and, in thanks, built a chapel on the spot. The more colourful version is that Haroun, a Saracen chief, raided the village and selected a Provençale for his harem. The chaste Agnès resisted her kidnapper until he converted to Christianity.

From the 12th century the village was fought over by the counts of Ventimiglia and Provence. In the 16th century the ancient château was dismantled and its stones incorporated into existing houses. The ruined **château** overlooks an Italianate cemetery and pine forest. The walk up is especially pungent in spring: woodsmoke wafts through the cherry blossom, herbs and damp pine trees. At the top, if the fog has lifted, there are views towards the Alps, the coast and even Corsica.

Just below the château ruins is the village, clustered around the foot of a cliff. Place de la Mairie is a compact square lined with medieval buildings, including **Notre-Dame-des-Neiges**, the 17th-century parish church. The honey and herb shops outside are a prelude to the main assault on Rue Longue. With its neat stone steps and flower-hung archways, well-restored houses and well-trained dogs, Ste-Agnès is almost too perfect. On a summer's day, however, **Rue Longue** mills with enamel-ists and herbalists, soap-sellers and crystal-engravers, jewellers and dried flower designers.

Rue Longue leads to **Square Ste-Agnès**, perched on the edge of a ravine. This is where the original chapel was carved into the rock. All that now remains is a small shrine and a cute statue of the saint. The chapel was destroyed during the construction of a wartime fortification system along the border. From 1930 the Italian threat was ever-present so an extension to the Maginot line was created from the coast to the mountains beyond Sospel. Designed as an updated model of a Vauban fortress, Fort Ste-Agnès remains an impressive defensive system, only accessible via a narrow drawbridge.

Villagers whimsically attribute their wartime escape to the spirit of Ste Agnès, still lurking in her grotto within the military fort. On 21 January, her saint's day, a dawn concert and carnival are followed by a procession to Notre-Dame-des-Neiges.

Rue des Comtes Leotardi leads out of the village, past covered passageways and medieval ramparts. Along here is the Vieille Auberge, with its promise of *raviolis maison, tarte agnèsoise* and panoramic views. If not leaving Ste-Agnès over-fed or laden with pine-scented cologne and Saracen jewels, then consider a walk along mule tracks to Gorbio. The Chemin du Pierre Rochard is named after the wartime parish priest who regularly walked to Menton to bring back rations.

Castellar, just east of Ste-Agnès, is perched on a hillside covered with orchards and olives. The village is an acquired taste, historically richer than Ste-Agnès yet somewhat neglected. Entirely lacking in arts and crafts, Castellar is guileless, a traditional hill-top village. To Niçois, its sole function is to serve Sunday lunch in a rural setting. The rectangular village was laid out with military precision by the Lascaris Seigneurs. It remained in their hands until the Revolution, with peasants continuing to pay such feudal dues as a shoulder of pork for a day's grazing rights. Not until 1792 did Castellar become part of France, an event celebrated by *l'arbre de la liberté* in the **Place de la Mairie**.

From here, the formal grid-pattern is clear: three parallel streets, linked by covered passageways, lead to the church at the end of the village. Two encircling paths trace the outline of the former city walls. **Rue de la République** is lined with sober medieval houses with roughly-hewn stone staircases. An old-fashioned bakery produces *fougasse*, biscuits made from almonds and pine kernels.

Equally pleasant aromas waft from La Tour Lascaris, a rustic restaurant housed in the **Palais Lascaris**, the counts' former residence. Although the *salle d'armes* has lost its frescoes, it retains an austere charm in keeping with the cuisine. Apart from *tourte de courge*, a courgette and aubergine pie, there is *Barba Juan, crêpes* stuffed with mushrooms, cheese and rice. Food is simple and vegetable-based, a reflection of Castellar's peasant roots.

At the end of Rue de la République is St-Pierre, a baroque church with an onion-domed bell tower and pinkish facade. From here, Rue Général Sarrail leads back to the Mairie. The first house on the left was a medieval prison but is being converted into a crafts workshop. Opposite is the **Chapelle des Pénitents Blancs**, a restored baroque chapel hemmed in by medieval houses. Further along is the **Chapelle des Pénitents Noirs**, sadly in need of restoration.

Covered passageways on the right lead to **Rue Arson**, the prettiest part of the village, bordering the countryside. A circular medieval tower backs on to the ramparts and, close to the church, is an olive-processing mill and an old wash house. Jean-Paul Albin, president of the *comité des fêtes*, is keen to attract visitors to his village but not at the expense of peace and quiet. In short, scruffy Castellar will not succumb to the prettified Ste-Agnès effect.

Heading for the mountains: The route to St-Martin-Vésubie from Nice takes in more perched villages as well as the spectacular Gorge de la Vésubie. Es-

A floral etreat.

caping Nice on the N202 going north, take the D414 to Colomars, where it becomes the ridge road to **Aspremont**, a charming village of concentric picturesque lanes with lots of little winding alleys leading from them. At the foot of the village stands the chapel of St-Claude, built in 1632 to guard the inhabitants against the plague. The church of St-Jacques has an unusual 13th-century Gothic nave, contrasting in style with the other village buildings. Like the rest of the village, the church has been recently restored. A castle once stood at the top of the village, but now only the ramparts remain.

Follow the Rue des Remparts around the top of the village to reach the Place Leandre Astraudo, a small square with a fountain; on one side is the highest remaining section of castle wall with corbels and blocked-up windows. There is a stairway to a little children's playground with a superb view of the mountains and a grove of trees marking the position of the castle keep.

Nearby **Castagniers** is a tiny village,

largely rebuilt in the 19th century. There is a wonderful view of the Var Valley from the small square in front of the 1817 church.

If you continue up the Var Valley, you will find **St-Martin-du-Var** just off the main highway; the old village is a small tangle of lanes tucked behind the huge main square. **La Roquette-sur-Var**, high on its hill, was built at a strategic position on the old international frontier with Italy and at the summit of the village there are the vestiges of a castle. The church of St-Pierre was completed in 1682.

Continuing north on the N202, you comte to Plan-du-Var, the last stop for pizza and cold drinks before the **Gorges de la Vésubie**, which lacks any kind of roadside refreshment. The gorge is stunning, its steep sides plummeting to the river far below, the road winding and tunnelling through the rock. In a car it can be difficult to stop safely to admire the view; cycling or rambling is a much better way to appreciate it all.

At **St-Jean-la-Rivière** the deep gorge is spanned by a dramatic bridge and the houses are built on top of each other either side of the river. Here the Vésubie canal, much of which is underground, begins. From here you can take the steep, winding road to Utelle, one of the villages on the original *route du sel* from the salt flats of Hyères to the Southern Alps, a route which was abandoned at the end of the 18th century.

This is real mountain country where you are more likely to meet a logging truck on a hairpin bend than a tourist coach. **Utelle** is a very pleasant little town, dependent mainly on olive cultivation. It is built like a star on a rocky outcrop, originally the crossroads of a number of mule paths over the mountains which surround it. The hillsides, covered in wild lavender and fragrant herbs, are perfect for walking and picnics. The 16th-century church of St-Véran replaced an earlier one destroyed by the earthquake of 1452. It is a curious mixture of architectural styles, with Romanesque columns and capitals, 18th-century baroque decoration, a Gothic loggia and 16th-century high altar. Don't

Ready for a stroll around La Turbie.

miss the 16th-century primitive painted altarpiece of the Annunciation in the north aisle or the doors with their 12 panels carved with dragons.

The village has some intriguing door lintels; near the post office there is one at knee level, carved with esoteric alchemical symbols.

The mountain road continues beyond the village, climbing higher and higher with hair-raising views to the valleys below, until you reach a magnificent wind-blown plateau and the sanctuary of Madone d'Utelle. According to legend, it was founded by sailors who were guided to safety during a tempest by a mysterious light on the mountain, and founded the sanctuary in gratitude. The chapel which is usually open, was restored in the mid-1970s, and the building next to it is used as a retreat.

There is a viewing platform with a spectacular 360-degree panorama of mountain peaks and valleys and beyond to the distant sea; on a clear day you can see as far as Cap d'Antibes and even Corsica.

The main road, D 2565, continues to Lantosque, climbing all the way. The gorge widens to meadows and pastures; this is an area of pony rides, horses, camping and caravaning.

There can be few things more pleasurable than sitting beneath a parasol at one of the cafés in the lively little square at **Lantosque**, with a distant view of the village of La Bollène Vésubie clinging to its hill-top further up the valley.

Lantosque itself is built on the rocky spine of the hill up which the streets climb in a series of staircases. There is a distinct Italianate influence in the architecture with open loggias on the top floors of many of the older houses.

A little further on is **La Bollène Vésubie**, a charming town with big, shady lime trees lining the wider streets. At the top of the village is a pretty baroque church dated 1525. There are no architectural highlights in the village; it is the total ensemble that makes it so delightful. Like many of these villages, it was badly flooded in 1993 and has taken some time to recover.

The D2565 leads on through trout fishing country to **Roquebillière Vieux**, an equestrian centre. A bridge leads over the river to new Roquebillière, attractively built with uniform red tiled roofs. High on the mountain, overlooking them both is **Belvédère**, a hill town with a rather good clock and sun dial on the bell tower and a large barn-like church. The houses are many-storeyed with balconies and top-floor loggias in the mountain tradition. Lavender and jasmine grows everywhere and the views are wonderful.

Once beyond Roquebillière, the architecture becomes noticeably alpine, with large overhanging roofs and balconies in the Swiss chalet style. Not for nothing is this area known as the "Suisse niçoise".

Located in the centre of it is **St-Martin-Vésubie**, the gateway to the Mercantour national park. It is a mountaineering centre and summer retreat, popular with the people of Nice. Even in high season it's a sleepy kind of place, certainly for the cat dozing in the window of the *boulangerie* along with loaves shaped like tortoises and crocodiles. The main shopping and restaurant street is the Rue du Dr-Cagnoli which runs the full length of the town. It has a fast-flowing gutter running down the middle and is lined with Gothic houses with corbels and balconies, the oldest of which are at the bottom, near the church. There is quite a mix of architectural styles, blending Swiss-style chalet roofs and wooden balconies with Italian loggias, Gothic doors and jettied roofs.

At No. 25 is the *maison Gothique* of the counts of Gubernatis, a national monument. It has a jettied first floor, ornamental frieze and arched ground floor. On one side of the street the buildings lean out over the river and the restaurants have tree-shaded dining terraces in the back. Near the 18th-century Chapelle-des-Pénitents-Blancs with its interesting bulb cupola, there is a tiny market place. The baroque church is 17th-century, but possesses a 13th-century virgin which is carried in procession on 2 July to the sanctuary of the

The total ensemble of La Bollène Vésubie.

Madone de la Fenestre, where she remains until the end of September.

From the terrace in front of the church door there is a view looking south to the perched village of Venanson and the surrounding mountains and forest. Behind the east end of the church, to the right, is the Place de la Frairie, a terrace looking out over the Madone de la Fenestre river, which has its origins in the Lac de la Fenestre in the mountains to the east on the Italian border. The steep river valley can be followed for 8 miles (13 km) along the D94, ending at the high mountain sanctuary of Madone de la Fenestre.

A variety of return routes to the coast are possible. You might go via **Peïra Cava**, which was originally a military camp but has developed into a winter sports and holiday resort. The view from the Pierre Plate, which is a half-mile walk or drive up the small road opposite the Hotel Truchi, is superb. There is parking near the top.

Lucéram is probably of Roman origin, situated at the crossroads of ancient paths, in particular the salt route from the coast. Until recently it depended on mountain farming for survival, mainly olive cultivation and also distilling wild lavender. Today the still fortified village, with its tall stacked houses in pastel colours of yellow, rose and almond green, and its sombre vaulted alleys, depends almost entirely on tourism. It is noted particularly for the church treasures in the 15th-century l'Église Ste-Marguerite, which include a silver reliquary and retables attributed to Niçois artist Louis Bréa.

Finally, **Coaraze** is worth a detour; a restored medieval perched village with concentric lanes, arches and covered passages and public gardens with cypress trees. The church is 17th-century in the *baroque-rustique* style and there are sundials in the square outside. Visit the graveyard which uses cement boxes for burials because the rock is so hard that graves are impossible to dig. At the summit of the village is the Place du Château, site of the now demolished castle.

Alpine view from Utelle.

BORDER COUNTRY

The **Haut-Pays** resembles Piedmont rather than Provence and, in accent, sounds Italian rather than French. The Italian influence colours the architecture: loggias, arcaded squares and onion-topped bell towers abound. A love of decoration is present in such flourishes as carved lintels, elegant balconies and madonnas in niches. The dreamy Italianate villages strive after colour, with painted facades, *trompe l'oeil* decoration and glinting fish-scale roofs. Sospel and the **Bévéra Valley** mark the transition from the outward-looking Mediterranean world to the inward-looking mountain world. Here olives, lavender and lemons give way to pine, oak, mountain laurel and vivid blue gentians.

The **Haute Roya Valley** begins just north of Sospel and from Breil-Sur-Roya the mountain atmosphere becomes more pronounced. The rural architecture acquires an alpine sturdiness, with dry stone barns and *cazouns*, the shepherds' primitive shelters.

Sleepy town: The natural gateway to the mountainous hinterland is **Sospel**, sprawling along the Bévéra Valley. As a great advocate of green tourism, Sospel offers a wide range of walks through classic hill country. Tourism is low-key and has not changed the character of this sleepy medieval town.

Sospel was an independent commune by the 11th century and an important trading post on the old salt route linking Piedmont with France. Medieval Sospel depended, in turn, on the counts of Ventimiglia, Provence and Savoy but retained a degree of autonomy. This was partly due to the presence of charitable confraternities which played a major role in city life. By the 17th century Sospel was a noted artistic and intellectual centre but fell into a gradual decline, not reversed by the town's return to France in 1860.

The town did, however, experience a brief period of glory, and much suffering, during World War II. In 1944–45 there were fierce battles in the area and occupying German forces only withdrew in April 1945. By then, many Resistance workers had been executed and other Sospellois had been deported to Italy. In recognition of Sospel's sacrifices, the town was awarded the *Croix de Guerre*.

The focal point of the town is the **Pont Vieux**, the 11th-century tollgate and bridge spanning the river Bévéra. It is the oldest tollgate in the Alpes-Maritimes and was still in use in the 18th century. Carriages from Nice transported salt, fish, citrus fruits, porcelain and silk towards Piedmont. In the opposite direction came rice, flax, muslin, lace and dry white wine.

Although the bridge was partly blown up in 1944, the stones were fished out of the river and the Pont Vieux was restored in 1953. The left bank of the river, originally outside the city walls, is lined with attractive pastel-coloured buildings.

Beside the old bridge is a small square with an arcaded medieval building and

fountain. This faded apricot-coloured building was the **Palais Communal** until 1810, housing both the town council and religious tribunals. Place Garibaldi, the adjoining square, has a series of medieval arcades incorporated into later buildings.

The riverside quarter, stretching from Place Garibaldi to Place Ste-Croix, consists of austere 14th-century houses, once home to Sospel's prosperous merchant class. The houses in Rue de la République contain vast interconnecting wine cellars. In the same street is the Maison de Toia, a sculpted Romanesque *hôtel particulier*.

Chapelle Ste-Croix, dating from 1518, is the oldest confraternity building and as the headquarters of the Pénitents Blancs still serves a charitable purpose. Medieval Sospel had five confraternities which offered hospitality to pilgrims and made loans to impoverished peasants. While most Franciscan confraternities were egalitarian, Sospel's were hierarchical: the Pénitents Noirs served the nobility while the Rouges only welcomed local dignitaries; the Blancs were for the bourgeoisie; the Bleus for the young; and the Gris for the poor.

From Place Ste-Croix it is a short stroll across the river to the main street, Avenue Jean-Médecin and Place St-Pierre, a market-place overlooking plantain trees. Rue St-Pierre, a medieval street leading to the **Cathedral**, is lined with dilapidated houses, including the Romanesque Maison Domérégo. This dingy passage astonishingly opens on to Place St-Michel, the most theatrical square in the region. Tucked into a graceful Romanesque clocktower is the cathedral's peaches-and-cream facade: frothy stucco and kitsch gladiatorial figures adorn the exterior.

Opposite the chapel is the Foyer Rural, also subject to the *trompe l'oeil* effect. This cultural centre used to be the Town Hall until an earthquake shattered the building in 1887. Next door is the Palais Ricci, an arcaded Romanesque mansion which in 1809 welcomed Pope Pius VII on his journey to Tuscany. Curiously, this baroque square echoes Pienza, the Tuscan Renaissance town built by Pius II.

Sospel's cathedral is in its element during a sudden summer thunderstorm. It is also magical in the late evening, when the bells chime and a sliver of moon is visible between the Lombard Tower and the baroque facade. The majestic interior is well-preserved and full of light. A touching invitation to prayer says, *"Cette lumière symbolise ma prière que je continue, tout en m'allant."*

The highlight is a 15th-century *Madonna* by Bréa, the renowned Niçois artist. The Virgin, dressed in a gold embroidered dress, stands in front of a Mediterranean coastal scene. Facing Bréa's work is a 15th-century depiction of the Virgin and Christ. The composition features the Pénitents Blancs, who commissioned the work. The painting, awkward and less idealised than Bréa's work, is also more moving.

Walks: From Place St-Michel, the Montée de Louis Saramito leads up to the ruined castle and abbey. From Sospel,

Mountain goatherd.

a signposted walk leads all the way through Provençal countryside to Olivetta in Italy. Longer hikes lead south to Castellar, or north to Moulinet and L'Authion, mountainous terrain where the Germans made their last stand at the Battle of Sospel.

War memorials are on every hill but the **Fort St-Roch** is the most impressive. Just south of Sospel, St-Roch was built in 1930 against the threat of an Italian invasion. It is virtually an underground village, protected by anti-tank defences where 250 soldiers, with artillery and equipment, could survive for at least three months. Local fears of an invasion were well-founded and although Sospel held out against superior Italian forces, occupation was inevitable, by the Italians in 1940 and the Germans in 1943. By September 1944 the Germans had lost Nice and Menton but hung on to Sospel, despite an Allied advance northwards.

Just 3 miles (5 km) south of Menton, the Allies were told to stay put and wait until the advance across northern Europe was established. As a result, Sospel suffered even longer in German hands and was exposed to American artillery attacks. In October the Germans retreated northwards and Hawaiians were the first Allies to enter Sospel. Cries of *"Vive Sospel! Vive La IV République!"* were shortlived, however, and the battle continued until April 1945.

Good *cuisine bourgeoise* is available at the *Hotel de France* but, for a foretaste of the Italianate Roya Valley, try the *tortellini* in *La Taverne Toscane*. Peaceful Sospel may lose some of its charm when the Menton-Sospel road is finally completed. So now is the time to sample the riverside walks and alpine liqueurs.

The Roya Valley: Compared with the Vallée de la Bévéra, the **Roya Valley** is wilder, poorer and more rugged. In the past, routes didn't follow the valley floor because of fears of flooding or landfalls in narrow gorges. Instead, paths were carved along the side of the mountains and through high mountain passes. The Roya's medieval villages, often

Heading down the Roya valley.

perched beside fearsome gorges, were linked only by the old salt route.

Until the 19th century this route was the only way through the region; the Roya Valley did not open up until 1860 when Napoléon III, newly in control of the Comté de Nice, wished to increase trade with Piedmont. The Italian influence, a troubled history, and terrible communications have all helped preserve the Roya in its splendid isolation.

Breil-sur-Roya makes an arresting first impression, particularly if reached by rail or via the precarious Col de Brouis. The train from Sospel emerges from a long mountain tunnel and suddenly there is a fish-shaped pattern of pastel houses clinging to a bend in the River Roya. The mountains bank steeply behind the red-tiled houses. A golden angel blows a trumpet from a chapel rooftop.

Breil likes to call itself the "French gateway to the Roya" since until 50 years ago the Italian border ran just north of the village. However, France is only skin deep. *Ciao* is a normal greeting; the *cuisine provençale* tastes of Piedmont; and Italy lies only a few miles east.

Breil was ruled by the counts of Provence, Ventimiglia and Genoa before becoming part of the House of Savoy until 1860. Unlike Sospel, Breil depended almost entirely upon olive growing and farming. The lower slopes are still given over to olives and 500 tonnes are harvested each year. As for farming, the village still operates traditional grazing rights: from October to April more than 2,000 Breil sheep and goats graze on communal land. It was a dispute about this issue that led to an 18th-century revolt against the feudal lords. The event is re-enacted every four years in *Staccada*, complete with mock battles and a show trial.

A gentle walk along the river leads to Place Brançion in the heart of the medieval village. Open to the river on one side, the square is dominated by an apricot-coloured church, **Sancta Maria in Albis**. This 17th-century baroque façade is echoed by a flamboyant Italianate **Serious mountain terrain.**

interior, with a vivid Bréa panel-painting and a fine organ. The church, like many others in the Roya Valley, has a glittering multi-coloured onion dome.

Breil is well-worn hiking country; signed walks lead to medieval watchtowers like La Cruella or to isolated chapels to the west of the village. Longer hikes lead to Sospel or Vesubie.

Although many Breillois are civil servants or coastal commuters, the village is enough of a retirement haven to radiate relaxation. Residents include poets, local historians and the foodwriter Mademoiselle Sassi whose book, *Recettes Breilloises*, provides a guide to Breil cuisine.

In April 1945 when General de Gaulle led the liberating French forces into Breil, he may have been tempted to stay behind. In its unspectacular way, Breil offers peace of mind.

Breil is, in many ways, untypical of the Roya Valley. The vegetation is lushly Mediterranean and blurs the impact of the brooding mountains. Relative prosperity and an influx of outsiders have diluted its Italian atmosphere. In the **Haute Roya**, however, the transition to mountainous terrain is complete. The dramatic Gorges de Saorge, immediately after Breil, announce serious terrain, with high waterfalls, deep forests, wind-blown alpine pastures and mauve-grey canyons.

Nor are Italian sentiments muted in the Upper Roya. From medieval times, the effects of epidemics and wars forced local *seigneurs* to recruit labour from further afield, particularly from Piedmont, Lombardy and Liguria. This influx of Italians continued until the 1950s and has left its mark on the language, culture and architecture.

In 1860, unlike the rest of the Comté de Nice, the Upper Roya remained with the House of Savoy, rulers since medieval times. La Brigue, Tende and the other villages in the Upper Roya were in an anomalous position. In the 1860 plebiscite they voted to rejoin France rather than remain with Piedmont but were refused permission by Cavour, Victor Emmanuel's astute Prime Minister. Cavour's subterfuge was to claim that

the region, bordering the game-rich Mercantour, formed part of the King's *terrains de chasse*. The reality had nothing to do with retaining hunting grounds and everything to do with controlling the vital mountain passes.

It was not until the 1947 plebiscite that the Haute Roya was incorporated into France. The head rather than the heart determined this political allegiance: trading links were with the French coast and the French standard of living was far higher. So, while Niçois rightly claim that they were never Italian but merely Piedmontese, the same cannot be said of the distinctly Italian Roya Valley. Since becoming French, there have been no great social changes to this self-sufficient mountain community. The dialects still remain resolutely *Piémontais*, as do the local crafts and traditions.

Shimmering tiles: The most spectacularly sited of all Roya villages is **Saorge**. At first sight it appears suspended between a hazy mountain sky and the lush valley floor. The village forms a vast

Saorge, perfect example of a "stacked village".

amphitheatre around a sheer cliff. Down below flows the Roya and on the other side of the canyon lie olive groves rising to terraced alpine pastures.

Saorge looks like a traditional *village perché*: it is perched on high for defensive reasons and favours a south-facing slope, both as winter shelter and summer sun-trap. The painted Venetian facades and the bell towers covered in a mosaic of shimmering tiles are also typical of Roya hill-top villages. But the height of the narrow medieval houses, the disparity of street levels and the complexity of the interlinking passages mark Saorge out as a perfect example of a *village empilé*, a "stacked village".

Saorge is set at right-angles to the slope so that the equivalent to a 30-storey tower separates the foundations of the lowest house from the roof of the highest one. Each house can be up to ten storeys high, with entrances at five different street levels. The heights are so varied that some streets are merely corridors linking individual apartments rather than houses. This is a medieval version of the complex walkways found in modern shopping malls.

As a fortified village controlling the Col de Tende, Saorge seemed impregnable but was finally captured by French forces in 1793. Even though it later returned to Piedmont, this former capital of the Roya never regained its prestige. The building of a valley road in the 19th century turned the village into a backwater; only valleys prospered. In 1806 the chief tax-collector visited Saorge and complained of "a road riddled with wolves and bandits, crossed in peril of one's life". The dangers may have gone but the isolation remains.

Saorge is a remarkable composition, making it difficult to single out individual attractions. The rough slate roofs, a feature of the Roya Valley, add a severe touch to the 15th-century houses below. The facades are tinted pink, ochre and russet, bathing the village in a warm Ligurian glow at odds with the stark setting. The deepest alleys never see any sunlight.

In the 1960s, at the height of the rural exodus, houses in Saorge sold for 2,000

francs; now the average price is 300,000 francs, a sign that many have been snapped up as *résidences secondaires*. The population, a mere 200 in winter, swells to 2,500 in summer. In winter, the shutters are closed and the village only stirs on market day.

At the entrance to the village is a panoramic view of the valley below. On the square itself is a group of peach-coloured buildings, including a chapel and a Mairie crushed against the cliff. From here, Rue Ste-Jeanne d'Arc winds upwards through covered passageways. (The names of streets are usually meaningless in Saorge since most have three names, usually after rival Resistance leaders.)

At the top is **St-Sauveur**, the 15th-century parish church. The forbidding exterior is not misleading; inside is a damp, mauve-tinged interior and a chilly atmosphere not redeemed by a fine Italian organ. Virtually next door is a cheerful cafe, *Lou Pountain*, a chance to sample *quiques*, a local variant on spinach *fettuccini*.

Cobbled streets lead up to a **Franciscan monastery** set amongst cypresses and olives. The sunny terrace is a place for contemplation, with telescopic views of Saorge below and of barren mountains beyond. Although the monastery is built around a Romanesque church, it is essentially baroque.

A former mule track leads from the monastery to **Madone del Poggio**, an isolated Romanesque church topped by an octagonal tower. This graceful sliver of a tower is supported by a honeycomb apse, all that remains of the original abbey. The church and surrounding estate have been in the Davio family for years so the vivid frescoes in the crypt cannot be visited. One consolation is the view of Saorge at sunset. The light shifts across the terraced crescent, colouring the facades sienna and casting deep shadows over the onion-domed towers.

Despite the wonderful scenery, the inhabitants are a disparate, warring group. The core of the winter community consists of doddering *vieux du pays*, hippies and young professionals. The *vieux* are happy to let run-down shepherds' shacks and outlying farms to the *marginaux*. The profit from these latter-day hippies is frittered away in Chez Gilon bar. The hippies lead a pioneer lifestyle, bee-keeping, weaving and tilling the soil. It is subsistence farming; the pastures are known locally as "Siberia" because they receive no sun for four months of the year.

The yuppies are shocked to see mules laden with olives and ill-dressed children. The young schoolteacher's wife complains that the hippies and the retired railway workers are lowering the tone. "What do we want with *boules*, hunting and silly festivals?" Born and bred in Saorge, she loves the quality of life, the landscape and the dialect, an old Ligurian language that pre-dates Latin. Still, she has nothing but scorn for the left-wing mayor who lives in Nice and visits the village only at weekends. "Along with China, we're the last place in the world to remain Communist."

Gorges: Between Saorge and La Brigue the landscape is ravaged by a series of gorges. The building of the Nice-Turin railway brought much-needed work to the Roya villages. Although the line was begun in 1910, work stopped in 1914 and the track was destroyed during World War II. Finally finished in 1972, the result is a spectacular feat of engineering. The 39 viaducts alone make it the most acrobatic line in Europe. The track often does a loop in mountain tunnels so that a train emerges from a tunnel just above its entry point.

Just before La Brigue is **St-Dalmas** station, an overbearing piece of Fascist architecture which served as a major communications centre in Mussolini's time. Despite its baroque church and sturdy architecture, St-Dalmas-de-Tende is an unremarkable village. It is best-known as a touring base for excursions into the **Vallée des Merveilles**. This remote valley lies in the heart of the protected zone known as the **Parc National du Mercantour**.

Alpine pastures: La Brigue is at once the richest and simplest of Roya villages. Set amidst alpine pastures, La Brigue has always been a remote place,

Breil, French gateway to the Roya.

VALLE DES MERVEILLES

Cradled in a majestic circle of the Alps, the Vallée des Merveilles is aptly named and no mere marketing ploy. The valley is a vast open-air museum of prehistory. It is also a Wagnerian landscape of rock-strewn valleys, jagged peaks and eerie lakes. Thanks to the presence of minerals, the lakes are green, turquoise, slate-grey and even black.

Just west of the Lac des Mèsches is the Minière de la Vallaure, an abandoned mine quarried from pre-Roman times to the 1930s. Early prospectors came in search of gold and silver but had to settle for copper, zinc, iron and lead instead. The Romans were beaten to the valley by Bronze Age settlers who carved mysterious symbols on the polished rock, ice-smoothed by glaciation. These carvings were first recorded in the 17th century but investigated only from 1879 by Clarence Bicknell, an English naturalist. He made it his life's work to chart the carvings and died in a valley refuge in 1918.

The rock carvings are similar to ones found in northern Italy, notably those in the

Camerino Valley near Bergamo. However, the French carvings are exceptional in that they depict a race of shepherds rather than hunters. The scarcity of wild game in the region forced the Bronze Age tribes to turn to agriculture and cattle-raising. Carvings of yokes, harnesses and tools depict a pastoral civilisation and these primitive inscriptions served as territorial markers for the tribes in the area.

However, the drawings are also open to less earth-bound interpretations. Anthropomorphic figures represent domestic animals and chief tribesmen but also dancers, devils, sorcerers and gods. Such magical totems are in keeping with Mont Bégo's reputation as a sacred spot. Given the bleakness of the terrain, it is hardly surprising that the early shepherds looked heavenwards for help. Now, as then, flocks of cows, sheep and goats graze by the lower lakes, especially at Fontanalbe. However, the abandoned stone farms and shepherds' bothies attest to the unprofitability of mountain farming.

The Vallée des Merveilles is accessible only by jeep or on foot, and now, due to increasing vandalism – even to the carvings themselves – you can visit the Vallée only if accompanied by an official guide. Given the mountain conditions, the drawings are only visible between the end of June and October. It is a 5-mile (8-km) drive west from St Dalmas to the information centre by the Lac des Mèsches. Then follows a 6-mile (10-km) trek through the woods to Lac Long and the start of the rock carving zone. To protect the engravings, the authorities now insist that visitors are accompanied by an approved guide. A range of different trips can be organised through Tende tourist office.

The Vallée des Merveilles is part of the Parc National du Mercantour, a vast conservation area worth visiting in its own right. Roughly 56 by 19 miles (90 by 30 km), Mercantour is a wilderness of pine forests, gorges and pastures. There are no permanent residents, just a few hamlets occupied by summer visitors. It is ideal rambling country with an amazing variety of flora and fauna. Wild geraniums, gentian violets and forest fruits are common on the lower slopes while orchids, edelweiss and rare saxifrage grow higher up.

The park is also a game reserve with huge ibex, wild boar and shaggy mountain goats. The only problem is illegal hunting on the edge of the Mercantour. The park is regularly raided to satisfy the Niçois penchant for venison or *marcassin*. ■

Animals inspire many of the rock carvings.

wholly dependent on the wool trade. Until the late 19th century, three-quarters of the population reared the sure-footed breed of sheep known as the Brigasque. After spending the summer in La Brigue, local shepherds took their flocks to winter pastures in Breil, Èze and Menton. The itinerant La Brigue shepherd, dressed in red velvet cap and green corduroy, has entered French folklore as a born storyteller.

The wealth created by the wool trade attracted Jewish merchants, money-lenders and goldsmiths to set up shop in the quarter known as Rû Ghetto. By the 15th century, wool merchants and notables could afford to indulge in artistic patronage. Italian craftsmen were commissioned to build new chapels and to adorn bourgeois homes with engraved lintels. The village was deeply influenced by the Italian Renaissance: the local architecture was enriched by arcaded streets and sculpted columns. Italian frescoes replaced traditional Niçois murals.

As late as the 19th century there was a flourishing crafts tradition in the village. However, La Brigue's return to France in 1947 divided the commune with scant regard for history. The "low" village of La Brigue became French while the "high" village, Briga Alta, remained Italian, along with virtually all the neighbouring hamlets. The population of La Brigue dropped from a peak of 4,000 to a mere 500, making it the same size as it was in the 12th century.

Still, there are compensations for such depopulation. With the exception of one ugly square, there has been little recent development. The remoteness of the location has deterred potential buyers of second homes, as has the impenetrable local dialect and the sense of a closed community. After the War, the villagers may have diversified into cattle-rearing but agriculture is the mainstay. Today's farmers are horse-breeders, cheese-makers and bee-keepers, not to mention amateur fishermen. The river Levenza is rich in rainbow trout and the speckled local variety.

La Brigue, lying along the Levenza

Lac Basto, Mercantour National Park.

river, is dwarfed by snow-capped mountains, including the majestic Mont Bégo. The oldest quarter fans out from Rio Secco, a dry river bed but the natural introduction to the village is Place St-Martin, an Italianate square. A cluster of trout restaurants border the square and the fast-flowing river. Apart from *truites vivantes* in their tanks, the rustic restaurants offer *gnocchi, lasagne* and *tantifauluza*, a leek tart.

A 17th-century chapel with a leaning *campanile* looms against mauve canyon walls. This is **L'Assuntà,** once the home of the *Pénitents Blancs*, a chapel which answered to Rome. Decorative Tuscan pillars adorn the facade, creating a purity of line which is not reflected in the interior.

Next door, bordering a more intimate square, is **St-Martin**, the village church. The Romanesque bell tower surmounts a mellow, stone structure. St Martin is said to have preached here before settling in the Loire Valley as bishop of Tours. The interior is the richest in the region, boasting Tuscan decor and striking 16th-century paintings. The ceiling, with its starry blue sky, is reminiscent of Siena Cathedral. Equally Italianate are the frescoes of angels in flight, the vaulted arches and the altar screen.

The works of art, including two attributed to Louis Bréa, are individualistic and memorable. Bréa's *Nativité* portrays a luminous Virgin and Child against a dark, craggy background resembling La Brigue. Like Bréa's *Assomption*, also in the church, the painting is a sober yet knowing work. The expressive faces and the delicate handling of drapery are typical of Bréa's artistic gifts.

Music: In summer, concert-lovers wallow in baroque waves of emotion as the church echoes to the sound of Boccherini and Respighi. The organs in La Brigue have been made by such masters as the Lingiardi brothers. Standard church organs weren't able to play baroque music and opera, still less Piedmontese airs and ballets. However, the church organs in the Roya were all adapted to respond to the 19th-century vogue for *Bel Canto*. On informal occasions the organs play shepherds' folk songs about love and war.

On the far side of the church is another fine Pénitents Blancs chapel, **L'Annonciade**. It has a lovely carved baroque facade, also built of the warm local stone. The interior is being transformed into a museum of religious art. From here, all alleys lead inwards, towards the medieval heart of the village. The cobbled streets are confusingly named in local dialect with Frenchified equivalents, so Rio Secco is also Rû Sec, a reference to the dry river bed that traces the arcaded street.

La Brigue has the greatest variety of decorative slate lintels in the Roya Valley. Made of green and black stone, these lintels are the work of 15th- and 16th-century Italian stonemasons. The lintels usually link a Biblical saying or a wise saw to a pictorial motif, such as a Renaissance dragon, cherubs, shepherds and lambs. Rue Filippi, Rue de la République and Rue Rusca are all good lintel-hunting grounds. The village is

The closed community of La Brigue.

304

completely unrestored and, depending on taste, either ripe for conversion or perfect as it is.

Gods and ghouls: Two miles (4 km) from La Brigue is **Notre-Dames-des-Fontaines**, arguably the most remarkable chapel in the Riviera hinterland. This simple medieval chapel, overlooking a mountain stream, has been a pilgrimage centre since the 14th century. The chapel is supposedly built over a Temple to Diana. Legend has it that after a serious drought, the region was saved by a miraculous outpouring of water from this spot. *Jean de Florette* legends aside, the chapel is celebrated for its 15th-century frescoes, painted by Jean Baleison and Jean Canavesio, Ligurian artists.

Baleison's frescoes, decorating the choir, are faded Marian images, painted as refined courtly figures. Jean Canavesio's frescoes, however, are more satisfying compositions, painted around a central figure. What sets his work apart is the drama and intensity of the moral message, designed to provoke pilgrims into repentance. A grotesque *Judas Iscariot* shows the traitor's disembowelment, performed by a demonic monkey. There is a Hieronymous Bosch quality to the most tormented work.

Elsewhere there are quieter scenes reflecting medieval daily life and landscapes. The *Garden of Gethsemane*, for instance, is full of lush Provençal plants. The artist's palette comes from the region too: the green is crushed slate; the white is limestone; and the black is burnt oak twigs.

Wooded walks: From Notre-Dame-des-Fontaines, walkers can hunt for mushrooms, strawberries and blackcurrants in wooded glades. The enchanting walk back to La Brigue is via a medieval bridge and small orchards owned by Filippi Frères, fruit farmers and beekeepers. A more strenuous hike leads to **Briga Alta**, the Italian village that once belonged to La Brigue. The villagers still meet during hunting and fishing competitions, a time to celebrate their common heritage: trout, *gnocchi* and *salumeria*, Italian salami.

Italian influence in La Brigue.

Tende is as strange as anywhere in the Roya Valley. Despite being a frontier post, it remains a musty, medieval town with its heavy wooden doors closed to the world. But what it lacks in charm, it certainly makes up for in atmosphere.

Tende guards the **Col de Tende**, the old mountain pass connecting Piedmont and Provence. Now bypassed by a road tunnel, the pass was once a fearsome experience. Smollett, crossing it in 1765, was "speechless in front of this celebrated and perilous mountain". His awe was not unjustified. Fears of bandits and smugglers aside, the crossing was undoubtedly beset with difficulties: it took six manservants to cut the ice with pick-axes before Smollett could get through.

Approached from La Brigue, Tende is still an impressive sight. The newer part of town hugs the river; behind is stacked the medieval town, rising in tiers to an Italianate cemetery and a stunted tower. The 14th-century tower is all that remains of the feudal château built by the Lascaris dynasty. The town's fortunes are a familiar story of a powerful church and the oppressed, poverty-stricken peasants.

At the beginning of the century, Tende's farmers and miners were still impoverished: travel was on foot or by mule; bread was a luxury and dried so that it lasted longer. Under Fascism, Tende became a garrison town with over 3,000 Italian soldiers throughout the war years. In 1947 Tende, newly French, was deserted by the military, as well as by Italian civil servants and manual workers.

The economic decline was only checked in the 1980s, with the opening of a new rail link and the creation of ski resorts. The Mercantour Park and the Vallée des Merveilles have also helped to attract visitors to the region. But Tende still remains oblivious to tourism; on the city map the *vieille ville*, the most interesting part of town, is paradoxically left blank.

The *vieille ville* is made of greyish-green schist, a type of slate still quarried nearby. Blackened by time and traffic

The vast amphitheatre of Saorge.

fumes, these sombre houses set the tone. The overhanging roofs are not decorative, as a glance at the snowy peaks will confirm. Nor is Tende ever hot: "*En été il y a toujours de l'air*," as the hardy locals say. Only the orange and pink belfries, decorated in Ligurian colours, generate any warmth.

The late Gothic **Cathedral**, tucked away down a dark alley, is made of blackened green stone and is badly in need of restoration. The sculpted Renaissance facade is framed by pillars propped on stone lions, an unusual feature in church architecture.

Ancient walnut doors lead to a majestic interior, adorned with a starry Tuscan ceiling and a nave emblazoned with the Lascaris arms, a two-headed eagle. Medieval houses and confraternity chapels are clustered around the cathedral.

The gloomy, claustrophobic atmosphere is intensified by a walk through the *vieille ville*. Thick oak doors are adorned with medieval lintels representing the medieval guilds. **Rue Béatrice Lascaris** climbs through the medieval quarter to the Lascaris tower, ruined ramparts and Italianate cemetery. At the end of covered passageways are blind alleys with views of terraced allotments beside a tinkling mountain stream.

Out of season *vieille* Tende feels medieval. *Les gens du pays* collect firewood and mule dung in hand-drawn carts; old men strip olive wood; chestnuts are roasted over open fires; dogs tear each other apart in dark corners. The air is rent with sounds of sawing, chopping and howling. Even the smells are unchanged since medieval times: sawdust and woodsmoke, dung and dog's piss, incense and roast chestnuts.

To dispel this oppressive atmosphere one can stroll down to the new town, centred on Place de la République. Here the aromas vary from *lasagne* and pizza to trout *soufflé* and Piedmontes *polenta*. The stodgy *polenta* dishes are a reminder of Tende's humble origins. Until recently, the poorest people lived on chestnut and cabbage soup or on a pasta made from flour, oil and potatoes. On Sundays, this was supplemented by *une bonne sauce*, generally rabbit.

Wild game, such as boar and deer, was caught in the woods then sold to wealthier citizens. Nowadays, the local cuisine is on a par with Sospel's but Tende still harbours hunters who stray into the Mercantour and wild boar are still caught in significant numbers. Certainly, it is best not to question the provenance of game in local restaurants.

Unusually for a frontier town, Tende is still a closed world, moulded by poverty and self-sufficiency. Until tourism makes a mark, Tende will continue to have few *résidences secondaires* or outsiders. Still tourism is beginning to make its mark slowly, and now a new museum is to open, the **Musée des Merveilles**.

But *les enfants du pays* have often kept a *pied à terre* here, wishing to return to their roots one day. In Tende, as in the rest of the Haut-Pays, there is a desire to perpetuate peasant traditions. It's a place to rear a few chickens and tend a garden in retirement. Underneath the glamour of the Côte d'Azur, the French provincial heart beats strongly.

Mountain huntsman.

INSIGHT GUIDES
Travel Tips

Insight Guides portray destinations in depth, providing the complete picture and the top photography

Insight Pocket Guides *focus on the best choices for places to see and things to do and include large fold-out maps*

Insight Compact Guides' portability makes them the perfect books to carry with you for on-the-spot reference

Three types of guide for all types of travel

INSIGHT GUIDES Different people need different kinds of information. Some want *background information* to help them prepare for the trip. Others seek *personal recommendations* from someone who knows the destination well. And others look for *compactly presented data* for on-the-spot reference. With three carefully designed series, Insight Guides offer readers the perfect choice. Insight Guides will turn your visit into an experience.

The world's largest collection of visual travel guides

CONTENTS

Getting Acquainted

The Place

The Côte d'Azur has a particularly varied landscape. In just 2 hours one can travel from the palm-fringed coast up to the high peaks of the Alps. In the east, the Mercantour National Park covers 265 sq. miles (686 sq. km) of forests, lakes, waterfalls and mountains. Its abundant flora is protected – as many as 30 different species are particular to this area.

While the popular resorts are fairly built up with hotels and apartments, the mountains and inland areas are mostly dotted with small villages and hamlets. The region was probably one of the first to be settled by humans, and even earlier evidence of Cro-Magnon man has been found in the caves around Grasse.

Along the coast the westernmost stretch is the least developed, dotted with fishing villages and behind them the maquis and cork-woods, which suffer so often from summer fires. This scenery is changing as more exotic trees are planted in an effort to save the woodland as the cork oaks are destroyed. Further inland are the olive groves, for which the region is famous, and the lavender-covered moorland.

Time Zones

For most of the year, France is one hour ahead of Greenwich Mean Time, so if it is noon in Nice, it is 11am in London, 5am in New York and Toronto and 8pm in Melbourne.

Climate

An extremely privileged region, both in its natural landscape and its climate, the Côte d'Azur is a popular resort all year round. It enjoys around 2,700 hours of sunshine a year, but the heat is never unbearable because of the sea breezes (nights can be cool). The highest temperatures are in July and August – around 24°C (75°F). Winter is mild and sunny – frost is a rarity.

There is snow on the mountains, but the heat of the sun means that it is quite possible to ski in a T-shirt. The wettest period is the autumn, but then the area is favoured with short, heavy downpours followed by bright sunshine. Spring, too, can have some wet spells when the sky becomes quite heavy and overcast. The worst aspect of the weather is that which only really affects the hinterland, the famous Mistral. This fearsome wind, said to be able to "blow the ears off a donkey", causes considerable damage and can have a depressing effect.

Temperatures

Temperatures are always given in celsius (centigrade). For conversion to fahrenheit, see below:

0°C	=	32°F
5°C	=	40°F
10°C	=	50°F
16°C	=	60°F
21°C	=	70°F
27°C	=	80°F

The People

CULTURE & CUSTOMS

The history of the region is ancient with evidence of early human and even Cro-Magnon settlements. Up in the mountains, in the archaeological sites of the Vallée des Merveilles and the Vallon de Fontanelbe, an extraordinary number of stone engravings (over 100,000) bear witness to man's early habitation. Its later history was inextricably linked with the Greeks, and then the Romans. With the coming of Christianity, Latin became the lingua franca of the area. The Italian influence on architecture, culture and cuisine has been considerable.

Religion plays a great part in the development of any culture and this region is no exception, with much of its religious art dating back to the 15th and 16th centuries.

Recent culture has benefited much from the contribution of artists drawn to the region. Since the arrival of Picasso, Chagall, Matisse *et al*, museums and art galleries have been established and become a magnet for other artists around the world. Indigenous arts and crafts, particularly the pottery and fabrics known as provençal can be seen all around the region.

Government

For much of its history, the Côte d'Azur, with Nice at its centre, was a disputed area. Its proximity to the Italian border meant that it was mostly controlled by the Italians under the House of Savoy and it did not become French until 1860.

For years the French were ruled by a very centralised form of government, but under the socialists (1981–86) the Paris-appointed *préfets* lost much of their power as the individual *départements* (or counties) gained their own directly elected assemblies for the first time, giving them far more financial and administrative autonomy. Each *département* still has a *préfet*, but the role is now much more advisory. The *préfecture* is based in the county town of each *département*: Digne in Alpes-de-Haute-Provence, Gap in Hautes-Alpes, Nice in Alpes-Maritimes, and Toulon in Var. These offices handle most matters concerned with the social welfare of their citizens.

Each French *département* has a number which is used as a handy reference for administrative purposes. For example, it forms the first two digits of the postcode in an address and the last two figures on licence plates. The *département* numbers for the Riviera are as follows: Alpes-de-Haute-Provence is 04, Hautes-Alpes is 05, Alpes-Maritimes is 06, Var is 83.

Each *département* is divided into a number of disparately-sized communes whose district councils control a town, village or group of villages under the direction of the local mayor. Communes are now responsible for local planning and environmental matters. Decisions relating to tourism and culture are dealt with at regional level, while the state still controls education, the health service and security.

The Principality of Monaco is generally included as part of the region, but it is largely autonomous. It is still ruled by the Grimaldi family, who acquired it from the Genoese as far back as 1308. In the early 20th century, the then Prince of Monaco signed a treaty with the French to retain its autonomy provided its citizens conformed to French law. This had the perhaps unforeseen effect of attracting tax exiles to the principality (where no income tax was levied).

Economy

The Côte d'Azur is heavily dependent on tourism, but efforts have been made to lessen that reliance. One of the major industries – which is almost an extension of tourism – is the conference trade. The area is probably the most popular in France for conventions, with the Cannes Film Festival and international music publishing fairs being the best known.

The area also has another glamorous industry: perfumes. Grasse is the world perfume capital.

There is hardly any heavy industry in the region; however, the Var valley in the west is continuing to attract electronics and related businesses. There is also an emphasis on scientific research, with centres set up for the study of astronomy, oceanography and health care. An off-shoot of the interest in health can be seen in the growth of treatment centres for thalassotherapy and balneotherapy.

Planning the Trip

What to Bring

MAPS

A first essential in touring any part of France is a good map. The Institute Géographique National is the French equivalent of the British Ordnance Survey and their maps are excellent; those covering the Riveria are listed below:

Red Series (1:250,000, 1 cm to 2.5 km) sheet 115 covers the region at a good scale for touring.

Green Series (1:100,000 (1 cm to 1 km) are more detailed, corresponding roughly to individual départements – sheet nos. 67 and 68 cover most of the region, for the far north, sheets 60 and 61 are necessary.

Also available is the IGN tourist map *Alpes Maritimes* and highly detailed 1:50,000 and 1:25,000 scales, which are ideal for walkers (*see also the Ramblers section*). For planning your route IGN 901 covers the whole of France at a scale of 1 cm to 10 km and is regularly updated.

The Michelin regional maps are published at a scale of 1:200,000 (1 cm to 2 km). The whole region is covered on sheet No. 245 or at the same scale on two separate sheets: south No. 84, north, No. 81. Michelin also publishes town plans, as does Blay, but local tourist offices often give away their own town plans free of charge. Michelin's Route Planning Map 911 shows motorways and alternative routes and other travel advice.

Good mountain maps for walkers and winter sports are produced by Didier Richard, mostly at a scale of 1:50,000, but a few at the more detailed 1:25,000 scale.

Stockists in London are: Stanfords International Map Centre, 12–14 Long Acre, Covent Garden WC2, tel: (0171) 836 1321; The Travel Bookshop, 13 Blenheim Crescent, London W11 2EE, tel: (0171) 229 5260; and The European Bookshop, 4 Regent Place, London W1R 6BH, tel: (0171) 734 5259.

Compass Books, Freepost, Dereham, Norfolk NR19 1TE, tel: (01362) 691623 offer a mail order service (7-day money-back guarantee) and carry a wide range of maps and guides for the region and the whole of France. IGN Maps are also available by mail order from the IGN sole agent in the UK, World Leisure Marketing, 9 Downing Road, West Meadows Industrial Estate, Derby, tel: 01322 343332. In France, most good bookshops should have a range of maps, but they can often be bought more cheaply in hypermarkets or service stations.

Electricity

Electric current is generally 220/230 volts, but still 110 in a few areas. Current alternates at 50 cycles, not 60 as in the US, so take a transformer for shavers, travel irons, hairdryers etc., which also takes care of the fact that outlet prongs are different.

Entry Regulations

All visitors to France require a valid passport and a visa except for citizens of EU countries, Andorra, Monaco, and Switzerland. If in any doubt check with the French consulate in your country, as the situation may change from time to time. If you intend to stay in France for more than 90 days, then a *carte de séjour* must be obtained (again from the French consulate) – this also applies to EU citizens until restrictions are relaxed.

Animal Quarantine

No animal under three months of age may be taken into France. It is not advisable to take animals to France from the UK because of the six-months' quarantine required by the British authorities on the animal's return. However, if you do wish to take a pet you need to have either a vaccination certificate for rabies or a certificate to show that your country has been free of the disease for three years. For further information contact the French consulate in your country.

Customs

All personal effects may be imported into France without formality (including bicycles and sports equipment). It is forbidden to bring into the country any narcotics, pirated books, weapons and alcoholic liquors that do not conform to French legislation. Certain items (e.g. alcoholic drinks, tobacco, perfume) are limited as to the amounts you can take in or out duty free, and these amounts differ depending on whether you are coming from another EU country, a non-EU European country, or outside Europe. From 1 January 1993, customs barriers within Europe for alcoholic drinks and tobacco (bought and duty paid in France) practically ceased to exist, but the old regulations still apply for goods bought at duty-free shops on the ferry or aeroplane. The current allowances are shown below (with on-board duty-free shop allowances in brackets, although these can be exceeded if you prove the goods are for personal consumption (e.g. a family wedding) and not for resale. For information contact HM Customs and Excise, Dorset House, Stamford Street, London SE1 9NG, tel: (0171) 928 3344.

Allowances for each person over 18 years old:
- 10 litres (1 litre) of spirits or liqueurs over 22 percent alcohol by volume
- 20 litres (2 litres) fortified wine
- 90 litres (2 litres) wine (no

more than 60 litres of it may be sparkling wine)
- 200 cigars (50 cigars) or 400 cigarillos (100 cigarillos) or 800 cigarettes (200 cigarettes).

Health Care

The International Association for Medical Assistance to Travellers (IAMAT) is a non-profit-making organization which anyone can join free of charge (a donation is requested). Benefits include a membership card (entitling the bearer to services at fixed IAMAT rates by participating physicians) and a traveller clinical record (a passport-sized record completed by the member's own doctor prior to travel). A directory of English speaking IAMAT doctors on call 24-hours a day is published for members.

EU nationals should check before leaving that they qualify for subsidised treatment in France under EU rules. Most British nationals do – check with the Department of Health and ask for the form E111. The E111 does not cover the full cost of treatment, so you may find it worthwhile to take out private insurance as well.

IAMAT OFFICES

Canada: 1287 St Claire Ave., W. Toronto, M6E 1B9, tel: (416) 652 0137 or 40 Regal Road, Guelph, Ontario, N1K 1B5, tel: (519) 836 0102.
New Zealand: PO Box 5049, Christchurch 5.
US: 417 Center Street, Lewiston, NY 14092, tel: (716) 754 4883.

Money

The French Franc is divided into 100 centimes. A 5-centime piece is the smallest coin and the F500 note the highest denomination bill.

Banks displaying the Change sign will change foreign currency and in general, at the best rates (you will need to produce your passport in any transaction). If possible avoid hotel or other independent bureaux which may charge a high commission. Credit

cards are widely accepted, but Visa is by far the most common and can now be used in hypermarkets and many supermarkets. Access (MasterCard/EuroCard) and American Express are also accepted in many places.

Credit cards and cash cards from many European banks can now be used in French cashpoint machines (ATMS) located outside banks. Check the validity of your cashcard with your home bank before departure.

Eurocheques, used in conjunction with a cheque card, drawn on your own bank account, can often be used, though some French banks do not accept them. Apply for these, or if you prefer, travellers' cheques, from your own bank, allowing a couple of weeks before your departure.

Public Holidays

A list of major public holidays is given below. It is common practice, if a public holiday falls on a Thursday or Tuesday for French business to *faire le pont* (bridge the gap) and have the Friday or Monday as a holiday too. Details of closures should be posted outside banks etc. a few days before the event but it is easy to be caught out, especially on Assumption day in August, which is not a holiday in the UK.

New Year's Day: 1 January
Easter Monday: (but not Good Friday)
Labour Day: Monday closest to 1 May
Ascension Day
8 May: (to commemorate the end of WWI)
Whit Monday: (Pentecost)
Bastille Day: 14 July
Assumption Day: 15 August
All Saints' Day – Toussaint: 1 November
Armistice Day: 11 November
National holiday in Monaco: 19 November
Christmas Day: 25 December, but not Boxing Day 26 December.

Getting There

BY AIR

Best options from Britain are British Midland (0345 554554), British Airways (0345) 222111, or via Paris with Air Inter Europe (0181 742 6600). The budget option is Easyjet from Luton. **Note:** the 20 minute taxi ride from the airport is not value for money – so take the bus instead.

Helicopter transfer services operate from Nice to Cannes and Monaco (transfers can be included in ticket prices).

Although there are some scheduled flights from the US, travellers from America and other countries outside Europe may find it cheaper to travel by charter via Paris or London. Numerous companies offer flights to these two cities; Nouvelles Frontières offers some of the most competitive fares on both scheduled and charter flights to Paris from the US and Canada. It also flies charters direct from London Gatwick to Nice. Availability of charter flights is variable; for details contact the company at:

Canada: 800 Boulevard de Maisonneuve Est., Montreal, Quebec H2L 4M7, tel: (5l4) 288 4800.

UK: 11 Blenheim Street, London W1, tel: (0171) 629 7772.

US: 125 West 55th Street, New York NY, tel: (212) 247 0100.

BY SEA

There are several ferry services operating from the UK, the Republic of Ireland and the Channel Islands to the northern ports of France. All of them carry cars as well as foot passengers. Hovercraft crossings are fast, but more dependent on good weather than the ferries. The new Seacat catamaran service offers the quickest crossing but, like the hovercraft, can only carry a limited number of cars. The ports of Boulogne, Calais and Le Havre offer direct access by motorway to Paris; there is almost direct motorway access also via Dunkerque and Caen.

Brittany Ferries sails from Portsmouth to Saint-Malo and Caen, Plymouth to Roscoff, Cork (Eire) to St Malo and Roscoff, and a cheaper Les Routiers service from Poole to Cherbourg (summer only). Contact Wharf Road, Portsmouth PO2 8RU, tel: (01705) 827 70l; or Millbay Docks, Plymouth PLl 3EW, tel: (01752) 22l 32l.

Hoverspeed operates hovercraft from Dover to Calais and Boulogne (crossing time approx. 30 minutes). The Seacat catamaran runs between Boulogne and Folkestone. Details of all services from Hoverspeed Ltd, Marine Parade, Dover CT17 9TG, tel: (01304) 240241.

North Sea Ferries connects travellers from the north of England and Scotland to France, via their Hull-Zeebrugge route. Situated 56 km (35 miles) from the French border, Zeebrugge gives good motorway access to Paris region. The overnight services offer entertainment; a five-course dinner and breakfast are included in the fare. Contact the company at King George Dock, Hedon Road, Hull HU9 5QA, tel: (01482) 795141.

P & O European Ferries operates the short sea routes from Dover to Calais, as well as Portsmouth to Le Havre and Cherbourg. Fares and schedules from P & O, Channel House, Channel View Road, Dover CT16 3BR, tel: (01304) 203388.

Sally Line ferries uses the smaller ports of Ramsgate and Dunkerque. Details from 81 Piccadilly, London W1V 9HF, tel: (0171) 409 2240; for reservations: Argyle Centre, York Street, Ramsgate, Kent CT11 9DS, tel: (01843) 595522.

Sealink Stena Line ferries operates from Dover to Calais (the fastest shipping route at 90 minutes), Southampton to Cherbourg, and Newhaven to Dieppe. Details and reservations for all services are available from Charter House, PO Box 121, Park Street, Ashford, Kent TN24 8EX, tel: (01233) 647047.

Irish Ferries offers a service from Rosslare to Le Havre and Cherbourg, with ferries leaving daily from 1 April to mid-September to one of the two ports. It currently runs a service once weekly from Cork to Le Havre and Cherbourg from June–August. Contact them at 2-4 Merrion Row, Dublin 2, tel: 661 511.

BY TRAIN

For visitors travelling from Paris, the train is a fast, efficient way to reach the region, especially with the high-speed express trains (TGV). All services leave from Paris-Gare de Lyon; the principal destinations in the region are Nice, Toulon, Fréjus/St-Raphaël and Cagnes-sur-Mer. Travel around the region by train is pretty good, although trains can be infrequent on some lines. Car and bicycle hire is available at most main stations – as a package with your rail ticket if you prefer (details from French Railways, below).

France has a fast efficient rail network operated by the SNCF (Société Nationale des Chemins de Fer de France). Its much praised TGV programme is developing all the time, offering comfortable express services from Paris to Lyon and the southeast and to Le Mans, Rennes and Bordeaux in the west and southwest.

For visitors travelling from Paris, the train is a comfortable way to reach any major destination in France with most express services offering refreshments (and even play areas for young children). There are five main stations serving the provinces from Paris, so check which one you need before setting off. Getting across country by rail is less easy. Car and bicycle hire is available at most main stations – as a package with your rail ticket if you prefer (details from French Railways).

Tickets may be booked for through journeys from outside France. In the UK, tickets can be booked from any British Rail Station, including ferry travel. British Rail travel centres can supply details of continental services or contact British Rail International Enquiries, International Rail Centre, Victoria Station, London SW1, tel: (0171)

834 2345. Students and young people under 26 years of age can get a discount. Eurotrain, tel: (0171) 730 3402, offers 30 percent off standard two-month return tickets for those under 26.

French Railways has opened a new telephone service, Rail Shop, in London to provide an instant booking service. The lines, however, are usually very busy and a little patience is required. A second Rail Shop is due to open in Manchester. The service includes ferry bookings, discounted tickets for young people,

Rail Passes

There are several rail-only and rail-combination passes available to foreign visitors. These must always be bought before departing for France. In the UK, a Eurodomino Pass offers unlimited rail travel on any 3, 5, or 10 days within a month. This can also be purchased in conjunction with an Air France Rail Ticket.

Visitors from North America have a wider choice of passes, starting with the basic France Railpass which offers four or nine days of unlimited travel within a month. Then there are various types of Eurail Pass which offer varying periods of first-class travel throughout Europe; the Eurail Youthpass offers a similar deal for young people under 26. The France Rail 'n' Drive pass offers a flexible rail and car-rental package, while the Fly Rail and Drive Pass combines internal flights on Air Inter with train travel and car hire.

Similar passes are available to travellers from other countries, although the names of the tickets and conditions may vary slightly.

SNCF has a central reservation office in Paris, tel: (1) 45 65 60 60 and information services in English, tel: (1) 45 82 08 41, and in French, (1) 45 82 50 50. The SNCF office in Paris is at 10 place de Budapest, 75436 Paris Cedex 09, tel: (1) 42 85 60 00.

Most French railway stations accept Visa and American Express.

a *Carte Vermeil* for senior citizens, which gives a generous discount on tickets and Eurodomino rail passes (*see below*). Lines are open Monday to Friday and Saturday morning, tel: (0891) 515 477 (information only) or (0171) 495 4433 (reservations only).

Any rail ticket bought in France must be validated by using the orange automatic date-stamping machine at the entrance to the platform. Failure to do so incurs a surcharge.

Channel Tunnel

The Channel Tunnel offers fast, frequent rail services between London (Waterloo), Lille (2 hours) and Paris (Gare du Nord – 3 hours). Connections to other destinations are available. Rail passenger services are run by Eurostar a consortium of the French, British and Belgian railway companies, and tickets are bookable through French or British railway companies.

Le Shuttle is the name of the service that takes cars and their passengers from Folkestone to Calais on a simple drive-on-drive-off system. The journey time through the tunnel is about 35 minutes. No tickets are needed – you just turn up and take the next service. Le Shuttle runs 24 hours a day, all year round, with a service at least once an hour through the night. Enquiries in UK, tel: 0990-353535.

Motorail is another, if somewhat pricey alternative, solution for travellers wishing to have the freedom of their own car on holiday but hoping to avoid the long haul from the northern coast. The following routes are available: Boulogne or Dieppe to Fréjus/St-Raphaël (summer only) and Calais to Nice. There is also a service from Paris to Fréjus/St-Raphaël.

BY COACH

Eurolines European coach services operate regular services from London (Victoria) to Nice, Cannes and Grasse. The ticket includes the ferry crossing (via Dover) and National Express coaches have connections with the London

departures from most major towns in the UK. For details contact Eurolines UK, 52 Grosvenor Gardens, Victoria, London SW1W 0AU, tel: (0171) 730 8235.

BY CAR

Many drivers are daunted by the thought of a long drive (745 miles/1,200 km from London and over 560 miles/900 km from Paris), before even starting their holiday. Indeed, in high season the roads can become very crowded. For those in a hurry, the autoroute from Paris to Nice (A6, A7, A8) takes about eight hours, but toll fees can add up. For travellers driving from the port of Calais, it is now possible to travel all the way to the Riviera by motorway.

However, if speed is not of the essence and you intend to make the drive part of your holiday, follow the green holiday route signs to your destination – these form part of a national network of *bison futé* routes to avoid traffic congestion at peak periods. You will discover parts of France you never knew existed and are more likely to arrive relaxed. The first weekend in August and the public holiday on the 15th are usually the worst times to travel, so avoid them if you can. For further details about driving in France, *see Getting Around* page 320.

Special Facilities

DOING BUSINESS

Business travel is now such an important part of the tourist economy that the French Government Tourist Office in London and Chicago (*see Useful Addresses*) have a department set up just to deal with business enquiries. They will help organise hotels, conference centres and incentive deals for any group, large or small.

On the Côte d'Azur in particular, business tourism is of vital importance to the region's economy, and has been developed alongside its regular tourist industry. Nice, Cannes and Monte-Carlo all attract visitors to the trade fairs and other events that take place annually, and the larger hotels depend on the conference trade for a major part of their business. The international airport at Nice, with direct flights to much of Europe and the US means that it is an ideal venue for top-flight companies who can afford to indulge their higher paid executives.

Cannes, Nice and Monte-Carlo all have huge, modern convention centres, in very attractive locations. The one in Cannes is at the west end of La Croisette and plays host to the annual Film Festival. In Nice, the **Acropolis** is set in splendid gardens studded with statues by famous artists while Monte-Carlo's **Convention Centre and Auditorium** is suspended over the Mediterranean. Most larger hotels also have conference facilities.

For general information about business travel and facilities contact the regional tourist offices (see Useful Addresses page 317). Another good source of business information and local assistance, are the **Chambres de Commerce et d'Industrie** in the individual départements. Here you can obtain details about local companies, assistance with the technicalities of export and import, interpretation/translation agencies and conference centres – indeed, most chambers of commerce have conference facilities.

There is also a **French Chamber of Commerce** in London (tel: 0171 225 5250) which exists to promote business between the two countries, and at the same address is **French Trade Exhibitions**: 2nd floor, Knightsbridge House, 197 Knightsbridge, London SW7 1RB, tel: (0171) 225 5566.

TRAVELLERS WITH SPECIAL NEEDS

Most disabled travellers will be keen to book accommodation in advance rather than arriving "on spec". Most of the official list of hotels (available from the FGTO or the regional tourist office – see Useful Addresses page 316) include a symbol to denote wheelchair access, but it is always advisable to check directly with the chosen hotel as to exactly what facilities are available. Balladins runs a chain of budget-priced hotels throughout France which all have at least one room designed for disabled guests. Restaurants and all other public areas are wheelchair accessible. For a complete list contact Hotels Balladins, 20 rue du Pont des Halles, 94656 Rungis Cedex, tel: 49 78 24 61, fax: 46 87 68 60.

An information sheet aimed at disabled travellers is published by the French Government Tourist Office: for a copy send a stamped addressed envelope. There is a guide – Où Ferons Nous Etape? (in French only) – which lists accommodation throughout France that is suitable for disabled people, including wheelchair users. Once again, if you have specific needs you should double check when booking. It is available for around FF40 by post from the Association des Paralysés, Service Information, 17 Boulevard August Blanqui, 75013 Paris, tel: (1) 40 78 69 00. This organization may also be able to deal direct with specific enquiries and can provide addresses of their branches throughout France. The

Travelling with Children

The Riveria is more the kind of place that attracts adults for its glamorous beaches and nightlife than a family resort, and young families could be well advised to stay away from the crowds (and high prices) of the high season. The coastal resorts to the west of the region are more easily approached by car and therefore more attractive to families. To get anywhere near the beaches of Nice or Cannes in August could be a nightmare with young children and their accompanying clutter in tow (remembering the difficulties of parking).

However, the private beaches of the Riviera do cater well for children, and have beach clubs providing various amusements (for a fee). Some of the public beaches also have the same kind of facilities (expect to pay a fee for the morning/afternoon session). There are also plenty of other places to take children: **Marineland** in Antibes, the **Museum of Oceanography** in Monaco, to name just two. Consult the Attractions section (page 332) for more ideas.

In France generally, children are treated as people, not just nuisances. It is pleasant to be able to take them into restaurants (even in the evening) without heads being turned in horror at the invasion. French children, being accustomed to eating out from an early age, are on the whole well behaved in restaurants so it helps if one's own offspring understand that they can't run wild.

Many restaurants offer a children's menu; otherwise, they will often split a prix-fixe menu between two children. If travelling with very young children, you may find it practical to order nothing specific at all for them but request an extra plate and give them tasty morsels to try from your own dish. It is a good introduction to foreign food for them, without too much waste. French meals are generally generous enough (nouvelle cuisine excepted) to allow you to do this without going hungry yourself, and you are unlikely to encounter any hostility from le patron (or la patronne). Another option is to order a simple, inexpensive dish from the à la carte menu, such as an omelette, which most childen like.

Most hotels have family rooms so children do not have to be separated from parents and a cot (lit bébé) can often be provided for a small supplement, it is a good idea to check availability if booking in advance.

Some of the hotels offer a baby listening or child-minding service.

Rousseau H Comme Handicapé guide may also prove useful. It is available from Hachette bookshops or at SCOP, 4 rue Gustave-Rouanet, 75018 Paris, tel: (1) 42 52 97 00.

Michelin's Red Guide *France* for hotels and its *Camping-Caravanning – France* both include symbols for disabled welcome.

The Royal Association for Disability and Rehabilitation (RADAR), 25 Mortimer Street, London W1N 8AB, tel: (0171) 637 5400, has some useful information for tourists, including a guide book, *Holidays and Travel Abroad*. This is a general country-by-country guide and provides information about France as a whole, including hotel chains offering suitable accommodation and tour operators offering specialist holidays.

France's sister organization to RADAR, the Comité National Français de Liaison pour la Réadaptation des Handicapés (CNFLRH) is based at 38 Boulevard Raspail, 75007 Paris, tel: (1) 45 48 90 13. It offers a good information service for visitors with special needs travelling to France, although it does not have any specific information about the regions of France.

The Holiday Care Service offers free information on travel accommodation and counterpart associations in France. Send a large stamped addressed envelope to: 2 Old Bank Chambers, Station Road, Horley, Surrey RH6 9HW, tel: (01293) 774 535, fax: (01293) 784 647, Minicom (for the hearing impaired): (01293) 776 943.

For young people, the Centre d'Information et de Documentation Jeunesse, 101 Quai Branly, 75740 Paris Cedex 15, provides information on services for young disabled travellers. It publishes *Vacances Personnes Handicapées* and annual leaflets on activity and sports holidays for young disabled people. Parents may also find the following organization helpful: Union Nationale des Associations de Parents d'enfants Inadaptés (UNAPEI), 15 Rue Coysevox, 75018 Paris, tel: (1) 42 63 84 33.

The Comité de Liaisons pour le transport des personnes handicapées, Conseil National des Transports, 34 avenue Marceau, 75009 Paris publishes a booklet called *Guide des Transport à l'usage des Personnes à Mobilité Réduite*. This gives brief information on the accessibility for less able passengers on all forms of public transport and contacts for special transport schemes throughout France.

Some concessionary ferry fares are available for members of the following organizations. The Disabled Drivers' Association, Ashwellthorpe, Norwich NR16 1EX, tel: (01508) 41449. Disabled Drivers' Motor Club, Coltingham Way, Thrapston, Northants NN14 4PL, tel: (01832) 734 724. The Disabled Motorists' Federation, Unit 2a Atcham Estate, Shrewsbury SY4 4UG, tel: (01743) 761 889.

More information about air and sea travel is available in a guide entitled *Door-to-Door*. For a free copy write to Department of Transport, Door-to-Dooor Guide, Freepost, Victoria Road, South Ruislip, Middlesex HA4 0NZ. There are also copies available on audio cassette for the vision impaired.

In the US, the following offer services to disabled travellers.

Travel Information Service, Moss Rehabilitation Hospital, 1200 West Tabor Road, Philadelphia, PA 19141–3099, tel: (215) 456 9600. General information for would-be travellers.

Society for the Advancement of Travel for the Handicapped (SATH), 26 Court Street, Brooklyn, New York 11242, tel: (718) 858 5483. Advice and assistance in travel matters.

Accessible Journeys, 35 W. Sellers Avenue, Ridley Park, Philadelphia, 19078-2113. Tours using wheelchair-accessible transport in Europe.

In Canada the following organisation may be of help.

Canadian Rehabilitation Council for the Disabled, 45 Sheppard Avenue E., Toronto, Ontario, M2N 5W9, tel: (416) 250 7490. National organization producing some material relating to travel.

Access to Places of Interest

Some places of interest in the area are fitted with a magnetic loop system to help the hearing impaired. These include the **Palais des Festivals** at Cannes, the **Nice Opera** and the **Le Forum Cinema**, also in Nice at 45 Promenade des Anglais. Some museums also have braille aids.

STUDENTS & YOUNG PEOPLE

Students and young people under the age of 26 can benefit from cut-price travel to France and rail cards for getting around the country (for details *see Getting There* page 312).

If you wish a prolonged stay in the region, it may be worth finding out about an exchange visit or study holiday. Several organizations exist to provide information or arrange such visits.

In the UK, the Central Bureau for Educational Visits and Exchanges, Seymour Mews House, Seymour Mews, London WIH 9PE, tel: (0171) 486 5101, produces three books: *Working Holidays* (opportunities in France are limited; the grape harvest is still a big draw for young people and employment opportunities are listed here); *Home from Home* (a wealth of useful information about staying with a French family) and *Study Holidays* (details of language courses). Another option, for those with decent French is to approach one of the UK-based camping holiday operators who employ students as site couriers (*see Where to Stay* page 323).

Organizations in the US include:

Council on International Educational Exchange (CIEE), 205 E. 42nd Street, New York, NY 10017, tel: (212) 661 1414 – many services, including travel.

American Council for International Studies Inc., 19 Bay State Road, Bost, Mass. 02215, tel: (617) 236 2051.

Youth for Understanding International Exchange, 3501 Newark Street, NW, Washington DC 20016, tel: (202) 966 6800.

Volunteers are welcome at the workcamps organised on several on the archaeological and cultural sites in Burgundy (mainly during the summer). For information contact the Direction Régionale des Affaires Culturelles, 39 Rue Vannerie, 21000 Dijon, tel: 80 72 53 53. Although unpaid, this is a good way of meeting other young people of all nationalities and an opportunity to learn the language.

There several French tour operators which organize study tours and language courses, some of the more reputable are listed here:

Accueil des Jeunes en France, 119 Rue St Martin, 75004 Paris, tel: (1) 42 77 87 80, fax: (1) 42 77 70 48. Offers French study programmes, inexpensive accommodation (or with a family), and tours for individuals or groups.

Centre des Echanges Internationaux, 104 Rue de Vaugirard, 75006 Paris, tel: (1) 45 49 26 25. Sporting and cultural holidays and educational tours for 15 to 30-year-olds. Non-profit making organization.

Séjours Internationaux Linguistiques et Culturels (SILC), 32 Remparts-de l'Est, 16002 Angoulême, tel: 45 95 83 56.

Union National des Organizations de Séjours Linguistiques (UNOSEL), 293/295 Rue de Vaugirard, 75015 Paris, tel: (1) 42 50 44 99.

A complete list of private language schools is obtainable from regional tourist offices (see Useful Addresses page 317).

Souffle is an organization created in 1991 which embraces 11 centres which specialise in teaching French as a foreign language, and have all signed a quality charter. Contact Souffle at BP 133, 83957 La Garde Cedex, tel: 94 21 20 92, fax: 94 21 22 17.

Once in France, students will find a valid student identity card useful to obtain discounts on all sorts of activities. including admission to museums, galleries, cinema and theatre. If you do not have your ID card with you reductions may sometimes be allowed by proving your status with a passport.

The Centre d'Information et Documentation de Jeunesse (CIDJ) at: 101 Quai Branly, 75740 Paris, tel: (1) 45 67 35 85, is a national organization which disseminates information pertaining to youth and student activities. The noticeboard in the Paris office is a mine of useful information regarding accommodation and events.

For individual holidays, the cheapest way to stay is generally under canvas, or in a hostel (expect to pay around FF55 a night without meals).

GAY LIFE

Gay organisations and social centres are advertised in the local press. More general information is available from the national *Gai Pied Guide* (published in French, sold in the UK). If you need urgent help or information, try the Paris-based gay switchboard (SOS Homosexualité), tel: 16 1-46 27 49 36) with English-speakers.

Note this service is only active Wednesday and Friday from 6pm until midnight.

Useful Addresses

IN THE UK & IRELAND
French Government Tourist Office, 178 Piccadilly, London W1V 0AL, tel: (0891) 244 123, fax: (0171) 493 6594.

Consulat Général de France, 21 Cromwell Road, London SW7 2DQ, tel: (0171) 838 2000, fax: (0171) 838 2001. Visa section: 6a Cromwell Place, London SW7, tel: (0171) 838 2050, fax: (0171) 838 2046.

Consulat Général de France, 11 Randolph Crescent, Edinburgh EH3 7TT, tel: (0131) 225 7954, fax: (0131) 225 8975.

French Embassy, 58 Knightsbridge, London SW1X 7JT, tel: (0171) 201 1000, fax: (0171) 201 1004. Commercial department: 21–24 Grosvenor Place, London SW1X 7HU, tel: (0171) 235 7080, fax: (0171) 235 8598. Cultural department: 23 Cromwell Road, London SW7, tel: (0171) 838 2055, fax: (0171) 838 2088.

Monaco Government Tourist and Convention Office, 3-18 Chelsea Garden Market, Chelsea Harbour, London SW10 0XE, tel: (0171) 352 9962, fax: (0171) 352 2103.

Useful Addresses in France

Comité Régional du Tourisme, 55 Promenade des Anglais, 06000 Nice. The tourist authority is very proud of their service, Com'Azur, a single phone number will put you in touch with any of the tourist offices in the region. Tel: 93 37 78 78 for queries to be dealt with in French or English.

Direction du Tourisme et des Congrès de la Principauté de Monaco, 2a Boulevard des Moulins, Monte-Carlo, MC 98030 Monaco Cedex, tel: 92 16 61 16.

Départemental tourist offices (Comité Départemental de Tourisme):

Alpes de Haute-Provence, 19 rue Honorat BP 170, 04005 Digne, tel: 92 32 29 79.

Var, Conseil Général, Boulevard Foch, BP 99, Draguignan Cedex, tel: 94 50 55 50.

Parc National du Mercantour, 23 Rue d'Italie, 06000 Nice, tel: 93 16 78 83. Information about the national park, its flora and fauna, excursions and activities.

Info-Montagne. Tel: 93 87 30 24. A specialist team providing good quality tourist information about the Alps.

Ligue Française pour la Protection des Oiseaux (LPO), La Corderie Royale, BP 263, I7305 Rochefort.

Nice Côte d'Azur International Airport. Tel: 93 21 30 12.

Cannes-Mandelieu International Airport. Tel: 93 90 40 40.

Monaco Heliport, Fontvieille. Tel: 93 30 83 88.

SNCF **Rail Shop**, 179 Piccadilly, London W1V 0BA, tel: (0891) 515 477 (for information only), (01345) 300 003 (for reservations only)
Air France, 158 New Bond Street, London W1Y 0AY, tel: (0171) 499 9511; 29-30 Dawson Street, Dublin 2, tel: 77 8272 (reservations: tel: 77 8899).

IN NORTH AMERICA

Maison de la France/French Government Tourist Office, 610 Fifth Avenue, Suite 222, New York, NY 10020-2452, tel: (310) 271 7838; 645 North Michigan Avenue, Suite 630, Chicago, Illinois 60611-2836, tel: (214) 720 4010, fax: (214) 702 0250; Cedar Maple Plaza, 2305 Cedar Springs Road, Suite 205, Dallas, Texas 75201, tel: (214) 720 4010, fax: (214) 702 0250.
Business Travel Division, 610 Fifth Avenue, Suite 222, New York, NY 10020-2452, tel: (212) 757 1125, fax: (212) 247 6464.
Maison de la France / French Government Tourist Office, 1981 Avenue McGill Collège, Tour Esso, Suite 490, Montreal H3A 2W9, Quebec, tel: (514) 288 4264, fax: (514) 845 4868; 30 St Patrick Street, Suite 700, Toronto M5T 3A3 Ontario, tel: (416) 593 4723.
Air France, 666 Fifth Avenue, New York, NY 10019, tel: (212) 315 1122 (toll-free reservations, tel: 1 800 237 2747); 8501 Wilshire Boulevard, Beverly Hills, Los Angeles, CA 90211, tel: (213) 688 9220.
Air France, 979 Ouest Boulevard de Maisonneuve, Montreal, Quebec H3A 1M4, tel: (514) 284 2825; 151 Bloor Street West, Suite 600, Toronto, Ontario M5S 1S4, tel: (416) 922 3344.

For information on railways, contact:
US: Raileurope Inc. at the following locations: 226–230 Westchester Avenue, White Plains, NY 10604; 360 Post Street, San Francisco, CA 94102, tel: (415) 982 1993; 100 Wilshire Boulevard, Santa Monica, CA 90401, tel: (213) 451 5151; IIE Adams Street, Chicago, IL 60603, tel: (312) 427 8691; 800 Corporate Drive, Suite 108, Fort Lauderdale, FL 33334, tel: (305) 776 2729; 6060 N. Central Expressway, Suite 220, Dallas, TX 75206, tel: (214) 691 5573.
Canada: Raileurope Inc. at the following locations: 2087 Dundas East, Suite 100, Mississauga, Ontario L4X IM2, tel: (416) 602 4195; 643 Notre Dame Ouest, Suite 200, Montréal, Quebec H3C 1HB, tel: (514) 392 1311; 409 Granville Street, Suite 452, Vancouver, BC V6C IT2.
For embassy and consulate offices in France, *see Practical Tips*.

Practical Tips

Emergencies

SECURITY & CRIME
Take sensible precautions regarding personal possessions. Tourists can be a target for petty thieves, so do not give them an open invitation by leaving valuables lying about on the beach or in hotel rooms. Drivers should follow the rules of the road and always drive sensibly. Heavy on-the-spot fines are given for traffic offences such as speeding, and drivers can be stopped and breathalysed during spot checks. Police are fairly visible on the main roads of France during the summer months.

To report a crime or loss of belongings, visit the local *gendarmerie* or *commisariat de police*. Telephone numbers are given at the front of local directories; in an emergency, dial 17. If you lose a passport, report first to the police, then to the nearest consulate (*see Useful Addresses*). If you are detained by the police for any reason, ask to telephone the nearest consulate for a member of the staff to come to your assistance.

Business Hours

Office workers normally start early – 8.30am is not uncommon, but often stay at their desks until 6pm or later. This is partly to make up for the long lunch hours (from noon or 12.30 for two hours) which are still traditional in banks, shops and other public offices. On the Riviera, while the smaller traders still keep to these hours – many closing until 3pm at lunchtime, the larger department stores now tend to stay open. Many companies, too, are beginning to change to shorter

Weights & Measures

The metric system is used in France for all weights and measures, although you may encounter old-fashioned terms such as livre (roughly 1 lb weight – 500 grams) still used by small shop-keepers.

For quick and easy conversion, remember that 1 inch is roughly 2.5 cm, 1 metre roughly equivalent to a yard, 4 oz is just over 100 gm and 2 lb is just under 1 kilo. As 5/8 of a mile is 1 kilometre, a handy reckoning whilst travelling is to remember that 50 miles = 80 km, thus 25 miles = 40 km. Accurate conversions are given below:

Weight
1 ounce (oz) = 28.3 grams (gm)
1 pound (lb) = 454.0 grams
2.2 pound = 1.0 kilogram (kg)
Length
1 inch (in) = 2.5 centimetres (cm)
1 yard (yd) = 0.914 metres (m)
1 mile = 1.6 kilometres (km)
Liquid
1 pint = 0.47 litre (l)
1 Imp. gallon = 4.54 litres
1 US gallon =3.785 litres

lunchbreaks as employees appreciate the advantages of getting home earlier to families in the evening.

Banks on the Riviera are normally open 8.30am–noon and 1.30–5pm, Monday–Friday. However, some bureaux de change are open on Sunday.

Office Provençal, 64 Avenue Jean Médecin, 06000 Nice, tel: 93 13 45 44. Open: 8am–midnight.

Office Provençal, 17 Rue Marechal Foch, 06400 Cannes, tel: 93 39 34 37. Open: 8am–8 pm.

Media

Regional **newspapers**, such as Nice Matin, with national and international as well as local news, have a far higher standing here than in the UK and are often read in preference to national dailies such as Le Monde, Libération and Le Figaro. British and American dailies, notably The Times and the International Herald Tribune, are widely available as are local English-language publications aimed at the tourist and expatriate community. Look out for the Riviera Reporter which gives an irreverent, insider's view of the region.

Television viewers in the region can receive two main national channels: TF1 (commercial) and France 2 (state-owned but largely financed by advertising); as well as FR3 which offers regional programmes. French houses are also beginning to be defaced by satellite dishes at about the same rate as their British counterparts. Cable TV provides access to BBC channels.

France Inter is the main national **radio** station (l892m long wave), it broadcasts English-language news twice a day in summer (generally 9am and 4pm). Essential (English) listening is Monte Carlo's Riviera Radio (106.3 and 106.5), 24 hours of world news, regional broadcasts, small ads for jobs, property and so forth.

Postal Services

Provincial post offices – Postes or PTTS (pronounced pay-tay-tay) are generally open Monday to Friday 9am–noon and 2–5pm, Saturday 9am–noon (opening hours are posted outside); in Paris and other large cities they are generally open continuously from 8am–7pm. Exceptionally, the main post office in Paris is open 24 hours every day, at 52 Rue du Louvre, 75001 Paris.

Inside major post offices, individual counters are marked for different requirements – if you just need stamps, go to the window marked Timbres. If you need to send an urgent letter overseas, ask for it to be sent par exprès, or through the Chronopost system which is faster, but very expensive. Stamps are often available at tobacconists (tabacs) and shops selling postcards. Letters within France and most of the EU are FF2.80 up to 20g; FF4.30 for airmail to Ireland, the US and Canada; and FF5.10 to Australia.

Telegrams (cables) can be sent during post office hours or by telephone (24-hours); to send a telegram in English dial 1614 233 2111. Expect to pay around FF75 for a minimum of 15 words to the US, Canada or the UK.

For a small fee, mail can be kept poste restante at any post office, addressed to Poste Restante, Poste Centrale (for main post office), then the town's postcode and name, e.g. 16000 Angoulême. A passport is required as proof of identity when collecting mail. Many post offices have coin-in-slot photocopying machines.

Telephone

Telex, Minitel information service (useful for directory enquiries) and fax facilities are available in the main post office in most major towns.

The French telephone system, once quirky, is now one of the most efficient in the world. That is not to say that you can be guaranteed to find telephone boxes (cabines publiques) that are always operational, but most are. Telephone numbers have been rationalised to ten figures, given in sets of two, e.g. 99 44 63 21 17, the only codes necessary are for dialling into or out of Paris or overseas. To dial Paris from the provinces, dial 16 1, then the subscriber's number; to dial out of Paris, just dial 16 then the number.

International calls can be made from most public booths, but it is often easier to use a booth in a post office – ask at the counter to use the phone, then go back to settle the bill – but you have no record of the cost of the call until the end.

Coin-operated phones take most coins and card phones are now very common and simple to use. It is worth purchasing a phone card (une télécarte – currently F50 or F120) if you are likely to need to use a public call box, as many are being converted to take cards and in some towns are far more numerous now than coin-operated ones. Cards are available from post offices, stationers, railway stations, some cafés and tobacconists. Several main post offices now also have telephones that can be used with credit cards.

If you use a phone (not a public call box) in a café, shop or restaurant you are likely to be surcharged. Some hotels and cafés now have computerised public telephones whereby the caller receives a printed statement of the details of his call on payment of the bill at the bar – a useful asset for business travellers.

MAKING CALLS

To make an international call, lift the receiver, insert the money (if necessary), dial 19, wait for the tone to change, dial the country code, followed by the area code (omitting any initial 0) then dial the telephone number.

International dialling codes: Australia 61; Canada 1; Ireland 353; UK 44; US 1.

Useful numbers: operator services 13; directory enquiries 12.

Note that numbers will be given in pairs of figures, unless you ask for them to be given *chiffre par chiffre* (singly).

If using a US credit phone card, dial the company's access number.
- Sprint, tel: 19 00 87
- AT & T, tel: 19 00 11
- MCI, tel: 19 00 19.

Most main post offices in France have now replaced the traditional telephone directories with the computerised Minitel system. Members of the public can use this free of charge to look up any number in the country. The instructions (in French) are fairly simple to understand, and you simply tap in the name of the town, *département* and person (or company) whose number you seek for it to be displayed on the small screen, connected to the telephone. It can also be used in the same way as yellow pages to find, for example, all the dry cleaners listed in a particular town.

If you need to make a phone call in rural areas, or small villages with no public phone, look out for the

blue plaque saying téléphone publique on private houses. This means the owner is officially required to allow you to use the phone and charge the normal amount for the call.

You cannot reverse charges (call collect) in France but you can to countries which will accept such calls. Go through the operator and ask to make a PCV (*pay-say-vay*) call. Telephone calls can only be received at call boxes displaying the blue bell sign.

The cheapest times to telephone are weekdays 10.30pm–8am and at weekends after 2pm on Saturday.

Note: The French telephone system was overhauled in 1996. Eight-digit numbers were extended to 10 digits and the following regional telephone numbers gained a prefix: Paris, Ile de France region 01; North West 02; North East 03; South East and Corsica 04, and South West 05.

When dialling Paris from outside France drop the (1).

Consulates

The nearest consular service may be in Paris.

American Embassy, 2 Avenue Gabriel, 75382 Paris, Cedex 08, tel: (16) 142 961202; Consulate: 31 Rue Maréchal Joffre, 06000 Nice, tel: 93 88 89 55.

Australian Embassy, 4 Rue Jean-Rey, 75015 Paris, tel: 01 40 59 33 00.

British Consulate, 9 Avenue Hoche, Paris 75008, tel: 1 42 66 91 42; 12 Rue de France, 06000 Nice, tel: 93 82 32 04. **Embassy:** 35 Rue du Faubourg-St-Honoré, 75008 Paris, tel: (16) 1 42 66 91 42.

Canadian Embassy, 35 Avenue Montaigne, 75008 Paris, tel: 1 44 43 29 00. **Consulate:** le Continental, Place des Moulins, Monte-Carlo, tel: 93 25 58 22.

Irish Embassy, 12 Avenue Foch, 75116 Paris, tel: 1 45 00 20 87.

Getting Around

Domestic Travel

Public transport on the Côte d'Azur is quite good and avoids the problem of finding a parking space. It is really only sensible to take a car if you are touring. Roads to and around the main resorts get completely choked up during July and August and you can spend as much time getting to the beach as you spend on it. Parking in the main resorts is costly. Some towns – Cannes, for instance – have no street meters and tickets must be purchased from a machine and displayed.

Car hire is expensive, but bikes are fairly readily available. Most railway stations hire them out and they do not necessarily have to be returned to the same station. Bikes are carried free of charge on buses and some trains (*Autotrains*); on other, faster services you will have to pay (check before you travel – some services have high charges for carrying cycles). Travelling by a combination of bike and bus or train can be an excellent way of touring and viewing the region.

BY BUS

Details of routes and timetables are generally available free of charge. The main source of information for bus travel is available from Agence Sunbus, 10 Avenue Félix Faure, and also from local tourist offices. There are good services from the airport to all the major resorts, but inland services can be infrequent.

BY TRAIN

Information on services is available from the Gare SNCF, Avenue Thiers, 06049 Nice Cedex, tel: 93 87 50

50 (information); 93 88 89 93 (bookings). The Metrazur rail network links all the coastal towns.

Further services run inland. If you intend to travel extensively by train it may be worth obtaining one of the rail passes available before leaving home (*see Getting There* page 313). These tickets can be used on any journey, otherwise individual tickets need to be purchased – but check on any discounts available, e.g. the *Carte Couple* for married couples travelling together on off-peak services. Children under 4 travel free, from 4 to 12 for half-fare. All tickets purchased at French stations have to be put through the orange machines at the stations to validate them before boarding the train. These are marked *compostez votre billet*.

The Chemin de Fer de Provence runs from Nice to Digne-les-Bains through some spectacular countryside (up to five services a day in each direction). Information from: Gare du Sud, 33 Avenue Malaussena, 06000 Nice.

BY CAR

British, US, Canadian and Australian licences are all valid in France and you should always carry your car's registration document and insurance (third party is the absolute minimum, but it is advisable to ask your insurance company to provide added cover).

Additional insurance cover, which can include a get-you-home service, is offered by a number of organizations including the British and American Automobile Associations and Europ-Assistance, Sussex House, Perrymount Road, Haywards Heath RH16 1DN, tel: (01444) 442211; in the US, Europ-Assistance Worldwide Services Inc., 1133 15th Street, Suite 400, Washington DC 20005, tel: (202) 347 7113. The Automobile Club National is the Umbrella organization of France's 40-odd motoring clubs. It will assist any motorist whose own club has an agreement with it. Details at: 9 rue Anatole-de-la-Forge, 75017 Paris, tel: (1) 42 27 82 00, fax: (1) 40 53 90 52.

CAR HIRE

Hiring a car is an expensive business in France, partly because of the high VAT (TVA) rate of 33 percent on luxury items. Some fly/drive deals work out reasonably well if you're only going for a short visit – Air France, for instance, offers a flydrive service to Nice, with daily departures. French Railways offer a good deal on combined train/car rental bookings.

Rules of the Road

The use of seat belts (front and rear if fitted) and crash helmets for motorcyclists is compulsory. Children under 10 are not permitted to ride in the front seat unless the car has no rear seat.

Priorité à la droite: An important rule to remember is that priority on French roads is always given to vehicles approaching from the right, except where otherwise indicated. In practice, on main roads the major road will normally have priority, with traffic being halted on minor approach roads with one of the following signs:

• STOP

• *Cédez le passage* – give way

Vous n'avez pas la priorité – you do not have right of way

• *Passage protégé* – no right of way

Particular care should be taken in towns, where you may wrongly assume you are on the major road, and in rural areas where there may not be any road markings (watch out for farm vehicles).

The French recently changed the rules concerning roundabouts – in theory, drivers already on the round-about now have priority over those entering it, but beware. Some drivers still insist that priority belongs to the drivers entering a roundabout.

Speed limits: Speed limits are as follows: 130 kph (80 mph) on toll motorways; 110 kph (68 mph) on other motorways and dual carriageways; 90 kph (56 mph) on other roads except in towns where the limit is 50 kph (30 mph). There is now a minimum speed limit of 80 kph (50 mph) on the outside lane of motorways during daylight with good visibility and on level ground. Speed limits are reduced in wet weather as follows: toll motorways: 110 kph, dual carriageways: 100 kph, other roads: 80kph.

On-the-spot fines can be levied for speeding. On toll roads, the time is printed on the ticket you take at your entry point; your average speed can thus be calculated and a fine imposed on exit. Nearly all motorways (*autoroutes*) are toll roads, so you will need to have some cash with you (especially small change) if you intend to use them, although toll booths will now accept payment by Visa and there is always a manned booth.

Autoroutes are designated "A" roads and national highways "N" roads. "D" roads are usually well maintained, while "C" or local roads, may not always be so.

You must carry a red triangle to place 50 metres (164 ft) behind the car in case of a breakdown or accident. In an accident or emergency, call the police (dial 17) or use the free emergency telephones (every 2 km/1 mile) on motorways. It is useful to carry an European Accident Statement Form (obtainable from your insurance company) which will simplify matters in the case of an accident.

Unleaded petrol (*essence sans plomb*) is now widely available in France. If in doubt, a map showing the location of filling stations is available from main tourist offices.

For information about current road conditions, contact: Autoroute, tel: 93 49 33 33; CRIR, tel: 91 78 78 78. In the Alps you may need snow chains, which can be bought cheaply at hypermarkets or hired from garages.

Weekly rates are often better than daily hire and it can be cheaper to arrange before leaving for France. Major car hire companies are listed below:

Avis
UK: 0181 848 8733
Nice: 0493 21 36 33

Budget
UK: 0800 181181
France: 0800 10 00 01

Europcar
UK: 0345 222525
Nice: 0493 21 36 44

Hertz
UK: 0181 679 1799
France: 0800 05 33 11

ROUTES

Following a tourist circuit, or route is a sure way of getting to see the major sites of a region. The *Carte Routière* of the Côte d'Azur is published free by UDOTSI des Alpes Maritimes (*see Useful Adresses* page 316) and gives 11 suggested itineraries. Local tourist offices will help with suggestions, some of the major routes are given below:

Route des Hauts Lieux de Provence: this covers an extensive area, in the west of the region, from Toulon to Fréjus and as far north as Draguignan. It takes in, among other sites, the Cité Episcopale de Fréjus and the Roman Arenas; the Château de Grimaud, the Château d'Entrecasteaux and the Palais des Comtes de Provence à Brignoles.

Côtes de Provence Wine Road: much of this route takes in the same area as the route des Hauts Lieux de Provence. For details of vineyards open to the public and offering tastings, contact the Syndicat des vins Côtes de Provence, 83460 Les Arcs-sur-Argens, tel: 94 73 31 01.

Circuit sans frontière de Nice à Turin: as its name suggests, this road leads all the way to Turin, and its aim is to cover in particular, all the major religious sites en route.

Ramblers

The hinterland behind the coast, the national parks of Mercantour and Luberon and of course, the mountains offer superb opportunities for walkers. There are also a number of coastal paths, for example the Sentier du Littoral which follows the coast south from La Favière (Var), and can easily be achieved in a day's walk. All the main footpaths in France form part of the national network of long distance footpaths (Sentiers de Grandes Randonnées or GR). The major footpaths in the region are the GR5 which goes from Nice all the way up to Amsterdam; the GR51, from Theoule to Castellar, overlooking the coast; the GR52 from Menton to the Vallée des Merveilles and the GR4 to the Gorges du Verdon.

It should be noted both the Parc National du Mercantour and the Vallée des Merveilles enforce a code of country behaviour and it is forbidden to enter many of the sites in the latter without a guide.

The French Ramblers' Association, Fédération Française de la Randonnée Pédestre (FFRP) in Paris publishes Topoguides (guide books incorporating IGN 1:50,000 scale maps) to all France's footpaths, in French. However there is a series of guide books in English published by Robertson-McCarta called *Footpaths of Europe*, which are based on the French topoguides with IGN maps and include information about accommodation along the way. Titles appropriate to the region are: Walking the GR5: Larche to Nice, and peripherally, Walking the GR5: Modane to Larche and Walks in Provence. All these titles are available by mail order from Compass Books.

IGN Blue series maps at a scale of 1:25.000 are ideal for walkers, and they also publish maps of the national parks. Didier-Richard are specialist publishers of walking maps, at a scale of 1:50,000. Useful sheets are No. 1 Alpes de Provence, No. 9 Mercantour, No. 19 Haute-Provence and No. 26 Au Pays d'Azur.

French topoguides are available from all good bookshops in the region.

The Comité Regional pour la Randonnée Pédestre organises a variety of activities throughout the year: guided walks taking a day, a weekend or more; as well as themed walks, flora or wildlife for example. For more information contact: CRRP, M. Chartier, 365 rue des Iris, 83230 Bormes-les-Mimosa, tel: 71 50 38.

For a list of qualified guides working in the Alps contact: M. Jacques Raoust, rue Basse, 04170 Saint André-les-Alpes, tel: 92 89 04 19.

Various walking holidays with accommodation either in hotels or under canvas are available. Some are organised through package operators in the UK, others are bookable through the French organisations such as Clés de France, the agency for the French National Parks.

Clés de France, 13 Rue Saint-Louis, 78100 Saint-Germain-en-Laye, tel: (1) 30 61 23 23. For holidays in the Mercantour and Luberon national parks.

Ramblers Holidays, Box 43, Welwyn Garden City, Herts AL8 6PQ, tel: (01707) 331133.

Waymark Holidays, 44 Windsor Road, Slough SL1 2EJ, tel: (01735) 516 477.

Hitchhiking

With sensible precautions, hitchhiking can be an interesting and inexpensive way to get around France. Would-be hitchhikers may be discouraged by the difficulty of getting a lift out of the Channel ports, so it may be worth taking a bus or train for the first leg of your journey. Hitching is forbidden on motorways, but you can wait on slip roads or at toll booths. Allostop is a nationwide organisation which aims to connect hikers with drivers (you pay a registration fee and a contribution towards the petrol). Tel: (1) 42 46 00 66 via Paris, or 0447 700201.

Where to Stay

Accommodation

A wide variety of accommodation exists for the millions who visit the Côte d'Azur every year. Here is an outline of all the different types of place to stay, with specific suggestions.

Hotels

This hotel list names the region's most famous hotels and also suggests others that have a certain interest or distinctive charm. It is by no means exhaustive. It should be noted that prices on the Côte d'Azur tend to be higher than in other regions of France, but it is still possible to find reasonably-priced accommodation. Opening and closing dates and room prices may vary.

Note: hotels are listed in accordance with the order of the *Places* chapters.

HYERES, ILES D'HYERES & MASSIF DES MAURES

Giens

Relais du Bon Accueil
Tel: 94 58 20 48
A member of the Relais de Silence group. A charming and simple establishment set in beautiful grounds with sea-view. Credit cards: Visa. Rooms from FF350.

Porquerolles

Mas du Langoustier
Tel: 94 58 30 09
An old Provençal *mas* with its own gardens and two tennis courts. Closed: November–April. Credit cards: Amex, Diners, MasterCard, Visa. Rooms: full-board only, from FF1000.

Port Cros

Le Manoir
Tel: 94 05 90 52
A tropical atmosphere with large garden and colonial-style family house. Comfortable rooms, some with balcony. Closed: early October–early May. Credit cards: MasterCard, Visa. Rooms: half-board from FF1000.

Aiguebelle

(just outside Le Lavandou)
Les Roches
Tel: 94 71 05 07
Set on the cliffs with fabulous sea-views, a luxurious modern hotel tastefully decorated and furnished. Private beach, fresh-water swimming-pool. Closed: mid November–mid December and early January–early March. Credit cards: Amex, Diners, MasterCard, Visa. Rooms from FF700.

ST-TROPEZ REGION: FROM LA CROIX VALMER TO LES ISSAMBRES

St-Tropez

Bastide de St-Tropez
Route des Carles
Tel: 94 97 58 16
The height of luxury in the heart of the vineyards. Some of the rooms and suites with private garden and jacuzzi. Open: all year round. Credit cards: Amex, Diners, MasterCard, Visa. Rooms: FF1,800–3,200.

La Ponche
3 rue des Remparts
St-Tropez
Tel: 94 97 02 53
Once a favourite of Picasso's, this hotel was originally a row of little fishermen's cottages in the old town. Excellent restaurant. Rooms from FF700.

Lou Cagnard
Avenue P. Roussel
8399
Tel: 94 97 04 24
New very reasonably-priced hotel near the port and with a pretty courtyard. No credit cards. Rooms from FF200.

Résidence de la Pinède
Plage de la Bouillabaisse
Tel: 94 97 04 21

On the famous Bouillabaisse beach, under the pine trees. The hotel has been refurbished to provide comfortable rooms and suites. A member of the Relais and Châteaux group. Closed: 25 October–20 March. Credit cards: Amex, Diners, MasterCard, Visa. Rooms from FF1000.

Le Yaca
1 Boulevard d'Aumale
Tel: 94 97 11 79
An attractive old Provençal residence in town, tastefully refurbished. Accommodation built around a swimming-pool and gardens. Closed: 15 October–20 December and 10 January–10 April. Credit cards: Amex, Diners, MasterCard, Visa. Rooms from FF1000.

Ramatuelle

La Ferme d'Augustin
Route de Tahiti
Tel: 94 97 23 83
An old farm with a beautiful Mediterranean garden. Rustic atmosphere and furniture. All rooms with sea-view. Closed: mid October–end March. Credit cards: Visa. Rooms from FF500.

Grimaud

La Boulangerie
Route de Collobrières
Tel: 94 43 23 16
Simple and comfortable, a small friendly hotel quietly situated in the Maures hills. Swimming-pool and tennis courts. Closed: mid October–early April. Credit cards: Visa. Rooms from FF400.

Gigaro (La Croix Valmer)

Souleias
Plage de Gigaro
Tel: 94 79 61 91
Modern hotel in extensive grounds overlooking the unspoilt beach of Gigaro. Spacious rooms, swimming-pool, tennis courts, private yacht. Closed: November–mid March. Credit cards: Eurocard, Diners, Visa.

Ramatuelle
(6 miles from Ste-Maxime)
Mas des Brugassières
Tel: 94 43 72 42
Away from the coast in the Maures hills. A small hotel with rooms on to either the terrace around the swimming-pool or a private terrace. Tennis courts. Open: all year round. Credit cards: Amex, Diners, Visa. Rooms: FF400–600.

ST-RAPHAEL, FREJUS & MASSIF DE L'ESTEREL
Frejus
Residence du Colombier
Route de Bagnols
Tel: 94 51 45 92
Separate villas with private terraces surrounded by pine woods. Swimming pool and sports facilities. Rooms from FF400.

Cannes
Carlton Intercontinental
58 Boulevard Croisette
Tel: 04 93 06 40 06
Cannes' world-famous waterfront luxury hotel. The rooms and lobby have recently been completely renovated and are now more splendid than ever. Health centre and casino on the top floor. Open: all year round. Credit cards: Amex, Diners, MasterCard, Visa. Rooms: FF2,000–3,500.

CAP 'ANTIBES FROM GOLFE JUAN TO LA BRAGUE
Cap d'Antibe
Grand Hotel du Cap
Boulevard Kennedy
Tel: 93 61 39 01
Beautifully set on the water's edge in extensive wooded grounds. Recently refurbished, very comfortable rooms. Heated sea-water swimming-pool, tennis courts. Closed: end October–end March. Credit cards: Amex, Diners, Mastercard, Visa. Rooms from FF3500.

Antibes
Mas de la Pagane
15 Avenue du Mas-Ensoleillé
Tel: 93 33 33 78
An attractive old Provençal mas in

surprisingly calm situation close to the town centre. Friendly family atmosphere. Open: all year round. Credit cards: Visa. Rooms: FF250–450.

Juan-Les-Pins
Belles Rives
Boulevard Baudoin
Tel: 93 61 02 79
Close enough to town to enjoy the lively atmosphere, yet sufficiently far away from the noise and crowds, a former 1930s villa that has retained all the charm of its era, when it was the home of Zelda and Scott Fitgerald. Closed: 10 September–Palm Sunday. Credit cards: Amex, Diners, MasterCard, Visa. Rooms from FF1000.
Garden Beach Hotel
15–17 Boulevard Baudoin
Tel: 93 67 25 25
On the site of the former casino, right in the centre of town and with a nice terrace overlooking the bay. Open: all year round. Credit cards: Amex, Diners, MasterCard, Visa. Rooms from FF500–2000.

GRASSE
Mougins
Le Mas Candille
Boulevard Rebuffel
Tel: 93 90 00 85
A beautiful 200-year-old farmhouse in the countryside outside Mougins, re-opened after extensive renovations that have respected its character. Swimming-pool, terrace with wonderful views of the Pre-Alps. Open: all year round. Credit cards: Amex, Diners, MasterCard, Visa. Rooms from FF900.
Les Muscadins
18 Boulevard Courteline
Tel: 93 90 00 43
On the edge of the village, an attractive hotel with a good view of the Bay of Cannes. Only 8 bedrooms, each different, all nicely furnished and decorated. Closed: 1 February–1 April and 1–15 December. Credit cards: Amex, Diners, MasterCard, Visa. Rooms from FF900.

VENCE, ST-PAUL, CAGNES & THE VAR VALLEY
Cagnes-Sur-Mer (Haut-de-Cagnes)
Le Cagnard
Rue du Pontis-Long
Tel: 93 20 73 21
Situated in the little winding back-streets not far from the Grimaldi Castle, a charming hotel with a rustic atmosphere. Wooden beams, low ceilings and attractive old furniture. Member of the Relais et Châteaux group. Open: all year round. Credit cards: Amex, Diners, MasterCard, Visa. Rooms FF550–1500.

Roquefort Les Pins
Auberge du Colombier
Tel: 93 77 10 27
A small friendly hotel set away from the coast in a beautiful well-established garden commanding a fine view down to the Mediterranean. Swimming-pool and tennis courts. Closed: 10 January–10 February. Credit cards: Amex, Diners, MasterCard, Visa. Rooms from FF200.

Vence
Château du Domaine St-Martin
Route de Coursegoules
Tel: 93 58 02 02
True luxury set on the hills above Vence, with a magnificent view of the coast. Extensive grounds, swimming-pool. A member of the Relais and Châteaux group. Closed: 20 November–10 March. Credit cards: Amex, Diners, MasterCard, Visa. Rooms: FF4000.
La Roseraie
Avenue Henri Giraud
Tel: 93 58 02 20
Small friendly hotel in a 1930s villa. Pretty garden and pool. Closed: January. Credit cards: Amex, Visa. Rooms from FF400.

St-Paul
La Colombe d'Or
Place du Général de Gaulle
Tel: 93 32 80 02
A lovely old building on the edge of the village, once frequented by artists such as Picasso, Matisse,

Miró and Léger, whose works still adorn the walls. Private courtyard and swimming-pool. Closed: mid November–mid December. Credit cards: Amex, Diners, MasterCard, Visa. Rooms from FF950.

Mas d'Artigny
Route de la Colle
Tel: 93 32 84 54
Beautifully situated in the woods between St-Paul and la Colle with a splendid 360° view of the sea and the mountains. Open: all year round. Credit cards: Amex, Visa. Rooms from FF600.

NICE
Hotel Négresco
37 Promenade des Anglais
Tel: 0493 166400
The last vestige of Nice's era of splendour at the end of the 19th century with its famous dome dominating the coastline of the Baie des Anges. Period furniture from the 16th and 18th century, and priceless paintings and tapestries. Open: all year round. Credit cards: Amex, Diners, MasterCard, Visa. Rooms from FF1300.

La Pérouse
11 Quai Rauba-Capéu
Tel: 93 62 34 63
At the east end of the Promenade des Anglais, conveniently situated between the old town and the port. The rooms have splendid views of the Baie des Anges. Swimming-pool. Open: all year round. Credit cards: Amex, Diners, MasterCard, Visa. Rooms from FF890.

Hotel Windsor
11 Rue Dalpozzo
Tel: 93 88 59 35
Centrally located, with garden, swimming-pool and fitness room. Spacious, nicely furnished rooms. Open: all year round. Credit cards: Amex, Diners, MasterCard, Visa. Rooms from FF550.

CAP FERRAT & THE GOLDEN TRIANGLE
Eze
Château Eza
Tel: 93 41 16 64
Accessible only on foot (baggage carried up by donkey), this 400-year-old castle is perched on top of the cliff and overlooks 250 km (160 miles) of coast. Beautifully decorated rooms with antique furniture, oriental rugs, some with fireplace. Closed: November–March. Credit cards: Amex, Diners, MasterCard, Visa. Rooms: FF1,500–3,500.

Beaulieu-Sur-Mer
La Réserve de Beaulieu
5 Boulevard Leclerc
Tel: 93 01 00 01
A luxurious late 19th-century villa, beautifully situated on the coast with private beach and harbour. Swimming-pool in the garden. Closed: mid November–mid December. Credit cards: Amex, Diners, MasterCard, Visa. Rooms from FF1000.

St-Jean Cap Ferrat
Brise Marine
58, Avenue Jean Mermoz
Tel: 93 76 04 36
A small hotel in an attractive terraced garden. Some of the rooms overlook the sea. Closed: end October–1 February. Credit cards: Visa. Rooms: FF250–600.

La Voile d'Or
Yachting harbour
Tel: 93 01 13 13
An Italian villa in a garden overlooking the yachting harbour. Rooms of all sizes, attractively decorated. Two pools. Closed: 31 October–1 March. Credit cards: Visa. Rooms from FF1000.

MONACO
Abela Hotel
23, Avenue des Papalins
Fontvieille
Tel: 92 05 90 00
A little way out of the centre, a comfortable modern hotel overlooking the new harbour. Open: all year round. Credit cards: Amex, Diners, MasterCard, Visa. Rooms from FF700.

Hotel Hermitage
Square Beaumarchais
Tel: 92 16 40 00
Beautiful Edwardian architecture, spacious comfortable rooms. Swimming-pool and fitness centre. Open: all year round. Credit cards:
Amex, Diners, MasterCard, Visa. Rooms from FF1300.

Hotel de Paris
Place du Casino
Tel: 92 16 30 00
The most prestigious of Monaco's luxury hotels. Indoor swimming-pool. Open: all year round. Credit cards: Amex, Diners, MasterCard, Visa. Rooms from FF1800.

MENTON & ROQUEBRUNE
Menton
Chambord
6, Avenue Boyer
Tel: 93 35 94 19
Three-star hotel just off the Promenade du Soleil. Open: all year round. Credit cards: Amex, Diners, MasterCard, Visa. Rooms from FF400.

Hotel de Londres
15, Avenue Carnot
Tel: 93 35 74 62
Small central hotel. Open: 23 December–31 October. Credit cards: Amex, Diners, MasterCard, Visa. Rooms from FF300.

Roquebrune Cap Martin
Vista Palace Hotel
Grande Corniche
Tel: 92 10 40 00
A modern luxury hotel high above Monaco with wonderful views. Spacious rooms, pool and fitness centre. Open: all year round. Credit cards: Amex, Diners, MasterCard, Visa. Rooms from FF1000.

Westminster
14, Avenue Laurent
Tel: 93 35 00 68
Closed: early January–early February and end October–25 December. Credit cards: Visa. Rooms from FF900.

PERCHED VILLAGES
Peillon
Auberge de la Madone
Tel: 93 79 91 17
A simple country hotel, whose rooms offer splendid views of the hill-top village and the valley. Closed: January, early November–20 December, and Wednesdays. Credit cards: not accepted. Rooms from FF430.

Lantosque
L'Ancienne Gendarmerie
Tel: 93 03 00 65
Once a police-station, now a small family inn. Rooms simple but comfortable. Closed: early November–31 December and Mondays. Credit cards: Amex, Diners. Rooms from FF350.

Utelle
Bellevue
Utelle
06450 Lantosque
Tel: 93 03 17 19
Quiet, family hotel with stunning views and swimming pool. Credit cards: not accepted. Rooms: from FF250.

BORDER COUNTRY
Sospel
Hotel de France
9 Boulevard de Verdun
Tel: 93 04 00 01
Friendly family-run hotel overlooking river; restaurant with local specialities. Open: all year round. Credit cards: Amex, Diners, MasterCard, Visa. Rooms: from

FF250 for demi-pension.
Hotel des Etrangers
7 Boulevard de Verdun
Tel: 93 04 00 09
Swimming pool on site, English spoken and proprietor is expert on local history. Credit cards: Amex, Diners, MasterCard, Visa. Rooms: from FF300 for demi-pension.

Tende
Le Prieuré
St-Dalmas-de-Tende
Tel: 93 04 75 70
Three-star hotel with good restaurant in lovely valley. Organises trips to Vallée des Merveilles. June–September. Credit cards: Amex, Diners, MasterCard, Visa. Rooms: from FF250.

Bed & Breakfast

Apart from members of the Fédération Nationale des Gîtes Ruraux de France who have always offered a few *chambres d'hôtes* (guest rooms), the notion of bed and breakfast is a fairly recent one in France. It has always been so

easy to find good, cheap hotels in France, that there has been less demand for this kind of accommodation. Now, however, visitors to the country are more keen to get to know the local people and enjoy their hospitality.
Bookings outside France
5 Worlds End Lane
Green St-Green
Orpington
Kent BR6 6AA
Tel: (01689) 855538
Offer a straightforward bed and breakfast service which can include ferry bookings.
Café-Couette
8 Rue de l'Isly
75008 Paris
Tel: (1) 42 94 92 00
Is a Paris-based organisation offering B&B, or *Hébergement chez l'habitant*.
For details of bed and breakfast accommodation offered by the Fédération des Gîtes Ruraux, write to the Relais, addresses listed under *Self-Catering*.

Self-Catering

France probably has the best network of self-catering cottages anywhere in Europe. The *Fédération des Gîtes Ruraux de France* was set up over 30 years ago with the aim of restoring rural properties (by means of offering grants to owners) on the condition that these properties would then be let as cheap holiday homes for the less well-off town and city dwellers. These gîtes (literally, a place to lay one's head) have now become extremely popular with the British as an inexpensive way of enjoying a rural holiday in France and properties range from very simple farm cottages to grand manor houses and even the odd château.

The properties are all inspected by the Relais Départemental des Gîtes de France (the county office of the national federation) and given an *épi* (ear of corn) classification. Gîtes are completely self-catering (in many cases expect to supply your

own bedlinen), but most have owners living nearby who will tell you where to buy produce (and if on a farm, often provide it).

One salutary note: many of these cottages are on farms, and as such, are surrounded by wildlife – so if you are squeamish about the odd mouse in the kitchen, stay in a hotel. The properties should be, and generally are, kept clean and in good order.

As gîtes are, by their nature, rural properties, there are very few to be found on the coast. Most are off the beaten track and a car, or at least a bicycle, is usually essential. Bicycles can often be hired locally or sometimes from gîte owners. Car hire is expensive, but some fly/drive packages still make this a relatively inexpensive way to visit the region, as gîtes can cost as little as F1,200 a week for the whole house.

Gîtes do get very heavily booked

in high season, so start the process in the new year. If you wish to deal directly with France, the Relais Départemental will send you a list of all the gîtes in their *département*. Most gîtes in the Alpes-Maritimes are in rural areas away from the coast; as the Var is less built-up, it has a wide selection, with a total of 850 gîtes. Contact: Maison des Gîtes de France, 35 rue Godot-de-Mauroy, 75439 Paris, tel: (1) 49 70 75 75

Tour operators offering package holidays include:
Cresta: (0161 927 7000)
British Airways Holidays: (01293 723100)
Travelscene: (0181 427 8800);
Inghams: (0181 780 7700)
French Life: (0113 239 0077)
French Expression: (0171 431 1312)
VSB: (0124 224 0340).

Club Méditerranée

The Club Med, as it is affectionately known, is almost an institution in France – a kind of upmarket holiday camp with meals (including unlimited wine) and all kinds of sports and leisure facilities laid on. The Club Med site at Opio is one of the most luxurious there is, with accommodation in a de-luxe hotel. For more information, contact the company at 106–110 Brompton Road, London SW3 1JJ, tel: (0171) 581 1161 or (01635) 38450 (brochure service), or in France: 2 Place de la Bourse, 75083 Paris Cedex 02, tel: (1) 42 96 10 00.

Camping

There is a good choice of campsites in the region. The Comité Régional du Tourisme (see Useful Addresses page 316) produces a list of all recognised sites, with details of star-rating and facilities.

In the Alpes-Maritimes in particular, the quieter campsites tend to be away from the coast. If you are looking for a young atmosphere with plenty of activity, there are several sites just outside Antibes at La Brague, but choose your pitch carefully to avoid ending up right next to the main road.

As with other types of holiday accommodation, the sites get heavily booked in high season, especially those closest to the coast so advance booking is advisable, if not essential. Members of the Camping Club or Camping and Caravanning Club of Great Britain can make use of their booking services. The Michelin Camping/Caravanning Guide lists sites which accept (or insist on) pre-booking. **The Camping Service** at 69 Westbourne Grove, London W2 4UJ, tel: (0171) 792 1944, can book sites either from their own brochure of 3 and 4-star sites or any other you may wish to book. They will also book ferries as part of the package.

A camping carnet is useful (some sites will not accept a booking without one). Available in the UK for members of the AA, RAC or the

Camping Clubs mentioned in this section; or from the GB Car Club, PO Box 11, Romsey, Hants SO5 8XX.

Campsites, like hotels, have official classifications from one-star (minimal comfort, water points, showers and sinks) to four-star luxury sites which allow more space to each pitch, and offer above-average facilities, often including a restaurant or takeway food, games areas and swimming-pools. Sites near the coast particularly have a lot to offer families, including children's clubs and entertainment and discos for teenagers. The majority of sites nationwide are two-star, but most of the four-star sites are by the coast.

If you really like to get back to nature and are unimpressed by the modern trappings of hot water and electric power, look out for campsites designated Aire naturelle de camping, where facilities will be absolutely minimal and prices to match. With a maximum of 25 pitches, they offer the opportunity to stay away from some of the more commercial sites (which can be huge). The FFCC Guide (see Useful Publications) lists over 2,000 such sites nationwide.

Do not be tempted to get back to nature by off-site camping. This is strictly forbidden because of the risk of fire.

Some farms offer "official" sites too, under the auspices of the Fédération Nationale des Gîtes Ruraux (see Self-catering) – these are designated Camping à la ferme. Again, facilities are usually limited but farmers are allowed to have only six pitches and if you are lucky you will get to enjoy the farm life and some of its produce.

Campsites to the west of the region are becoming increasingly popular. They avoid some of the crowds of the fashionable resorts and are often right by the beach. Sites to the east of St-Tropez tend to be further inland, involving a drive from the site to the coast and inevitable parking problems.

Packaged camping holidays are now very popular, as all the

camping paraphernalia is provided on the site – you bring only your personal luggage. Many companies now offer this type of holiday, mostly with ferry travel included in the all-in price. Like other package tours, the companies have couriers on the sites to help with any problems. Where such companies have taken over sections of existing sites facilities have improved to meet the demands of their customers and so benefit all campers. Many companies offer opportunities for sports and leisure, such as wind-surfing or surfing; often the equipment, and sometimes instruction too is covered by the cost of the package. Be warned that some of the sites are very large, so might not suit those seeking peace.

A selection of the package operators is listed below, for others check the Sunday press.

Canvas Holidays
12 Abbey Park Place
Dunfermline KY12 7PD
Tel: (01383) 621 000
Pioneers in the field; offers a nanny service.

Eurocamp Travel
Canute Court
Toft Road
Knutsford
Cheshire WA16 0NL
Tel: (01565) 626262

Keycamp Holidays
Ellerman House
92-96 Lind Road
Sutton SM1 4PL
Tel: (0181) 395 4000

USEFUL PUBLICATIONS & ADDRESSES

French Federation of Camping and Caravanning Guide (FFCC), lists 11,300 sites nationwide, and also shows which have facilities for disabled campers. Available from Springdene, Shepherd's Way, Fairlight, E. Sussex TN35 4BB; or 78 rue de Rivoli, Paris, tel: 01 42 72 84 08.

Michelin Green Guide – Camping/Caravanning France. Very informative and also lists sites with facilities for the disabled. Published annually in March.

Good Camp Guide for France by Alan Rogers (Deneway Guides) lists 200 inspected sites nationwide, mostly around the coast.
Camping and Caravanning Club
11 Lower Grosvenor Place
London SW1
Tel: 01203 422024
Caravan Club
East Grinstead House
East Grinstead
Sussex RH19 1UA

Naturism

With its wonderful climate, the Côte d'Azur is an ideal resort for naturists. Indeed, the world's first nudist centre was established on the Île du Levant in 1931 by two doctors, Gaston and André Durville. The island still attracts naturists and there are many other sites in the region. The following is a selection:
La Grande Terre la Baume
04120 Castellane
Tel: 92 83 64 24
20 caravans and places for 100 tents at the edge of the Grand Canyon of Verdon. Open: Easter to the end of October.
Les Lauzons
04300 Limans
Tel: 92 76 00 60
20 mobile homes and 180 camping places, plus a gîte rural at 500 metres. Open: all year.
Domaine d'Enriou
04480 Saint-Laurent-du-Verdon
Tel: 92 74 41 02
Four houses to let, plus 100 camping places, at the edge of the Verdon Gorge. Open: mid-May to mid-September.
Nice Nature
77 Boulevard Virgile Barel
06300 Nice
Tel: 93 55 60 50
Campsite plus chalet and dormitory accommodation in the heart of Nice. Open: all year.
Centre Naturisme Origan
06260 Puget-Therniers
Tel: 93 05 06 00
Fifteen mobile homes and 100 camping places in the region of the gorges by the river Var. Open: 1 May–30 October.

Youth Hostels

Holders of accredited Youth Hostel Association cards may stay in any French hostels which are in fact run by two separate organisations; Fédération Unie des Auberges de Jeunesse (FUAJ), 27 Rue Pajol, 75018 Paris, tel: 01 44 89 37 27, which is affiliated to the International Youth Hostel Federation, and the Ligue Française pour les Auberges de Jeunesse (LFAJ), 38 Boulevard Raspail, 75007 Paris, tel: (1) 45 48 69 84.

There are about half a dozen accredited hostels on the coast and more inland. Information locally about hostels is available from Centre Information Jeunesse Côte d'Azur, 19 Rue Gioffredo, 06000 Nice, tel: 93 80 93 93; fax: 93 80 30 33. Open: Monday–Friday, 8.45am–6.45pm.

Auberges de Jeunesse are open to members of the Youth Hostel Association or holders of a youth card (*carte jeune*).
Tende (06430): Chemin Ste-Cathérine, tel: 93 04 62 74.
The British YHA publishes the International Youth Hostel Handbook, Vol I (revised each March), which includes all the hostels in the region, price £5.99 by post from Youth Hostel Association, 14 Southampton Street, London WC2E 7H7, tel: (0171) 836 8541. They also handle membership queries, tel: (0171) 836 1036.

In the US apply to the American Youth Hostels Inc, PO Box 37613, Dept USA, Washington DC 20013/7613, tel: (202) 783 6161.
Gîtes d'Etapes offer hostel accommodation and are popular with ramblers, climbers and horse riders (some offer stabling). All official gîtes d'étapes come under the auspices of the Relais Départementaux des Gîtes Ruraux (for addresses *see Self-catering*). Prices are similar to youth hostels but can be expensive in the more luxurious establishments. You do not have to be a member of any organisation to use them.

Where to Eat

Where to Eat

As with the hotels, the purpose of this list is to mention some of the region's most famous restaurants, and to recommend others that are particularly attractive or interesting.

HYÈRES, ILES D'HYÈRES & MASSIF DES MAURES

Aiguebelle, Le Lavandou
Les Roches
1 Avenue des Trois Dauphins
Tel: 93 71 05 07
Beautiful beach setting and good food inspired by the flavours of Provence. Closed: early November–end March. Credit cards: Visa, Amex, Eurocard. Menus FF280 and FF480, à la carte FF550.

ST-TROPEZ REGION: FROM LA CROIX VALMER TO LES ISSAMBRES

St-Tropez
La Bouillabaisse
Quartier la Bouillabaisse
Tel: 04 94 97 54 00
In an old fisherman's cottage serving excellent fresh fish from the terrace right by the beach, and you can even arrive by boat. Credit cards: Visa, Amex. Menu up to FF180.
La Cascade
5, Rue de l'Eglise
Tel: 94 54 83 46
Lively Caribbean atmosphere and Caribbean specialities. Credit cards: Visa. Menu FF129, à la carte FF200.
L'Olivier
Route des Carles
Tel: 94 97 58 16
A country house restaurant serving elegant cuisine based on the

flavours of Provence. Closed: mid November–third week December, Monday and Tuesday lunchtimes out of season. All credit cards accepted. Menus: FF200 and FF350, à la carte FF300.

Gassin
Villa de Belieu
Tel: 94 56 40 56
Credit cards: Amex, Visa, MasterCard, Diners. A beautiful setting in a wine domain. Four excellent menus. Menus FF250–600, à la carte FF500–600.

Grimaud
Café de France
Place Neuve
Tel: 94 43 20 05
Simple Provençal food, shady terrace set back from the village square. Closed: end October–February, Tuesday. Credit cards: Visa. Menu: FF105, à la carte FF200.

ST-RAPHAEL, FRÉJUS & MASSIF DE L'ESTEREL

St-Raphael
Pastorel
54, Rue de la Liberté
Tel: 94 95 02 36
Good traditional food with a Provençal touch. Closed: 15 November–15 December, Sunday evenings and Mondays. Credit cards: Visa, Amex, Diners. Menus: FF130, FF190 and FF230, à la carte FF250.

Les Adrets
Auberge des Adrets
Route Nationale 7, towards Mandelieu
Tel: 94 40 36 24
Good food in a pleasant setting. Closed: Mondays. Credit cards: Visa. Menu: FF195, à la carte FF350.

Auribeau sur Siagne
Auberge de la Vignette Haute
Tel: 93 42 20 01
Rustic setting and romantic atmosphere. The dining room is lit by 400 oil lamps. Credit cards: Visa, Amex, Diners. Menus: FF280–430.

CANNES

La Côte
Hotel Carlton Intercontinental
58, Boulevard de la Croisette
Tel: 93 06 40 06
Elegant dining-room and excellent cuisine. Closed: mid November–end December. Credit cards: Visa, Amex, Diners. Menus: FF190 (weekday lunchtimes), and FF330, à la carte FF450.

L'Eléphant Bleu
4, Rue Batéguier
Tel: 93 38 18 70
Good and imaginative Thai cuisine at reasonable prices, right in the heart of restaurant-land.

La Palme d'Or
Hotel Martinez
73, Boulevard de la Croisette
Tel: 92 98 30 18
Imaginative gastronomic cuisine with a taste of the Mediterranean. One of Cannes' top restaurants, with a view of the Bay and the Lérins Islands. Credit cards: Visa, Amex, Diners. Menus FF280 and FF480, à la carte FF520.

Le Petit Carlton
93, Rue d'Antibes
Tel: 93 39 27 25
This used to be just a bar, but has opened up a very French-style unpretentious restaurant. Typical French food, quick service, very reasonable prices. À la carte around FF100.

La Pizza
3, Quai St-Pierre
Tel: 93 39 22 56
The best-known pizza place in the region, which always has plenty of atmosphere.

Le Royal Gray
Hotel Gray d'Albion
6, Rue des Etats-Unis
Tel: 92 99 79 60
Master chef Jacques Chibois has been voted chef of the year many times. Widely recognised as the best restaurant in Cannes. Credit cards: Visa, Amex, Diners. Menus: FF210 (weekday lunch only), FF340–500, à la carte FF500–700.

CAP D'ANTIBES, FROM GOLFE JUAN TO LA BRAGUE

Golfe Juan
Le Bistrot du Port
53, Boulevard des Frères Roustan
Tel: 93 63 70 64
Mainly fish dishes. Attractive terrace on the old port. Closed: Sunday evenings and Monday. Credit cards: Visa, Eurocard. Menus FF220 and FF250, à la carte FF300.

Juan-Les-Pins
Belles Rives
Boulevard Baudointel: 93 61 02 79. Set right on the water's edge, once the residence of Scott Fitzgerald. Closed: mid October–mid March. Credit cards: Visa, Amex. Menus: FF280, FF380 and FF480, à la carte FF450.

La Terrasse, La Pinède, Avenue Gallice, tel: 93 61 08 70. Recognised as one of the region's best restaurants. Closed: end October–Easter. Menus: FF320 (lunchtime), FF450 and FF520, à la carte from FF600.

Antibes
Auberge Provençale
Place Nationale
Tel: 93 34 13 24
Attractive dining-room and beautiful courtyard in summer. Closed: mid April–mid May, mid November–mid December and Mondays. Credit cards: Visa, Amex, Diners, Eurocard. Menus: from FF135–230.

Bacon
668 Boulevard de Bacon
Tel: 04 93 61 50 02
Celebrated restaurant famous for its fish dishes and in particular its superlative bouillabaisse. Credit cards: Visa, Amex, Diners. Menus from FF250.

La Bonne Auberge
Route Nationale 7
Tel: 93 33 36 65
One of the best restaurants in the area. Credit cards: Visa, Amex. Menus: FF390, FF490 and FF560, à la carte FF650.

Don Juan
17, Rue Thuret, tel: 93 34 58 63.
Excellent service, good, reasonably-priced pizzas, Italian and provençal dishes.
Casa Pabl
1, Rue de la Touraque
Tel: 93 34 21 54
An unpretentious, pretty restaurant near the ramparts. Closed: mid January, early November and Mondays. Credit cards: Visa, Amex, Diners. Menu: FF90, à la carte from FF200.

Biot
Les Arcades
16 Place des Arcades
Tel: 93 65 01 04
Classical Provençal cuisine in the dining room of a 15th-century house, which doubles as an art gallery. Menus: FF140 and FF150, à la carte FF200.
Auberge du Jarrier
30, Passage de la Bourgade
Tel: 93 65 11 68
Elegant French cuisine with a Mediterranean flavour. Credit cards: Visa, Eurocard. Menus: FF190–320, à la carte FF400.
Le Café Brun
44 ter
Impasse St-Sébastien
Tel: 93 65 04 83
A typical Dutch "brown café" serving Indonesian dishes. Lively atmosphere. Credit cards: Visa, MasterCard. No menu, à la carte FF200.
Les Terraillers
11, Route du Chemin Neuf
Tel: 93 65 01 59
An elegant restaurant just outside the village in a beautiful vaulted cellar. Attractive terrace in summer. Closed: November and Wednesdays. Credit cards: Visa, Amex, Diners. Menus: FF150, FF220 and FF260, à la carte FF350.

GRASSE

Mougins
Le Moulin de Mougins
424, Chemin du Moulin
Tel: 93 75 78 24
The most famous restaurant in this village full of famous restaurants. Roger Vergé's "*cuisine du soleil*" is known worldwide. Closed: end January–early April, Mondays and Thursday lunchtimes. Credit cards: Visa, Amex, Diners. Menu: FF650, à la carte FF800.
L'Amandier
Place du Commandant Lamy
Tel: 93 90 00 91
This is Roger Vergé's second restaurant, in the old village. Closed: Wednesdays and Saturday lunchtimes. Credit cards: Visa, Amex, Diners. Menu: FF330, à la carte FF500.
Le Bistrot de Mougins
Place du Village
Tel: 93 42 05 59
Set in a beautiful vaulted stone cellar, excellent Provençal cuisine. Closed: December–mid January, Tuesdays and Wednesdays. Menu: FF150.
La Ferme de Mougins
10, Avenue Saint Basile
tel: 93 90 03 74
A Provençal residence built of stone, set in an idyllic garden. Closed: February, Saturday lunchtimes and Thursdays. Credit cards: Visa, Eurocard, Diners, Amex. Menus: FF230 and FF380, à la carte FF500.

Valbonne
L'Auberge Fleurie
1016 Route de Cannes
Tel: 93 12 02 80
Excellent value for money. Particularly good desserts. Closed: Wednesdays. Credit cards: Visa. Menus: FF98, FF125 and FF155.

Cabris
Auberge du Petit Prince
15, Rue Frédéric Mistral
Tel: 93 60 51 40
A country inn serving good food and offering an attractive terrace. Closed: mid November–mid December, Thursday evenings and Fridays. Credit cards: Visa, Amex, Diners. Menus: FF98, FF140 and FF180, à la carte FF250.

VENCE, ST-PAUL, CAGNES & THE VAR VALLEY

Bar Sur Loup
La Jarrerie
Route de Grasse
Tel: 93 42 92 92
Offers a traditional and elegant atmosphere and good cuisine, plus an atmospheric setting in a former monastery. Closed: January, Monday evenings and Tuesdays. Credit cards: Visa. Menus: FF135–FF250.

Tourrettes Sur Loup
Chez Grand'Mère
Place Mirabeau
Tel: 93 59 33 34
Very popular for North African specialities and meats grilled on the open fire. Reservations recommended. Closed: November, Saturday lunchtimes and Wednesdays. Menu: under FF100, à la carte FF150.
Le Petit Manoir
21, Grand'Rue, tel: 93 24 19 19.
Elegant restaurant serving fine cuisine. Closed: November and February school holidays, Wednesdays and Sunday evenings (except July and August). Credit cards: Visa, Eurocard. Menus: FF120–200.

Vence
Le Château des Aromes
2618 Route de Grasse
Tel: 93 58 70 24
The château also houses a perfume museum, where the emphasis is on the essences used to flavour the cuisine. Fragant terrace and beautiful views. Closed: November–February, Sunday evenings. Credit cards: Visa, Amex.
La Roseraie
Avenue Henri Giraud
Tel: 93 58 02 20
Specialities from the southwest of France. Beautiful terrace around the swimming-pool.Closed: January, Tuesdays and Wednesdays. Credit cards: Visa, Amex. Menus: FF100 and FF150, à la carte FF200.

St-Paul
La Colombe d'Or
1, Place du Général de Gaulle
Tel: 93 32 80 02
The dining-room is hung with the works of Matisse, Picasso, Léger, Delaunay and others, the terrace must be the most beautiful in the region. Good, traditional cuisine. Closed: early November–third week in December. Credit cards: Amex, Diners, Visa. No set menu, à la carte FF350.

Coursegoules
L'Escaou
Tel: 04 93 59 11 28
Restaurant in a mountain village near the coast, serving rustic Provençal cuisine with superb views from its terrace. Credit cards: Visa. Menus: FF90–180.

La Gaude
La Seguinière
tel: 93 24 42 92
An attractive villa with plenty of atmosphere. Jazz on Saturday evenings. Garden in summer. Menu: FF260.

Cagnes-sur-Mer
Le Cagnard
Rue du Pontis Long
Haut-de-Cagnes
Tel: 93 20 73 21
The cuisine is elegant and beautifully presented. Charming dining-room in what was once the 14th-century castle's guardroom. Closed: early November–mid December and Thursday lunchtimes. Credit cards: Visa, Amex, Diners. Menus: FF340 and FF430, à la carte FF500.

Entre Cour et Jardin
102 Montee de la Bourgade
Tel: 04 93 20 72 27
Friendly restaurant in a little village street with art exhibitions in the courtyard twice a year. Credit cards: Visa. Menus: up to FF180.

Le Picadéro
3, Boulevard de la Plage
Cros de Cagnes
Tel: 93 22 32 84
Bistrot-style, excellent value for money. Closed: Mondays. Menus : FF170 and FF280, à la carte FF320.

Nice
Auberge de Bellet
St-Roman de Bellet
Tel: 93 37 83 84
In Nice's most famous vineyard of the same name. Vintage wines and delicacies such as lobster and pigeon and garlic stew. Closed: end of January and Tuesdays. Credit cards: Visa, Eurocard. Menus: FF195 and FF280, à la carte FF400.

Le Chantecler
Hotel Negresco
37, Promenade des Anglais
Tel: 93 16 64 00
Nice's finest restaurant, in the Negresco hotel. Elegant cuisine with a Mediterranean touch. Closed: mid November–mid December. Credit cards: Visa, Amex, Diners, Eurocard. Menus: FF260 (weekday lunch), FF390 and FF550. A la carte FF600.

Le Safari
1 Cours Saleya
Tel: 93 80 18 44
Big café with outside tables in flower market street. Try the *bagna cauda*, a hot anchovy dip with raw vegetables. Credit cards: Visa, Amex. Menus: FF90–180.

Le Comptoir
20 rue Saint-Francois-de-Paule
Tel: 93 92 08 80
A 1930s-style bar and restaurant, excellent for late-night dining. Credit cards: Visa, Amex, Diners. Menus: up to FF180.

Nissa-Socca
5, Rue Ste-Réparate
Tel: 93 80 18 35
Arrive early or be prepared to wait. Popular and unpretentious, serving Niçois specialities: fresh pasta, vegetable fritters. Excellent value. Closed: Sundays and Monday lunchtimes. Credit cards not accepted. À la carte: FF60–70.

CAP FERRAT & THE GOLDEN TRIANGLE

St-Jean Cap Ferrat
Le Provençal
2, Avenue Denis Semeria
Tel: 93 76 03 97
Imaginative, gastronomic cuisine with a Mediterranean flavour.

Closed: Sundays. Credit cards: Visa, Amex Menus: FF150 (lunchtime only), FF250 and FF450, à la carte FF400–500.

La Voile d'Or
Yachting harbour
Tel: 93 76 11 17.
High prices justified by the idyllic setting overlooking the pretty harbour and the exquisite cuisine. Closed: November–March. Credit cards: Visa, Amex. Menus: FF400, FF460 and FF550, à la carte FF700–800.

Beaulieu-sur-Mer
Le Metropole
15, Boulevard Leclerc
Tel: 93 01 00 08
Fish specialities in a discreetly luxurious setting. Closed: November–20 December. Credit cards: Visa, MasterCard. Menus: FF380 and FF450, à la carte FF500.

La Réserve
5, Boulevard Leclerc
Tel: 93 01 00 01
Excellent cuisine in an elegant setting. Emphasis on fish dishes. Credit cards: Visa, Diners, Amex, Eurocard, MasterCard. Menus: FF280–450, à la carte FF500.

Eze
Château de la Chèvre d'Or
Moyenne Corniche Rue du Barri
Tel: 92 10 66 66
Light, classical cuisine in a medieval château. Closed: December, January, February and Wednesdays. Credit cards: Visa, Amex, Diners. Menu: FF330 (lunchtime), à la carte: FF600–800.

Chateau Eza
Tel: 93 41 12 24
Former residence of the Prince of Sweden, suspended high above the sea. Closed: late October–early April. Credit cards: Visa, Amex, Diners, Eurocard. Menus: FF250 (lunchtime) and FF490, à la carte FF500.

Peillon
Auberge de la Madone
Tel: 93 79 91 17
A true Provençal inn offering authentic regional cuisine. Closed:

end October–end December and
Wednesdays. Credit cards: not
accepted. Menus: FF120 and
FF280, à la carte FF300.

MONACO

Le Café de Paris
Place du Casino
Tel: 92 16 36 36
Recently completely renovated in
1920s style, this deserves a visit
as one of the sights of Monte-Carlo.
Open: every day for lunch and
dinner. Credit cards: Visa, Amex,
Diners. No set menu, à la carte
from FF250.
   Polpetta
   2, Rue Paradis
   Tel: 93 50 67 84
   Offering among the best value for
money in Monaco. Italian food.
Closed: mid October, late Febru-
ary–mid March, Saturday
lunchtimes and Tuesdays. Credit
cards: Visa, Eurocard. Menu:
FF120, à la carte FF200.
   Rampoldi
   3, Avenue des Spélugues
   Tel: 93 30 70 65
   Simple cuisine: grills and Italian
specialities. Popular with locals.
Closed: November. À la carte:
FF300.

MENTON & ROQUEBRUNE

Roquebrune
Au Grand Inquisiteur
Rue du Château
Tel: 93 35 05 37
Restaurant in a medieval setting in
the old village. Closed: mid March,
mid November–December,
Mondays. Credit cards: Visa.
Menus: FF125 and FF210, à la
carte FF250.
Le Vistaero
Grande Corniche
Tel: 93 35 01 50
Fabulous view over Monaco and the
coast towards Nice. Credit cards:
Visa, Amex, Diners, Eurocard.
Menus: FF300 and 490, à la carte
FF500.

Menton
L'Oursin
3, Rue Trenca
Tel: 93 28 33 62
Fish specialities. Closed: mid December–mid February and Wednesdays. Credit cards: Visa, Amex. À la
carte only: FF250–300.

PERCHED VILLAGES & BORDER COUNTRY

Labrigue
Le Mirval
Rue St-Vincent Ferrier
Tel: 93 04 63 71
Most charming restaurant in La
Brigue, outside village, by the river.
Local specialties include trout,
spinach ravioli and game. Open
April –November only. Credit cards:
Amex, Diners, MasterCard, Visa.

Breil-sur-Roya
Castel du Roy
Route de Tende
Tel: 04 93 04 43 66
Charming riverside restaurant with
tranquil tree-shaded terrace serving
specialities of the region, such as
roasted pigeon. Credit cards: Visa.
Menus: up to FF180.

Attractions

Places of Interest

The Côte d'Azur is renowned for its
luxurious resorts and glamorous
lifestyle. You could spend your
whole holiday just lazing on the
beach, celebrity-spotting. However,
you would be doing yourself and the
region an injustice. There are all
kinds of different activities on offer
and places to visit.
   This section covers a variety of activities: technical visits, parks and
gardens, *caves* (wine cellars) open
to the public and steam railways
etc. Some of the venues are particular to the region and are well worth
seeking out.
   All places listed (in alphabetical order) are open daily, morning and afternoon (not including public
holidays) except where otherwise
specified. Most close for a long
lunch break – noon or 12.30 until 2
or 2.30pm. Expect to pay an
entrance fee at most venues. A list
of museums and art galleries are in
Culture (page 331).
   Many of the major towns in the
region offer guided tours of the
town – enquire at the Office de
Tourisme or Syndicat d'Initiative.

Antibes
Marineland/Aquasplash
306 Avenue Mozart
Tel: 93 33 49 49
The biggest marine show in Europe
with dolphins, whales, sealions,
etc. Sea museum and aquaria.
Separate entrance fee for the water
park (Aquasplash) with waterchutes,
wave pool and other attractions.
Restaurant. Marineland open: all
year; Aquasplash: June–September.
The Marineland complex includes:
La Petite Ferme Provençale. The

re-creation of a local farm with animals, an oil mill, displays of honey and a perfumery. Open: 10am–6pm. Also the **Butterfly Jungle**. A vast indoor tropical environment where butterflies can be observed in a "natural" habitat.
Villa Thuret
has 5 hectares (12 acres) of gardens and an arboretum with 2,000 different species.

Biot

Biot is noted for its traditional earthenware pottery and also for hand-blown glass. There are several ceramics studios all along the Route de la Mer, such as: La Poterie Provençale, le Lavandier, Martine Polisset and Aux Jarres de Provence.
For glassworks visit La Verrerie de Biot, Chemin des Combes, 06410 Biot, tel: 93 65 03 00.

Cannes

The town and its surrounding area have some splendid gardens open to the public: the **Parc de la Croix des Gardes**, set above Le Suquet; **La Roseraie de la Croisette**, thousands of rose trees, right on the seafront; **Forêt Dominiale de l'Ile Sainte Marguerite**, 420 acres of indigenous Mediterranean vegetation with an herbarium and botanic trail; visit too the Cistercian **Abbey of Lérins** on Île St-Honorat where the land is still cultivated by the monks using medieval methods.

Contes

Moulin à Huile, 06390 Contes, tel: 93 79 00 01. Olive oil mill in operation during the grinding period from November to February and open to the public on Saturdays (all year).

Eze

The **Jardin Exotique**, tel: 04 93 41 10 30 and the perfumeries of Gallimard and Fragonard (see Grasse) are also worth visiting.

Frejus

Aquatica, on the RN 98. A water park, and nearby, **Aquatigolf**. There are also several formal **gardens** in the town: **Villa Aurélienne**, Route de

Cannes; **Villa Marie**, Avenue Aristide Briand; **Parc de Sainte Croix**, Avenue du XVe Corps; and **Jardin Havana**, boulevard Alfred de Musset, Saint Aygulf.
For the younger visitors, the **zoo** – Safari de l'Esterel, Le Capitou, tel: 94 40 70 65.
You can also visit the **nurseries** where exotic plants are produced.

Gonfaron

Village des Tortues, Route des Mayons, les Plaines, tel: 94 78 26 42. Wild tortoise preserve.

Grasse

Grasse is internationally famous for its perfumes, which grew up out of the glove-making and tanning industries. Many of the **perfumeries** offer free guided tours all year round; the most important have their own museums, and of course you are invited to buy the products at the end of your tour. Try any (or all) of the following (please make appointments for group visits). (See also Museums and Art Galleries page 331.) Both Fragonard and Gallimard also have perfumeries which can be visited in Èze.
Fragonard, Boulevard Fragonard, Route de Cannes, tel: 93 36 02 71.
Gallimard, 73 Route de Cannes, tel: 93 09 20 00.

Hyeres

Observatoire du Pic des Fées, overlooking the bay de l'Almanarre, just outside the town, the observatory is open to the public every Saturday evening. Allée des Pinson, Le Mont des Oiseaux, 83400 Hyères, tel: 94 38 69 03 (Tuesday evening only).
Magic World, a leisure park with fairground amusements and other attractions; regular firework displays and son-et-lumière shows, plus a restaurant and bars. Free entry, open every evening 8pm–1am, June–September. Port de Hyères Les Palmiers. Outside the town is Cave **Gasperini**, a wine cellar, offering tastings of its Côtes de Provence AOC wines, 42 Avenue de la Libération, 83260 La Crau, tel: 94 66 70 01.

La Londe Les Maures

Tropical Bird Garden, Quartier St-Honoré, tel: 94 35 02 15.

Le Lavandou

Parc de Loisirs, a big leisure park with amusements for all ages: practice golf, tennis, adventure playground, big chess boards, Mediterranean garden.
Domaine de l'Anglade, Avenue Vincent Auriol, 83980 Le Lavandou, tel: 94 71 10 89. The wine cellars are open to the public.
Niagara Parc Nautique, just to the north of the town on the D27 Route du Canadel, lies Le Môle, the oldest village in the region, and the Niagara water park whose huge swimming-pool offers many watery amusements, tel: 94 49 58 85.

Menton

Known as the "Lemon Capital", the sedate town of Menton has many **gardens** open to the public: **Parc Gorre**; **Parc du Pian**, an ancient olive grove; **Jardins Bioves** where citrus fruits are displayed for the International Lemon Festival in February; **Palais Carnoles** with 50 varieties of citrus fruits; **Les Colombières**, the creation of Ferdinand Bac, a Mediterranean garden covering 15 acres and finally the botanical garden of the **Natural History Museum** at Val Rahmeh.

Monaco

The tiny principality has some lovely **gardens** to visit. Apart from those of the casino itself, there is the Jardin Exotique, tel: 93 30 33 65 with its notable collection of cheese plants; **Parc de Fontvieille**, landscaped gardens surrounding the Princess Grace rose garden (150 different varieties) and several new museums; the **Zoological Gardens** at La Condamine; and the pine woods of the **Parc-Promenade du Portier**.

Nice

Confiserie du Vieux Nice, Quai Papacino, tel: 93 55 43 50. Confectioners open to the public for guided tours (in English), sampling and a visit to the shop. Admission: free.

Closed: Sundays in winter.

Moulin Alziari, 14 rue St. Francois de Paule, tel: 93 85 76 92. Legendary olive oil shop.

Observatoire de Calern, Centre of Geodynamic and Astronomic Research, offers astronomy shows May–October; tours daily at 3pm in July and August, at other times by appointment. Information from PARSEC, 2 Passage du Petit Parc, 06000 Nice, tel: 93 42 66 16.

Observatoire de Nice, Boulevard Bischoffsheim (Grande Corniche), tel: 93 00 30 11. Visits by appointment and every Saturday at 3pm.

Parc des Miniatures, Avenue Impératrice Eugenie, tel: 93 44 67

74. Fascinating history of Nice in miniature, laid out over more than 7 acres. Restaurant. Open: till dusk.

Nice is famed for its gardens, the oldest being **les Jardins du Monastère de Cimiez**, hardly changed since 1546. Visit too the **Jardin des Arènes de Cimiez**, the olive grove where the Grande Parade du Jazz takes place each July.

The **Parc du Château** is set in 20 hectares (50 acres), with superb views of the coast.

The **Jardins d'Acropolis** display modern sculpture in 6 acres around the Palais des Congrès. The **Parc Floral** at Phoénix de l'Arénas on the Promenade des Anglais offers many

attractions such as an aquarium, astronomical garden, musical fountains and other features particularly appealing to children, tel: 93 18 03 33.

Opio

Moulin d'Opio, 2 Route de Chateauneuf, 06650 Opio, tel: 93 77 23 03. Fifteenth-century olive oil mill offering free guided tours in French. Closed: Sundays and 15 October–15 November; in operation November to March.

St-Cezaire

Les Grottes de St-Cézaire, tel: 93 60 22 35. Spectacular underground caves and also a picnic site with a

Excursions

Boat trips are the most obvious excursions that come to mind on the Côte d'Azur and many companies offer trips for a just a few hours or a whole day. However, you may prefer to take a trip on a steam train, a jeep or in the air. Some possibilities are listed below:

Sea

Take a trip to Monaco, the Iles de Lérins (where the "Man in the Iron Mask" was confined in the fortress on Ste-Marguerite Island), the Hyères Islands, or even a day trip to Corsica. Or go out in the evening to watch the fireworks from the sea.

From Lavandou: Compagnie des transports Maritimes, 15 Quai Gabriel Péri, 83980 Le Lavandou, tel: 94 71 01 02.

From Sainte Maxime/St-Tropez: Transports Maritime, Plan de la Tour, 83120 St. Maxime, tel: 94 96 51 00.

Saint Raphael/St. Tropez, Bateau Bleu, tel: 94 95 17 46.

Calanques de la Corniche d'Or (Esterel), Departures from St. Raphael, tel: 94 95 17 46.

SNCM **Ferryterranée**, Quai du Commerce, 06005 Nice cedex, tel: 93 13 66 66. Day trips to Corsica with two hours ashore (ports vary).

Photo Safari: Trips from June–October (according to the movements

of the whales) from Antibes or Beaulieu-sur-Mer, lasting 10–12 hours. Cost includes boat hire and a two-man crew (maximum 8 passengers). Contact: Guigo Marine, Port Vauban, Avenue du 11 Novembre, 06600 Antibes, tel: 93 34 70 70.

Train

The "Train des Pignes" run by Chemins de Fer de Provence line goes from Nice to Digne and a trip on it is a grand way to take in some of the sights. It climbs as high as 900 metres (2,950 ft) at Saint-André les Alpes. All-inclusive day trips, 150 km (95 miles) each way (Tuesday–Thursday) include a meal, wine and coffee and a guided village tour.

On most Sundays from mid-May to mid-October, a steam train runs from Puget-Theniers to Annot and back. Information from Chemins de Fer de Provence, 33 Avenue Malaussena, 06000 Nice, tel: 04 93 88 34 72.

It is also worth taking a trip along the SNCF Nice-Cuneo line which passes through splendidly wild landscapes and also offers sights of spectacular engineering in the form of bridges and viaducts. Information from Nice station or SNCF. Tel: 93 87 50 50.

Overland

Access to many of the sites of the Vallées des Merveilles is now forbidden unless a guide is conducting a tour. One way of getting around is by jeep, although it can be costly – upwards of FF1,000 a day. The Association des Taxis Accompagnateurs des Merveilles will take you up to the Vallée des Merveilles (from late June to late October) for a day trip, including a guided tour of the archaeological site. Information from M. J. Bresso, Place de la Mairie, 06430 Tende, tel: 93 04 60 31.

In the Air

Heli-Air-Monaco operate 10-minute trips every day for up to five people. Héliport de Monaco Fontvieille, 98000 Monaco, tel: 93 21 34 95.

Provence Aéro Service offer tourist flights. RN 8, 83330 Le Castellet, tel: 94 90 79 79.

Héli-Air St-Tropez, helicopter flights. 83990 St-Tropez, tel: 94 97 15 12.

Coach Trips

Day or half-day trips with commentary take in many of the sights along the coast and inland, and are less expensive than going by sea or air. Details of the many coach operators are available from local tourist offices or bus/coach stations.

bar. Closed: October to mid-February except Sunday afternoons.

St-Roman-De-Bellet
Château de Bellet, Château de Bellet, St-Roman-de-Bellet, 06200 Nice, tel: 93 37 81 57. Vineyard open on request and by appointment, situated in a very old wine-growing area, now reduced to just 40 hectares (100 acres).

St-Tropez
Once a pretty little fishing port much beloved of painters and other artists, St-Tropez is now perhaps better known as a playground for filmstars (Brigitte Bardot started the trend) and for its nudist beaches. Visit the two hill-villages nearby (Ramatuelle and Gassin), and the **Annonciade Museum** (*see Museums* page 331).

Vallauris
Vallauris is a magnet for local potters, with many opening their studios to the public. A complete list is available from local tourist offices and also from the Syndicat des Potiers, Espace Grandjean, Avenue du Stade, 06220 Vallauris, tel: 93 64 17 93.
    Parfumerie Jean Bouis, 50 bis Avenue G. Clémenceau, tel: 93 64 38 27. Open: all year.

Vence
The medieval town is well worth a visit.
At **Château Notre Dame Des Fleurs**, the Foundation Maurice Lavoillet invites visitors to its gardens where plants are grown for the production of perfumes and liqueurs; there is also a **Museum of Perfume** and a restaurant specialising in aromatic cooking. See too the **Matisse chapel** (*see Archaeology/Architecture*).

Culture

Some of the greatest artists of the past two centuries have been drawn to the Côte d'Azur by its sunshine, light, colour and freedom. They have all left their mark and the region now has more than 100 art galleries. And the tradition continues: painters still flock to the area to follow in the footsteps of their idols, and many contemporary studios and galleries are just as exciting as the established national museums.
    The range of collections in the region's museums is not confined to works of art. There are equally fascinating exhibitions of the history of the area as well as more particular collections such as the Escoffier Museum of culinary arts in Villeneuve-Loubet and the Museum of Oceanography in Monaco (the eighth most visited museum in the whole of France).

MUSEUMS & ART GALLERIES

Most museums charge an entrance fee; for those that are state-owned expect to pay between FF10 and FF25 (half price on Sundays). Reductions are usually given for children, senior citizens and students – on production of a valid card. Those listed here are open every day, morning and afternoons (except public holidays) except where otherwise specified. Remember, most close for a long lunch, from noon or 12.30 to around 2.30pm.
    Municipal museums generally have local exhibits and show the history of the area.

Antibes
Musée Picasso, Château Grimaldi, Place du Château, tel: 93 34 91 91. Entirely devoted to the works of

Picasso. Closed: Tuesday and public holidays.

Biot
Musée National Fernand Léger, Chemin du Val-de Pome, tel: 93 65 63 61. Known as the "Cathedral of Modern Art", reopened in 1989 with the addition of a new building, houses modern works, in particular stained glass, mosaics and ceramic. Closed: Tuesday. In the same square is an interesting little **museum of local history**, open Thursday, Saturday and Sunday. Tel: 93 65 05 85.

Breil-sur-Roya
Ecomusée du Haut Pays, tourist information, tel: 93 04 99 76. Exhibitions of the natural environment, history and life of the Roya and Bevera valleys.

Cagnes-sur-Mer
La Maison de Renoir, Les Collettes, tel: 93 20 61 07. The house where Renoir lived for the 12 years before his death in 1919. Since 1989 has had on display 10 of his best works, plus drawings and sculpture. Closed: Thursday and mid October–mid November. Visit too the 6 acres of **gardens**, with ancient olive trees and a rose garden.
    Also in the town visit the **civic museum** housed in a former château of the Grimaldi family: among is displays are 40 portraits of the local singer Suzy Solidor by 40 different artists (including Cocteau and Dufy) as well as an exhibition devoted to the olive tree.

Cannes
Musée de la Castre, le Suquet, tel: 93 38 55 26. Exhibitions of modern and primitive art in a former château enjoying splendid views over the bay. Closed: Tuesday. Admission: free Wednesday and Sunday. The town also boasts many small **private galleries**, showing mainly the work of contemporary artists. See too the **Musée de la Mer** on Ste-Marguerite Island. Closed: Tuesday and in January and February.

Draguignan

Musée Art Tradition Populaire de Moyenne Provence, 15 Rue Joseph Roumanille, tel: 94 47 05 72. Also at the same address, **Musée Arts et Traditions Populaires**. Museums dedicated to local crafts and rural way of life, the latter has a reconstructed olive mill and displays of provençal cuisine. Closed: Sunday morning and Monday. See too, the **Musée Municipal**, 9 Rue de la République, tel: 94 472880. Closed: Monday. Admission: free.

Fréjus

Fondation Templon, ZI du Capitou, tel: 94 40 76 30. This foundation advertises itself as housing one of the best collections of modern art in Europe, principally showing works no more than 30 years old.

Grasse

Musée International de la Parfumerie, 8 place du Cours, tel: 93 36 80 20. One of only three museums of its kind in the world, explaining the development and techniques of the industry. Closed: Monday, Tuesday and November.
 Villa-Musée Fragonard, 23 Boulevard Fragonard, tel: 93 36 02 71. A 17th-century villa surrounded by a park, former home of M. Maubert, glove-maker, where Fragonard took shelter during the Revolution. Staterooms and paintings by the artist. A **Rose Festival** is held in May and a **Jasmine Festival** in August. Closed: most Saturdays and Sundays and November.
 Musée de la Marine, Hôtel de Pontèves, 2 Boulevard du Jeu de Ballon, tel: 93 40 11 11. Dedicated to the career of Admiral de Grasse and naval history. Closed: Sunday and November.

Hyères

Musée Municipal, Place Th. Lefebvre, tel: 94 35 90 42. Includes collections of archaeology, fine arts, local history and natural history. Closed: Tuesday. Admission: free.

Menton

Musée Jean Cocteau, Vieux Port, tel: 93 57 72 30. Entirely devoted to the life and works of Cocteau. Closed: Monday and Tuesday. Also worth a visit is the **Salle de Mariages** in the town hall, decorated by Cocteau in 1957–58.
 Musée des Beaux Arts, Palais Carnoles, 3 Avenue de la Madone, tel: 93 35 49 71. Situated in the former summer palace of the Princes of Monaco, which itself stands in a magnificent garden (**parc de la Madone**), this museum houses collections dating from the 13th to the 19th centuries, as well as contemporary works. Closed: Tuesday. Admission: free.
 Musée de Préhistoire Régionale, Rue Loredan Larchey, tel: 93 35 84 64. Closed: Tuesday. Admission: free.

Monaco Town

Musée Océanographie, Avenue Saint-Martin, tel: 93 15 36 00. A million visitors a year are drawn to this exciting museum created in 1901 by Prince Albert who was fascinated by the subject. Exhibits of marine technology are complemented by possibly the best aquarium in Europe.
 Palais du Prince, tel: 93 25 18 31 (open to the public when the prince is not in residence).

Monte-Carlo

Musée National, 17 Avenue Princesse Grace, tel: 93 30 91 26. Housed in a fine 19th-century villa by the sea and surrounded by the Princess Grace rose garden, perhaps the most fascinating aspect of this museum is the collection of antique dolls and working automats from the 18th century.

Mougins

Musée de l'Automobiliste, Aire des Breguières, Autoroute A8, tel: 93 69 27 80. Appealing to both adults and children alike, a superb collection of cars spanning the century. Easiest access is via the motorway exit between Cannes and Antibes, or from the Vallauris–Le Cannet Road.

Musée de la Photographie, tel: 93 75 85 67. Noted in particular for its display of portraits of Picasso by different photographers. Open: Wednesday–Sunday (daily in July and August), afternoons.

Nice

Right in the centre of Nice stands the new arts and theatre complex which includes the **Musée d'Art Moderne et Contemporain**, Promenade des Arts, tel: 93 62 61 62. It has wide-ranging collections of artists mostly from the 1960s on, as well as sculptures in the surrounding gardens. Also includes a library, shop and café. Admission: free.
 Musée d'Archéologie, 160 Avenue des Arènes, tel: 93 81 59 57. Set up in 1989 on the site of the baths dating from the 3rd century, this museum offers a superb evocation of the region's ancient history, as one of the oldest known sites of human habitation. Access is via the archaeological site, Avenue Monte Croce. Closed: Sunday afternoon, Monday and November. For prehistory, visit too the **Musée de Terra Amata**, 25 Boulevard Carnot, tel: 93 55 59 93.
 Musée d'Art et d'Histoire, Palais Masséna, 65 Rue de France/35 Promenade des Anglais, tel: 93 88 11 34 or 93 55 15 24. Important collections of decorative and religious art and history of the region. Closed: Mondays and November. Admission: free.
 Musée Barla, 60 bis Boulevard Risso. Natural history museum; visit too its fascinating annex the **Galerie de Malacologie** at 3 Cours Saleya (by the flower market), with its fine display of shells and underwater creatures. Main museum closed: Tuesday and mid August–mid September; the Galerie closed: Sunday, Tuesday and November. Admission: free.
 Musée des Beaux-Arts, 33 Avenue des Baumettes, tel: 93 44 50 72. Vast collections of European fine arts from the 17th century on, including the impressionists and important collections of Chéret, Ziem and Van Dongen. Closed:

Mondays. Admission: free.

Musée International d'Art Naïf Anatole Jakovsky, Château Sainte-Hélène, Avenue Val-Marie, 06200 Nice, tel: 93 71 78 99. A villa once owned by the founder of the casino at Monte-Carlo houses a fine collection of naïve art, established by a gift of the Jakovskys of 600 works, but now much expanded with art from all over the world. Closed: Tuesdays. Admission: free.

Musée Matisse, 164 Avenue des Arènes, tel: 93 81 08 08. With the building of a new extension, this museum houses the personal collection of the celebrated artist who died in Nice in 1954. It covers works from all periods of the painter's career.

Musée National Marc Chagall, Avenue du Docteur-Ménard, tel: 93 53 87 20. Built to house Chagall's "Biblical Message" of which 12 canvases (the Creation) are in one room and the other five (Song of Songs) in another. His other work is also well represented in all its various forms: paintings, stained glass, sculptures, mosaics, tapestries, and so forth. Also a library. Closed: Tuesday.

Musée Naval, Tour Bellanda, Parc du Château, tel: 93 80 47 61. A small museum in a building that is itself an historic monument showing the history of Nice as both a naval and pleasure port. Closed: Tuesday and mid-November to mid-December. Admission: free.

Nice also has a large number of **private galleries**, open to the public for viewing and sales.

Peille

Musée du Terroir, Mairie de Peille, tel: 93 79 90 32. One of three "ecomuseums". Open: Wednesday, Saturday and Sunday summer afternoons (winter: Sunday only). Admission: free.

St-Jean Cap Ferrat

Musée Ephrussi de Rothschild, tel: 93 01 33 09. Varied and sumptuous collection which was bequeathed to the nation by Baroness de Rothschild who had the Italianate villa specially

Diary of Events

January
Cannes: MIDEM (International Disc and Music Publishing Festival)
Menton: Theatre season
Monaco: Monte-Carlo Rally; International Circus Festival
Nice: Festival of Birds

February
Isola 2000: Snow Carnival
Menton: International Lemon Festival
Nice: Carnival and Battle of Flowers

March
Antibes: Café Theatre Festival
Grasse: Carnival
Monte-Carlo: MANCAS (Contemporary and film music festival); Spring Arts Festival (continues until end April).

April
Cannes: MIP-TV (International TV Programmes festival)
Roquebrune-Cap-Martin: Costumed procession of lanterns to the castle on Good Friday.
Monte-Carlo: Biennial of Sculpture (odd numbered years, until end of September).

May
Cannes: Film Festival
Fréjus: Fleuriades – flower festival
Grasse: Expo Roses – international rose show
Monaco: Grand Prix
Nice: May Festival and International Youth Folk Festival; Art Jonction International
St-Tropez: The Bravades festival is in honour of the Roman soldier Torpes from whom St-Tropez takes its name.

June
Antibes: International Young Soloist Festival
Cannes: International Cabaret-theatre Festival
Fréjus: Arènes de l'Automobile: exhibition of collector's cars
Monte-Carlo: Fires of Saint Jean folk festival

Nice: Sacred Music Festival
Roquebrune-Cap-Martin: Theatre Festival.

July
Antibes: International Jazz Festival
Fréjus: Forum des Arts et de la Musique: concerts, classical dance, theatre
Golf Juan: Jean Marais Festival (theatre and music)
Grasse: International Festival of Military Music
Monte-Carlo: Season of concerts in the Princes Palace courtyard; Fireworks Festival and Monaco carnival
Nice: International Folk Festival; "Grande Parade du Jazz"
Vence: Classical concerts in the cathedral and open-air
Villefranche-sur-Mer: Venetian Festival

August
Antibes: International Fireworks Festival
Fréjus: Fête du Raisin – wine-tasting and feasting
Grasse: Festival of Jasmine
Menton: International Chamber Music Festival
Monte-Carlo: Feast of Saint Roman folk festival
Roquebrune-Cap-Martin: Costumed procession to the castle
Vallauris: Pottery Festival

September
St-Tropez: Grape-picking festival

October
Monte-Carlo: Season of Symphony Concerts

November
Monte-Carlo: 19 November national holiday: parades, ceremonies and spectacles (fireworks the previous evening)

December
Fréjus: Foire aux Santons: Provençal craftsmen exhibit *santons* – small clay figures of saints used for religious purposes.

designed to house it. The ornamental gardens are worth a visit. Closed: Sunday and Monday mornings and November.

Ste-Maxime
Musée des Traditions Locales, Place des Aliziers, Route du Muy, St-Donat, tel: 94 96 50 52. Closed: Monday and Tuesday.

St-Paul-de-Vence
Fondation Maeght, tel: 93 32 81 63. Just northwest of the town this notable building houses the museum of modern art established in 1964 by art dealer Aimé Maeght. Apart from the works of Chagall, Braque, Bonnard etc. inside, the **gardens** are a backdrop to sculptures and other works, including Miró's fountains.
   Musée d'Histoire Locale, Place de la Castre, tel: 93 32 41 13. Costumes and sets showing the history of St Paul.
   There are also many private art galleries in the town.

St-Raphael
Musée Archéologique, Place de la Vieille Eglise, tel: 94 19 25 75. Archaeological collections and in particular exhibitions of submarine archaeology. Closed: Tuesday in summer (Sunday mid-September to mid-June).

St-Tropez
Musée de l'Annonçiade, Rue de l'Annonçiade, tel: 94 97 04 01. Housed in a 16th-century chapel, the collection in this museum bears witness to the attraction of St-Tropez and its surrounding area to artists who came specifically to capture its colour and exceptional light. Works by Matisse, Bonnard, Braque, Utrillo and Seurat are among those featured. Closed: Tuesday and November.
   Musée Naval de St-Tropez, tel: 94 97 59 43.

Vallauris
Musée National Picasso, Place de la Libération, tel: 93 64 97 42. Similar to the one in Antibes, this museum is dedicated to the life and

works of the artist, in particular his work *La Guerre et la Paix* (War and Peace). Closed: Tuesday. More of Picasso's works can be seen in the **Musée Municipal,** Place de la Libération, tel: 93 64 16 05. Also houses a good collection of ceramics. Closed: Tuesday; entry to both museums by the same ticket.

Villeneuve-Loubet
Musée Escoffier, 3 Rue Escoffier, tel: 93 20 80 51. A Museum of Culinary Art, in the house where Escoffier, one of France's most famous chefs, was born. Closed: Mondays and November

Live Arts

The playground of film stars, musicians and artists, the Côte d'Azur offers a wide variety of live arts: music, from jazz to a programme of opera and symphony concerts; festivals of film and café theatre. In all, the region stages some 500 major cultural events each year.

ARCHAEOLOGY & ARCHITECTURE
It has been noted that the Riveria was settled by humans early in its history. Included in this listing therefore are some of the earliest prehistoric sites yet discovered. The later civilisations of the Greeks and Romans are also still very much in evidence and there are some very well preserved sites.
   In its more recent history, the region was largely dominated by the Italians, with the result that many of its important buildings are either of original Italian construction, or more latterly, designed in an Italianate style in keeping with their surroundings.
   In the hinterland, there isplenty of rural Provençal architecture: the stone-built hill villages, some with their defending walls, and the solid farmhouses, or *mas*. Efforts are being made to prevent the spoiling of this rural landscape; in many areas it is forbidden to build new houses unless in traditional fashion, using traditional materials.

In all the listings, opening times are as for museums, unless otherwise specified. Expect to pay an entrance fee (except cathedrals and churches).

Antibes
Although a modern resort, the old town of Antibes still has much of interest. Visit the **Rue Fourmillière,** the "most flowered street in Antibes". By the ramparts stands the medieval **Château Grimaldi,** now housing the **Picasso museum** (*see listing*) and nearby is the **cathedral** built in the 17th century, but housing a fine altarpiece by Louis Bréa (1515). Overlooking the harbour is the 16th-century **Fort Carré,** open to the public in July and August. Also worth a visit, at Cap d'Antibes, is the **Hôtel du Cap d'Antibes** which featured in Scott Fitzgerald's *Tender is the Night.* **Musée d'Histoire et d'Archéologie,** Bastian St-André, tel: 92 905435.

Auron
Although a modern ski resort, Auron has a notable Romanesque (12th-century) chapel with striking frescoes. Visit too the **Museum of Religious Art.**

Brignoles
Palais des Comtes de Provence Musée du Pays Brignolais, tel: 94 69 45 18. A 12th-century former palace of the Counts of Provence. Some of it is ruined but what remains is interesting, including a typical provençal kitchen. It houses the local museum which shows the history of bauxite mining in the area. Closed: Monday and Tuesday.
   Château de Vins, Vins-sur-Caramy, 83170 Brignoles, tel: 94 72 50 40. Restoration work has been going on for some years now to save this Renaissance castle. Visitors are admitted to parts of it, including the courtyard and terraces.

Cannes
The resort boasts the smartest promenade on the Riviera. **La Croisette** is lined with elegant hotels, among which is the **Carlton,**

the ultimate in wedding-cake architecture. The town is overlooked by the 11th-century **Le Suquet tower**, now housing the **Le Castre Museum**, tel: 93 38 55 26.

Collobrières
Ancienne Chartreuse de la Verne, 83610 Collobrières. A charterhouse founded around 1174 in the Maures Mountaines. Green serpentine stone used for ornamental motifs gives its a remarkable appearance. It resumed its original vocation in 1983 and now houses a religious community of Bethlehem monks. Closed: Tuesdays and October.

Entrecasteaux
This tiny, typically provençal village dating back to the Middle Ages boasts a heavily fortified **castle**, which was bought in the 1970s by a Scot, Ian McGarvie-Munn who won awards for its restoration, and installed his rather eccentric collections (including Scottish bagpipes). See too the formal **garden** designed by Le Nôtre, France's answer to Capability Brown, tel: 94 04 43 95.

Eze
This hill village enjoys a fantastic location, perched right above the sea and offering breathtaking views. Visit the **church** with its baroque interior and the **Chapel of the White Penitents**.

Frejus
Amphithéâtre and Arènes, Rue Henri Vadon, tel: 94 17 05 60. Dating back to the end of the 1st or the beginning of the 2nd century, this is one of the largest amphitheatres built in Gaul. Built for the use of the Roman garrison, it can accommodate 10,000 people. Closed: Tuesday.
   Cité Episcopal, Rue du Fleury, tel: 94 51 26 30. Episcopal city comprising a palaeo-Christian baptistry, one of the oldest Christian monuments of ancient Gaul, the 18th-century **cathedral** (which includes the remains of an older building and an interesting

belltower), and the cloister, noteworthy for its fine gothic columns. Closed: Tuesday. The **Musée Archéologique** on the same site houses the ancient Roman forum.

Grasse
The cathedral, **Notre-Dame-du-Puy**, dates back to the 12th century, although much restored in the 17th century. Of particular note are paintings by Rubens, Bréa and a rare Fragonard. Also the 17th-century **Villa Fragonard** (*see Places of Interest* page 329).

Grimaud
This attractive hill village near St-Tropez is dominated by the ruined **Château de Grimaud**. Built on a Gallo-Roman site, the present castle dates back to the 13th century. Restoration work is being carried out, but its is open to visitors at all times.

Hyères
Settled by both the Greeks and Romans, and then important in the Middle Ages, the old town is still enclosed by fortified ramparts. Of particular note is the 12th-century **Tour St-Blaise** and the **Tour des Templiers** in the market place. Vist too the church of **St-Paul** (1572) on a hill just outside the town, and the ruined **St-Bernard Château** and gardens.

Iles De Lerins
Just off the coast and accessible from many of the small ports (*see Excursions in the Things to do section*), these two islands both have notable buildings. **St-Honorat** is named after a 4th-century monk who founded one of the first monasteries in France on the island. It was acquired by the Cistercians after the Revolution. Its museum is open to the public. On the **Île St-Marguerite** stands a 17th-century fortress built by Richelieu, and famous for the imprisonment of the "Man in the Iron Mask", whose identity is still in question. It is now used as a sports and cultural centre; *son-et-lumière* displays are held in season.

La Brigue
In the upper Roya valley sits this unspoilt medieval village with a Romanesque **church**. Also nearby is the **Sanctuary of Notre-Dame-des-Fontaines**, a small chapel with some fine frescos.

La Turbie
Set behind Monaco, this old town boasts a roman landmark, **la Trophée des Alpes**, which has been partly restored by an American patron. See too the **Museum of Roman Provence**, tel: 93 41 10 11.

Le Thoronet
Abbaye du Thoronet, 83340 Le Thoronet, tel: 94 60 43 90. Set in a verdant valley, this Cistercian abbey was founded in the 12th century, and has been preserved practically in its orginal state. Visit the church, cloister, dormitory and chapter house.

Lorgues
Collégiale St-Martin de Lorgues, 83510 Lorgues, tel: 94 73 92 37. A majestic, classic religious building, remarkable because of its size, built by the town in the 18th century. Admission: free.

Mandelieu-La-Napoule
The 14th-century **castle** was bought in 1918 by the rather eccentric American sculptor, Henri Clews, who restored it and lies buried there. Now a museum, housing much of his work, and a Franco-American cultural centre. The **gardens** are also worth a visit.

Mougins
Just north of Cannes, this old fortified village provides a panoramic view of the coast. Of particular note are the 15th-century **gateway**; the romanesque **Saint Barthélémy chapel** and the **chapel of Notre-Dame-de-Vie** on a hilltop nearby. Picasso spent his last years at the *mas* (farmhouse) of Notre-Dame-de-Vie and died there.

Nice
Many of the town's notable buildings have already been mentioned

in the Museums listing. Also of note is the **Opera House** and the **Palais Lascaris**, 15 rue Droite, tel: 93 62 05 54. There are some wonderful Italian baroque churches, as well as the Russian Orthodox **Cathedral of Saint Nicholas**, which once served a sizeable Russian community in Nice. It has sumptuous decorations both inside and out. Also on the hill of Cimiez the old Roman settlement has been excavated, showing in particular, the **temple of Apollo** and the **amphitheatre**.

Roquebrune
The well-restored medieval village is dominated by its feudal **castle** where villages proceed each year in traditional costume to give thanks for being saved from the plague in the Middle Ages.

Saint-Cezaire
The village itself has a **Romanesque chapel**, housing a Roman sarcophagus, but of more interest are the **grottoes**, just north of the village. Discovered in the late 19th century, they have remarkable stalactites and stalagmites.

St-Jean-Cap-Ferrat
The home of many of the Riviera's wealthier residents and thus dotted with elegant villas. The **Villa Mauresque** (not open to the public) was the home of Somerset Maugham; but the most notable building is the Italianate mansion which houses the **Rothschild Museum**.

St-Jeannet
At 2,500 ft (760 metres), this village offers splendid views of the whole coast from the Baou peak (easy access to the viewing table). Also the 17th-century **church** and **Templars' castle**.

St-Maximin-La-Sainte-Baume
Basilique et Couvent Royal de St-Maximin, 83470 St-Maximin, tel: 94 78 00 09. Over a Gallo-Roman crypt containing some richly embellished sarcophagi, Charles II of Anjou built this Gothic basilica, the best of its kind in the region, to

serve as the reliquary of Mary Magdalen, patron saint of Provence. At the same time (1295) a vast Dominican monastery was built. See too the **medieval town** below with its arcaded Jewish quarter.

St-Paul-de-Vence
A charming hill village, famous for its modern art collections (see Museums). You can still walk around the 16th-century **ramparts**; also of note are the alleyways paved with mosaics and piazzas graced by fountains. Visit too the 12th-century hilltop **church** with its wealth of paintings.

St-Tropez
Citadelle de St-Tropez, tel: 94 97 59 43. High above the town this mighty 16th-century fortress affords a breathtaking view from the Alps to the Maures Mountains and the sea. Now houses a naval museum. Closed: Thursdays.

Valbonne
Well-preserved, picturesque village, its main square is bordered by Romanesque arcades. Also nearby is the **Roman aqueduct** of Claussones and to the south, the modern science park of **Sophia-Antipolis**.

Vence
Chapelle du Rosaire, 466 Avenue Henri Matisse, tel: 93 58 03 26. Just outside the town stands a small chapel, also known as the **Matisse Chapel** as it was entirely designed and decorated by the artist. Open: Tuesday and Thursday, or on request with 24 hours' notice. Closed: November to mid-December. Also worth visiting is the **church** in the medieval town itself which houses a mosaic by Marc Chagall.

Villefranche-sur-Mer
Delightful Italianate houses line the harbour of this old fishing port. Visit the **Chapelle Saint Pierre** (tel: 93 76 90 70), by the harbour, which was decorated by Jean Cocteau.

Nightlife

Apart from Paris, the Côte d'Azur has the most exciting nightlife in France. The casino at Monte-Carlo was the first in the country to open in 1865 (at a time when they were not permitted in the rest of France). It saved the principality from bankruptcy and the rich and famous came flocking to try their luck. What started as a Victorian novelty has now been tinged by a touch of Las Vegas and it has been joined by plenty of other casinos along the coast, some of them incorporating nightclubs or cabarets.

CAFÉ THEATRES & PIANO BARS
If gambling is not your style, you can enjoy your evenings at a café theatre, discothèque or piano bar, or by soaking up the atmosphere at a pavement café. There are firework displays during the summer, and everywhere on 14 July.

Local tourist offices will keep you up to date with what is going on, as will the local English-language and French papers. Following is a list of cafés/restaurants where you can be entertained as you dine. Many of the luxury hotels also have piano bars. You will need a healthy bank account for most of them.

Antibes
La Siesta, Pont de la Brague, tel: 93 33 31 31. Shows June–September.

Le Sucrier, 6 Rue des Bains, tel: 93 34 22 00. Café-theatre with performances Thursday–Saturday.

Cagnes-sur-Mer
Le Liberty, 52 Avenue de la Gare, tel: 93 20 69 17. Piano bar and dancing.

Cannes

Palm Beach, Place Franklin D. Roosevelt, tel: 93 43 91 12. Famous venue. Open: 1 June–31 October.
  Les Ambassadeurs, Esplanade Georges Pompidou/La Croisette, tel: 93 39 01 01.

Grasse

Restaurant les Parfums, Rue Eugene Charabot, tel: 93 36 03 15.

Hyères

Cafeteria DM, Centre Commercial du Pyanet, tel: 94 65 79 64. Weekend dinner-dances.
Lord's, Rue Joseph Clotis, tel: 94 35 47 00.
  Royal Cocktails Club, 32 Rue de Limans, tel: 94 65 62 20.

Casinos

Note that entrance to most casinos is around FF80–100 (although some are free) and restricted to those aged over 21 years of age. Many require you to show your passport.
  The main venues are as follows:

Antibes

La Siesta, Route de Bord de Mer, tel: 93 33 01 18. Open: June–September.

Cannes

Carlton Casino Club, Carlton Intercontinental, 58 la Croisette, tel: 93 68 00 33. Open: every day 4pm–4am. Also has restaurants, piano bar and disco.
Casino Municipal, 1 Jetée Albert-Edouard, tel: 93 38 12 11. Open: daily from 11am , plus Le Galaxy nightclub every evening (except Monday) at 11pm.
Palm Beach Casino, Place Franklin D. Roosevelt, tel: 93 43 91 12. Open: daily from 1 June–31 October.

Juan-Les-Pins

Eden Casino, Boulevard E Baudoin, tel: 92 93 71 71. Refurbished.

Isola 2000

Auberge de la Lombard, tel: 93 23 11 67. Open: for the winter sports season, December–May and then from June–September.

Ste-Maxime

  Café de Paris, Place du Casino, tel: 93 25 59 60.
  Le Cygne, 7 Avenue Princesse Grace, tel: 93 25 59 60. Closed: Sundays and in January.

Roquebrune-Cap-Martin

Le Vista Palace, Grande Corniche, tel: 93 35 01 50. Open: all year. Dinner is served around the pool.

Saint-Laurent-du-Var

Le Trotteur, Plage de St-Laurent,

Mandelieu-La-Napoule

Loews Hotel, Boulevard Général de Gaulle, tel: 93 49 90 00. Open: daily 8pm–4am. Also restaurant and floor show.

Monte-Carlo

Casino de Monte-Carlo, Place du Casino, tel: 04 92 16 21 21. The original and still the most famous where formal dress is required. Open: all year: main salon from noon, private rooms from 3pm. Also has a separate cabaret, as does SBM **Loews Casino**, Loews Hotel, Avenue des Spelugues, tel: 93 50 65 00. Less formal than its presitigious older brother, with free admission. Open: from 11am.

Nice

Casino Ruhl de Nice, 1 Promenade des Anglais, tel: 93 87 95 87. Open: daily 5pm–5am (4pm–4am in winter). Also offers a restaurant, discoand cabaret.

Ste-Maxime

Casino Beach, 13 Avenue De Gaulle, tel: 94 96 12 90.

St-Raphael

Casino, Square de Gant, tel: 94 95 01 56.

tel: 93 31 10 76. And the **Cocody Beach**, tel: 93 07 52 10 are right on the seafront.

Vence

  Le Vieux Moulin, 661 Chemin Ste-Colombe, tel: 93 58 96 96. Piano-bar and show. Closed: Sunday.

DISCOTHEQUES

Those listed are open all year unless otherwise indicated. They mostly open late (10 or 11pm).

Antibes

La Siesta, Route du Bord de Mer, tel: 93 33 31 31.
Shock, Avenue du 11 Novembre, tel: 93 33 69 93.

Fréjus

La Playa, Boulevard Libération, Fréjus Plage, tel: 94 52 22 98.
L'Odyssée, Boulevard Libération, Fréjus Plage, tel: 94 51 27 54.

Juan-Les-Pins

Les Pecheurs, Avenue Baudoin, tel: 93 67 30 30.
Voom-voom, Boulevard de la Pinède, tel: 93 61 18 71.
Whisky à Gogo, La Pinède, tel: 93 61 26 40.

Monte-Carlo

La Boccaccio, 39 Avenue Princesse Grace, tel: 93 30 15 22.
Jimmy'z, Place du Casino, tel: 93 50 80 80. Open: nightly, September–June. Also **Jimmy'z de la Mer**, Avenue Princesse Grace, tel: 92 16 22 77. Open: July and August.
The Living Room, 7 Avenue des Spélugues, tel: 93 50 80 31.
Parady'z, Avenue Princesse Grace, tel: 93 30 71 71. Open: July and August.
Tiffany's, 3 Avenue des Spélegues, tel: 93 30 70 55.
L'X Club, 13 Avenue des Spélegues, tel: 93 30 70 55.

St-Tropez

Les Caves du Roy, Hôtel Byblos, Place des Lices, tel: 94 56 68 00.
Le Papagayo, Résidence du Port, tel: 94 97 07 56.

Shopping

Shopping Areas

Over the years most major towns in France have made the sensible decision to keep the town centre for small boutiques and individual shops. Many of these areas are pedestrianised and so rather attractive (although beware – some cars ignore the *voie piétonnée* signs). The large supermarkets, hypermarkets, furniture stores and do-it-yourself outlets are grouped on the outskirts of the town, mostly designated as a Centre Commercial. This laudable intent is, however, somewhat marred by the horrendous design of some of these centres – groups of garish functional buildings which make the town's outskirts very unattractive. In the case of Nice, for example, there are vast hypermarkets, out by the airport to the west of the town.

These centres are fine for bulk shopping, for self-catering or for finding a selection of wine to take home at reasonable prices, but otherwise the town centres are far more interesting. It is here that you will find the individual souvenirs that give a taste of the region, alongside the beautifully dressed windows of delicatessens and pâtisseries.

Nice itself has glamorous shopping districts to attract its wealthy tourists. The **Masséna quarter** is a pedestrianised area of chic boutiques, where you will also find the main department stores, Galeries Lafayettes and La Riviera. In **Cannes**, head for the city centre, particularly Rue d'Antibes with its irresistible confectioners and luxury boutiques.

Markets

The heart of every French town is its market, and the markets of the Côte d'Azur and Provence are possibly the most colourful and lively of any in the whole of France. In many towns the market is held every day (except Monday); they mostly start early in the morning and close at midday. The French themselves usually visit early to get the best of the produce.

Some of the best general daily markets are in **Nice** (cours Saleya), **Antibes** (cours Masséna, covered market), **Cannes** (Marché Forville, also the flower market, Jardin des Allées – not Saturday), **Grasse** (Place aux Aires), **Menton** (Esplanade du Carei, and covered market), **Toulon** (Cours Lafayette), **Monte-Carlo** (Place d'Armes), **St-Maxime** (covered market, Rue Fenand Bessy, open all day in summer). Other markets which are well worth a visit, but not held daily are as follows (mornings): **St-Tropez** (Tuesday and Saturday), **Fréjus** (Wednesday and Saturday, Place des Poivriers, also **Fréjus Plage**, Place de la République, Tuesday and Friday, June–September), **Hyères** (Tuesday, Place de la République, Saturday, Avenue Gambetta), **Le Lavandou** (Thursday), **Draguignan** (Wednesday and Saturday), **Ste-Maxime** (Old Town, Thursday; marché du Capet, Avenue Georges Pompidou, Monday).

Another attraction are the specialist markets. All the above have flower stalls, but Nice, where the flower market is open all day, and **Cannes** are especially colourful. Antique and second-hand (*brocante*) markets are also very popular; those listed below are held regularly and open all day unless otherwise indicated.

Antibes: Place Audiberti, Thursday; also Cours Masséna for bric-à-brac and crafts, Tuesday and Friday afternoons.

Cagnes: Place du Château, Sunday.

Cannes: Allées de la Liberté, Saturday.

Buying Wine Direct

You may be tempted by all the signs you see along the road for *dégustations* – tastings. Many wine producers and farmers will invite you to try their wines and other produce with the aim of making a sale. This is a good way to try before you buy and can sometimes include a visit to a wine cellar. Often farm produce is more expensive to buy this way than in the supermarkets – do not forget that it is freshly produced, and not factory processed. However, this should not be true of wine and it can be more reliable, as well as cheaper to buy something you have tried and know you like. For a selection of wine cellars open to the public, *see Places of Interest*.

Menton: Place aux Herbes, Friday.
Nice: Rues A. Gauthier/C. Ségurane/E. Philibert, also the flea market, Place Guynemer, both daily except Sunday; philatelist's market, Square Durandy, Rue Pastorelli, Sunday morning.
Ste-Maxime-sur-Mer: Marché des Artisans (craft market), Thursday.
La Seyne-sur-Mer: Les Sablettes, Saturday, plus a flea market, Place B. Frachon, alternate Sundays except in July.
Vence: L'Ara, Wednesday.
Villefranche-sur-Mer: Place A. Pollonais, Sunday.
There are also antique and craft fairs and *marchés exceptionnels*, held at various points throughout the year, such as harvest times. Check with the local tourist office for details.

Shopping Tips

Food shops, especially bakers, tend to open early; boutiques and department stores open from 9am, but sometimes not until 10am. In town centres, just about everything closes from noon until 3pm apart from the department stores which usually stay open. Most shops close in the evening at 7pm. Out of town, the hypermarkets are usually open all day until 8 or even 9pm. Most shops are closed Monday mornings and large stores generally all day. If you want to buy a picnic lunch, remember to buy everything you need before midday. Good delicatessens (*charcuterie*) have a selection of delicious ready-prepared dishes, which make picnicking a delight.

On most purchases, the price includes TVA (VAT or purchase tax). The base rate is currently I8.6 percent, but can be as high as 33 percent on luxury items. Foreign visitors can claim back TVA paid and this may be worth doing if you spend more than FF4,200 (FF2,000 for non-EC residents) in one place. Some large stores and hypermarkets have information bureaux where you can obtain a refund form. This must be completed to show (with the goods purchased) to customs officers on leaving the country (pack the items separately for ease of access). Then mail the form back to the retailer who will refund the TVA in a month or two. Certain items purchased (e.g. antiques) may need special customs clearance. For more information contact the Service de Détaxe et de la Réglementation, tel: 93 85 27 55.

COMPLAINTS

If you have a complaint about any purchase, return it in the first place to the shop as soon as possible. In the case of any serious dispute, contact the Direction Départementale de la Concurrence et de la Consommation et de la Répression des Fraudes.

Sport

Participant Sports

WATER SPORTS

It is not necessary to be a millionaire and member of the most fashionable yacht club to enjoy the pleasures of the sea. Of course, if you wish to hire a luxury yacht for a week's cruise, being a millionaire might help. You also need money to enjoy some of the beaches. Only 70 percent are open to the public, the rest (nearly 150 beaches) are privately owned (usually by hotels) and an entrance fee is charged. Most of the private beaches have a good range of equipment for hire: windsurfers, dinghies, catamarans, water skiing, parascending etc.

To hire a boat, or a yacht, for a day or longer, all you need really do is stroll around the pleasure ports of the resorts and ask. Another source of information is the local syndicat d'initiative or tourist office (*see Useful Addresses* page 317).

See also the *Excursions* page 330, for scheduled cruises. There are too many operators offering boats for cruising and sailing to list them all here, hence a selection. Most offer them for hire with or without a crew .

Sailing & Windsurfing

Comité Régional de Voile Côte d"Azur, Espace Antibes 2208 Route de Grasse, 06600 Antibes, tel: 93 74 77 05.
Cannes: Station Voile, 9 rue Esprit Violet, tel: 04 92 18 88 87.
Juan les Pins: Nautique 2000, tel: 04 93 61 20 01.

Scuba Diving

Fédération française d'études et de sports Sous-Marins, tel: 93 65 11 64.

Antibes: Sondyle Club 62 allé des Pins du Cap, tel: 93 61 45 45.
Nice Centre inter de Plongée, 2 Ruelle des Moulins, tel: 04 93 55 59 50.
Cannes: Plongé Club de Cannes, 46 rue Georges Clemenceau, tel: 93 38 67 57.

Canoeing & Kayaking

Ligue Régionale Alpes-Provence, 14 Avenue Vincent Auriol, 30200 Bagnols-sur-Ceze, tel: 66 89 47 71.

Sea Fishing

Antibes: Avec Lucien, du Port d'Antibes, tel: 93 64 28 39.
Nice: Atout Pêche, 67 Avenue St-Augustin, tel: 93 71 30 35.
Cannes: Cannes Pêche, 44 rue Georges Clemenceau, tel: 93 39 76 17.

SKIING

Club Alpin: 14 rue Mirabeau, Nice, tel: 93 62 59 99.

Downhill Skiing

Auron: Office du Tourisme, tel: 04 93 23 02 66.
Isola 2000: Office du Tourisme, tel: 04 93 23 15 15.

Cross-Country Skiing

Val Casterino, tel: 93 04 73 71.
Le Boréon, St-Martin-de-Vesubie, tel: 93 03 33 77.

TENNIS

Nice: Nice Leader Apollo, 66 Route de Grenoble, tel: 04 93 18 00 95.
Antibes: Tennis Club municipal d'Antibes, Avenue Jules Grec, tel: 93 33 74 49.
Tennis municipal de Cannes: Avenue Francis Tonnere, tel: 93 47 05 82.

GOLF

Biot: Golfe du Biot La Basride du Roy, tel: 93 65 08 40.
Victoria Golf Club: Domaine du Val Martin, Valbonne, tel: 93 12 23 26.
Cannes: Golf de Cannes, Route du Golf, Mandelieu, tel: 04 93 49 55 39.
Golf de Nice: 198 Route de Grenoble, tel: 93 29 82 00.

Spectator Sports

Probably the most famous event in the whole region is the prestigious **Monte-Carlo Car Rally**, held in January. First staged in 1911, this road trial continues to attract the top names in the sport. Another lesser-known rally is held in November at St-Tropez; the 20 km (12 miles) **Rolls-Royce Rally**. The other big motoring event is the **Monte-Carlo Grand Prix** in May, one of the most decisive contests in the competition for the world motor racing championship.

April is the time for the International Tennis championships in Monte-Carlo, the **Monte-Carlo Open**, which is complemented by another "open", this time the **Golf Tournament** which takes place in early July. Another golfing event is the **Professional Golf Open** at Mougins (Cannes) which is held every April.

The major horse-racing venue is the **Côte d'Azur Hippodrome** at Cagnes-sur-Mer where meetings are held during the day from December to May and in the evenings in July and August. One of its major events takes place in February. There is also an **international show-jumping competiton** in Cannes during May. Hyères is popular for racing, and meetings are held at the **Hippodrome** there during the spring and autumn. Fréjus hosts a **horse show** in June.

There are all kinds of sailing and other water-sport events, with most of the major competitions taking place at Mandelieu-la-Napoule, just west of Cannes, including the **Grand Prix de la Corniche d'Or** (April), "**Les Vieilles Ecoutes**" (July), the **International Rowing Regatta** (August) and the **Grand Prix de la Ville** (October). Other events are the **International Marathon** in the Baie des Anges, Nice in April, the **Transgolfe Windsurf Regatta** in St-Tropez in July and the **Royal Regattas** in September in Cannes to coincide with the **International Pleasure Boat Festival**; there is also a **Boat Show** at Beaulieu-sur-Mer in May.

Language

French is the native language of more than 90 million people and the acquired language of 180 million. It is a Romance language descended from the Vulgar Latin spoken by the Roman conquerors of Gaul. It still carries the reputation of being the most cultured language in the world and, for what it's worth, the most beautiful. People often tell stories about the impatience of the French towards foreigners not blessed with fluency in their language. In general, however, if you attempt to communicate with them in French, they will be helpful.

Since much of the English vocabulary is related to French, thanks to the Norman Conquest of 1066, travellers will often recognise many helpful cognates: words such as *hôtel*, *café* and *bagages* hardly need to be translated. You should be aware, however, of some misleading "false friends" (*see above right*).

Words & Phrases

How much is it? *C'est combien?*
What is your name? *Comment vous appelez-vous?*
My name is... *Je m'appelle...*
Do you speak English? *Parlez-vous anglais?*
I am English/American *Je suis anglais/américain*
I don't understand *Je ne comprends pas*
Please speak more slowly *Parlez plus lentement, s'il vous plaît*
Can you help me? *Pouvez-vous m'aider?*
I'm looking for... *Je cherche*
Where is...? *Où est...?*
I'm sorry *Excusez-moi/Pardon*
I don't know *Je ne sais pas*

No problem *Pas de problème*
Have a good day! *Bonne journée!*
That's it *C'est ça*
Here it is *Voici*
There it is *Voilà*
Let's go *On y va. Allons-y*
See you tomorrow *A demain*
See you soon *A bientôt*
Show me the word in the book *Montrez-moi le mot dans le livre*
yes *oui*
no *non*
please *s'il vous plaît*
thank you *merci*
(very much) *(beaucoup)*
you're welcome *de rien*
excuse me *excusez-moi*
hello *bonjour*
OK *d'accord*
goodbye *au revoir*
good evening *bonsoir*
here *ici*
there *là*
today *aujourd'hui*
yesterday *hier*
tomorrow *demain*
now *maintenant*
later *plus tard*
this morning *ce matin*
this afternoon *cet après-midi*
this evening *ce soir*

On Arrival

I want to get off at... *Je voudrais descendre à...*
Is there a bus to the Louvre? *Est-ce qui'il ya un bus pour le Louvre?*
What street is this? *A quelle rue sommes-nous?*
Which line do I take for...? *Quelle ligne dois-je prendre pour...?*
How far is...? *A quelle distance se trouve...?*
Validate your ticket *Compostez votre billet*
airport *l'aéroport*
train station *la gare*

Time

At what time? *A quelle heure?*
When? *Quand?*
What time is it? *Quelle heure est-il?*
● Note that the French generally use the 24-hour clock.

False Friends

False friends are words that look like English words but mean something different.

le car motorcoach, also railway carriage
le conducteur bus driver
la monnaie change (coins)
l'argent money/silver
ça marche can sometimes mean walk, but is usually used to mean working (the TV, the car etc.) or going well
actuel "present time" (la situation actuelle the present situation)
rester to stay
location hiring/renting
personne person or nobody, according to context
le médecin doctor

bus station la gare routière
Métro stop la station de Métro
bus l'autobus, le car
bus stop l'arrêt
platform le quai
ticket le billet
return ticket aller-retour
hitchhiking l'autostop
toilets les toilettes
This is the hotel address C'est l'adresse de l'hôtel
I'd like a (single/double) room... Je voudrais une chambre (pour une/deux personnes) ...
....with shower avec douche
....with a bath avec salle de bain
....with a view avec vue
Does that include breakfast? Le prix comprend-il le petit déjeuner?
May I see the room? Je peux voir la chambre?
washbasin le lavabo
bed le lit
key la cléf
elevator l'ascenseur
air conditioned climatisé

On the Road

Where is the spare wheel? Où est la roue de secours?
Where is the nearest garage? Où est le garage le plus proche?
Our car has broken down Notre voiture est en panne

I want to have my car repaired Je veux faire réparer ma voiture
It's not your right of way Vous n'avez pas la priorité
I think I must have put diesel in the car by mistake Je crois que j'ai mis du gasoil dans la voiture par erreur
the road to... la route pour...
left gauche
right droite
straight on tout droit
far loin
near près d'ici
opposite en face
beside à côté de
car park parking
over there là-bas
at the end au bout
on foot à pied
by car en voiture
town map le plan
road map la carte
street la rue
square la place
give way céder le passage
dead end impasse
no parking stationnement interdit
motorway l'autoroute
toll le péage
speed limit la limitation de vitesse
petrol l'essence
unleaded sans plomb
diesel le gasoil
water/oil l'eau/l'huile
puncture un pneu de crevé
bulb l'ampoule
wipers les essuies-glace

Shopping

Where is the nearest bank (post office)? Où est la banque/Poste/ PTT la plus proche?
I'd like to buy Je voudrais acheter
How much is it? C'est combien?
Do you take credit cards? Est-ce que vous acceptez les cartes de crédit?
I'm just looking Je regarde seulement
Have you got...? Avez-vous...?
I'll take it Je le prends
I'll take this one/that one Je prends celui-ci/celui-là
What size is it? C'est de quelle taille?
Anything else? Avec ça?
size (clothes) la taille

The Alphabet

Learning the pronunciation of the French alphabet is a good idea. In particular, learn how to spell out your name.
a=ah, **b**=bay, **c**=say, **d**=day **e**=er, **f**=ef, **g**=zhay, **h**=ash. **i**=ee, **j**=zhee, **k**=ka, **l**=el, **m**=em, **n** =en, **o**=oh, **p**=pay, **q**=kew, **r**=ehr, **s**=ess, **t**=tay, **u**=ew, **v**=vay, **w**=dooblah vay, **x**-=eex, **y** ee grek, **z**=zed

size (shoes) la pointure
cheap bon marché
expensive cher
enough assez
too much trop
a piece un morceau de
each la pièce (eg ananas, 15F la pièce)
bill la note
chemist la pharmacie
bakery la boulangerie
bookshop la librairie
library la bibliothèque
department store le grand magasin
delicatessen la charcuterie/le traiteur
fishmonger's la poissonerie
grocery l'alimentation/l'épicerie
tobacconist tabac (can also sell stamps and newspapers)
markets le marché
supermarket le supermarché
junk shop la brocante

Emergencies

Help! Au secours!
Stop! Arrêtez!
Call a doctor Appelez un médecin
Call an ambulance Appelez une ambulance
Call the police Appelez la police
Call the fire brigade Appelez les pompiers
Where is the nearest telephone? Où est le téléphone le plus proche?
Where is the nearest hospital? Où est l'hôpital le plus proche?
I am sick Je suis malade
I have lost my passport/purse J'ai perdu mon passeport/porte-monnaie

Slang

métro, boulot, dodo nine-to-five syndrome
McDo McDonald's
branché trendy (literally "connected")
C'est du cinéma It's very unlikely
une copine/un copain friend/chum
un ami friend but **mon ami,** boyfriend; also **mon copain**
un truc thing, "whatsit"
pas mal, not bad, good-looking
fantastic! fantastic! terrible!

Sightseeing

town *la ville*
old town *la vieille ville*
abbey *l'abbaye*
cathedral *la cathédrale*
church *l'église*
keep *le donjon*
mansion *l'hôtel*
hospital *l'hôpital*
town hall *l'hôtel de ville/la mairie*
nave *la nef*
stained glass *le vitrail*
staircase *l'escalier*
tower *la tour (La Tour Eiffel)*
walk *le tour*
country house/castle *le château*
Gothic *gothique*
Roman *romain*
Romanesque *roman*
museum *la musée*
art gallery *la galerie*
exhibition *l'exposition*
tourist *l'office de*
information *tourisme/le*
office *syndicat d'initiative*
free *gratuit*
open *ouvert*
closed *fermé*
every day *tous les jours*
all year *toute l'année*
all day *toute la journée*
swimming pool *la piscine*
to book *réserver*

Dining Out

Table d'hôte (the "host's table") is one set menu served at a set price. **Prix fixe** is a fixed price menu. **A la carte** means dishes from the menu are charged separately.

breakfast *le petit déjeuner*
lunch *le déjeuner*
dinner *le dîner*
meal *le repas*
first course *l'entrée/les hors d'oeuvre*
main course *le plat principal*
drink included *boisson compris*
wine list *la carte des vins*
the bill *l'addition*
fork *la fourchette*
knife *le couteau*
spoon *la cuillère*
plate *l'assiette*
glass *le verre*
ashtray *le cendrier*

...au bacon **bacon and eggs**
...au jambon **ham and eggs**
...sur le plat **fried eggs**
...brouillés **scrambled eggs**
tartine **bread with butter**
crêpe **pancake**
croque-monsieur **ham and cheese toasted sandwich**
*croque-madame ...***with a fried egg on top**
galette **type of pancake**
pan bagna **bread roll stuffed with salad Niçoise**
quiche **tart of eggs and cream with various fillings**
quiche lorraine **quiche with bacon**

Basic Rules

Even if you speak no French at all, it is worth trying to master a few simple phrases. The fact that you have made an effort is likely to get you a better response. More and more French people like practising their English on visitors, especially waiters in the cafés and restaurants and the younger generation. Pronunciation is the key; they really will not understand if you get it very wrong. Remember to **emphasise each syllable**, but not to pronounce the last consonant of a word as a rule (this includes the plural "s") and always to drop your "h"s. Whether to use **"vous"** or **"tu"** is a vexed question; increasingly the familiar form of "tu" is used by many people. However it is better to be too formal, and use "vous" if in doubt. It is very important to be polite; always address people as **Madame** or **Monsieur**, and address them by their surnames until you are confident first names are acceptable. When entering a shop always say, "Bonjour Monsieur/ Madame," and "Merci, au revoir," when leaving.

Breakfast and Snacks

baguette **long thin loaf**
pain **bread**
petits pains **rolls**
beurre **butter**
poivre **pepper**
sucre **sugar**
confiture **jam**
oeufs **eggs**
...à la coque **boiled eggs**

First course

An *amuse-bouche, amuse-gueule* or appetizer is something to "amuse the mouth", served before the first course

anchoiade **sauce of olive oil, anchovies and garlic, served with raw vegetables**
assiette anglaise **cold meats**

Numbers

0 *zéro*	**11** *onze*	**30** *trente*	**1,000,000** *un million*
1 *un, une*	**12** *douze*	**40** *quarante*	
2 *deux*	**13** *treize*	**50** *cinquante*	
3 *trois*	**14** *quatorze*	**60** *soixante*	● *The number*
4 *quatre*	**15** *quinze*	**70** *soixante-dix*	*1 is often*
5 *cinq*	**16** *seize*	**80** *quatre-*	*written like an*
6 *six*	**17** *dix-sept*	*vingts*	*upside down V,*
7 *sept*	**18** *dix-huit*	**90** *quatre-*	*and the number*
8 *huit*	**19** *dix-neuf*	*vingt-dix*	*7 is crossed.*
9 *neuf*	**20** *vingt*	**100** *cent*	
10 *dix*	**21** *vingt-et-un*	**1000** *mille*	

potage **soup**
rillettes **rich fatty paste of
shredded duck, rabbit or pork**
tapenade **spread of olives and
anchovies**
pissaladière **Provençal pizza with
onions, olives and anchovies**

Meat and Fish
La Viande Meat
bleu **rare**
à point **medium**
bien cuit **well done**
grillé **grilled**
agneau **lamb**
andouille/andouillette **tripe
sausage**
bifteck **steak**
boudin **sausage**
boudin noir **black pudding**
boudin blanc **white pudding
(chicken or veal)**
blanquette **stew of veal, lamb or
chicken with a creamy egg sauce**
boeuf à la mode **beef in red wine
with carrots, mushroom and onions**
à la bordelaise **beef with red wine
and shallots**
à la **cooked in red**
Bourguignonne **wine, onions and
mushrooms**
brochette **kebab**
caille **quail**
canard **duck**
carbonnade **casserole of beef, beer
and onions**
carré d'agneau cassoulet **rack of
lamb stew of beans, sausages,
pork and duck, from southwest
France**
cervelle **brains (food)**
chateaubriand choucroute **thick
steak Alsace dish of sauerkraut,
bacon and sausages**
confit **duck or goose preserved in
its own fat**
contre-filet **cut of sirloin steak**
coq au vin **chicken in red wine**
côte d'agneau **lamb chop**
daube **beef stew with red wine,
onions and tomatoes**
dinde **turkey**
entrecôte **beef rib steak**
escargot **snail**
faisan **pheasant**
farci **stuffed**
faux-filet **sirloin**
feuilleté **puff pastry**
foie **liver**

foie de veau **calf's liver**
foie gras **goose or duck liver pâté**
gardiane **rich beef stew with olives
and garlic, from the Camargue**
cuisses de grenouille **frog's legs**
grillade **grilled meat**
hachis **minced meat**
jambon **ham**
lapin **rabbit**
lardon **small pieces of bacon, often
added to salads**
magret de canard **breast of duck**
médaillon **round meat**
moelle **beef bone marrow**
mouton navarin **stew of lamb with
onions, carrots and turnips**
oie **goose**
perdrix **partridge**
petit-gris **small snail**
pieds de cochon **pig's trotters**
pintade **guinea fowl**
Pipérade **Basque dish of eggs,
ham, peppers, onion**
porc **pork**
pot-au-feu **casserole of beef and
vegetables**
poulet **chicken**
poussin **young chicken**
rognons **kidneys**
rôti **roast**
sanglier **wild boar**
saucisse **fresh sausage**
saucisson **salami**
veau **veal**

Poissons Fish
Armoricaine **made with white wine,
tomatoes, butter and cognac**
anchois **anchovies**
anguille **eel**
bar (or loup) **sea bass**
barbue **brill**
belon **Brittany oyster**
bigorneau **sea snail**
Bercy **sauce of fish stock, butter,
white wine and shallots**
bouillabaisse **fish soup, served
with grated cheese, garlic
croutons and** rouille, **a spicy sauce**
brandade **salt cod purée**
cabillaud **cod**

calmars **squid**
colin **hake**
coquillage **shellfish**
coquilles Saint-Jacques **scallops**
crevette **shrimp**
daurade **sea bream**
flétan **halibut**
fruits de mer **seafood**
hareng **herring**
homard **lobster**
huître **oyster**
langoustine **large prawn**
limande **lemon sole**
lotte **monkfish**
morue **salt cod**
moule **mussel**
moules marinières **mussels in
white wine and onions**
raie **skate**
saumon **salmon**
thon **tuna**
truite **trout**

Days and Months

Days of the week, seasons and
months are not capitalised in
French.
● **Days of the week**
　Monday lundi
　Tuesday mardi
　Wednesday mercredi
　Thursday jeudi
　Friday vendredi
　Saturday samedi
　Sunday dimanche
● **Seasons**
　spring le printemps
　summer l'été
　autumn l'automne
　winter l'hiver
● **Months**
　January janvier
　February février
　March mars
　April avril
　May mai
　June juin
　July juillet
　August août
　September septembre
　October octobre
　November novembre
　December décembre
● **Saying the date**
　20th October 1999, le vingt
　octobre, dix-neuf cent quatre-
　vingt-dix-neuf

Table Talk

I am a vegetarian *Je suis végétarien*
I am on a diet *Je suis au régime*
What do you recommend? *Que'est-ce que vous recommandez?*
Do you have local specialities? *Avez-vous des spécialités locales?*
I'd like to order *Je voudrais commander*
That is not what I ordered *Ce n'est pas ce que j'ai commandé*
Is service included? *Est-ce que le service est compris?*
May I have more wine? *Encore du vin, s'il vous plaît?*
Enjoy your meal *Bon appétit!*

Légumes Vegetables

ail **garlic**
artichaut **artichoke**
asperge **asparagus**
aubergine **eggplant**
avocat **avocado**
bolets **boletus mushrooms**
céleri **grated celery**
rémoulade **with mayonnaise**
champignon **mushroom**
cèpes **boletus mushroom**
chanterelle **wild mushroom**
cornichon **gherkin**
courgette **zucchini**
chips **potato crisps**
chou **cabbage**
chou-fleur **cauliflower**
concombre **cucumber**
cru **raw**
crudités **raw vegetables**
épinard **spinach**
frites **chips, French fries**
gratin dauphinois **sliced potatoes baked with cream**
haricot **dried bean**
haricots verts **green beans**
lentilles **lentils**
maïs **corn**
mange-tout **snow pea**
mesclun **mixed leaf salad**
navet **turnip**
noix **nut, walnut**
noisette **hazelnut**
oignon **onion**
panais **parsnip**
persil **parsley**
pignon **pine nut**

poireau **leek**
pois **pea**
poivron **bell pepper**
pomme de terre **potato**
radis **radis**
roquette **arugula, rocket**
ratatouille **Provençal vegetable stew of aubergines, courgettes, tomatoes, peppers and olive oil**
riz **rice**
salade Niçoise **egg, tuna, olives, onions and tomato salad**
salade verte **green salad**
truffe **truffle**

Fruits Fruit

ananas **pineapple**
cavaillon **fragrant sweet melon from Cavaillon in Provence**
cerise **cherry**
citron **lemon**
citron vert **lime**
figue **fig**
fraise **strawberry**
framboise **raspberry**
groseille **redcurrant**
mangue **mango**
mirabelle **yellow plum**
pamplemousse **grapefruit**
pêche **peach**
poire **pear**
pomme **apple**
raisin **grape**

On the Telephone

How do I make an outside call? *Comment est-ce que je peux téléphoner à l'exterieur?*
I want to make an international (local) call *Je voudrais une communication pour l'étranger (une communication locale)*
What is the dialling code? *Quel est l'indicatif?*
I'd like an alarm call for 8 tomorrow morning. *Je voudrais être réveillé à huit heures demain martin*
Who's calling? *C'est qui à l'appareil?*
Hold on, please *Ne quittez pas s'il vous plaît*
The line is busy *La ligne est occupée*
I must have dialled the wrong number *J'ai dû faire un faux numéro*

prune **plum**
pruneau **prune**
Reine claude **greengage**

Sauces Sauces

aioli **garlic mayonnaise**
béarnaise **sauce of egg, butter, wine and herbs**
forestière **with mushrooms and bacon**
hollandaise **egg, butter and lemon sauce**
lyonnaise **with onions**
meunière **fried fish with butter, lemon and parsley sauce**
meurette **red wine sauce**
Mornay **sauce of cream, egg and cheese**
Parmentier **served with potatoes**
paysan **rustic style, ingredients depend on the region**
pistou **Provençal sauce of basil, garlic and olive oil; vegetable soup with the sauce.**
provençale **sauce of tomatoes, garlic and olive oil.**
papillotte **cooked in paper**

Puddings Dessert

Belle Hélène **fruit with ice cream and chocolate sauce**
clafoutis **baked pudding of batter and cherries**
coulis **purée of fruit or vegetables**
gâteau **cake**
île flottante **whisked egg whites in custard sauce**
crème anglaise **custard**
pêche melba **peaches with ice cream and raspberry sauce**
tarte tatin **upside down tart of caramelised apples**
crème caramel **caramelised egg custard**
crème Chantilly **whipped cream**
fromage **cheese**
chèvre **goat's cheese**

In the Café

If you sit at the bar (*le zinc*), drinks will be cheaper than at a table. Settle the bill when you leave; the waiter may leave a slip of paper on the table to keep track of the bill. The French enjoy bittersweet aperitifs, often diluted with ice and fizzy water.

drinks *les boissons*

coffee *café*
...with milk or cream *au lait or crème*
...decaffeinated *déca/décaféiné*
...black/espresso *express/noir*
...American filtered coffee *filtre*
tea *thé*
...herb infusion *tisane*
...camomile *verveine*
hot chocolate *chocolat chaud*
milk *lait*
mineral water *eau minérale*
fizzy *gazeux*
non-fizzy *non-gazeux*
fizzy lemonade *limonade*
fresh lemon juice served with sugar *citron pressé*
fresh squeezed orange juice *orange pressé*
full (eg full cream milk) *entier*
fresh or cold *frais, fraîche*
beer *bière*
...bottled *en bouteille*
...on tap *à la pression*
pre-dinner drink *apéritif*
white wine with cassis, black-currant liqueur *kir*
***kir* with champagne** *kir royale*
with ice *avec des glaçons*
neat *sec*
red *rouge*
white *blanc*
rose *rosé*
dry *brut*
sweet *doux*
sparkling wine *crémant*
house wine *vin de maison*
local wine *vin de pays*
Where is this *De quelle région*
wine from? *vient ce vin?*
pitcher *carafe/pichet*
...of water/wine *d'eau/de vin*
half litre *demi-carafe*
quarter litre *quart*
mixed *panaché*
after dinner drink *digestif*
brandy from Armagnac region of France *Armagnac*
Normandy apple brandy *calvados*
cheers! *santé!*
hangover *gueule de bois*

Further Reading

General

Ardagh, John. *France Today*. London: Secker and Warburg. Up-to-date, hefty tome on modern France.
Braudel, Fernand. *The Identity of France*. Fontana Press.
Cole, Robert. *A Traveller's History of France*. London: The Windrush Press. Slim volume for background reading.
Connolly, Cyril. *The Rock Pool*. Oxford University Press.
Fitzgerald, F. Scott. *Tender is the Night*. Penguin.
Forbes, Leslie. *A Table in Provence*. Webb & Bower. Recipes plus.
Grey-Wilson C. & Blamey M. *The Alpine Flowers of Britain and Europe*. Collins. Comprehensive reference book.
Guinsberg S. & E. *The Perched Villages of the Alpes-Maritimes*. Editions Edisud. Detailed guide to over 90 mountain villages, often ignored by tourists.
Hamilton, Ronald. *A Holiday History of France*. London: The Hogarth Press. Illustrated guide to history and architecture.
Howarth, Patrick. *When the Riviera was Ours*. Century Hutchinson. History of the development of the riveria as a tourist resort.
Sagan, Françoise. *Bonjour Tristesse*. Penguin.
Schonfelder & Schonfelder. *Wild Flowers of the Mediterranean*. Collins. Over 1,000 species described and hundreds of photographs.
Stendhal. *Travels in the South of France*. John Calder. Record of a journey made by the author in 1838.
Tomkins, Calvin. *Living Well is the Best Revenge*. E.P. Dutton.
Zeldin, Theodore. *The French*. How the French live today.

Other Insight Guides

Among the 192 companion **Insight Guides** to this book, the following highlight French destinations: *France, Paris, Normandy, Brittany, Loire Valley, Burgundy, Provence* and *Alsace*.
Apa Publications has two complementary series:
Insight Pocket Guides are specifically designed for the short-stay visitor and contain full-size fold-out maps. Titles in this series include: *Paris, Brittany, Loire Valley, Côte D'Azur, Provence* and *Alsace*.
Insight Compact Guides are handy mini-encyclopedias packed with facts, photographs and cross-referenced maps; titles include: *Paris, Normandy, Brittany, Burgundy* and *Provence*.

ART & PHOTO CREDITS

Index

The World of Insight Guides

400 books in three complementary series cover every major destination in every continent.

Insight Guides

Alaska
Alsace
Amazon Wildlife
American Southwest
Amsterdam
Argentina
Atlanta
Athens
Australia
Austria
Bahamas
Bali
Baltic States
Bangkok
Barbados
Barcelona
Bay of Naples
Beijing
Belgium
Belize
Berlin
Bermuda
Boston
Brazil
Brittany
Brussels
Budapest
Buenos Aires
Burgundy
Burma (Myanmar)
Cairo
Calcutta
California
Canada
Caribbean
Catalonia
Channel Islands
Chicago
Chile
China
Cologne
Continental Europe
Corsica
Costa Rica
Crete
Crossing America
Cuba
Cyprus
Czech & Slovak Republics
Delhi, Jaipur, Agra
Denmark
Dresden
Dublin
Düsseldorf
East African Wildlife
East Asia
Eastern Europe
Ecuador
Edinburgh
Egypt
Finland
Florence
Florida
France
Frankfurt
French Riviera
Gambia & Senegal
Germany
Glasgow

Gran Canaria
Great Barrier Reef
Great Britain
Greece
Greek Islands
Hamburg
Hawaii
Hong Kong
Hungary
Iceland
India
India's Western Himalaya
Indian Wildlife
Indonesia
Ireland
Israel
Istanbul
Italy
Jamaica
Japan
Java
Jerusalem
Jordan
Kathmandu
Kenya
Korea
Lisbon
Loire Valley
London
Los Angeles
Madeira
Madrid
Malaysia
Mallorca & Ibiza
Malta
Marine Life in the South China Sea
Melbourne
Mexico
Mexico City
Miami
Montreal
Morocco
Moscow
Munich
Namibia
Native America
Nepal
Netherlands
New England
New Orleans
New York City
New York State
New Zealand
Nile
Normandy
Northern California
Northern Spain
Norway
Oman & the UAE
Oxford
Old South
Pacific Northwest
Pakistan
Paris
Peru
Philadelphia
Philippines
Poland
Portugal
Prague

Provence
Puerto Rico
Rajasthan
Rhine
Rio de Janeiro
Rockies
Rome
Russia
St Petersburg
San Francisco
Sardinia
Scotland
Seattle
Sicily
Singapore
South Africa
South America
South Asia
South India
South Tyrol
Southeast Asia
Southeast Asia Wildlife
Southern California
Southern Spain
Spain
Sri Lanka
Sweden
Switzerland
Sydney
Taiwan
Tenerife
Texas
Thailand
Tokyo
Trinidad & Tobago
Tunisia
Turkey
Turkish Coast
Tuscany
Umbria
US National Parks East
US National Parks West
Vancouver
Venezuela
Venice
Vietnam
Wales
Washington DC
Waterways of Europe
Wild West
Yemen

Insight Pocket Guides

Aegean Islands★
Algarve★
Alsace
Amsterdam★
Athens★
Atlanta★
Bahamas★
Baja Peninsula★
Bali★
Bali Bird Walks
Bangkok★
Barbados★
Barcelona★
Bavaria★
Beijing★
Berlin★

Bermuda★
Bhutan★
Boston★
British Columbia★
Brittany★
Brussels★
Budapest & Surroundings★
Canton★
Chiang Mai★
Chicago★
Corsica★
Costa Blanca★
Costa Brava★
Costa del Sol/Marbella★
Costa Rica★
Crete★
Denmark★
Fiji★
Florence★
Florida★
Florida Keys★
French Riviera★
Gran Canaria★
Hawaii★
Hong Kong★
Hungary
Ibiza★
Ireland★
Ireland's Southwest★
Israel★
Istanbul★
Jakarta★
Jamaica★
Kathmandu Bikes & Hikes★
Kenya★
Kuala Lumpur★
Lisbon★
Loire Valley★
London★
Macau
Madrid★
Malacca
Maldives
Mallorca★
Malta★
Mexico City★
Miami★
Milan★
Montreal★
Morocco★
Moscow
Munich★
Nepal★
New Delhi
New Orleans★
New York City★
New Zealand★
Northern California★
Oslo/Bergen★
Paris★
Penang★
Phuket★
Prague★
Provence★
Puerto Rico★
Quebec★
Rhodes★
Rome★
Sabah★

St Petersburg★
San Francisco★
Sardinia
Scotland★
Seville★
Seychelles★
Sicily★
Sikkim
Singapore★
Southeast England
Southern California★
Southern Spain★
Sri Lanka★
Sydney★
Tenerife★
Thailand★
Tibet★
Toronto★
Tunisia★
Turkish Coast★
Tuscany★
Venice★
Vienna★
Vietnam★
Yogyakarta
Yucatan Peninsula★

★ = Insight Pocket Guides with Pull out Maps

Insight Compact Guides

Algarve
Amsterdam
Bahamas
Bali
Bangkok
Barbados
Barcelona
Beijing
Belgium
Berlin
Brittany
Brussels
Budapest
Burgundy
Copenhagen
Costa Brava
Costa Rica
Crete
Cyprus
Czech Republic
Denmark
Dominican Republic
Dublin
Egypt
Finland
Florence
Gran Canaria
Greece
Holland
Hong Kong
Ireland
Israel
Italian Lakes
Italian Riviera
Jamaica
Jerusalem
Lisbon
Madeira
Mallorca
Malta

Milan
Moscow
Munich
Normandy
Norway
Paris
Poland
Portugal
Prague
Provence
Rhodes
Rome
St Petersburg
Salzburg
Singapore
Switzerland
Sydney
Tenerife
Thailand
Turkey
Turkish Coast
Tuscany
UK regional titles:
Bath & Surroundings
Cambridge & East Anglia
Cornwall
Cotswolds
Devon & Exmoor
Edinburgh
Lake District
London
New Forest
North York Moors
Northumbria
Oxford
Peak District
Scotland
Scottish Highlands
Shakespeare Country
Snowdonia
South Downs
York
Yorkshire Dales
USA regional titles:
Boston
Cape Cod
Chicago
Florida
Florida Keys
Hawaii: Maui
Hawaii: Oahu
Las Vegas
Los Angeles
Martha's Vineyard & Nantucket
New York
San Francisco
Washington D.C.
Venice
Vienna
West of Ireland